MEMORIESOFJESUS

A Critical Appraisal of James D. G. Dunn's *Jesus Remembered*

ROBERT B. STEWART
& GARY R. HABERMAS
EDITORS

ACADEMIC
www.BHacademic.com

ISBN: 978-0-8054-4840-5

Published by B&H Publishing Group
Nashville, Tennessee

Dewey Decimal Classification: 232
Subject Heading: JESUS CHRIST\BIBLE. N.T. GOSPELS—CRITICISM

Scripture quotations marked RSV are from the *Revised Standard Version of the Bible*, copyrighted 1946, 1952, © 1971, 1973.

Journal, periodical, major reference works, and series abbreviations follow *The SBL Handbook of Style* (Peabody, MA: Hendrickson, 1999).

Printed in the United States of America

1 2 3 4 5 6 7 8 9 10 11 12 • 18 17 16 15 14 13 12 11 10

VP

For my children, Ray, Bethany, and Rebekah,
who brighten my life everyday

To my colleagues at Liberty University in the
Department of Philosophy and Theology

CONTENTS

CONTRIBUTORS

Craig L. Blomberg (PhD, University of Aberdeen) is a Distinguished Professor of the New Testament at Denver Seminary in Littleton, Colorado. He holds a BA from Augustana College in Rock Island, Illinois, an MA from Trinity Evangelical Divinity School in Deerfield, Illinois, and a PhD from the University of Aberdeen, Scotland. He is the author of 12 books and has coauthored or coedited seven more, along with dozens of journal articles and chapters in multiauthor works. His books include three on the historical reliability and interpretation of the gospels (one specializing in John), two on interpreting and preaching the parables, three commentaries (on Matthew, 1 Corinthians, and James), a textbook on Jesus and the Gospels and another on Acts through Revelation, and two books on material possessions in the Bible.

Markus Bockmuehl (PhD, University of Cambridge) is a Fellow of Keble College and Professor of Biblical and Early Christian Studies at the University of Oxford, having previously held chairs at Cambridge and St. Andrews. Among his books are *The Epistle to the Philippians* (Hendrickson, 1998); *Jewish Law in Gentile Churches: Halakhah and the Beginning of Christian Public Ethics* (Baker Academic, 2003); and *Seeing the Word: Refocusing New Testament Study* (Baker Academic, 2006). He has recently edited volumes on the Gospels: *The Written Gospel* (Cambridge University Press, 2005), with D. A. Hagner; on Messianism, *Redemption and Resistance* (T & T Clark, 2007), with J. Carleton Paget; and on the New Testament and Christian dogmatics, *Scripture's Doctrine and Theology's Bible* (Baker Academic, 2008), with A. J. Torrance.

Samuel Byrskog (ThD, Lund University) is a Professor of New Testament Studies at Lund University, Sweden. He has published several books and articles in the area of eyewitness testimony, tradition, memory, identity formation, and orality/scribality in early Christianity and its Greco-Jewish environment. His publications include *Jesus the Only Teacher: Didactic Authority and Transmission in Ancient Israel, Ancient Judaism and the Matthean Community* (Almqvist & Wiksell, 1994); *Story as History—History as Story: The Gospel Tradition in the Context of Ancient Oral History* (Mohr Siebeck, 2000); and the first volume of a commentary on Romans (EFS-förlaget, 2006). He has recently edited *Jesus in Memory: Traditions in Oral and Scribal Perspectives* (Baylor University Press, 2009) with Werner Kelber.

Stephen T. Davis (PhD, Claremont Graduate University) is the Russell K. Pitzer Professor of Philosophy at Claremont McKenna College. His degrees are from Whitworth University (BA), Princeton Theological Seminary (MDiv), and the Claremont Graduate University (PhD in Philosophy). He writes mainly on the philosophy of religion and Christian theology and is the author or editor of some fifteen books, including *Encountering Evil* (John Knox Press, 1981); *Risen Indeed* (Eerdmans, 1993); *God, Reason, and Theistic Proofs* (Eerdmans, 1997); *The Trinity* (Oxford University Press, 2002); and *Christian Philosophical Theology* (Oxford University Press, 2006).

James D. G. Dunn (PhD, DD, University of Cambridge) is Emeritus Lightfoot Chair of Divinity at Durham University, where he taught for over 20 years until 2003, and a Methodist Local Preacher. He has authored more than 20 volumes, including *Baptism in the Holy Spirit* (Westminster John Knox, 1970); *Jesus and the Spirit* (Eerdmans, 1997); *Unity and Diversity in the New Testament* (3d ed.; SCM Press, 2006); *Christology in the Making* (2d ed.; Eerdmans, 2003); commentaries on Acts, Romans, Galatians, Colossians, and Philemon; *Jesus, Paul and the Law* (Westminster John Knox, 1990); *The Partings of the Ways between Christianity and Judaism* (Trinity Press International, 1992); *The Theology of Paul the Apostle* (Eerdmans, 2006); *The New Perspective on Paul* (Eerdmans, 2007); *A New Perspective on Jesus* (Baker, 2005); *New Testament Theology: An Introduction* (Abingdon, 2009); and the first two volumes of a trilogy on *Christianity in the Making* (Eerdmans, 2003, 2008).

Paul Rhodes Eddy (PhD, Marquette University) is Professor of Biblical and Theological Studies at Bethel University in St. Paul, Minnesota, and Teaching Pastor at Woodland Hills Church in St. Paul. He has authored, coauthored, or coedited a number of books, including *John Hick's Pluralist Philosophy of World Religions* (Ashgate, 2002); *The Jesus Legend: A Case for the Historical Reliability of the Synoptic Jesus Tradition* (Baker Academic, 2007); and *The Historical Jesus: Five Views* (InterVarsity, 2009). He has also authored a number of articles and essays related to the historical study of Jesus.

Craig A. Evans (PhD, Claremont; DHabil., Budapest) is a Payzant Distinguished Professor of the New Testament at Acadia Divinity College in Nova Scotia, Canada. He is the author of a number of books, including *Jesus and His Contemporaries* (Brill, 1995) and *Jesus and the Ossuaries* (Baylor University Press, 2003). He is also the editor of the *Encyclopedia of the Historical Jesus* (Routledge, 2008). Professor Evans has appeared in many television documentaries concerned with Jesus and his world. His interests include the historical Jesus, the Dead Sea Scrolls, and archaeology.

Gary R. Habermas (PhD, Michigan State University) is a Distinguished Research Professor and Chair of the Department of Philosophy and Theology at Liberty University. He has authored or coauthored 36 books (18 on the subject of Jesus' resurrection) and contributed more than 65 chapters or articles to additional books. He has also written well over 100 articles of various sorts. He has frequently been a Visiting or Adjunct Professor, teaching over 40 courses at 15 graduate schools and seminaries during the last 15 years.

Charles L. Quarles (PhD, Mid-America Baptist Theological Seminary) is Vice President for the Integration of Faith and Learning, Chair of the Division of Christian Studies, and Research Professor of New Testament and Greek at Louisiana College. He has published scholarly articles in such journals as *New Testament Studies, Novum*

Testamentum, Journal for the Study of the Historical Jesus, Bulletin for Biblical Research, Catholic Biblical Quarterly, and many others. He is the editor or author of several books, including most recently *Buried Hope or Risen Savior: The Search for the Jesus Tomb* (B&H Academic, 2008) and the forthcoming book *An Illustrated Life of Paul* (B&H Academic). He is coauthor, with Andreas Köstenberger and Scott Kellum, of *The Cradle, the Cross, and the Crown: An Introduction to the New Testament* (B&H Academic, 2009).

Scot McKnight (PhD, University of Nottingham) is a Karl A. Olsson Professor in Religious Studies at North Park University in Chicago, Illinois. He is the author of more than 20 books, including *The Jesus Creed: Loving God, Loving Others* (Paraclete, 2004); *Embracing Grace: A Gospel for All of Us* (Paraclete, 2005); *The Story of the Christ* (Baker, 2006); *A Light among the Gentiles* (Fortress, 1992); *A New Vision for Israel* (Eerdmans, 1999); *Interpreting the Synoptic Gospels* (Baker, 1988); and he is a coeditor with J. B. Green and I. H. Marshall of the award-winning *Dictionary of Jesus and the Gospels* (IVP, 1992) as well as the coeditor, with J. D. G. Dunn, of *The Historical Jesus in Current Study* (Eisenbrauns, 2005).

Jens Schröter (PhD, Ruprecht-Karls University Heidelberg) is a Professor of New Testament exegesis and theology, including the New Testament Apocrypha, at the Humboldt University of Berlin. His Habilitation was at Humboldt University. Among his publications are *Erinnerung an Jesu Worte. Studien zur Rezeption der Logienüberlieferung in Markus, Q und Thomas* (Neukirchener Verlag, 1997); *Jesus und die Anfänge der Christologie* (Neukirchener Verlag, 2001); *Das Abendmahl. Frühchristliche Deutungen und Impulse für die Gegenwart* (Katholisches Bibelwerk Stuttgart, 2006); *Jesus von Nazaret. Jude aus Galiläa—Retter der Welt* (Evangelische Verlagsanstalt Leipzig, 2006); and *Von Jesus zum Neuen Testament. Studien zur urchristlichen Theologiegeschichte und zur Entstehung des neutestamentlichen Kanons* (Mohr Siebeck, 2007). His main areas of academic interest are historical Jesus research, the Acts of the Apostles, theology of the New Testament, and early Christian Apocrypha.

Robert B. Stewart (MDiv, PhD, Southwestern Baptist Theological Seminary) is Associate Professor of Philosophy and Theology at New Orleans Baptist Theological Seminary where he is the Greer-Heard Professor of Faith and Culture. He is editor of *The Resurrection of Jesus: John Dominic Crossan and N. T. Wright in Dialogue* (Fortress, 2006); *Intelligent Design: William A. Dembski and Michael Ruse in Dialogue* (Fortress, 2007); and *The Future of Atheism: Alister McGrath and Daniel Dennett in Dialogue* (Fortress, 2008); and author of *The Quest of the Hermeneutical Jesus: The Impact of Hermeneutics on the Jesus Research of John Dominic Crossan and N. T. Wright* (University Press of America, 2008). A contributor to the *Cambridge Dictionary of Christianity* and the *Revised Holman Bible Dictionary*, he has published articles or chapters in numerous books.

Bill Warren (MDiv, PhD, New Orleans Baptist Theological Seminary) is Professor of New Testament and Greek at New Orleans Baptist Theological Seminary where he holds the Landrum P. Leavell II chair of New Testament Studies. He is the founding director of the H. Milton Haggard Center for New Testament Textual Studies. He is the editor of *La Teología de la Liberación: Una Respuesta Evangelica* (SBTI Press, Cali, Colombia, 1990); translator of *Introducción a la Crítica Textual* (Cuba and Colombia, 2004); author of *Luke: A Study Guide* (Seminary Extension, 1997); and Senior Project Director and Editor for the CNTTS Textual Apparatus, an electronic textual apparatus for the Greek New Testament (OakTree Software, 2003 to present). A contributor to the *Revised Holman Bible Dictionary*, he has published articles and book reviews in numerous journals in both Spanish and English.

Ben Witherington III (MDiv, Gordon Conwell; PhD, University of Durham, UK) is Amos Professor of New Testament for Doctoral Studies at Asbury Theological Seminary and on the doctoral faculty at St. Andrews University in Scotland. Witherington has also taught at Ashland Theological Seminary, Vanderbilt University, Duke Divinity School, and Gordon-Conwell. He has written over 40 books, including *Jesus the Sage* and *Jesus, Paul and the End of the World* plus a host of commentaries. Two of his books, *The Jesus Quest* and *The Paul Quest*, were selected as top biblical studies works by *Christianity Today*. He also writes for many church and scholarly publications and is a frequent contributor to the Beliefnet Web site. Along with many interviews on radio networks across the country, Witherington has been seen on the History Channel, NBC, ABC, CBS, CNN, the Discovery Channel, A&E, and the PAX Network.

PREFACE

ROBERT B. STEWART AND GARY R. HABERMAS

Life is full of strange truths: models want to be actors, athletes want to be musicians, actors want to be politicians—and philosophers want to be New Testament specialists. At least it seems that way to me (Stewart). Despite the fact that we are philosophers, not New Testament professors, for most of our academic careers we have been fascinated with historical Jesus studies. And we have noticed on numerous occasions that we frequently run into other philosophers at the professional meetings we have attended that deal with issues related to the historical Jesus. In fact, to the best of our recollection, we have never attended a session dealing with the historical Jesus at either the Society of Biblical Literature or the Evangelical Theological Society where several philosophers were not in attendance. But this should not really surprise us because Jesus is indeed the most interesting of men.

This book grew out of our fascination with Jesus. Both of us attended the Synoptic Gospel section of the 2005 annual meeting of the Evangelical Theological Society in Valley Forge, Pennsylvania, where James D. G. Dunn was the featured scholar. Dunn spoke on his book *Jesus Remembered* and then responded to a slate of papers critiquing the book. The time we invested was well spent. The discussion was witty and in-depth, and nobody was in a hurry to leave the room when the session was finally over.

A few days later, Dunn again was the featured scholar, this time at an Evangelical Philosophical Society session at the annual meeting of the American Academy of Religion in Philadelphia, Pennsylvania. The topic was the resurrection of Jesus. Dunn again presented his position on the issue and then replied to response papers by Gary Habermas and Stephen Davis. When the session was over, Gary Habermas approached me (Stewart) to ask if I would be interested in editing a book on the presentations. I was open to the idea, and we both spoke to Dunn and Davis about it that evening. We all thought it a good idea, and events were set in motion for me to edit a little book on that one section of a rather large meeting.

When I got back in touch with Jimmy via e-mail about the idea, he suggested that I invite the others who presented on *Jesus Remembered* to participate in the book as well. Given the fact that the focus of the Valley Forge meeting had been on oral tradition and historical memory, it seemed like a few more papers were in order. Jimmy suggested some writers, and I added a few whom I knew would make a significant contribution. And all of a sudden, we were no longer talking about a little book. As the project grew, I asked Gary to join me in editing this project. No doubt his agreeing to do so has significantly improved this book. Two are stronger than one and more likely to see clearly what is overlooked by one alone. It has been a privilege for us to work with scholars like those who have contributed to this book. We would be remiss not to thank Terry Wilder and Ray Clendenen for their belief in this project and excellent work in behalf of it. Finally, we must express our gratitude to Rhyne Putman for constructing the index. We are proud to present the fruit of their labors to you and hope that you enjoy this book as much as we do.

INTRODUCTION

ROBERT B. STEWART AND GARY R. HABERMAS

The historical Jesus is a bit like Elvis—a lot of people claim to have found him. But it seems like he always looks different. According to some, the historical Jesus was a prophet of some sort;[1] according to others, he was a sage;[2] still others see him as the promised Messiah;[3] others think he is best understood as a Cynic,[4] whereas others mix and match these categories. These are just a few broad sketches that have been drawn of the historical Jesus—there are many more from which to choose. This plurality of Jesuses is reflected in the questions that are asked of him. The questions are different today than in the recent past. Carey Newman notes, "The question that drove research throughout

---

[1] Chief among those who view Jesus as an apocalyptic prophet is E. P. Sanders, *Jesus and Judaism* (Philadelphia: Fortress, 1985). G. Theissen, *The Shadow of the Galilean: The Quest of the Historical Jesus in Narrative Form* (Philadelphia: Fortress, 1987); and R. A. Horsley, *Jesus and the Spiral of Violence: Popular Jewish Resistance in Roman Palestine* (San Francisco: HarperSanFrancisco, 1987) and idem, *Sociology and the Jesus Movement* (New York: Crossroad, 1989) are leading proponents of understanding Jesus as a social prophet rather than an apocalyptic prophet.

[2] B. Witherington III, *Jesus the Sage: The Pilgrimage of Wisdom* (Minneapolis: Augsburg Fortress, 1994), argues for viewing Jesus as a sage, a teacher of divine wisdom, but more "the embodiment of Wisdom on earth." Idem, *The Jesus Quest: The Third Search for the Jew of Nazareth* (Downers Grove: InterVarsity, 1995), 193.

[3] A few who hold that Jesus in some way understood himself as Israel's Messiah include M. N. A. Bockmuehl, *This Jesus: Martyr, Lord, Messiah* (Edinburgh: T & T Clark, 1994); and J. P. Meier, *A Marginal Jew: Rethinking the Historical Jesus* (vols. 1 and 2 of *The Roots of the Problem and the Person*; New York: Doubleday, 1991).

[4] Two who have written of a Cynic Jesus include G. F. Downing, *Christ and the Cynics: Jesus and Other Radical Preachers in First-Century Tradition* (Sheffield: Sheffield Academic Press, 1988); and J. D. Crossan, *The Historical Jesus: The Life of a Mediterranean Jewish Peasant* (San Francisco: HarperCollins, 1991).

the middle years of the twentieth century and was fiercely argued and typically answered in either minimalist or maximalist ways is this: What can be assuredly known about the historical Jesus? Today, however, the question has been reformulated: Which Jesus should be remembered?"[5]

It is also unsettling that those who purportedly have discovered him seem to find him in wildly different locations. Some have found him in traditional settings, like the Synoptic Gospels. Others have found him, or at least heard his voice, in new venues like the *Gospel of Thomas*, the *Gospel of Peter*, the Dead Sea Scrolls, or Secret Mark.

Ben Witherington III notes that the original quest of the historical Jesus began "not because any new or exciting data had surfaced but because the canonical Gospels were being reread in new ways."[6] This statement describes the current context in part: new reading methods are playing a role in Jesus research, but new sources—that is, new places to look for him (and possibly find him)—are also available to scholars. Like Elvis, there seems to be no end to reports of him. Unlike Elvis, many of these reports merit serious investigation.

Even the tools for the quest are different, or at least more numerous, than in times past. In addition to source, form, and redaction criticism, scholars are bringing anthropological, archaeological, sociocritical, and numerous literary critical methods to the task and mixing these methods together in imaginative and interesting ways. This has the potential effect of not only shining light on the historical figure of Jesus but also of offering historians a clearer picture of Jesus' world. Of course, as is the case with Elvis, imagination unchecked can be a frightening thing. The potential exists not only for great enlightenment but also for great distortion. And there is the reality of numerous, conflicting reports on the historical Jesus.

Books thus seem to fly off the scholarly presses faster than stores can stock them and certainly faster than readers can purchase and read them. Jesus, it must be said, like Elvis, is big business. So, why this book about Jesus? Or even more importantly, why a book like this book—why a book about a book about Jesus?

---

[5] C. C. Newman, ed., *Jesus & the Restoration of Israel: A Critical Assessment of N. T. Wright's Jesus and the Victory of God* (Downers Grove, IL: InterVarsity, 1999), 13.
[6] Witherington, *The Jesus Quest*, 9.

The answer to this question is primarily twofold: because of the book itself and because of the author of the book. James D. G. Dunn is a rarity among New Testament scholars. Rare is the scholar who can master even one field sufficiently to be viewed by all parties as an expert. Rarer still is the scholar who can master two areas to that extent. Such is the case with James D. G. Dunn. Most New Testament specialists would be more than satisfied to have accomplished all that Dunn has achieved in the area of New Testament pneumatology. World-class scholars have based their careers on much less. But Dunn has gone on to write one of the most important works on Pauline theology in the latter half of the twentieth century, *The Theology of Paul the Apostle*, besides writing a number of other important works on Paul, to say nothing of significant commentaries or books on particular Pauline epistles, or serving as editor of the prestigious *Cambridge Companion to St. Paul*. One after another, works flow forth from his pen that could rightfully be deemed his *magnum opus*. But the term *magnum opus* is singular. Should we thus speak of Dunn's "magnum opera"? Any mature work of James D. G. Dunn is certain to receive close scrutiny from all in his field (a sure sign of academic achievement) and thus any book that brings together significant responses to Dunn in one volume is a worthy project.

The second reason is Dunn's book, *Jesus Remembered*, itself. *Jesus Remembered* is a monumental work that leaves almost no stone unturned. Dunn meticulously works through the issues involved in the search for Jesus and, with a surgeon's skill and patience, provides step-by-step answers to each in turn. This sort of precision might be tedious if not for Dunn's ability as a writer.

I (Stewart) remember well a conversation over breakfast with a leading light of the Jesus Seminar at the 2004 Society of Biblical Literature meeting in San Antonio, Texas, in which *Jesus Remembered* came up. I said that I had heard good things about the book and looked forward to reading it. He replied that reading it was "like being beaten to death by ping-pong balls." I took that then, and still do, to mean either that it was a lightweight work or that it was very precise in its handling of issues. The book is no lightweight treatment of the subject. It does, however, proceed in a very systematic and detailed way toward its destination (which is not really its ultimate destination, given that it is just the first in a three-volume series, *Christianity in the Making*, on the origins of Christian faith). I, on the other hand, happen to love ping-pong and believe that precision is no reason not to appreciate a book. Precision is, in fact, what keeps good scholarship headed in the right direction. *Jesus Remembered* is as precise as John P. Meier's series and nearly as all encompassing as that of N. T. Wright. It rightfully belongs, along with John Dominic Crossan's works on Jesus, on the upper shelf of contemporary Jesus scholarship.

But a remarkably well-written, learned, and precise book would not in and of itself be a sufficient reason to publish a book about that book. The book must also be groundbreaking. And *Jesus Remembered* is surely that. Dunn's thesis that the only Jesus historians have access to is the remembered Jesus, coupled with his insistence that any solution to questions of gospel origins must first of all address the oral tradition rather than the literary tradition, is indeed a bold and striking one. If he is correct, then there is much that must change in contemporary gospel studies. If he is wrong, then others owe it to Dunn and the academy to show where and why.

Finally, a word must be said about the contributors to this volume. We have brought together a world-class team of scholars to probe and critique Dunn's work. Some are Dunn's former students, others near or distant admirers. Among our contributors are scholars working in the United States, Canada, Great Britain, Germany, and Sweden. Some are quite critical of Dunn's method and his conclusions; others are not. All respect his scholarship. Doubtless, we have left some stones unturned. There are surely important issues that are not addressed in this book. With a work as wide-ranging as *Jesus Remembered*, how could it be otherwise? (One goal for this book was to make it shorter than the 992 pages that constitute *Jesus Remembered*.) Nevertheless, important issues are addressed throughout. We are grateful for the opportunity to bring you this book and hope that you enjoy it as much as we do— and that it will drive you to read (or reread) *Jesus Remembered*. James D. G. Dunn will have the last word in this book as he responds to our authors. But certainly this will not be the last word on Dunn's Jesus.

1

FROM REIMARUS TO DUNN

SITUATING JAMES D. G. DUNN IN THE
HISTORY OF JESUS RESEARCH

ROBERT B. STEWART

A Brief History of Jesus Research

According to James D. G. Dunn, "The key issue in any attempt to talk historically about Jesus of Nazareth has been and continues to be the tension between faith and history, or more accurately now, the *hermeneutical* tension between faith and history" (emphasis added).[1] In this chapter, I intend to lay out broad contours of the historical methods—paying particular attention to hermeneutical issues—of certain key thinkers in the history of historical Jesus research and to situate Dunn within a broad continuum of contemporary Jesus scholars. Significant thinkers and their methods in the history of Jesus research thus need to be briefly examined to understand more fully how they impacted Jesus research. The amount of space that can be allotted to any individual in this section is limited. Some significant scholars will

---

[1] J. D. G. Dunn, *Jesus Remembered* (vol. 1 of *Christianity in the Making*; Grand Rapids: Eerdmans, 2003), 125.

1

be overlooked entirely, a matter that is unavoidable. It is hoped, however, that enough of a sketch will be provided that one may make out the general features of historical Jesus research over approximately the past 230 years.

The Original Quest[2]

Albert Schweitzer dates the beginning of the quest of the historical Jesus to 1778, when G. E. Lessing's edition of Hermann Samuel Reimarus's essay "On the Aims of Jesus and His Disciples" was published.[3] Prior to Reimarus, there were many harmonies of the Gospels,[4] but there had been no scholarly attempt to study the Gospels as historical documents.[5] All that changed with Lessing's posthumous publication of Reimarus's work in a series Lessing named *Fragmente eines Ungenannten* (*Fragments from an Unnamed Author*), commonly referred to today as the *Wolfenbüttel Fragments*.[6]

H. S. Reimarus was born in Hamburg in 1694 and taught in Wittenberg and Wismar before spending 1720 to 1721 in Holland and England, where he became acquainted with Deism.[7] The influence of

---

[2] It is doubtless that the Enlightenment played a seminal role in motivating the study of Jesus as a purely historical figure. Chief in importance in this regard is Baruch (Benedict) Spinoza and his critique of biblical studies in "Of the Interpretation of Scripture," in *Tractatus Theologico-Politicus*. The latter work is found in B. Spinoza, *The Chief Works of Benedict de Spinoza* (trans. R. H. M. Elwes; New York: Dover, 1951), 1:98–119.

[3] A. Schweitzer, *The Quest of the Historical Jesus: A Critical Study of Its Progress from Reimarus to Wrede* (trans. W. Montgomery; New York: Macmillan, 1968; repr., Baltimore: The Johns Hopkins University Press, 1998), 15. Cf. H. S. Reimarus, "Concerning the Intention of Jesus and His Teaching," in *Reimarus: Fragments* (ed. C. H. Talbert; trans. R. S. Fraser; Lives of Jesus Series, ed. L. Keck; Philadelphia: Fortress, 1970), 59–269.

[4] Cf. Schweitzer, *The Quest of the Historical Jesus*, 13–15; W. B. Tatum, *In Quest of Jesus* (2d ed.; Nashville: Abingdon, 1999), 39–40.

[5] Schweitzer briefly mentions a life of Jesus that predated Reimarus that was written in Persian by the Jesuit Hieronymus Xavier, a missionary to India for a Moghul emperor. Schweitzer concludes that it was a "skilful falsification of the life of Jesus in which the omissions, and the additions taken from the Apocrypha, are inspired by the sole purpose of presenting to the open-minded ruler a glorious Jesus, in whom there should be nothing to offend him." Schweitzer, *The Quest of the Historical Jesus*, 13–14.

[6] See Reimarus, "Concerning the Intention of Jesus and His Teaching." At the time of publication, Lessing was librarian to the Duke of Brunswick at the ducal library in Wolfenbüttel, hence the name of the series.

[7] C. Brown, "Reimarus, Hermann Samuel," in *Major Biblical Interpreters* (ed. D. K. McKim; Downers Grove: InterVarsity, 1998), 346.

Deism may be seen in his attempt to ground understanding of the historical Jesus in deistic *Vernunft* (reason). Reimarus is consumed with answering one basic question: "What sort of purpose did Jesus himself see in his teachings and deeds?"[8] Reimarus concludes that the preaching of Jesus was separate from the writings of the apostles. He thus argues that the Gospels, not the New Testament epistles, are where one finds the historical Jesus.

> However, I find great cause to separate completely what the apostles say in their own writing from that which Jesus himself actually said and taught, for the apostles were themselves teachers and consequently present their own views; indeed, they never claim that Jesus himself said and taught in his lifetime all the things that they have written. On the other hand, the four evangelists represent themselves only as historians who have reported the most important things that Jesus said as well as did. If now we wish to know what Jesus' teaching actually was, what he said and preached, that is a *res facti*—a matter of something that actually occurred; hence this is to be derived from the reports of the historians. . . . Everyone will grant, then, that in my investigation of the intention of Jesus' teaching I have sufficient reason to limit myself exclusively to the reports of the four evangelists who offer the proper and true record. I shall not bring in those things that the apostles taught or intended on their own, since the latter are not historians of their master's teaching but present themselves as teachers. Later, when once we have discovered the actual teaching and intention of Jesus from the four documents of the historians, we shall be able to judge reliably whether the apostles expressed the same teaching and intention as their master.[9]

Reimarus defines the essence of religion as "the doctrine of the salvation and immortality of the soul."[10] This generic liberal description of the essence of religion masks Reimarus's eventual conclusions concerning Jesus. He concludes that Jesus (a) was a pious Jew; (b) called Israel to repent; (c) did not intend to teach new truth, found a new religion, or establish new rituals; (d) became sidetracked by embracing a political position; (e) sought to force God's hand; and (f) died alone, deserted

---

[8] Reimarus, "Concerning the Intention of Jesus and His Teaching," 64.

[9] Ibid., 64–65.

[10] Ibid., 61.

by his disciples. What began as a call for repentance ended up as a misguided attempt to usher in the earthly, political kingdom of God.[11]

He also posits that after Jesus' failure and death, his disciples stole his body and declared his resurrection in order to maintain their financial security and ensure themselves some standing.[12] Peter Gay writes that this sort of conspiracy theory is typical of Deism: "Even the sane among the deists had a paranoid view of history and politics: they saw conspiracies everywhere."[13]

In typical deistic fashion, Reimarus insists that there are "no mysteries" or "new articles of faith" in the teachings of Jesus.[14] This grows out of his conviction that Jesus was essentially Jewish, not Christian. The uniquely Christian doctrines that one finds in the New Testament originate with the apostles, not Jesus. Reimarus maintains that Jesus' mind-set was eschatological in nature. He correctly discerns that the historical Jesus is never to be found in a non-Jewish setting but wrongly sees Christianity as discontinuous with Judaism.

Reimarus explicitly rejects the twin pillars of traditional Christian apologetics concerning the deity of Jesus: miracles and prophecy.[15] He accepts the basic historicity of the Gospels but reasons the supernatural away through the use of deistic explanations. In short, his rejection of portions of the Gospels is not the result of literary criticism but rather of a prior commitment to the deistic worldview. In this sense, his project can be said to be *precritical*. Reimarus is critical of supernaturalism and the miracle stories in the Gospels, but he does not read the Gospels critically as literature.

Friedrich Daniel Ernst Schleiermacher is best known for his pioneering contributions to modern theology: *Der christliche Glaube* (*The Christian Faith*) and *Über die Religion: Reden an die Gebildeten unter ihren Verächtern* (*On Religion: Speeches to Its Cultured Despisers*).[16] He

---

[11] Ibid., 61–150.

[12] Ibid., 243–50.

[13] P. Gay, *Deism: An Anthology* (Princeton: Princeton University Press, 1968), 10.

[14] Reimarus, "Concerning the Intention of Jesus and His Teaching," 71–76.

[15] Ibid., 229–37.

[16] F. D. E. Schleiermacher, *The Christian Faith* (ed. H. R. Mackintosh and J. S. Stewart; Edinburgh: T & T Clark, 1928); idem, *On Religion: Speeches to Its Cultured Despisers* (ed. and trans. R. Crouter; Cambridge and New York: Cambridge University Press, 1996).

was, however, also a pioneer in hermeneutical method and life-of-Jesus research. Schleiermacher was the first scholar to lecture on life of Jesus research in a university. Although he never wrote a book on the historical Jesus, the notes from his class lectures, along with the comments of five of his students, were edited by K. A. Rütenik and published in 1864, 30 years after his death.[17]

Schleiermacher divides the exegetical task into two subcategories: higher and lower criticism. His higher criticism is concerned with establishing the New Testament canon. His lower criticism is concerned with arriving at an accurate original reading of a particular text. In other words, he practiced something approaching canonical criticism and textual criticism.[18]

For Schleiermacher, the Old Testament was not normative in the same way as the New Testament. It was the Scripture of Judaism, not Christianity. It could serve to help one understand the New Testament Scriptures but could not serve as the basis for Christianity, which was, in his estimation, an entirely new faith. Furthermore, the Christian interpreter was prone to read foreign ideas and concepts into the Old Testament and thus to obscure its original historic sense. Nevertheless, he concluded that it could be a useful appendix in Christian Bibles rather than part of the Christian Scriptures.[19]

Hermeneutics, as opposed to exegesis, consists of two parts: the grammatical (universal) and the psychological (particular). The former focuses on the syntactical structure of a text, whereas the latter addresses the intentions of the author. In practice, however, the two are interwoven. The role of the interpreter is first to recognize distinctive markings of a particular biblical author. This is the comparative reading of a text. The second role of the reader is to intuit or divine the thought processes involved in writing the text.[20]

---

[17] J. C. Verheyden, introduction to *The Life of Jesus*, by Friedrich Schleiermacher (ed. J. C. Verheyden; trans. S. M. Gilmour; Lives of Jesus Series, ed. L. E. Keck; Philadelphia: Fortress, 1975), xv–xvi.

[18] D. DeVries, "Schleiermacher, Friedrich Daniel Ernst," in *Major Biblical Interpreters* (ed. D. K. McKim; Downers Grove: InterVarsity, 1998), 351.

[19] Ibid. It is thus not difficult to see how Schleiermacher is hesitant to situate Jesus within Judaism.

[20] Ibid., 352.

Schleiermacher primarily focuses on Jesus' proclamation and the time period of his public ministry. He considers issues such as the virgin birth, crucifixion, and resurrection unhistorical. For Schleiermacher, what matters most in interpretation is the intention of the writer (or the historical person written about). He thus inquires of Jesus' intentions and his perfect God-consciousness.[21]

In summary, Schleiermacher understood the importance of grammatical-historical exegesis of texts and anticipated critical methods to come. Yet, in good romanticist style, he was most concerned with intuiting Jesus' intentions and religious consciousness.

David Friedrich Strauss wrote three best-selling books about Jesus (or perhaps three different versions of one book). Each of the three was different. In retrospect, his first book has proven to be most significant. Therefore, this section will primarily focus on his first offering, *The Life of Jesus Critically Examined*.[22]

In his first *Life of Jesus*, Strauss seeks to apply Hegel's historical dialectic to understanding Jesus. To this end, he applies the concept of myth to the Gospels, something his teacher F. C. Baur had already done in Old Testament studies. Jesus understood mythically is the synthesis of the thesis of supernaturalism and the antithesis of rationalism. As a committed Hegelian, Strauss maintains that the inner nucleus of Christian faith is not touched by the mythical approach.

> The author is aware that the essence of the Christian faith is perfectly independent of his criticism. The supernatural birth of Christ, his miracles, his resurrection and ascension, remain eternal truths, whatever doubts may be cast on their reality as historical facts. The certainty of this alone can give calmness or dignity to our criticism, and distinguish it from the naturalistic criticism of the last century, the design of which was, with the historical fact, to subvert also the religious truth, and which thus necessarily became frivolous. A dissertation at the close of the work will show that the dogmatic significance of the life of Jesus remains inviolate: in the meantime let the calmness and *sang-froid* with which in the course of it, criticism undertakes apparently dangerous operations, be explained solely by

---

[21] Schleiermacher, *The Life of Jesus*, 87–123.
[22] D. F. Strauss, *The Life of Jesus Critically Examined* (ed. P. C. Hodgson; trans. G. Eliot; Life of Jesus Series, ed. L. E. Keck; Philadelphia: Fortress, 1972).

the security of the author's conviction that no injury is threatened to the Christian faith.[23]

One can easily see then that, at least at this point, Strauss intends not to destroy the Christian faith but only to critique the Gospels historically.

Strauss emphasizes not the *events* (miracles) in the Gospels (although the book is structured as an analysis of Jesus' miracles) but the *nature* of the Gospels. Unlike Reimarus, he is not primarily interested in explaining (away) how events in the Gospels took place. Neither is he interested in uncovering the sequence in which the Gospels were produced. His interest lies in revealing the nature of the Gospels as literature. By focusing on the literary nature of the Gospels, he anticipates several crucial issues in twentieth-century New Testament studies.

This represents a paradigm shift in Gospel studies. Whereas Reimarus had proposed two possibilities—natural or supernatural—Strauss proposes two different categories for interpreting the Gospels: mythic or historical. Unlike Reimarus, Strauss does not attribute the nonhistorical to deliberate deception on the part of the apostles but to their unconscious mythic imagination.[24] Strauss maintains that the biblical narratives were written well after they occurred and were embellished through years of oral retelling and religious reflection.[25] Strauss thus insists that the key to understanding Jesus historically is being fully aware of the differences between then and now.[26] The Gospel stories, according to Strauss, are poetic in form, not historical or philosophical.[27]

Although Strauss is certainly critical in questioning the supernatural events one finds in the Gospels, he is not methodologically "critical" in the sense of questioning the order or authorship of the Gospels. Ben Meyer comments that Strauss's first *Life of Jesus* is consistently less a literary discovery than a Hegelian deduction.[28] Doubtless, this is one reason that he ignores the synoptic question.

---

[23] Ibid., lii.

[24] Ibid., 39–92.

[25] Ibid., 49.

[26] Ibid., 39–44.

[27] Ibid., 53.

[28] B. F. Meyer, *The Aims of Jesus* (London: SCM, 1979), 34. Cf. Strauss, *The Life of Jesus Critically Examined*, 779.

Strauss's *Life of Jesus* was immediately a source of controversy. He was forbidden to teach theology any longer. Furthermore, when he took a post at another school, the controversy he created was so great that he was let go before beginning his teaching duties. In his second book on Jesus, *Das Leben Jesu: für das deutsche Volk*[29] (The Life of Jesus: for the German People), Strauss abandons Hegelian categories for moral categories. Eventually, Strauss repudiated entirely any attachment to Christianity. David Strauss died a committed materialist.[30]

In summary, Reimarus, Schleiermacher, and Strauss all played important roles in life of Jesus research. All of them, however, ignored what became the most consuming question for a generation of Jesus scholars to follow: in what order were the Gospels written?

Stephen Neill writes concerning the Synoptic Problem: "The first scholar to approach the correct solution of the problem on the basis of careful observation of the facts seems to have been Karl Lachmann."[31] In 1835, Lachmann wrote an article proposing that Mark was the earliest of the four canonical Gospels.[32] The philosopher Christian Hermann Weisse soon echoed Lachmann's opinion on the matter.[33] Yet both Lachmann and Weisse were approaching the matter apart from a clearly stated and justified methodology.

It was left to Heinrich Julius Holtzmann to treat the matter in a systematic fashion. Against Strauss, he is adamant that in order to understand Jesus historically, one must first undergo a thorough investigation of the Synoptic Gospels. Holtzmann understands the primary problem in historical Jesus research to be the order of sources. Therefore, the primary task is solving the Synoptic Problem. In *Die Synoptischen Evangelien: Ihr Ursprung und geschichtlicher Charakter* (The Synoptic

---

[29] D. F. Strauss, *Das Leben Jesu: für das deutsche Volk. Bearb. von David Friedrich Strauss* (Leipzig: F. A. Brockhaus, 1874).

[30] R. Morgan, "Strauss, David Friedrich," in *Major Biblical Interpreters* (ed. D. K. McKim; Downers Grove: InterVarsity, 1998), 367.

[31] S. Neill and N. T. Wright, *The Interpretation of the New Testament 1861–1986* (Oxford: Oxford University Press, 1988), 116–17.

[32] K. Lachmann, "*De Ordine Narrationum* in *Evangeliis Synopticis*," *TSK* 8 (1835): 570.

[33] C. H. Weisse, *Die evangelische Geschichte kritische und philosophisch bearbeitet Leipzig* (2 vols.; Leipzig: Breitkopf and Härtel, 1838); idem, *Die evangelienfrage in ihrem gegenwärtigen Stadium* (Leipzig: Breitkopf und Härtel, 1856).

Gospels: Their Origin and Historical Character), Holtzmann proposes that two written sources containing sayings of Jesus, *Urmarcus* and *Urmatthäus*, were available to the evangelists.[34]

To the degree that Holtzmann shared the basic presuppositions of nineteenth-century German liberalism, he represents the mainstream of the first quest. Behind the fascination with sources lay the liberal presupposition that the theological elements in the Gospels were later accretions from the early church. It was assumed, therefore, that the further back one goes, the less theological and the more historical the picture of Jesus becomes. Behind this expectation lay the liberal presupposition that Jesus preached a timeless ethic.[35] They fully expected to find that Jesus was a teacher of moral truths who had a unique awareness of God working through him. They also thought that by determining the order of the earliest sources, they could discern a noticeable shift in the personality of Jesus.[36] It is not going too far to say that the first quest, the liberal quest, was based largely on an unwarranted optimism concerning how much historical knowledge of Jesus one could acquire from the proper application of source criticism.

Both Albrecht Ritschl and Adolf Harnack understood Jesus primarily in ethical terms. According to Ritschl, the proper object of study is the observable experience of the church because the statements in Scripture become "completely intelligible only when we see how they are reflected in the consciousness of those who believe in Him."[37] He also taught not only that the kingdom of God and the message of Jesus were ethical in nature but also that Jesus was the bearer of God's ethical Lordship over humanity.[38]

> The delineation of the ethical connection between the sufferings and the vocation of Christ already give place to *the religious view* of the same, apart from which Christ Himself was not conscious of His

---

[34] H. J. Holtzmann, *Die Synoptischen Evangelien: Ihr Ursprung und geschichtlicher Charakter* (Leipzig: Wilhelm Engelmann, 1863), 64–67.

[35] Ibid., 470.

[36] Ibid., 1–9.

[37] A. Ritschl, *The Christian Doctrine of Justification and Reconciliation: The Positive Development of the Doctrine* (ed. H. R. Mackintosh and A. B. Macaulay; Clifton, N.J.: Reference Book Publishers, 1966), 1.

[38] Ibid., 385–484.

unique and independent vocation among men. The business of His vocation was the establishment of the universal ethical fellowship of mankind, as that aim in the world which rises above all conditions included in the notion of the world.[39]

For Harnack, Jesus' message of the kingdom emphasized (a) the kingdom of God and its coming, (b) God the Father and the infinite value of the human soul, and (c) the higher righteousness and the commandment of love.[40]

Meyer comments that most Jesus scholars of that day coupled the liberal emphasis on ethics with an equally liberal "hermeneutic of empathy."[41] In turn, a host of imaginative theses were put forward in an effort to understand more fully the nature of Jesus' religious experience by tracing out the psychological development of Jesus' messianic awareness.[42] This was very attractive in that it allowed the authors to write something akin to a *biography* of Jesus.[43] The weakness of this approach lay in that it was dependent more on imagination than historical method. Concerning this, Otto Pfleiderer writes,

> We may never forget how much, with the poverty of the ascertained historical materials is left to the uncontrolled power of combination and divination; in other words, to the imagination, which at best can do no more than roughly and approximately arrive at the truth, while it may no less easily go far astray. . . . Yet this advance is manifestly attended by the temptation to sacrifice the caution of historical criticism to the production of a biography as rich in detail and as dramatic in movement as possible, and to represent things as the ascertained results of critical examination, which are really nothing more than subjective combinations of the writers, to which a certain degree of

---

[39] Ibid., 449.

[40] A. Harnack, *What Is Christianity?* (trans. T. B. Saunders; New York: Harper & Row, 1957), 19–78.

[41] Meyer, *The Aims of Jesus*, 40.

[42] T. Keim, *The History of Jesus of Nazara* (trans. A. Ransom; 2 vols.; London: Williams and Norgate, 1876); K. Hase, *Geschichte Jesu Nach Akademischen Vorlesungen* (Leipzig: Breitkopf and Härtel, 1876); K. H. Weizsäcker, *Untersuchungen über die evangelische Geschichte, ihre Quellen und den Gang ihrer Entwicklung* (Leipzig: Gotha, 1864); B. Weiss, *Das Leben Jesu* (2 vols.; Berlin: Wilhelm Hertz, 1882).

[43] The first truly significant biography of Jesus was Renan's. E. Renan, *La Vie de Jesus* (Paris: Michel Lévy Frères, 1863).

probability will always remain, that the actual facts were something quite different.[44]

In 1901, William Wrede published *The Messianic Secret in the Gospels*.[45] Wrede insisted that the psychological theories of nineteenth-century-life-of-Jesus work were derived from somewhere other than the text.

> And this is the malady to which we must here allude—let us not dignify it with the euphemism "historical imagination." *The Scientific study of the life of Jesus is suffering from psychological "suppositionitis"* which amounts to a sort of historical guesswork. For this reason interpretations to suit every taste proliferate. The number of arbitrary psychological interpretations at the same time form the basis for important structures of thought; and how often do people think that the task of criticism has already been discharged by playing tuneful psychological variations on a given factual theme![46]

Wrede further maintained that the Gospels were not to be understood as biographies. The issue that he directly addressed was how best to explain the presence of the messianic theme in the Gospels. For Wrede, this messianic theme was best understood as a creation of the evangelist that reflected his attempt to harmonize two streams of thought in the early church concerning the truth that was clearly perceived in the post-Easter church. That truth was that Jesus was the Messiah but that nobody had heard him declare that prior to his death. He believed that the early church understood historically that Jesus *was made* Messiah at his resurrection, not that he *was revealed* as Messiah through the resurrection.[47] The idea that Jesus was the Messiah before his resurrection was merely the result of the early church's theological reflection on his then-evident messiahship.[48]

---

[44] O. Pfleiderer, introduction to *The Life of Jesus Critically Examined*, by David Friedrich Strauss (trans. G. Eliot; London: Swan Sonnenschein, 1902), xxiv–xxv.

[45] W. Wrede, *The Messianic Secret: Forming a Contribution also to the Understanding of Mark* (trans. J. C. G. Greig; Cambridge: James Clarke, 1971). For German, see *Das Messiasgeheimnis in den Evangelien*, 3te unveränderte Auflage (Göettingen: Vandenhoeck & Ruprecht, 1963).

[46] Ibid., 6.

[47] Ibid., 216–19.

[48] Ibid., 219–30.

Simply put, the messianic secret was Mark's attempt to harmonize history with theology.[49] Although Wrede allowed that Jesus' words and actions might have caused some to question if he might be the Messiah prior to his death and resurrection, he would not allow that Jesus *ever* taught that he was the Messiah.[50] The messianic secret was the product of a theological idea, not historical facts.[51]

According to Wrede, one must distinguish between historical and literary-critical questions, and literary-critical questions should be dealt with before historical ones. In this way, Wrede was able to point to messianic passages in the Gospels as support for his hypothesis, and problematic texts were thus neatly excised in the interest of historical tidiness. The result was predictable: truncated Gospels resulted in a truncated picture of Jesus. Wrede's Jesus lacked both messianic consciousness and theological creativity. But Wrede's conclusions have been influential in both form and redaction criticism. Consistent with the emphasis of the *religionsgeschichtliche Schule*, of which Wrede is a representative, the result of Wrede's work was to shift the focus from Jesus onto the communities the evangelists represent. Discerning the nature of the tradition behind a text thus became the focus of biblical interpretation.

On the same day in 1901 that Wrede published his book on the messianic secret, Albert Schweitzer published his *The Mystery of the Kingdom of God*.[52] In this brief sketch of Jesus' life, Schweitzer pictured Jesus as thoroughly conscious of his messianic role. In fact, it

---

[49] While Wrede insists that Mark is not solely responsible for the content of his Gospel in that it reflects the theology of the early church, he does nevertheless see Mark as providing a distinctive touch. Ibid. From this, one can see how both form and redaction criticism are well in line with Wrede's skepticism.

[50] Ibid., 230. H. Rollmann mentions a letter from Wrede to Harnack, written shortly before Wrede's death, in which Wrede writes that he had changed his mind concerning Jesus' messianic consciousness but saw no point in abandoning his tradition-historical approach to interpretation. H. Rollmann, "Wrede, William," in *Major Biblical Interpreters* (ed. D. K. McKim; Downers Grove: InterVarsity, 1998), 397.

[51] Wrede, *The Messianic Secret*, 67.

[52] A. Schweitzer, *The Mystery of the Kingdom of God: The Secret of Jesus' Messiahship and Passion* (trans. Walter Lowrie; New York: Macmillan, 1950). For German, see idem, *Das Messianitäts-und Leidensgeheimnis: Ein Skizze des Lebens Jesu* (Tübingen: J. C. B. Mohr, 1901). Originally Schweitzer's *Mystery* was part 2 of his *Das Abendmahl im Zusammenhang mit dem Leben Jesu und der Geschichte der Urchristentums* (Tübingen: J. C. B. Mohr, 1901).

was this messianic consciousness that motivated Jesus to do all that he did. In contrast to Wrede, Schweitzer understood Jesus as a messianic hero, along the lines of Nietzsche's cult of the hero (*Übermensch*).[53] Schweitzer's Jesus is a heroic figure, seeking to usher in the kingdom through his decisive sacrifice of himself. Schweitzer saw the messianic themes, which Wrede took to be later creations, as central to any understanding of Jesus. According to Schweitzer, one could not begin to understand Jesus without correctly perceiving that his messianic consciousness drove him to do all that he did.[54] Tragically, although the idea of resurrection is clearly in the mind of Schweitzer's Jesus, his summary concludes, "On the afternoon of the fourteenth of Nissan, as they ate the Paschal lamb at even, he uttered a loud cry and died."[55]

Schweitzer's first offering was not overly well received.[56] This prompted him to publish *The Quest of the Historical Jesus* (German: *Von Reimarus zu Wrede: eine Geschichte der Leben-Jesu-Forschung*) in 1906.[57] Eventually, this work became the standard by which all other histories of life of Jesus research would be measured.

Schweitzer is often cited as one who advocated the end of historical Jesus research. Such is not the case. Schweitzer did not intend to end the quest but to redirect it. Although Schweitzer did maintain that

---

[53] Schweitzer wrote of his philosophy of reverence for life as a superior version of Nietzsche's concern for life lived to fullest degree. A. Schweitzer, *The Philosophy of Civilization* (trans. C. T. Campion; London: A. & C. Black, 1946), 174–76.

[54] Schweitzer was not the first to advocate an eschatological Jesus. Johannes Weiss, Ritschl's son-in-law, had previously written that Jesus' proclamation of the kingdom of God was eschatological in nature. J. Weiss, *Jesus' Proclamation of the Kingdom of God* (ed. and trans. R. H. Hiers and D. L. Holland; Lives of Jesus Series, ed. Leander E. Keck; Philadelphia: Fortress, 1971). The primary difference between Weiss and Schweitzer is that while Weiss understood eschatology as the central motif of Jesus' teaching, Schweitzer saw it as the key to Jesus' personality and ministry.

[55] Schweitzer, *The Mystery of the Kingdom*, 173. Following Schweitzer's summary of the life of Jesus, there is a one page postscript that focuses on the recognition that the nature of Jesus is bound forever to be a mystery to modern man and that modern culture can only be revived by grasping the nature of his conscious sacrifice for others. It fittingly concludes with a sentence reminiscent of Nietzsche: "Only then can the heroic in our Christianity and in our *Weltanschauung* be again revived." Ibid, 174.

[56] For a thorough treatment of the response to Schweitzer's work, see W. P. Weaver, *The Historical Jesus in the Twentieth Century, 1900–1950* (Harrisburg, Pa.: Trinity Press International, 1999), 31–38.

[57] Schweitzer, *The Quest of the Historical Jesus*. For German, see idem, *Von Reimarus zu Wrede: eine Geschichte der Leben-Jesu-Forschung* (Tübingen: J. C. B. Mohr, 1906).

one could not use history to write a biography of Jesus, he believed that historical research could destroy false constructs of Jesus, including the most monstrous one of all—Jesus as a modern man. For Schweitzer, Jesus was the product of first-century Jewish apocalyptic expectation, not Enlightenment rationalism. In short, although Schweitzer believed that knowledge of the historical Jesus could not afford one a foundation upon which to ground Christian faith, he saw historical Jesus research as useful in destroying the fictional platforms that had been built by ecclesiastical dogma and Enlightenment historicism. The value of historical knowledge of Jesus was to be found in the recognition of one's inability to know him through investigation. Instead, Jesus is known most fully in decisive individual commitment. Again, the voice of Nietzsche is heard in the conclusion of *The Quest of the Historical Jesus*:

> He comes to us as One unknown, without a name, as of old, by the lake-side, He came to those men who knew Him not. He speaks to us the same word: "Follow thou me!" and sets us to the tasks which He has to fulfil for our time. He commands. And to those who obey Him, whether they be wise or simple, He will reveal Himself in the toils, the conflicts, the sufferings which they shall pass through in His fellowship, and, as an ineffable mystery, they shall learn in their own experience Who He is.[58]

From the standpoint of biblical criticism and interpretive method, Schweitzer's work is fairly simplistic. For one as concerned with critical history as he is, his approach to interpreting Scripture is surprisingly noncritical. In contrast to his predecessors, he is not especially concerned with answering source-critical questions. He accepts the general synoptic narrative as historical and interprets the Gospels in light of his one guiding principle: thoroughgoing eschatology.

The Abandoned Quest

It is often assumed that Schweitzer's *Quest* ended the first phase of historical Jesus research, but such a position is simplistic. Although it

---

[58] Ibid., 403. Those familiar with Schweitzer's life and philosophy will immediately see that this was for Schweitzer not simply a pithy phrase but a credo for life.

is true that Schweitzer offered up a devastating critique of the liberal quest, it was left to others to provide a positive diversion from liberal historical Jesus research. Several factors contributed to bringing the first quest to an "end."

In 1896, Martin Kähler argued that "the entire Life-of-Jesus movement is a blind alley"[59] because the necessary sources were not available. His basic premise was that the certainty of faith could not rest on the unavoidable uncertainties of history. He declared that the accuracy of Scripture cannot be based "on the success or failure of the inquiries of historical research; for these are always limited and only provisionally valid, that is, their validity endures only until new sources of knowledge appear on the horizon."[60] Instead of searching for the *historical* Jesus, one should seek the *historic* Jesus, the one who has molded history and contributed to it.[61]

Also in addition to Schweitzer's critique of the liberal historical Jesus project, there was the influence of the *religionsgeschichtliche Schule*, the history of religions school. Two names often associated with the history of religions school are Ernst Troeltsch and Wilhelm Bousset.

Troeltsch served as the philosopher for the movement. He insisted that Christianity was not historically unique. Like all religions, it was a historical phenomenon within its own time. Consequently, Jesus was no different than any other figure in history. To insist, like Kähler, that faith in Jesus is not subject to historical critique is simply naive, according to Troeltsch.[62] The historian is bound to explain movements in terms of causal events in the natural world.[63] Therefore, the historian's role in relation to Christian origins is simply to explain how Christianity came to be, not to answer theological or metaphysical

---

[59] M. Kähler, *The So-Called Historical Jesus and the Historic Biblical Christ* (ed. and trans. C. Braaten; Philadelphia: Fortress, 1964), 46.

[60] Ibid., 111.

[61] Ibid., 63.

[62] E. Troeltsch, *Die Bedeutung der Geschichtlichkeit Jesus für den Glauben* (Tübingen: J. C. B. Mohr, 1929), 34. For an insightful discussion of Troeltsch's significance for biblical interpretation, see A. C. Thiselton, *The Two Horizons: New Testament Interpretation and Philosophical Description* (Grand Rapids: Eerdmans, 1980), 69–74.

[63] E. Troeltsch, *Gesammelte Schriften* (Tübingen: J. C. B. Mohr, 1912–25), 2:734. Troeltsch is particularly critical of Christian theologians who attempt to use part of the historical-critical method but reject the presuppositions of it. Ibid., 2:730.

questions concerning Jesus. The hermeneutical result of applying this
principle to the study of Christian origins was that the referent of the
Gospels became the early church, not Jesus. Therefore, the question
changed from "Who was Jesus?" to "How did the early church come
to think of Jesus in this way?"

Bousset's answer in *Kyrios Christos: Geschichte des Christusglaubens
von den Anfängen des Christentums bis Irenaeus* was that the church came
to deify Jesus through a historical process of transformation due to
its encounter with Hellenism, an encounter in which alien ideas were
grafted into Christianity. He maintained that the earliest traditions concerning Jesus contained nothing miraculous and did not proclaim Jesus
to be divine.[64]

The shadow of Rudolf Bultmann falls over any attempt to understand New Testament theology in the twentieth century. Along with
K. L. Schmidt and Martin Dibelius, he pioneered New Testament
form criticism.[65] He understood the Gospels as collections of fragments edited together that addressed particular needs of the early
church, not as single documents chronicling the life of Jesus. Therefore,
Bultmann understood the primary purpose of form criticism to be the
discovery of the origin of the particular units of oral tradition that
lay behind the written pericopae of the Gospels, not simply identifying different forms of Gospel sayings.[66] In *Jesus and the Word*, he
declares, "I do indeed think that we can now know almost nothing
concerning the life and personality of Jesus, since the early Christian
sources show no interest in either, are moreover fragmentary and often
legendary; and other sources about Jesus do not exist."[67] Bultmann
posits that the early church was filled with controversy and infighting
between Hellenistic Jewish believers and Palestinian Jewish believers.
This results in a situation where sayings are attributed to Jesus that he

---

[64] W. Bousset, *Kyrios Christos: A History of Belief in Christ from the Beginnings of Christianity to Irenaeus* (trans. J. E. Steely; Nashville: Abingdon, 1970).

[65] C. Brown, "Historical Jesus, Quest of," in *Dictionary of Jesus and the Gospels* (ed. J. B.
Green, S. McKnight, I. H. Marshall; Downers Grove: InterVarsity, 1992), 334.

[66] R. Bultmann, *The History of the Synoptic Tradition* (trans. J. Marsh; Oxford: Basil
Blackwell, 1963), 3–4.

[67] R. Bultmann, *Jesus and the Word* (trans. L. Pettibone Smith and E. Huntress Lantero;
New York: Scribner's, 1958), 8.

did not utter. This led him to declare, "One can only emphasize the uncertainty of our knowledge of the person and work of the historical Jesus and likewise of the origin of Christianity."[68] The result was not only that form criticism, like the history of religions school, focused on something other than Jesus, the *Sitz im Leben* of the early church, but also that its foremost proponent announced that historical Jesus research could not succeed.

Bultmann's objections to historical Jesus research were not only methodological but also philosophical and theological. Influenced as he was by Kierkegaard and Heidegger, as well as the early Karl Barth,[69] Bultmann thought that historical knowledge of Jesus' *persönlichkeit* (personhood) was secondary in importance to existential knowledge of his word.[70] Bultmann's approach is first to recognize that the New Testament is mythological in nature and second to demythologize the New Testament myths. Bultmann openly draws on Heidegger's categories of existence and being to interpret the New Testament. But what often is missed in his method is that he adopts these categories because he believes that the New Testament demands to be demythologized—that such was the intention of the authors.[71]

Bultmann thus contributed to a decline in historical Jesus research in several ways: (a) his form critical method shifted the emphasis from Jesus onto the early Christian communities, (b) his form critical conclusions led to a sense of pessimism concerning historical Jesus research in general, (c) his demythologization shifted the emphasis from history to anthropology, and (d) his commitment to existentialism assigned historical knowledge of Jesus to a secondary status and thus undermined the entire project in general.

In summary, several factors were influential in the abandonment of the original quest of the historical Jesus. Among them were (a) Wrede's

---

[68] R. Bultmann, "The Study of the Synoptic Gospels," in *Form Criticism: Two Essays on New Testament Research* (ed. R. Bultmann and K. Kundsin; trans. F. C. Grant; n.p.: Willett Clark, 1934; repr., New York: Harper Torchbook, 1962), 17.

[69] Other influences on Bultmann include Luther, Collingwood, and the history of religions school as well as the liberal theology of his teacher, Harnack. For a general discussion of influences on Bultmann, see Thiselton, *The Two Horizons*, 205–51.

[70] Bultmann, *Jesus and the Word*, 9–12.

[71] R. Bultmann, "New Testament and Mythology," in *Kerygma and Myth* (ed. H. W. Bartsch; trans. R. Fuller; London: S.P.C.K., 1953), 11–12.

skepticism, (b) Schweitzer's critique of nineteenth-century lives of Jesus, (c) the influence of Martin Kähler, (d) the influence of the history of religions school, (e) the rise of form criticism, (f) Bultmann's demythologizing hermeneutic, and (g) the influence of existentialism on dialectical theology.

The New Quest of the Historical Jesus

The movement in historical Jesus research that is commonly called the "New Quest of the Historical Jesus" began in 1953 with a speech by Ernst Käsemann to a group of Bultmann's former students.[72] Käsemann agreed with Bultmann about the earlier quest: it was largely impossible and at least partially irrelevant. Käsemann also insisted that the primary interest of the primitive church was not historical verification of facts concerning Jesus but rather the proclamation of the kerygma. He held that the primitive church sought to rescue historical facts from obscurity through appeal to the reality of their present experience of Jesus as Lord. Käsemann concludes that this was not only the experience of the primitive church but also the task of Christians today.[73] But he also insists that to disregard Jesus entirely as a historical figure is to lapse into docetism.[74] Käsemann thus argues for a new type of historical inquiry concerning Jesus: one that recognizes that mere history apart from hermeneutics is insignificant.

> For mere history becomes significant history not through tradition as such but through interpretation, not through the simple establishment of facts but through the understanding of the events of the past which have become objectified and frozen into facts. . . . Mere history only takes on genuine historical significance in so far as it can address both a question and an answer to our contemporary situation; in other words, by finding interpreters who hear and utter this question and answer. For this purpose primitive Christianity allows mere history no vehicle of expression other than the kerygma.[75]

---

[72] E. Käsemann, "The Problem of the Historical Jesus," in *Essays on New Testament Themes* (trans. W. J. Montague; London: SCM, 1964), 15–47.

[73] Ibid., 20.

[74] Ibid., 46.

[75] Ibid., 21.

Historical inquiry is thus more difficult than either the super-naturalists or the rationalists imagined it to be. Käsemann's solution is to focus on the language of Jesus by separating the authentic from the inauthentic in the preaching of Jesus by applying the criterion of dissimilarity to his preaching.[76]

Although Käsemann was the initiator of the New Quest, James M. Robinson was the popularizer and historian of the movement. His 1959 book, *A New Quest of the Historical Jesus*,[77] gave the label "New Quest" intelligibility in the vocabulary of contemporary historical Jesus research. Robinson was primarily concerned to answer the question of how Jesus the proclaimer became Jesus Christ the proclaimed.[78] Also recognized with Käsemann and Robinson as participants in the New Quest were Günther Bornkamm, Norman Perrin, Hans Conzelmann, Ernst Fuchs, and Gerhard Ebeling.

Redaction criticism was primarily developed by Bornkamm and Conzelmann.[79] Although redaction criticism presupposes the results of source and form criticism, it also differs in several respects. It focuses on whole Gospels as well as the individual pericope. It stresses the role of the evangelist before that of the community or tradition. In doing so, it seeks to answer the question "What is the theology of this gospel?"[80] The hermeneutical effect of redaction criticism has been to focus on how the Gospel stories relate to each other, which has led to reading the Gospels as whole stories, not just as disparate fragments. This has led to a renewal of interest among biblical scholars in theology. But as seen before with form criticism and the history of religions school, the focus is still not on Jesus but on the theology of the editors of the Gospels.

The effect of the New Quest of the historical Jesus was to focus on the language of Jesus and the theological intentions of those who

---

[76] Ibid., 37.

[77] J. M. Robinson, *A New Quest of the Historical Jesus and Other Essays* (London: SCM, 1959; repr., Philadelphia: Fortress, 1983).

[78] Ibid., 22–25.

[79] G. Bornkamm, G. Barth, and H.-J. Held, *Tradition and Interpretation in Matthew* (trans. P. Scott; Philadelphia: Westminster, 1963); H. Conzelmann, *The Theology of St. Luke* (trans. G. Buswell; New York: Harper & Row, 1960).

[80] G. R. Osborne, "Redaction Criticism," in *New Testament Criticism and Interpretation* (ed. D. A. Black and D. S. Dockery; Grand Rapids: Zondervan, 1991), 199–224.

edited his message for later readers. Through it all, the New Quest still maintained Bultmann's existential concerns and was relatively short-lived because it was perceived to be much the same in nature as the Bultmannian "No Quest."

The Present State of the Quest: Situating Dunn

Less than a century ago, the historical quest for Jesus was widely believed by many to be if not dead then at least at a dead end. Even when I began seminary in the mid-1980s, the quest was still thought of largely in terms of the "New Quest," and that quest viewed as a relatively small group of scholars working with post-Bultmannian presuppositions that had run low on steam. Such is clearly not the case today. There has never been more activity and variety in the field of historical Jesus research than there has been in the last 25 years. I do not think it is going too far to say that the last 25 years have been the most fruitful in all the years of scholarly investigation of the historical figure of Jesus. In other words, more significant work from a wider array of perspectives has been produced in the last two and a half decades than at any time since Reimarus's fragments were first published. We are truly living in the golden age of research on the historical Jesus. Mostly this is because of the variety of historical and interpretive methods that are used today in New Testament scholarship.

In the last part of his *Quest*, Schweitzer concluded that there were only two live options for those wishing to find the historical Jesus: Wrede's thoroughgoing skepticism or his own thoroughgoing eschatology.[81] Wrede's approach led to historical skepticism and non-Jewish, modernist conclusions concerning Jesus, based mostly on his willingness to treat messianic texts as inventions of the evangelists. Schweitzer's approach, on the other hand, led to wholly eschatological, Jewish conclusions concerning Jesus, mostly due to his refusal to assign messianic statements to the early church.

N. T. Wright holds that Schweitzer's words, written at the beginning of the century, have proven prophetic in that most who are

---

[81] Schweitzer, *The Quest of the Historical Jesus*, 398.

seeking the historical Jesus may be grouped into two camps: those who have followed Wrede (thoroughgoing skepticism) and those who have followed Schweitzer (thoroughgoing eschatology). In recognizing these two distinct groups, Wright distinguishes between the Third Quest and the Renewed New Quest.[82] The Renewed New Quest has adopted the thoroughgoing skepticism of Wrede concerning the Gospels as sources and has sought to discover a non-Jewish Jesus. The Third Quest has sought to ground Jesus within the Judaism of the first century and has been far less skeptical than the Renewed New Quest concerning the value of the canonical Gospels as sources for the life of Jesus. The most obvious expression of the Renewed New Quest is the Jesus Seminar, led by the late Robert Funk. Some prominent advocates of the Third Quest include Wright, E. P. Sanders, John P. Meier, Ben Witherington III, the late Ben F. Meyer, and James D. G. Dunn. This does not mean, of course, that all contemporary parties in historical Jesus research fit neatly into one of these two categories. But recognition that these two overarching categories are not perfect does not render them useless.

While recognizing the validity of Wright's observations concerning Wrede and Schweitzer, skepticism and eschatology are not mutually exclusive categories. One can be skeptical about the chances of significant success in discovering a historical basis for knowledge of Jesus and still hold that Jesus had an eschatological orientation (e.g., as Bultmann did). Still, in recognizing the diversity of approaches in present-day Jesus scholarship, one must provide some way to measure or classify various approaches that different authors take in seeking him. To this end, I suggest that we think in terms of "modern" approaches on the one hand and "postmodern" on the other, recognizing that these two overarching categories are somewhat ill defined and that the terms are more broadly descriptive than specifically definitive.

Historians adopting an essentially modernist approach seek to be as scientific and as objective as possible in the doing of history. They are thus optimistic about the possibility of discovering what history

---

[82] N. T. Wright, *Jesus and the Victory of God* (vol. 2 of *Christian Origins and the Question of God*; Minneapolis: Fortress, 1996), 28–124. Wright coined the term "Third Quest." Neill and Wright, *The Interpretation of the New Testament, 1861–1986*, 363.

can tell us of Jesus, although they may be somewhat pessimistic about how close history can take us to the actual person of Jesus of Nazareth. A modern approach insists that some pictures of Jesus are right and others are wrong or, at the very least, that some pictures of Jesus more accurately describe the historical figure of Jesus than do others. The modern approach also insists that there is a right way to conduct historical research and of reading texts about Jesus, although different scholars disagree about historical method and how texts should be read or what they mean.

Postmodern historians are pessimistic about the possibility of ever engaging in historical research with a sufficiently objective mind-set. Furthermore, they doubt that any historian can arrive at a single picture of Jesus that is correct or better than any other picture. Texts about Jesus are thus essentially open. The postmodern position says that Jesus is now, and forever has been, a construct—and that this is not a bad thing for historians because we live in a world that is composed of stories and symbols. Whereas modernist historians see history as being essentially a scientific task, postmodern historians view it either as a literary task or perhaps a quest for self-realization, better suited to the school of humanities than the science department.

The projects of John P. Meier and E. P. Sanders serve as good examples of an essentially modern approach to the quest. Meier optimistically declares that he hopes to find the Jesus that a symposium composed of a Roman Catholic scholar, a Protestant scholar, a Jewish scholar, and an agnostic scholar could agree on.[83] On the other hand, he pessimistically declares, "By the Jesus of History I mean the Jesus whom we can 'recover' and examine by using the scientific tools of modern historical research,"[84] and "both method and goal are extremely narrow and limited: the results do not claim to provide either a substitute for or the object of faith."[85]

E. P. Sanders also brings an essentially modernist approach to the task. Sounding like a scientist, he spends a great deal of time talking

---

[83] J. P. Meier, *A Marginal Jew: The Roots of the Problem and the Person* (vol. 1 of *Rethinking the Historical Jesus*; New York: Doubleday, 1991), 1.

[84] Ibid., 25.

[85] Ibid., 30–31.

about evidence, facts, and hypotheses.[86] He also seeks to be as objective and impartial as possible. In doing so, he intends not to raise questions or provide answers of theological significance but to be *purely historical*.[87] Finally, he intends to focus on "facts" about Jesus rather than "sayings" of Jesus.[88]

The postmodern end of the continuum is ably represented by John Dominic Crossan. Crossan has no illusions about being objective. He forthrightly declares, "I am concerned, not with an unattainable objectivity, but with an attainable honesty. My challenge to my colleagues is to accept those formal moves or, if they reject them, to replace them with better ones. They are, of course, only *formal* moves, which then demand a *material* investment."[89] He further sees a plurality of equally valid positions concerning the historical Jesus[90] (although his own reconstruction presents Jesus as a peasant, Jewish cynic). Recognizing that there will be differing valid responses to, and readings of, Jesus does not in any way lead him to be pessimistic about either history or faith or to conclude that the historical Jesus is not relevant to Christian faith.

> But there is not in my work any presumption that the historical Jesus or earliest Christianity is something you get once and for all forever. And that is not because Jesus and Christianity are special or unique. No past of continuing importance can ever avoid repeated reconstruction. . . .
>
> In every generation, the historical Jesus must be reconstructed anew, and that reconstruction must become by faith the face of God for here and now.[91]

Many have commented, however, on the apparent contradiction between Crossan's seemingly objective evaluation of sources and his

---

[86] E. P. Sanders, *Jesus and Judaism* (Philadelphia: Fortress, 1985), 3–13.

[87] Ibid., 2.

[88] Ibid., 3–13.

[89] J. D. Crossan, *The Historical Jesus: The Life of a Mediterranean Jewish Peasant* (San Francisco: Harper & Row, 1991), xxxiv.

[90] Crossan, *The Historical Jesus*, 423; and idem, "The Historical Jesus in Earliest Christianity," in *Jesus and Faith: A Conversation on the Work of John Dominic Crossan* (ed. Jeffrey Carlson and Robert A. Ludwig; Maryknoll, N.Y.: Orbis, 1994), 3–4.

[91] J. D. Crossan, *Four Other Gospels: Shadows on the Contour of the Canon* (Minneapolis: Seabury, 1995), 7–11.

postmodern preference for perspectivalism.[92] Simply put, in my estimation, Crossan's supposedly objective manner of treating sources is subjec-
tively colored by his esoteric selection of which sources belong to which
historical strata. Yet Crossan is happy to allow others to reach their own
conclusions regarding who they believe the historical Jesus was so long
as they seek him, are confronted by him, and respond appropriately
to the Jesus they find. In the 2005 Greer-Heard Point-Counterpoint
Forum dialogue between Crossan and Wright on the resurrection of
Jesus, Crossan repeatedly declared that the *mode* of Jesus' resurrection
was secondary in importance to the *meaning* of his resurrection.[93]

The work of Wright falls in between these two extremes. On the
one hand, giving a nod to the postmodern approach, he forthrightly
declares that the historian plays a role in the creation of the history
to which contemporary readers have access when he distinguishes
between history as events that actually happened (history-E) and history as what people write about what actually happened (history-W).[94]

> Part of the point of all historical study is to recognize that all "his-
> tory-W" is written from one particular angle, involving particular
> selection and arrangement. Nobody ever "tells it like it was," because
> all events from the fall of a leaf to the fall of an empire, are too
> complex for that. All "history-W" therefore involves fresh selection,
> fresh rearrangements, not in order to prove that previous "history-
> W" "got it wrong" as regards "history-E" but in order that people of

---

[92] See especially N. T. Wright, "Taking the Text with Her Pleasure: A Post-Post-Mod-
ernist Response to J. Dominic Crossan's *The Historical Jesus: The Life of a Mediterranean Jewish
Peasant,*" *Theology* 96 (July/August 1993): 303–10; P. R. Eddy, "Response by Paul Rhodes
Eddy," in *The Resurrection: An Interdisciplinary Symposium on the Resurrection of Jesus* (ed. S. T.
Davis, D. Kendall, and G. O'Collins; New York: Oxford University Press, 1997), 285–86. For
an evaluation of the impact of Crossan's postmodern hermeneutic on his Jesus research, see
my *The Quest of the Hermeneutical Jesus: The Impact of Hermeneutics on the Jesus Research of John
Dominic Crossan and N. T. Wright* (Lanham, Md.: University Press of America, 2008), 27–75.

[93] N. T. Wright and John Dominic Crossan, "The Resurrection: Historical Event or
Theological Explanation: A Dialogue," in *The Resurrection of Jesus: John Dominic Crossan and
N. T. Wright in Dialogue* (ed. R. B. Stewart; Minneapolis and London: Fortress and SPCK,
2006), 16–47, esp. 27–29.

[94] N. T. Wright, "In Grateful Dialogue," in *Jesus and the Restoration of Israel: A Critical
Assessment of N. T. Wright's Jesus and the Victory of God* (ed. C. C. Newman; Downers Grove:
InterVarsity, 1999), 246; cf. N. T. Wright, *The New Testament and the People of God* (vol. 1 of
Christian Origins and the Question of God; Minneapolis: Fortress, 1992), 81–120.

our own generation may glimpse afresh the "history-E" that previous "history-W" was trying to unveil.[95]

Wright also maintains that all history is storied in nature, again sounding postmodern in terms of favoring narrative over propositions. History is, Wright insists, "neither 'bare facts' nor 'subjective interpretations,' but is rather *the meaningful narrative of events and intentions.*"[96] Accordingly, Wright appeals to a type of narrative analysis similar to that of A. J. Greimas.[97]

On the other hand, Wright rejects the postmodern skepticism that says that all that individuals can know are stories, which order their (constructed) world but do not actually depict past (or present) reality. Furthermore, Wright is clearly a historical realist, albeit a critical realist. As such, he acknowledges "the *reality of the thing known, as something other than the knower* (hence 'realism'), while also fully acknowledging that the only access we have to this reality lies along the spiraling path of *appropriate dialogue or conversation between the knower and the thing known* (hence 'critical')."[98] Accordingly, he rejects a strong version of postmodernism: "To those for whom the study and writing of history is their everyday concern, the qualms of postmodernism will seem incredibly, almost impossibly, over-cautious, shy and retiring. We simply *can* write history. We can know things about what has happened in the past."[99]

---

[95] Wright, "In Grateful Dialogue," 246–47.

[96] Wright, *The New Testament and the People of God*, 82. Wright's concern for intentionality parallels speech-act theory in some ways. Both argue that intentionality is a vital component in determining meaning. In other words, it is through "doing things,'" whether with words (speech-act theory), physical actions (action theory), or both (Wright's worldview analysis), that one's intentions become clear to interpreters and historians. On speech-act theory, see J. L. Austin, *How to Do Things with Words* (Cambridge, Mass: Harvard University Press, 1962); J. Searle, *Speech Acts: An Essay in the Philosophy of Language* (London: Cambridge University Press, 1969).

[97] Wright, *The New Testament and the People of God*, 69–70. Recognizing that Greimas's method is decidedly antihistorical, Wright's intention is not so much to follow it slavishly but to reuse a particular aspect of it. For more on Greimas's method, see A. J. Greimas, *Structural Semantics: An Attempt at a Method* (trans. D. McDowell, R. Schleifer, and A. Veile; Lincoln: University of Nebraska Press).

[98] Wright, *The New Testament and the People of God*, 35.

[99] Ibid., 81.

So, where does James D. G. Dunn's work fit in relation to those who surround him today? Dunn's work is sophisticated and therefore not simple to pin down. Like his Durham neighbor Wright, Dunn holds to a highly nuanced view that recognizes some validity from both sides of the continuum while not tilting strongly to one side or the other. He grants that there are no "bare facts" that exist as "objective artifacts"[100] and there are no raw data that have not been selected by the historical process or arrive on the scene without a historical context.[101] On the other hand, he cautions against a strong view of "textual autonomy."[102] The text alone is never enough for historical research because there is always a hermeneutical circle (or spiral) at work or, to use Gadamer's terminology, dual horizons of interpretation. Historical texts depend on more than themselves as they draw on (a) wider linguistic usage of the time (as well as appealing to other texts outside themselves), (b) language as well as words, and (c) the horizon of the reader as well the horizon of the text. Accordingly, understanding is always provisional and subject to clarification as the whole is illuminated by the parts and vice versa.[103]

Pessimistically he notes that there is always a hermeneutical distance or gap but optimistically he appeals to Gadamer's concept of *Wirkungsgeschichte* (history of effect) and notes that "the gap between text and reader is not empty; it is filled by the effect which the text has exercised in the in-between time between 'an historically intended, distanced object and belonging to a tradition,'" which actually conditions a reader to understand the text by producing an "historically effected consciousness."[104]

Sounding fairly modern, he maintains that there are three "norms" for interpreters of the Jesus tradition: (1) the Greek text for translation, (2) the "plain meaning" for interpretation, and (3) the synoptic tradition

---

[100] Dunn, *Jesus Remembered*, 108–9.

[101] Ibid., 111.

[102] Ibid., 114.

[103] Ibid., 118–22.

[104] Ibid., 122. This section brings to mind thoughts of speech-act theory but apart from a single note saying that Anthony Thiselton referred him to John R. Searle (referred to as R. Searle in both the note and the index) and Nicholas Wolterstorff, there is nothing at all on speech-act theory or the apparent similarity between Gadamer on this point and speech-act theorists. Ibid., 117n63.

for any attempt to illuminate the origins of Christianity. But this should not be taken to mean that he believes that certainty is achievable in historical research if only one observes these norms. Insisting that certainty is not attainable for the historian, he prefers to speak of probability but notes that in history, probability is a "very positive verdict."[105]

Memory and oral tradition are the two concepts that immediately leap off the page when reading *Jesus Remembered*. At the heart of Dunn's declaration in this regard is not simply that what we have in the Jesus tradition is the product of memory or that we cannot get back to Jesus himself or what he did or said, having access only to what his disciples remembered about him. I think Dunn would affirm all of the above but not *merely* all of the above. What we have in the earliest Jesus tradition is a reaction to Jesus by his earliest disciples—indeed a pre-Easter reaction to what he did and said. Historically speaking, I find this to be an extremely optimistic and balanced position. He is not declaring *a la* postmodernism that all one can ever know of Jesus is some sort of construct or that any take on Jesus is as good as any other. But neither is he saying that one can find a Jesus who is purely the product of reasoned—that is, scientific—historical investigation. As a theologian, I find this to be a tremendously positive way of saying that faith and history are not at odds but are in fact comrades. Dunn forthrightly declares, "In short, the tension between faith and history has too often been seen as destructive of good history. On the contrary, however, it is the recognition that Jesus can be perceived *only* through the impact he made on his first disciples (that is, their faith) which is the key to a historical recognition (and reassessment) of that impact."[106]

It "sounds" like Dunn is not taking us back as far as we would like, but in reality he is saying that the synoptic tradition *arises from an encounter* with Jesus. He boldly asserts that this is as good as it gets for historical figures who wrote nothing: "In one sense, of course, we are simply recognizing the nature of the evidence which any biographer has to weigh who has no access to any writings of the biography's subject."[107] One thing that is abundantly clear—and often overlooked by

---

[105] Ibid., 103.
[106] Ibid., 132.
[107] Ibid., 131.

those responding to Dunn—is that he firmly believes that the synoptic tradition takes us back *before Jesus's crucifixion,* which is something many would be hesitant to affirm. He confidently concludes, "However great the shock of Good Friday and Easter for the first disciples, it would be unjustified to assume that these events marked a discontinuity with their initial disciple-response, that they brought about complete disruption of their earlier disciple faith and that the traditioning process began only from that point on."[108] This leads to Dunn's third norm: the priority of the synoptic tradition for getting at the origins of Christianity.[109] Granting that there were differing faith responses to Jesus from the start, Dunn nevertheless insists that there was a unified (not uniform) core of belief that embraced and held together "a diversity of faith responses from the first" and that this is the explanation for the homogeneity one finds in the synoptic traditions.[110]

In emphasizing the role of faith in the development of the synoptic tradition, Dunn recognizes the danger of retreating into a postmodern enclave of a purely communal reading of texts about Jesus. This leads him to insist that history be a public discipline and to desire, like the vast majority of those historians who have sought for Jesus before him, that the Jesus of history have a voice to address contemporary culture.[111]

So, where to situate Dunn? He is neither purely modern nor postmodern in his method or hermeneutic. He not only recognizes some of postmodernism's critiques of modernism as valid, but he also rejects many common postmodern positions such as the autonomy of the text, perspectivalism, or communalism. He falls in the middle ground with Wright, with both affirming critical realism. He is more skeptical than Wright as to the usefulness of narrative criticism[112] and rejects Wright's big idea of the "return from exile."[113] They both reach fairly traditional conclusions concerning Jesus and do so with a fair amount of epistemological humility. They both also offer bold ways

---

108 Ibid., 133.
109 Ibid., 135.
110 Ibid., 134.
111 Ibid., 136.
112 Ibid., 119.
113 Ibid., 331–32.

forward that have been met with a good bit of commentary and criticism. At the end of the day, I see Dunn as depending a bit less on postmodern methods than Wright does but a bit more postmodern in his expectation—that is, a bit more pessimistic about getting Jesus right than Wright is.

Concerning his method and hermeneutic, I think Dunn's approach could be more fully supported by some discussion and appeal to speech-act theory. The distinction between locutionary, illocutionary, and per-locutionary acts would enable him to be more clear in expressing his program. (I think he is already broadly thinking in such ways.) I would also like to see more explicit discussion of worldviews, particularly the worldview of second-temple Judaism and the role that understanding it plays in interpreting texts about Jesus. I think he does go partway down this path with his insistence that texts, like children, have rights, such as knowing their parentage and place of origin.[114] I think his project could be more fully supported by explicitly addressing the role that worldviews play in communication and interpretation. Finally, I have some suspicions as to how specialists in philosophical hermeneutics would read his reading or use of Hans-Georg Gadamer. I am in agreement with what Dunn *says* when he appeals to Gadamer. I just wonder if Gadamer or those specializing in his thought would also agree.

At each and every point along the way, the quest of the historical Jesus has been impacted not only by various philosophical presuppositions but also by different critical and hermeneutical methods. The conclusions and methods of Reimarus, Strauss, and Schleiermacher were impacted by their philosophical presuppositions. The historical Jesus of the first quest (after Schleiermacher) was the product of liberal theology coupled with source criticism. The (non)historical Jesus of the No Quest period was the product of the history of religions school, Bultmann's existentialism, and form criticism. The Jesus of the New Quest was the result of the post-Bultmannian emphasis on the language of Jesus coupled with redaction criticism's concern to discover the theological motivation of the evangelists. Similarly, contemporary quests of Jesus, whether of the Renewed New Quest or Third Quest variety, modern or postmodern variety, are at least in part the product

---

[114] Ibid., 114.

of the philosophical mood of our day and contemporary interpretive methods brought to bear on historical data concerning Jesus. It has always been and always will be thus. I am grateful for Dunn's important and impressive contribution to the field. I look forward to the completion of his massive project with great interest.

2

WHOSE MEMORY?
WHOSE ORALITY?

A CONVERSATION WITH
JAMES D. G. DUNN ON
JESUS AND THE GOSPELS

MARKUS BOCKMUEHL

For over a quarter of a century, Durham University's Professor James D. G. Dunn has been known as one of the world's leading scholars on St. Paul, whose expertise came to its fullest expression in *The Theology of Paul the Apostle*[1] along with a range of other monographs and commentaries.[2] More recently, however, he has turned his attention to a large project on the subject of the "historical Jesus," touched upon in several earlier works[3] but now designed to occupy him for some years to come. *Jesus Remembered*, which aims to articulate a second "new

---

[1] J. D. G. Dunn, *The Theology of Paul the Apostle* (Grand Rapids: Eerdmans, 1998).

[2] Especially J. D. G. Dunn, *The Theology of Paul the Apostle*; idem., *The Epistle to the Galatians* (BNTC; London: A&C Black, 1993); and idem., *A New Perspective on Jesus: What the Quest for the Historical Jesus Missed* (Grand Rapids: Baker Academic, 2005).

[3] J. D. G. Dunn, *Jesus and the Spirit: A Study of the Religious and Charismatic Experience of Jesus and the First Christians as Reflected in the New Testament* (Philadelphia: Westminster, 1975); and idem, *The Evidence for Jesus* (Philadelphia: Westminster, 1985).

perspective" (in keeping with its influential predecessor on Paul), is the subject of the present volume.[4]

The preface shows that, like the Pauline theology, this work arises out of the author's long and distinguished career of teaching at the universities of Nottingham and especially Durham, as well as active contributions to the international lecture circuit. Although a major work in its own right, *Jesus Remembered* is merely the first of three projected volumes on *Christianity in the Making*, designed to provide "a comprehensive overview of the beginnings of Christianity," covering its first 120 years.[5] Volume 2 will survey the historical communities (with a strong emphasis on Paul), whereas volume 3 is intended to address the period of AD 70 to 150. It does also, however, stand on its own as a major original contribution to debate about the "historical Jesus."

The first part of the book, "Faith and the Historical Jesus," lays out the project vis-à-vis earlier Jesus scholarship, a kind of "history of the historical quests." Dunn asserts that the study of Christian beginnings programmatically concerns "three great questions":

1. What explains both Jesus' crucifixion and his impact on his disciples?
2. How and why did the Jesus movement after his death move beyond Judaism?
3. Was second-century Gentile Christianity fundamentally continuous or discontinuous?

Dunn views the history of the quest as characterized by a tension between the "flight from dogma" (chap. 4) and the "flight from history" (chap. 5). In doing so, he ignores, either inadvertently or deliberately, the possibility that aversion to dogma might be merely an instance of aversion to history, or indeed vice versa. (On that reading most of the discussion in each of these chapters would merit cross-referencing in the other.) The misguided eighteenth-century notion that doctrinal perception is somehow intrinsically inimical to historical affirmation

---

[4] This chapter represents a revision and expansion of material first published in M. Bock-muehl, "Review of James D. G. Dunn, *Jesus Remembered*," *JTS* 56 (2005): 140–49. Relevant material is reused here by permission of the *Journal of Theological Studies*. I am grateful to my doctoral student David Lincicum for a number of suggestions for improvement.

[5] J. D. G. Dunn, *Jesus Remembered* (vol. 1 of *Christianity in the Making*; Grand Rapids: Eerdmans, 2003), xiii, 6.

remains surprisingly widespread in contemporary biblical scholarship, even among interpreters who ostensibly understand the text's living footprint as potentially a help rather than a hindrance to circumspect historical study.

Dunn's historical survey of the Quests finds tentative beginnings in the Renaissance and Reformation.[6] Although much of this (e.g., on the rise of historical and textual study) is standard fare, there are some poignant insights here (e.g., following Jaroslav Pelikan's observations about the influence of Franciscan piety's "new realism" in relation to the humanity and passion of Jesus). The "Flight from Dogma" is characteristically associated with the Enlightenment, here said to begin a century earlier than usual, circa 1650. The rejection of divine revelation and miracle eventually ushers in the romantic reaction that in turn gave birth to liberal Protestantism, whose Jesus of timeless unobjectionable morality went hand in hand with great advances in historical-critical study of the Gospels. The (temporary) demise of the liberal approach is informatively chronicled via the usual reference points of Schweitzer, Kähler, and others—but with a curious virtual embargo, both here and in chapter 5, on the role played in that demise by Karl Barth and other champions of dialectical theology.

Somewhat unexpectedly (but perhaps sensibly), liberalism's downfall is followed without further ado by the much more recent sociological approaches of Gerd Theissen, Richard Horsley, and the revival of the liberal Jesus among North Americans like Robert Funk, John Dominic Crossan, Helmut Koester, and Marcus Borg.

The "Flight from History" here begins with a survey of the historical-critical method's epistemology and dwells more fully on Bultmann and the "second quest," rightly depicted as dragging on without significant epistemological refinements among certain contemporary German scholars of the older generation. The "Third Quest" is discussed extensively but supplied with a deliberate question mark: although welcoming its emphasis on Jesus' Jewishness, Dunn appears to view it as ultimately hamstrung by the same familiar weaknesses of the historical method—and thus vulnerable to the assault of postmodernism's radically ahistorical relativism.

---

[6] Ibid., 17–97.

Setting out his own methodological stall in chapter 6, Dunn affirms the vital necessity of historical inquiry in the context of hermeneutics and faith. History allows an appreciation of issues like readerly distance, probable rather than certain knowledge, and a "critical realism" in the dialogue between present and past. In spelling out the presuppositions of his hermeneutical circle, Dunn underscores the need to respect the historical integrity of texts, their "right" to speak in their own terms and to be heard primarily in terms of their contextual "plain meaning." He tips his hat in passing to Gadamer's model of "two horizons" (and, less persuasively, to *Wirkungsgeschichte*) while wanting to stress that interpretation is a genuine two-way encounter. Faith is seen to be the very fabric of the Gospel tradition from the beginning, witnessing to the impact made by the remembered Jesus (an impact construed in organic continuity with Jesus' intention). Here lies Dunn's major thesis in a nutshell, although he wisely takes care to safeguard this against a fideistic collapse into a purely intraecclesial discourse.

Part 2 moves on from issues of hermeneutics and the history of scholarship to the methods of Gospel study more strictly speaking. It begins with a useful survey of well-known canonical, hypothetical, and external sources for the study of Jesus (chap. 7) and sketches the historical context of first-century Judaism in Galilee and elsewhere (chap. 9), culminating in a preliminary outline of the life and mission of Jesus.[7]

The "key thesis of the whole volume," however, is chapter 8 on the Jesus tradition.[8] Here Dunn presents the parameters for his overall argument: continuity between Jesus and his background links to continuity with his aftermath, and it is the didactic, witnessing, remembering, and quasi-biographical nature of the Jesus tradition itself that confirms an essential continuity with the personal impact of Jesus as the founder of Christianity. A review of prior scholarship on the remembered Jesus tradition is followed by illustrations of the tradition's orality, drawn from the three Pauline conversion stories in Acts as well as specific narrative and teaching pericopae in Mark and Q, the common source (German *Quelle*). Other significant features of

---

[7] Ibid., 312–26.
[8] Ibid., 173–254.

this chapter include an emphasis on narrative *sequences* of oral tradition and, perhaps more interestingly, an understandable preference for variations in "performance" rather than sequential editorial "layering" as the most appropriate mode of expressing the "remembered Jesus." The transition to writing is on this view not an individual author's unprecedented creation for a particular community but the commitment to a public literary form of a widely shared traditional remembrance of Jesus with which the recipients were already quite familiar.

To privilege the tradition's "characteristic" Jesus in this fashion will, in Dunn's view, legitimize a modest but realistic quest for the "historical Jesus" as the "historic Jesus," who is above all "Jesus remembered" by and among those first involved with him (chap. 10). The emphasis thus moves decisively away from Gospel origins as by default a *literary* problem and toward an understanding of the *oral* form of tradition as original and most formative of the shape the Gospels take (although Dunn continues to operate with the assumption of Q and Marcan priority).

The outline attempted in chapter 9 is then developed in a very much fuller form in parts 3 to 5 on the mission of Jesus (Jesus and John the Baptist, the Kingdom of God as metaphor, the audience of Jesus and his practice and teaching on discipleship), on the Question of Jesus' self-understanding (as echoed first in the way he was understood, and then in the terms of the Sonship of God and of Man in which he described himself), and then finally on the climax of Jesus' mission (crucifixion and resurrection).

The distinct emphasis on orality surfaces repeatedly to good effect, aided by numerous close synoptic readings of texts. Illustrations of the benefits include the suggestion that the treatments of the hand-washing episode of Mark 7 (par. Matthew 15) may reflect contextually varied settings of the same oral teaching—in which quite possibly Jesus was "heard differently."[9] Another example is the "Son of Man" issue: contrary to recent interpretative fashion, Dunn quite plausibly traces the opaqueness and pluriformity of the evangelists' usage not in the first instance to their literary creativity but to the deliberate ambiguity of Jesus' *own* parlance. His ambiguous usage was received

---

[9] Ibid., 574–76.

and understood in diverse oral contexts that came inter alia to "reverse the direction of travel" implied in the Danielic Son of Man's "coming" while heightening the Christological significance in view of Psalm 110 (with an explicit preference for "roles" rather than "titles").[10]

Replete with erudite critical engagement in recent scholarly debates, these extensive and often detailed textual discussions cover what will be well-traveled territory to many readers. At the same time, Dunn's characteristically pragmatic and common-sense deployment of his theory lends the whole work a lightness of touch, which often allows old debates to appear in a fresh luminance even when the coordinates of the discussion are more conventional and less specifically tied to orality. One key example of this is support for the suggestion, which has been gaining scholarly ground in recent years, that Jesus anticipated his quasi-sacrificial death in a way that also linked it with a hope of vindication and resurrection.[11]

The treatment of the resurrection accounts itself stands in significant contrast to John P. Meier's explicit refusal to include the resurrection as among the "historical Jesus" questions. On the other hand, Dunn's treatment is compatible with much in N. T. Wright's magnum opus published in the same year: he concludes quite rightly that resurrection is intelligible, not as secondary effect or reflection, but only as experiential (and metaphorical) cause of Christology, a core of the tradition from the start and "the *beginning* of belief in Jesus as exalted."[12] On this point, the argument might have benefited from closer interaction with the carefully argued thesis of Horbury[13] and others about pre-Christian Jewish expectations of an exalted or heavenly Messiah. Attempting to explain the resurrection of Jesus as "metaphor," on the other hand, seems a hermeneutically questionable judgment that is not redeemed by appeal to metaphorical applications of such language elsewhere.[14] The necessarily revolutionary paradox of the early Christians' affirmation was that Easter Sunday confronted them with

---

[10] Ibid., 724–62.

[11] Ibid., 796–824.

[12] Ibid., 875–76.

[13] William Horbury, *Jewish Messianism and the Cult of Christ* (London: SCM, 1998).

[14] Dunn, *Jesus Remembered*, 878, with note 230, including references to national "resurrection."

resurrection *stricto sensu*, indeed with precisely the event from which all knowledge and hope of resurrection would henceforth derive.

Summing up in chapter 19, Dunn returns, above all, to the emphases of chapter 8. Realistically, the object of any historical quest can only be Jesus as he was actually remembered and had his impact on the disciples. This remembered Jesus is the de facto focus of the Jesus tradition itself, which derives its actual shape, above all, from local repertoires of oral performance and transmission. Dunn closes his argument by drawing out the continuity of Jesus' impact past the apostolic tradition to its life in the church, suggesting that through the Jesus tradition, it still remains possible today to encounter "the Jesus from whom Christianity stems."[15]

A shared tendency among contemporary British authors of books in the "historical Jesus" genre has been the belief that in order to say anything at all on this topic, one must say everything. This is perhaps particularly true of the pair of present-day "Durham masters of the big book," as one recent interlocutor put it.[16] At one level, Dunn himself would readily concede that the notion of essential patterns of continuity between the historical Jesus and the grain of the Gospel tradition is not strikingly new, not least among contributors to the Third Quest for the historical Jesus. At the same time, however, in a phrase deliberately echoing his earlier work on Paul, he claims to be presenting nothing less than "a new perspective on Jesus."[17]

Even in a book-length assessment like the present volume, a work of the size and ambition of *Jesus Remembered* compels one to be selective. The critical difficulties surrounding many of the issues under debate here have been such that a full-length monograph on each one would be required to do them justice. Therefore, my remaining remarks will focus primarily on five questions related to Dunn's "new perspective"—specifically, what it is that in his view makes it new or distinctive.

---

[15] Dunn, *Jesus Remembered*, 893.

[16] R. Morgan, "Christian Faith and Historical Jesus Research: A Reply to James Dunn," *ExpTim* 116 (2005): 218.

[17] Dunn, *Jesus Remembered*, 881. Cf. now idem, *A New Perspective on Jesus*, and see previously idem, "The New Perspective on Paul," *BJRL* 65 (1983): 95–122; and idem, *The New Perspective on Paul: Collected Essays* (WUNT 185; Tübingen: Mohr Siebeck, 2005).

1. My first query relates this issue of newness to previous New Testament study. Early reviewers have repeatedly pointed out that Dunn's analysis of scholarship on oral tradition significantly underplays the extensive contributions of writers like Harald Riesenfeld, Birger Gerhardsson, Joachim Jeremias, Rainer Riesner, Samuel Byrskog, and others in favor of a somewhat disproportionate emphasis on Werner H. Kelber (rightly criticized for ideological overinterpretation) and especially on the contemporary and largely anecdotal evidence adduced by Kenneth E. Bailey (here supplemented by one MPhil student's "hopes to carry out more scientifically controlled fieldwork"[18]). Byrskog and Riesner, in particular, seem to be largely ignored, although in response to a Scandinavian reviewer, Dunn has subsequently conceded that Gerhardsson may in fact be "much closer" to the preferred position of Bailey.[19] As it happens, Gerhardsson's proposals about the more formal techniques of transmission in Jewish tradition have been considerably extended and refined by the work of Byrskog and Riesner: the latter worked with particular emphasis on the Jewish context of Jesus' *teaching* of his followers (NB *mathētai, talmidim*; i.e., "learners"), whereas the former has significantly advanced our understanding of the role of "(eye)witness" terminology in a context of oral history and memory.[20]

2. British New Testament scholarship has a long and sometimes distinguished history of pragmatic resistance to the continental and American penchant for theory—and for losing the object of inquiry behind acres of elaborate, but doubtfully productive, theoretical scaffolding. At times, however, the British approach certainly has its own

---

[18] Dunn, *Jesus Remembered*, 209n187.

[19] J. D. G. Dunn, "On History, Memory and Eyewitnesses: In Response to Bengt Holmberg and Samuel Byrskog," *JSNT* 26 (2004): 483n21. Contrast the skeptical reaction of Gerhardsson himself in B. Gerhardsson, "The Secret of the Transmission of the Unwritten Jesus Tradition," *NTS* 51 (2005): 1–18.

[20] See now the emphasis on the gospels' long-neglected stress on named individuals in R. Bauckham, "The Eyewitnesses and the Gospel Tradition," *JSHJ* 1 (2003): 28–60; and idem, *Jesus and the Eyewitnesses: The Gospels as Eyewitness Testimony* (Grand Rapids: Eerdmans, 2006). See also my own studies in M. Bockmuehl, *Seeing the Word: Refocusing New Testament Study* (Grand Rapids: Baker Academic, 2006), 161–88; idem, "Peter's Death in Rome? Back to Front and Upside Down," *SJT* 60 (2007): 1–23; and idem, "New Testament *Wirkungsgeschichte* and the Early Christian Appeal to Living Memory," in *Memory and Remembrance in the Bible and Antiquity* (ed. L. T. Stuckenbruck et al.; Tübingen: Mohr Siebeck, 2007).

drawbacks. In the present case, it is hard not to feel that Dunn has left his welcome stress on remembrance somewhat starved of theoretical definition and support—he himself has subsequently wondered if at least the *title* of his book left him "vulnerable to criticism on that score."[21] Despite occasional doffings of the cap to one or two classic reference points of oral history (B. Vansina, A. B. Lord), the 2003 *mega biblion* left unclear whether early Christian remembering is to be conceptualized in terms of a theory of "oral history," of "eyewitness testimony," of "collective" or "cultural memory," or of some other primary focus. The complexity of the subject matter is clearly such that no one off-the-shelf theoretical framework can be expected to "do the trick." Still, it remains puzzling that although in a subsequent exchange Dunn claims to "recognize the importance" of Maurice Halbwachs,[22] *Jesus Remembered* never mentions either Halbwachs or Philippe Ariès on collective memory, Pierre Nora on "places of memory," Jan Assmann on "cultural memory," Jocelyn Small on memory in antiquity, or John Lukacs on "historical consciousness" and the "remembered past." Aside from a recognition of the fragility of personal and social memory, one of the implications of attending to such studies might be to give more explicit credence to the nature of memory's particularity as attaching most fruitfully to persons, places, or objects that may persist or mutate where individual recollection merely pales. Since our age of virtual reality has pretty much brought to fulfillment Jorge Luis Borges's famously depressing prophecy about the infinite library,[23] it is no doubt unreasonable to expect sustained engagement with *all* these approaches. But in a work of this magnitude and ambition, it was a little surprising to encounter *none* of them.[24]

---

[21] Dunn, *A New Perspective on Jesus*, 45.

[22] Dunn, "On History, Memory and Eyewitnesses," 481.

[23] J. L. Borges, *Ficciones (1935–1944)* (Buenos Aires: Sur, 1944).

[24] Some of this has since been remedied in more recent publications, including, for example, Dunn, *A New Perspective on Jesus*, 43–45; idem, "Social Memory and the Oral Jesus Tradition," in *Memory in the Bible and Antiquity: The Fifth Durham-Tübingen Research Symposium (Durham, September 2004)* (WUNT 212; ed. L. T. Stuckenbruck et al.; Tübingen: Mohr Siebeck, 2007), 179–94, with passing reference to Assmann and Halbwachs. Cf. Dunn's students, including T. C. Mournet, *Oral Tradition and Literary Dependency: Variability and Stability in the Synoptic Tradition and Q* (WUNT 2; Tübingen: Mohr Siebeck, 2005), 195; and A. LeDonne, "Theological Memory Distortion in the Jesus Tradition: A Study in Social

3. Further on the conceptualization of memory, another issue concerns Dunn's view of the nature of the early Christian "remembering" and the *identity* of those who remembered. There is a fleeting reference to "Apostolic Custodians,"[25] but we hear rather too little about who they were, how they were regarded within the oral and written tradition, and so on. For Dunn, memory of Jesus is a matter of the "living tradition," of numerous and largely anonymous communities who appear to possess and animate this memory almost innately or by default.[26] It seems ironic, given the explicit stress on the "impact" of the memory of Jesus, that in 1,000 pages Dunn never uses more than a passing footnote to discuss the significance of Justin's view on the Gospels as "memoirs *of the apostles*" (indeed, of *specific* apostles) or, for that matter, the analogous comments of Papias and the Elder, Irenaeus and Polycarp, Polycrates, and any number of others on the remarkably specific and concrete *apostolicity* of the tradition's witness to Jesus. Dunn quite rightly acknowledges the role of Peter, James, and John as the Gospel tradition's "principal witnesses,"[27] and for Peter and John, at any rate, that is also the clear testimony of the New Testament and the early church. What such early Christian preference for the apostolicity of individual memory might mean, however, is perhaps insufficiently explored in this book. Thus it seems significant, for example, that despite its displacement by Matthew and virtual absence from the manuscript and commentary traditions for several centuries, the Gospel of Mark's canonicity was never in doubt because it was firmly linked with an evangelist whose Petrine apostolic imprint neither friend nor foe in antiquity would bother to question.

Similarly, Richard Bauckham rightly stresses the key question of *whose* memory is in view: "who does the controlling, and how" in "informal controlled" tradition—and why should the Gospel tradition's balance between stability and flexibility not be applicable to a "*formal* controlled tradition" just as easily as to an "informal" one?[28]

Memory Theory," in *Memory and Remembrance in the Bible and Antiquity* (ed. L. T. Stuckenbruck et al.; Tübingen: Mohr Siebeck, 2007); and idem, *The Historiographical Jesus: Memory, Typology and the Son of David* (Waco: Baylor University Press, 2008).

[25] Dunn, *Jesus Remembered*, 180–81.
[26] Cf. Dunn, "History, Memory and Eyewitnesses," 482–87.
[27] Dunn, *Jesus Remembered*, 181.
[28] Bauckham, *Jesus and the Eyewitnesses*, 257–63 and passim.

This point is also notable in that "memory" for Dunn means almost exclusively *synoptic* memory: the list of relevant Christian sources expressly highlights Mark, Q, Matthew and Luke, and the *Gospel of Thomas*.[29] The Fourth Gospel is expressly sidelined in less than two pages, as "a secondary source"[30] keeping company with "other gospels" and agrapha. The eyewitness memory of the Beloved Disciple strikingly arises in the text only in the form of a *question* (thrice in passing,[31] otherwise it is relegated to the forthcoming volume 3 in a couple of footnotes).[32] The index shows each of the Synoptics to be referenced more than twice as often as the Fourth Gospel (even if in practice the latter does unexpectedly fare rather better than either Q or *Thomas*). In a book of this size, this is where the motif of *apostolicity* and of eyewitness testimony inextricably rooted above all (but by no means only) in John and Mark would seem to call for a good deal of further discussion. The earliest recipients in the Great Church at any rate recognized this theme and made much of its importance for apostolic faith, by no means discounting John's witness as opposed to Mark's. We must await volume 3 with interest, not least for the attention it will presumably give to challenges like that of Richard Bauckham on the subject of the Beloved Disciple's eyewitness testimony.

4. A further question concerns how the "new" of this perspective relates to scholarship it implicitly designates as "old"—and therefore, as someone has said somewhere, "obsolete and passing away." Although I find myself in considerable sympathy with Dunn's proposed approach, specialists in synoptic criticism may wonder how they are meant to work with what is on offer here. More conventional practitioners will inevitably find that the emphasis on orality seems to come at the cost of precision about such classic matters as sources, redaction, even authenticity and historicity. Dunn would perhaps respond, not unreasonably, that in too many cases that aim of precision was illusory and misguided from the start, dependent as it was on an excessively literary "cut-and-paste" paradigm. Nevertheless, might not Synopticists argue

---

[29] Dunn, *Jesus Remembered*, 143–65.
[30] Ibid., 167.
[31] Ibid., 843, 846, 854.
[32] Ibid., 510n98; 834n33.

in return that even if one grants a good many of Dunn's illustrations of orality, on his own assumption of Q and Marcan priority, there still remains a significant proportion of pericopae in which the very consistency of Matthean and Lucan developments makes the "old perspective" of quasi-literary analysis seem quite reasonable?

A similar quandary may beset those accustomed to asking standard questions about the historical Jesus, including his authentic teaching, identity, and intentions. Despite Dunn's generally laudable recognition that the past is knowable only through memory, and "the real Jesus" only through the impact he had, his project does not always maintain with sufficient clarity the distinction between Jesus' historical impact and his historical intention—between Jesus himself and the memory of him. I am in full agreement about the inescapable priority of memory, and therefore somewhat less troubled by that slippage than other critics may be. But Dunn's repeated and emphatic prioritization of Jesus' "impact" as opposed to "Jesus himself" will inevitably leave some readers wondering to what extent "the historical Jesus" remains a viable object of inquiry at all. Perhaps the answer is that apart from the earliest memory, he does not. That could be a perfectly defensible point of view; indeed, if Dunn is right, one could argue that there is really no such thing as "the historical Jesus" in the old-fashioned sense. But to say this would be explicitly to limit the extent to which one can speak sensibly about how Jesus thought of himself (as chaps. 16 and 17 do extensively). More than one critic has noted the tension between the seemingly slippery emphasis on an oral tradition's "living performance" and, on the other hand, the recurring confident appeals to that tradition's "stable core."[33] The only way to address this question, it seems to me, is by way of a closer analysis of the (largely personal) apostolic *vehicles* of that stability.

5. My final query raises the question of how "new" this perspective really is, or whether, despite all its best intentions, the essential scope of inquiry does not in fact continue within certain well-trodden paths of the prior historical Quests—especially the Third.

---

[33] D. J. Harrington, "Who Do You Say That I Am," *America* 189 (2003): 22. Cf. A. F. Gregory, "An Oral and Written Gospel? Reflections on Remembering Jesus," *ExpTim* 116 (2005): 7–12.

By definition, quests are a function of the questions they ask. And so it is worth returning to the three concerns that were stated at the beginning to define the study of Christian origins: (1) the reasons for Jesus' crucifixion and his impact on his disciples, (2) the reasons for the Jesus movement's expansion beyond Judaism, and (3) the question of second-century Gentile Christianity's continuity or discontinuity from the Jesus movement. Questions 2 and 3 address matters to be covered extensively in subsequent volumes, and we ought not perhaps to prejudge the answers they will receive. Doubtless, all three questions remain among the worthy and interesting tasks for scholarly study. Nevertheless, if we are to take seriously Dunn's timely call to prioritize the actual impact of Jesus on his followers, then it seems right to wonder if these remarkably traditional historical-critical topics really constitute the "three great questions" for an understanding either of Jesus or of Christianity in the making.

As has been the custom in all three conventional Quests, the questions posed are exclusively "etic" rather than "emic"—positing modernism's phenomenological, outsider's point of view that seems constitutionally incapable of addressing the sorts of "great questions" about the remembered Jesus that the tradition itself actually raised consistently from the very beginning. "Who do you say that I am" is not merely a clever synoptic narrative yarn but is the question the New Testament poses unrelentingly for believing and unbelieving readers alike. Who is Jesus of Nazareth? Is he dead or alive? In what sense, if any, is he "Lord and Messiah" (Acts 2:36) or "the Messiah who is above all, God blessed forever" (Rom 9:5)? Was the God of Israel in Christ reconciling the created world to himself? And what present and future reality do such assertions effect or entail? Why is there church, baptism, or absolution in his name?

One may be permitted to wonder if, and indeed why, these are perhaps rather more prominent among the questions that the memory of Jesus *did in fact* generate in the earliest tradition. Awkward they may be for the contemporary heirs of classic historical *Wissenschaft*. But what if, notwithstanding their awkwardness, these questions in fact retain the best potential to guide a "new" perspective to a properly historical understanding of Jesus remembered? It is here that the classic Quests have arguably been found most wanting and that attention to the historical impact of Jesus might in principle gain significant new ground. An argument that ignores them, as Robert Morgan rightly insists,[34] can only ever *seem* to produce "a Jesus congruent with the biblical witness": while it may seek to preserve the biblical picture of Jesus' humanity, in fact it "disregards the biblical belief in his divinity"—a belief, I would add, that for the biblical and patristic authors is neither extricable from his humanity nor somehow thinkable in a sort of second-order abstraction from it.

Dunn will no doubt shed much further light on these and related matters in his forthcoming volumes in this series. Here it remains for me to affirm my great admiration for a most impressive and attractive synthesis of scholarship on Jesus and the Gospels, which the editors of the present volume rightly considered an appropriate subject for this extended scholarly engagement. Dunn's *Jesus Remembered* not only distils a distinguished lifetime of teaching and learning but also provides excellent stimulus for a long-overdue reappreciation of the apostolic memory of the early church as the trustworthy place of access to Jesus of Nazareth. I offer these remarks as a contribution to that task, in grateful acknowledgment of Professor Dunn's stimulus.

---

[34] Morgan, "Christian Faith and Historical Jesus Research," 221.

3

TELLING THE
TRUTH OF HISTORY

A RESPONSE TO JAMES D. G. DUNN'S
JESUS REMEMBERED[1]

SCOT MCKNIGHT

What the great Southern writer Flannery O'Connor said to Mary McCarthy, a modern-day female Prometheus who railed against the Church, pertains to what many historical Jesus scholars think about the Gospels. When O'Connor was informed that McCarthy thought the eucharist was useful for fiction and nothing more than symbolic hocus-pocus, O'Connor said, "Well, if it's [the eucharist's] a symbol, to hell with it."[2] As a Protestant, I am smitten with the symbolic meaning of the eucharist, so I am in trouble with O'Connor. And, as an Evangelical with, to use Stan Grenz's terms, a convertive piety background,[3] I am forbidden to use her language, which might (in

---

[1] This chapter is a response paper read at the annual meeting of the Evangelical Theological Society, 2005, in Philadelphia (Valley Forge Convention Center). I participated along with Donald A. Hagner and Craig A. Evans in responses to James D. G. Dunn. The paper was written for that occasion, and I have left it largely unedited.

[2] F. O'Connor, *Collected Works* (ed. S. Fitzgerald; New York: The Library of America, 1988), 977.

[3] See S. Grenz, *Renewing the Center: Evangelical Theology in a Post-Theological Era* (Grand Rapids: Baker Academic, 2000), 44–47.

my experience) even make a Lutheran nervous. But, I am aware that many of my friends who are historical Jesus scholars would say the same thing about passages in the Gospels that are judged "inauthentic." They may not assign such sayings to hell, but they would clearly assign them to Robert Funk's purgatory of grayish matter. They think that much of the tradition in the Gospels is flawed history wrapped in the illusion of faith.

Tell the Truth but . . .

We are here to discuss the central theses of *Jesus Remembered*, and I would like to quote O'Connor again to give us a handle for a discussion of historiography. "*Tell the truth,*" she once told Miller Williams, a nationally recognized poet, "*but understand that it is not necessarily what happened.*"[4] Williams's essay is apposite to this chapter and setting: his essay is a listing of things O'Connor said to him, and they are recorded as he "remembers" them. I would like to use this O'Connor line, "Tell the truth, but understand that it is not necessarily what happened," as a *leitmotif* of this chapter. What I want to do most of all is connect Jimmy Dunn's[5] theory of history and oral tradition to a postmodernist historiography and suggest that he is helping us see what we have in front of us in the Gospels: here we have a story about Jesus, which really is the Church's story about Jesus, and this second layer is in essence the story that the Spirit prompted the Church to tell about Jesus and *it is the only story about Jesus that has final authority for the Church.*

If I read Jimmy aright (and his book has a clever Dickensian beginning),[6] he is saying that all we have in the Gospels is, to use

---

[4] From S. Gordon, *Flannery O'Connor: In Celebration of Genius* (Athens, Ga.: Hill Street Press, 2000), 3. The quotation is from Williams's essay, "Remembering Flannery O'Connor," 1–4.

[5] Perhaps I should explain my use of "Jimmy." I was Jimmy's student. When he came to our newly rented flat in Toton (near Nottingham) just hours after we had arrived in England from the United States, I asked him politely how I should address him. He said, "Jimmy." I have done so ever since, but I might use "Professor Dunn" when the stakes are higher in my disagreement.

[6] See J. D. G. Dunn, *Jesus Remembered* (Christianity in the Making 1; Grand Rapids: Eerdmans, 2003), 11. "It began with Jesus—'it' being Christianity. Whether *he* began it, or

Kähler's infamous terms, *Geschichte* and that any attempt to find *Historie* is either misguided (which is how I read him) or useless for the theology of the Church (which is also how I read him).[7] In Jimmy's masterful survey of the history of historical Jesus studies,[8] whether we look to the old-fashioned liberals of the days before Schweitzer or to the more recent scholarly neoliberal quests for Jesus, the same stricture applies: the Gospels are not amenable to a patient historical analysis that will yield an *ungeschichtlicher* Jesus. The only thing the student of the Gospels can and will find is the *geschichtliche Christus*. In Jimmy's own words, "All we have in the NT Gospels is Jesus seen with the eye of faith."[9]

This premise leads to Jimmy's major conclusion: what we have in the Gospels is the *remembered* Jesus. He says, "The Synoptic tradition provides evidence not so much for what Jesus did or said in itself, but for what Jesus was *remembered* as doing or saying by his first disciples, or as we might say, for the *impact* of what he did and said on his first disciples."[10] There is, therefore, no *historical* Jesus who can be distinguished from and set over against the portrait of Jesus in the Gospels. The only Jesus one can find in the Gospels is either a Jesus who generated the faith or a faith-generated Jesus—the Jesus of what Jimmy calls the "impact."

It is perhaps easiest for me to put my questions on the table now and then proceed to an extension and confirmation of *Jesus Remembered*.

My Questions about *Jesus Remembered*

My first question is, If the remembered Jesus is the core memory of the Church that is performed over and over in a variety of settings, and the core memory can be distinguished from the redactional/literary performances, what is the distinction between a "remembered" Jesus and

---

it looked back to him as its beginning, are matters to be clarified." Here I am reminded of Charles Dickens's *A Christmas Carol*, and I think the opening salvo of Jimmy's is exquisite.

   [7] M. Kähler, *The So-Called Historical Jesus and the Historic Biblical Christ* (trans. C. E. Braaten; Philadelphia: Fortress, 1964).
   [8] Dunn, *Jesus Remembered*, 11–136.
   [9] Ibid., 127.
   [10] Ibid., 130.

a "historical" Jesus? Is there any historical figure who is not a "remembered" historical figure?

My second question is, What is the distinction between a "remembered" Jesus and the redactor's theology? Is the "remembered" Jesus prior to and distinguishable from the evangelist's theological performance?

My third question, and the one I am most concerned about, is, What value is there in a "remembered" Jesus, either in himself or over against a "historical" Jesus, or over against the "Church's" Jesus? In other words, is not Professor Dunn perilously close to doing historical Jesus work once he distinguishes the "remembered" Jesus from the Gospels' Jesus? One would have to use illustrations to work with this question but take anything Jimmy sees as, at some level, "inauthentic" (the ransom saying of Mark 10:45) as an example.[11] Specifics do not matter; what matters is that there are times that Jimmy thinks the tradition, as we now have it in the Gospels, is not "authentic."[12] At this point, as I understand him, the "remembered" Jesus differs from what Jesus said. Now, what do we do with this remembered Jesus who differs from Jesus or who differs from the evangelist? What good is the remembered Jesus?

My fourth question is, How can Professor Dunn suggest that the historical Jesus scholars have not taken seriously the faith impact on the nature of the Gospel traditions when, as I see it, it is precisely the faith-impact nature of the traditions that gave rise to the question of whether there is another way to look at Jesus? Was it not the faith impact on the traditions that gave rise to the quest in the first place?[13]

My fifth question is, In his view, what is ultimately redemptive— the historical event (e.g., Jesus' death) or the remembered telling of that historical event?

Finally, a word about method: Jimmy seems to have two prevailing methodological stances at work, and I wonder if the one can be maintained with the other. Here is what I mean: Jimmy argues that

---

[11] See his discussion in *Jesus Remembered*, 812–15.

[12] I am using "authentic" here as it is customarily used, for it seems to me Jimmy is intent on helping us redefine the very meaning of this term in his entire project. In a sense, all is authentic in a "remembered" Jesus or oral traditioning theory.

[13] A nice summary of his approach can be found in his *A New Perspective on Jesus: What the Quest for the Historical Jesus Missed* (Grand Rapids: Baker Academic, 2005), and I am referring here to p. 34.

the "core" of the Gospel pericopae is often the oral tradition. At the same time, he argues that Mark is the first and that Matthew and Luke both used Mark and the common source (German *Quelle*) we call Q. Now, if the oral "core" happens to be nearly the same as the literary Markan elements that are common in Matthew and Luke, I am curious to know if he has in fact given away the sole foundation for his oral traditioning theory. That is, if the core is Markan, how can we *know* it is also oral?[14]

The Feasibility of a Historical Jesus

My next statement will surprise Jimmy because in Denver one day we walked down some long, cold street disagreeing about this very thing. I agree that the Gospels present *Geschichte*, and, more importantly, I agree that the only Jesus that matters for the Church is the *geschichtliche Christus*. But Jimmy contends that there is no historical Jesus to be found and that the quest is an illusion: the only data we have are the facts as effected through the faith of the first Christians, beginning in the very lifetime of Jesus.

I disagree that one cannot find a *historische Jesus*, and I do so for a very simple reason: scholars have been doing so for 200 years or more.[15] If we posit that there was a Jesus and that the Jesus who existed is not equivalent with the Gospels themselves, then there is, in fact, a reality known as Jesus. If the Gospels can somehow be proven to be "additional," "redacted," "overlaid," or anything of the sort, then we have the makings of a "historical" Jesus who is either less than or more than what we have in the Gospels. I see no way around the logic of Jesus as a historical figure and the Gospels as literary effects of that Jesus. The two are distinguishable.

Not only are they distinguishable, but also the evidence of the Gospels is not entirely the same sort: a "faith" sort of evidence. In Jimmy's

---

[14] Jimmy's response to this question in our session was this, and I quote from memory: "Of course, we can't know if it is oral."

[15] The most important survey now is that of W. P. Weaver, *The Historical Jesus in the Twentieth Century: 1900–1950* (Harrisburg, Pa.: Trinity Press International, 1999). I have sketched the trends in "Jesus of Nazareth," in *The Face of New Testament Studies* (ed. S. McKnight and G. R. Osborne; Grand Rapids: Baker, 2004), 149–76.

haste to say the Gospels are documents of faith, I sense that he has overdrawn his lines. I do not dispute that "faith" shaped the traditions, but there are bits in the tradition that are opposed to faith (criticism by opponents), and other bits are simply filler (he went into a boat), and some other bits are more robustly theological (Peter's confession, worship, etc.). Historical Jesus scholars have been keen on delineating the more robustly theological from the less and even nontheological bits.

Not only have historical Jesus scholars have been doing this for a long time, but also the historical Jesus they have been finding has nourished their own kind of faith, whether suborthodox or another brand. And they have used the Jesus they found to criticize the Church's Jesus over and over again. The reason I think scholars can find a historical Jesus and the reason that I think that sort of Jesus is useful for that kind of faith is because these scholars have been doing so for a long time. I think here of three recent examples: Dom Crossan's adventurous study into the Galilean peasant, Marc Borg's discovery of Jesus the religious genius, and Bruce Chilton's uncovering of—well, I am not quite sure how to describe his Jesus.[16]

So, we see these sojourners on the quest for the historical Jesus have found something behind it all. They have concluded that a lot of what we read in the Gospels did not in fact happen, but we also know that they have found the truth in the Jesus they found. And their own faith is rooted in such reconstructions. Now Jimmy is telling us that they are either seriously mistaken or that they should not be doing such a thing.

I disagree *and* agree with this: I do think they can find a historical Jesus (for they do) but I think they should not be doing such a thing if they think they are doing "Christian" faith.

The reason I disagree with Jimmy but ultimately agree with him is historiography, and I wish now to turn to what I think we can learn from recent historiographical studies for doing historical Jesus studies.

---

[16] I do not intend to disparage Bruce Chilton's study, but what he has said about Jesus is more than difficult to classify. On these studies, see J. D. Crossan, *The Historical Jesus: The Life of a Mediterranean Jewish Peasant* (San Francisco: HarperSanFrancisco, 1991); M. Borg, *Jesus: A New Vision. Spirit, Culture, and the Life of Discipleship* (San Francisco: HarperSanFrancisco, 1988); and B. Chilton, *Rabbi Jesus: An Intimate Biography* (New York: Doubleday [Peekamoose], 2000).

I think it will tell us that we can, in fact, get back there in the murky waters of pre-Gospel materials, but it will call into question the usefulness of such for Christian faith. It will tell us that the truth is in the Christian story and that story tells us why what happened happened.

Theories of History and Telling the Truth

Let me now set out three theories of history as we approach the Gospels and examine the historical Jesus. *Neoliberal historical Jesus scholars* think they *tell the truth* because *the Gospels are not what happened*. *Ecclesial Jesus scholars*, like Kähler, it is well known, and his more recent incarnation in Luke Timothy Johnson,[17] *tell the truth, whether it happened or not*. The truth, they say, transcends what happened for it is the significance of what happened that is the truth. *Modernistic historical Jesus historians*, some of whom would be Evangelicals, often believe that *the Gospels tell the truth about what happened, and what happened is the truth*,which, as is also well known, puts a big twist in their knickers if they discover that what they thought was the truth—that is, what happened—was not what happened, for it is therefore not the truth.

"History" has been equated here by both the neoliberal historians and the modernistic historians with "what happened," whereas the ecclesial historians define "history" in a different sense. I would like to explore this distinction by examining both modernistic historiography and *postmodernist historiography* and how each defines "history" and then suggest that ecclesial historians, such as Jimmy and I, offer for Evangelicals a noble path for participation in the historical Jesus debate. I will adapt and reuse material that is now published in my book *Jesus and His Death*.[18]

Before I do that, let me remind us of what Jimmy is saying: Jimmy is saying that what we have in the Gospels is the *remembered* Jesus, the Jesus of the impact, the Jesus who created the sort of faith that came to

---

[17] L. T. Johnson, *The Real Jesus: The Misguided Quest for the Historical Jesus and the Truth of the Traditional Gospels* (San Francisco: HarperSanFrancisco, 1996).

[18] S. McKnight, *Historiography, the Historical Jesus, and Atonement Theory* (Waco: Baylor University Press, 2005), esp. pp. 3–46. I am summarizing points made there, and the reader is invited to read a more complete discussion there.

expression in oral traditions that were eventually crystallized in written form in the Gospels. In other words, the Jesus of the Gospels is at one and the same time the Jesus who created faith and the Jesus who was shaped by that faith. And yet, in other words, the Jesus of the Gospels is an interpreted Jesus, for hermeneutics is at play from the very beginning.

Jimmy's *Jesus Remembered* raises a profound question: What is "history"? What are we talking about? Are we talking about "what really happened" or "the meaning of what happened"? And if so, is there more than one meaning? Can history be written from various angles to tell various stories but all somehow be in touch with what happened to render a judgment that each is historical and each is valid?[19]

Modernist Historiography: Sir G. R. Elton

Modernist historiography offers an alternative. It contends that all ancient texts leave residues of history and clues to history. Trained detachment, so this view contends, enables the historian to achieve a fair measure of objectivity in order to avoid bias of analysis and selection. Objects can be studied "for their own sake" in modernistic historiography. Patient analysis enables a historian to discover what really happened and then to describe what happened or, to use the old terms, *wie es eigentlich gewesen ist*. No single modern historiographer stands more for this line of thinking than Sir Geoffrey Elton, famous for his two books *The Practice of History* and *Return to Essentials*.[20]

It would be fun to quote Elton at length here, but let me simply just encourage you to read his two short books and come to terms with one of the most influential historiographers of the last century and to recognize in him a paradigm of how much of historical Jesus studies have operated.

Most historical Jesus scholars are Eltonian in stance and method. The telling stance of modernist historiography is detachment, objectivity,

---

[19] See also the discussion of D. L. Denton Jr., *Historiography and Hermeneutics in Jesus Studies: An Examination of the Work of John Dominic Crossan and Ben F. Meyer* (JSNTSS 262; London: T&T Clark/Continuum, 2004).

[20] G. Elton, *The Practice of History* (New York: Crowell, 1967); *Return to Essentials* (Cambridge: Cambridge University Press, 1991).

or disinterestedness, and the prevailing method is to clarify a method and scientifically apply that method until results are achieved and described. The results ought to be unassailable. No one represents this approach more than Norman Perrin in his *Rediscovering the Teaching of Jesus*.[21] I think John P. Meier's *A Marginal Jew* fits along the same line.[22]

Meaning and theology are left for others—the business of the historian is to discern the facts and approximate their meaning. In historical Jesus studies, this has given birth to "criteriology" and a supposed lack of interest in "theology" when one studies Jesus and, most especially, an alertness to what the Church believes and a steadfast commitment to say something different.[23] These are the marks of modernist historiography when applied to the historical Jesus.

"Tell us what happened," the modernist says. "And if you use a rigorous method, you'll be able to tell us the truth."

Postmodernist Historiography: Keith Jenkins

The issue for the postmodernist historiographer is the relation of the Subject (the historian) and the Object (Jesus as mediated through the Gospels). My examples, to make matters clear for this setting, will come from extremist historiographers: Hayden White and Keith Jenkins.[24] They are both, especially the latter, radical postmodernist historians.

Hayden White, an American historian, ran the gauntlet through this very issue. He contended in a bundle of books and articles that history is little more than literature. History is little more than a historian spinning a narrative out of "discrete facts" in the guise of antiquity or the past—with the radical implication that it could be argued there is no "good" or "bad" history. White himself backed off this conclusion

---

[21] N. Perrin, *Rediscovering the Teaching of Jesus* (New York: Harper & Row, 1967).

[22] Esp. visible in J. P. Meier, *A Marginal Jew* (ABRL; New York: Doubleday, 1991), 1:21–40.

[23] A comprehensive study of the criteria can be found in S. E. Porter, *The Criteria for Authenticity in Historical-Jesus Research: Previous Discussion and New Proposals* (JSNTSSS 191; Sheffield: Sheffield Academic Press, 2000).

[24] For H. White, see *The Content of the Form: Narrative Discourse and Historical Representation* (Baltimore: John Hopkins University Press, 1987). For K. Jenkins, see *On "What Is History?": From Carr and Elton to Rorty and White* (London: Routledge, 1995).

when confronted with its implications for the Holocaust, but still his point was heard.

And the one who perhaps heard it most clearly was Keith Jenkins, an English historian, who combined White with Richard Rorty to contend that history is a "language game all the way down." It is nothing but language, and in fact, it is the language of power and ideology to control what is there for the control of the present. History amounts to little more than autobiography and politics.

Here is a memorable line from Jenkins: "We now just have to understand that we live amidst social formations which have no legitimising ontological or epistemological or ethical grounds for our beliefs or actions beyond the status of an ultimately self-referencing (rhetorical) conversation." Or, "only theory can give history any unity of significance."[25]

Not all are as radical as either Hayden White or Keith Jenkins. F. R. Ankersmit, in his book *Historical Representation*, contends that "representation" is a better term for what historians do with facts: historians use facts that tell us "about" the past rather than "refer" to the past.[26] Still, Ankersmit joins the others in the postmodernist camp in recognizing that it is the historian's job to create meaning through narrative.

In my estimation, the major contribution of postmodernist historiography is the recognition that, in general, *discrete facts (or data) do not carry meaning but that meaning is shaped by the narrative into which they are placed*. "Don't even think you are telling the truth," the postmodernist might say, "but do what you can to put together a narrative that will tell your truth for your own reasons."

There are milder versions of this, of course—especially Joyce Appleby, Lynn Hunt, and Margaret Jacobs's *Telling the Truth about History*[27]—but the postmodernist side, whether on the starboard side with the critical realists or on the port side with Jenkins and White, still contends that the narrative attributes meaning to events.[28]

---

[25] Jenkins, *On "What Is History?"* 7, 83.

[26] F. R. Ankersmit, *Historical Representation: Cultural Memory in the Present* (Stanford: Stanford University Press, 2002).

[27] J. Appleby, L. Hunt, and M. Jacobs, *Telling the Truth about History* (New York: W. W. Norton, 1994).

[28] My own reading of historical Jesus scholars is that "critical realism" is perceived as a form of modernism; I'm not sure this is the case. See, for example, L. Beck, "Critical Realism,"

When it comes to Jesus, a postmodernist historiography has something to say. I will let Jimmy's words do the work: "Almost without many second and third questers noticing, the spring tide of postmodernism has built up against the dykes of the historical method, threatening to obliterate most of the familiar landmarks on which historical critics have depended for finding their way."[29] Here Jimmy uses to great effect what John Lewis Gaddis, a masterful historiographer, suggests in his valuable study, *The Landscape of History*: the need for good metaphors to understand where we are.[30] Postmodernity, it is here suggested, is threatening to overwhelm classical historical Jesus studies. Why? Because it is calling into question the simple separation of Subject and Object.

The Gospels themselves, carrying on the oral traditioning behind them, shaped the "data" and the "facts" into a narrative, and that narrative imposed "meaning" in order to create a credible and ecclesial "story" of who Jesus was, what Jesus did, and what he said. There is, in my judgment, no way around this meaning direction of narrative and that we will not find either "data" or "facts" that are just there without interpretation.

In other words, Professor Dunn's "remembered" Jesus is in alignment with the bedrock perception of postmodernist historiography: the Gospel writers effected meaning in their story, and this "meaning" is the Church's only story about Jesus. And, for my take, it is the only story worth telling when it comes to theologizing about Jesus.

It should be observed that N. T. Wright's *Jesus and the Victory of God*[31] is a mixture of both modernistic and postmodernistic historiography—for Tom is keen on using criteria, but he is also quite clear that a "critical realism" is not a simple detachment and application of method. The gradual coming to terms with what is really out there (a realism) requires time, essays, and attempts (critical), but eventually we approximate and get closer to the "real Jesus" (modernism).

---

in *The Oxford Companion to Philosophy* (2d ed.; New York: Oxford University Press, 2005), 183–84.

[29] Dunn, *Jesus Remembered*, 92.

[30] J. L. Gaddis, *The Landscape of History: How Historians Map the Past* (London: Oxford University Press, 2002).

[31] N. T. Wright, *Jesus and the Victory of God* (Minneapolis: Fortress, 1996).

Jimmy Dunn's own *Jesus Remembered* is, in my estimation, more clearly postmodernist than it is modernist. In this sense, it becomes a "nonhistorical" Jesus book that sets itself apart from all other historical Jesus books.

So, What Is History?

Here is Jimmy's definition of the *task* of the historian: "The task of the historian is to explain not only what happened, but why it happened and why it happened in the way it did."[32] To this, let me offer a definition of what history is that I think is consistent with the thesis of *Jesus Remembered*: history is a narratival ordering of (data that are embedded in) facts that, when ordered as they are, structure meaning. In the case of the Gospels, they structure meaning for the sake of faith and instruction in the way of Jesus.

In other words, the reason I like the *remembered* Jesus theory is because in it Jimmy recognizes that from the very beginning, the narrative performances of the first followers of Jesus shaped meaning, and it is their shaped meanings that set the parameters for Christian faith. Only Jesus presentations that are established by those parameters can be called "Christian" interpretations of Jesus.

The Remembered Jesus as the Christian Jesus

Now let me add what I think is the most significant reason I adhere to a critical realist or a mild postmodern theory of history when it comes to the Gospels and our understanding of Jesus.

I do think we can distinguish the real Jesus and a historical Jesus from the remembered Jesus and the Gospels' Jesus, but the *only Jesus who matters for Christian faith is the Jesus of the Gospels*. And this puts me into a position where I think the Jesus of the Gospels is an interpreted Jesus, a Jesus whose meaning has been shaped by the narratives that have been handed down to us in the shape of the Gospels; that is, as Jimmy clearly states, the hermeneutical process is not something

---

[32] Dunn, *Jesus Remembered*, 101.

preachers do now for the first time. Instead, "they continue a dialogue which began in the initial formation of the tradition."[33]

This is important to me because I think the *anamnēsis* (memory) theory of Jimmy Dunn needs to be wedded to a *pneumatology* that guided and directed the storytelling and narrative shaping of the earliest followers of Jesus. They eventually performed that story into the shape of the Gospels that now sits in front of us and shapes our own stories and identities.

On top of this *anamnēsis* and *pneuma*, we also have *graphē*. As Jimmy says, "The interpreter of the Jesus tradition has to acknowledge a degree of normativity to particular forms of that tradition."[34] He calls our NT, and, I assume, largely the Gospels in this context, the *norma normans*, the norming norm.

In addition to *anamnēsis*, *pneuma*, and *graphē*, we also need to add *pistis*: faith is not certainty, and faith is not simply a logical conclusion. As Jimmy states in *Jesus Remembered*,[35] faith deals in trust and commitment instead of certainty, and the story of Jesus as told by the first followers of Jesus and now found in our Gospels invites us to trust the Person who is the Story in order to come to know the truth that can set us free.

"Tell the truth," to borrow one final time from O'Connor's inimitable line, because the story we tell is why what happened did happen.

---

[33] Ibid., 129.
[34] Ibid., 135.
[35] Ibid., 104.

4

A New Perspective on the Jesus Tradition

Reflections on James D. G. Dunn's *Jesus Remembered*

Samuel Byrskog

During the annual meeting of the *Studiorum Novi Testamenti Societas* in Bonn, Germany, in the summer of 2003, the seminar on the historical Jesus arranged a panel discussion on the occasion of James D. G. Dunn's newly published book *Jesus Remembered*. An elaborated version of my introduction to that discussion was published the next year, with a response from Dunn himself.[1] The debate continued, and Dunn has clarified his view on several occasions. Time does not permit me to update the entire discussion. In what follows, I will present a somewhat revised version of my initial reaction to his book about seven years ago. I will integrate some of his responses and restate the issues that still, in my view, have not been addressed satisfactorily.

As previously, I will make no attempt at summarizing the book, even less to evaluate it comprehensively. By now, most readers are

---

[1] S. Byrskog, "A New Perspective on the Jesus Tradition: Reflections on James D. G. Dunn's *Jesus Remembered*," *JSNT* 26 (2004): 459–71; J. D. G. Dunn, "On History, Memory and Eyewitnesses: In Response to Bengt Holmberg and Samuel Byrskog," *JSNT* 26 (2004): 473–87.

familiar with its content. Rather, I wish again to focus on the most distinctive aspect of the book, namely, its approach to the Jesus tradition.
Dunn summarizes the main thrust of the book in four propositions:

> (1) The only realistic objective for any "quest of the historical Jesus" is
> Jesus *remembered*. (2) The Jesus tradition of the Gospels confirms *that*
> there was a concern within earliest Christianity to remember Jesus.
> (3) The Jesus tradition shows us *how* Jesus was remembered; its char-
> acter strongly suggests again and again a tradition given its essential
> shape by regular use and reuse in oral mode. (4) This suggests in turn
> that that essential shape was given by the original and immediate
> *impact made by Jesus* as that was first put into words by and among
> those involved as eyewitnesses of what Jesus said and did. In that key
> sense, the Jesus tradition *is* Jesus remembered.[2]

Two items are especially important. First, Dunn insists that the
Jesus tradition was communicated mainly orally. This is a vital insight
that challenges scholars of today to free themselves from one-sided
literary modes of working with ancient texts. Second, Dunn avoids the
naïveté of historical positivism without losing himself in postmodern
relativism. In this way, he captures the nature of the oral mode of communication and indicates the complex synthesis between Jesus as past
and present during the traditioning process. At the moment of oral
performance, past and present merge while, at the same time, being
paradoxically distinct. Most of the issues that are in need of further
discussion relate to this tricky synthesis between the past and the present in the oral Jesus tradition.

New and Old

Before reflecting critically on various aspects of these issues, I wish to
bring attention to Dunn's claim of presenting a "new perspective" on
Jesus and the Jesus tradition.[3] In order to set the stage for his approach,

---

[2] J. D. G. Dunn, *Jesus Remembered* (vol. 1 of *Christianity in the Making*; Grand Rapids: Eerdmans, 2003), 882; cf. also 335.
[3] Cf. also J. D. G. Dunn, *A New Perspective on Jesus: What the Quest for the Historical Jesus Missed* (Grand Rapids: Baker Academic, 2005).

Dunn refers to D. S. Du Toit's call for a comprehensive theory of the process of transmission of tradition in early Christianity.[4] Dunn realizes that there exists a perspective on the Jesus tradition that has hardly begun to be tapped and hopes to make the first step toward establishing a theory that would meet the need indicated by Du Toit.

I remain puzzled over this bold claim. Dunn has indeed been one of the leading scholars in the development of a new perspective on Paul. Although the Pauline debate defined what was new in relation to previous studies and clearly introduced a fresh perspective, today moving toward a balanced combination of new and old, it is less evident, at least to Swedish scholars, which aspects that represent a new perspective on the Jesus tradition. The label "new perspective" contains a claim that previous scholarship has not seen what is now to be seen or that there are new data or new ways to evaluate the data. But what is new in the "new perspective" on the Jesus tradition? That Jesus made an impact before Easter? That the impact was remembered? That the tradition was oral? That the tradition was performed and celebrated collectively? Biblical scholars have already noticed most of the basic features of this perspective, which are indeed very important. For Dunn, the new perspective is an attempt to "break out from the centuries-old cultural conditioning of a literary, print-dominated mindset which has determined how the early transmission of the Jesus tradition has been conceived by NT scholarship generally."[5] The old masters, several Scandinavians (e.g., Harald Birkeland, Ivan Engnell, Birger Gerhardsson, Sigmund Mowinckel, Eduard Nielsen, H. S. Nyberg, and Helmer Ringgren), who tried long ago to bring the implication of this vital insight to the international audience, will be, or would have been, curious to see if it finally catches on.[6]

---

[4] Dunn, *Jesus Remembered*, 173.

[5] Ibid., 883.

[6] B. Gerhardsson has presented his critique of Dunn's book in two articles: "Innan evangelierna skrevs," *SEÅ* 69 (2004): 167–89; and "The Secret of the Transmission of the Unwritten Jesus Tradition," *NTS* 51 (2005): 1–18. Dunn responds to the critique in "Eyewitnesses and the Oral Jesus Tradition," *JSHJ* 6 (2008): 85–105. He acknowledges that he overreacted to Gerhardsson's emphasis on memorization and failed to take account of the degree to which his model allows for variation (ibid., 88). To be noted is that Gerhardsson never denied that other forms of preserving and elaborating tradition existed in early Christianity but focused deliberately on the aspect that included memorization.

Dunn's contribution has the same kind of dialogical character that is distinctive of most of his previous work, even central to his understanding of scholarship. Several theories of the process of transmission already exist, older ones as well as more recent ones. There is certainly a need to discuss and refine them. Dunn rehearses existing theories and is more or less critical of them.[7] What emerges is a prolific way of evaluating an old debate and bringing it up to date with the current scholarly situation.

To this critique, Dunn responds that it is the combination of emphases that constitutes the new perspective.[8] He also points out that modern scholarship needs to be reminded that the tradition was oral and that previous attempts to envisage the oral period have been inadequate or sidetracked. In other words, previous attempts do exist (e.g., Bultmann, Gerhardsson, Kelber, Schröter). He certainly uses Kenneth Bailey's model in a way that has not been done before, but Bailey's model is not new to biblical scholarship (e.g., N. T. Wright). I might at first have read more into Dunn's claim than he intended, looking for a discussion with the old masters of my own scholarly tradition and understanding it to imply that the new perspective would change the paradigm of scholarship entirely and dramatically. My reaction was that what Dunn says is not new but nonetheless extremely important for the international scholarship on Jesus and the Jesus tradition.

Intention and Impact

One of the features that points to the interplay between past and present in the oral Jesus tradition is Dunn's insistence that Jesus made a profound impact on the disciples and that this impact was remembered and celebrated as oral tradition. It is essential for Dunn that we can reach back to Jesus of history by describing how his impact was remembered by the disciples and in the early churches. In a sense, the remembered Jesus *is* Jesus. As Dunn himself puts it, "I emphasize again that I do not envisage 'getting back to Jesus himself,'"[9] or as he

---

[7] Dunn, *Jesus Remembered*, 192–205.
[8] Dunn, "On History, Memory and Eyewitnesses," 478–80.
[9] Dunn, *Jesus Remembered*, 329.

states elsewhere, "And the Jesus thus remembered *is* Jesus, or as close as we will ever be able to reach back to him."[10]

Dunn envisions a close relationship between the intention and the impact of Jesus, speaking of "the original and immediate impact made by Jesus."[11] Already the notion of "original impact" is problematic. How can we ever reach to the "original" impact of one person on another? What is the original impact? Are not all impacts filtered by a person's or a group's various and multidimensional dispositions concerning how to understand that person from the very beginning and by the subsequent dynamics of the social and collective memory?

In later publications, Dunn has clarified his view on the impact of Jesus and stressed that it depended, to some extent, on Jesus' teaching methods.[12] "Impact" is, however, a broader term than "teaching," he maintains, in that it includes the total life-shaping effect that Jesus' ministry in word and deed and his death had on the disciples. This is helpful. I endorse his idea that Jesus' impact went beyond what can be measured only by analyzing his role as teacher. It is, however, evident that the didactic aspect of Jesus' impact has implications for Dunn's overall perspective. It suggests that the impact was partly structured from the beginning and therefore influenced the way the tradition at first developed, at least as far as the sayings tradition goes.

It is thus surprising that Dunn, in his book, blurs the distinction between impact and intention and fails to show how the intention was communicated to the disciples by means of teaching in word and deed. In chapter 9, he describes the primary historical context of Jesus the Jew, as is commonly done in books trying to get back to the historical Jesus. Such a context might be helpful for reconstructing historical intentionality, but the reception of Jesus' impact among the disciples and the traditioning process included settings with various cultural modes of remembering and performance. Dunn does not depict this broad context of traditioning. Large parts of the rest of the book elaborate

---

[10] Ibid., 335.

[11] Ibid., 335, 882.

[12] J. D. G. Dunn, "Social Memory and the Oral Jesus Tradition," in *Memory in the Bible and Antiquity: The Fifth Durham-Tübingen Research Symposium (Durham, September 2004)* (WUNT 212; ed. L. T. Stuckenbruck, S. C. Barton, and B. G. Wold; Tübingen: Mohr Siebeck, 2007), 179–94, esp. 185–89; idem, "Eyewitnesses and the Oral Jesus Tradition," 90.

the old search for Jesus' intention as part of what Jesus' was thinking. The questions addressed in chapter 13, "For Whom Did Jesus Intend His Message?" are, according to Dunn himself, subsets of the one over-arching question ("What was Jesus' intention?"[13]) posed long ago by Reimarus. Other sections in the book seek to find out why Jesus went up to Jerusalem, what meaning he gave to his anticipated death, his hope for vindication, and so on.[14] Here Dunn investigates what was going on in the mind of Jesus, what he thought of himself and his destiny. He is, as he says himself, trying to do the impossible, "to 'get inside' the head of a historical figure."[15] What about his emphasis that he does not envision getting back to Jesus himself but only to the remembered impact?

Dunn agrees with Werner Kelber in considering any talk of "sources" as inappropriate with oral tradition and adds that the label "oral transmission" can mislead the discussion since it envisages oral performance as intended primarily to transmit rather than to celebrate tradition.[16] This is an important point, and Dunn's insistence on the celebration of tradition as a form of "traditioning" is helpful in that it broadens the concept of tradition and transmission. Nevertheless, it is not entirely clear how his own enquiry as presented in the main bulk of the book differs from all the previous attempts to use the tradition as a source for reconstructing the history behind the way Jesus was remembered and interpreted. Dunn's focus on the oral tradition and the traditioning, as well on the impact of Jesus, is often transformed into a claim that Jesus' own intention was remembered by the impact he made on the eyewitnesses. This might be historically correct, in a general sense, but Dunn's theoretical agenda and conception of oral tradition do not articulate the sophisticated kind of interplay between the past and the present that would justify his curiosity for the Jesus of history.

In response, Dunn realizes that his attempt to inquire into Jesus' intention might seem at odds with his insistence that we cannot get back to Jesus himself.[17] His point, he says, is simply that it is possible to discern the thrust and character of Jesus' message from the

---

[13] Dunn, *Jesus Remembered*, 489.

[14] Ibid., 790–824.

[15] Ibid., 818.

[16] Ibid.

[17] Dunn, "On History, Memory and Eyewitnesses," 480.

transformative impact that it made. This is a more modest ambition than to get into the head of Jesus and discern his inner intentions. It would have benefited from an articulated agenda concerning the character of Jesus' teaching, of oral tradition and of orality and memory.

Such agendas exist, but Dunn does not make much of the insights of the oral history approach[18] and works with one-dimensional correlation between intention-impact-memory. He objects that the oral history approach ignores the role of oral transmission. This is correct, in a sense. It includes significant deliberations on the role of memory, but it is not interested in transmission as a technical and separate act, because oral history focuses on the same kind of dynamics that cause Dunn himself to be skeptical of the label "oral transmission" and tries to account for history as a personally and socially remembered and performed story. There is a widespread misunderstanding among biblical scholars that the oral history approach as applied to the Jesus tradition is nothing but a naive (re)turn to the innocent mind of eyewitnesses and a positivistic notion of history in new disguise. Nothing could be further from the truth. It is, in fact, a socialist perspective on history, a way of deconstructing the innocence of historical positivism and acknowledging history as a story that is communicated orally and that always is part of the significant social setting of the eyewitnesses.[19] The oral history approach and studies of social memory might have added significant theoretical discernment and examples of Dunn's discussion as to how the intention differed from or resembled the impact and how the impact from the very moment of observation and hearing was remembered as part of selective interpretative processes.[20]

---

[18] Cf. Dunn, *Jesus Remembered*, 198–99n138; 244n284.

[19] For the most influential presentation of what oral history is, see P. Thompson, *The Voice of the Past: Oral History* (3d ed.; Oxford: Oxford University Press, 2000).

[20] I have used the oral history approach in several studies. See S. Byrskog, *Story as History—History as Story: The Gospel Tradition in the Context of Ancient Oral History* (WUNT 123; Tübingen: Mohr Siebeck, 2000); idem, "Talet, minnet och skriften: Evangelietraditionen och den antika informationsteknologin," *SEÅ* 67 (2001): 139–50; idem, "History or Story in Acts—A Middle Way? The 'We' Passages, Historical Intertexture, and Oral History," in *Contextualizing Acts: Lukan Narrative and Greco-Roman Discourse* (SBL Symposium Series 20; ed. T. Penner and C. V. Stichele; Atlanta: Society of Biblical Literature, 2003), 257–83. I try to relate it to theories of social memory in "A New Quest for the *Sitz im Leben*: Social Memory, the Jesus Tradition and the Gospel of Matthew," *NTS* 52 (2006): 319–36.

Remembering and Interpreting

Dunn calls his book *Jesus Remembered* and puts much emphasis on the fact that Jesus was remembered and how he was remembered. It is essential for Dunn that this process of remembering and celebration of tradition—"traditioning"—included an actual act of recall, lest it would be entirely impossible to use it as an avenue back to Jesus of history.

As I have already indicated, it is all the more surprising that Dunn nowhere defines what he means by memory and remembrance. One of the basic marks of an oral culture, even when writing and reading have been introduced, is the cultivation of the faculty of memory. It is worthwhile repeating that *Mnēmosynē* was a goddess to the Greeks, being the mother of the muses, of both history writing (Clio) and rhetoric (Polyhymnia), and divinely sanctioned. Furthermore, Aristotle wrote an essay *de Memoria* (on memory), distinguishing between *mnēmē* (memory of the past) and *anamnēsis* (recollection in the present). There was also the widespread notion of the memory as a wax tablet, as something on which an impression was made. There are anecdotes of various people's exceptional memory. It was a matter of honor and shame. Children at school competed for memorization prizes. The rhetoricians used sophisticated visual techniques traced back to Simonides of Ceos, Hippias, and Theodectes the Tragedian to strengthen the memory as they delivered speeches, distinguishing between *memoria rerum* and *memoria verborum*. The rabbis are famous for their extreme attention to memory.

Dunn mentions none of it but thinks of remembering in terms of collective or corporate memory. In fact, his way of using the label "remembered" is sometimes hard to distinguish from the more general term "interpreted." What is the difference, according to Dunn, between corporate memory and corporate interpretation? Interpretation relates to something that already exists. When Dunn separates "tradition" from individual memory, he points out that corporate memory gives identity to the group "which thus remembers";[21] elsewhere, he speaks of "shared memory."[22] One might argue that it is not memory of the

---

[21] Dunn, *Jesus Remembered*, 173n1.
[22] Ibid., 241.

past that gives this kind of identity but the *interpretation* of the past within the frame of a shared symbolic universe. In order to clarify the notion of collective memory and to avoid emptying it of significant connotations, it is necessary to reflect more on the kind of mnemonic negotiation that takes place in the group and distinguish it carefully from the notion of interpretation.

The Collective and the Individual Memory

It is also necessary to specify how the collective memory relates to the memory of individuals. It was the Durkheimian sociologist Maurice Halbwachs, in his influential work *Les cadres sociaux de la mémorie* (The social frameworks of the memory) from 1925, who taught us to speak of the collective memory of a group or culture.[23] It was also Halbwachs who realized that there is a subtle interplay between the collective and the individual memory.[24] The popular stress on "collectivistic" and "dyadic" selves might have caused us to neglect the individualistic traits of persons in the ancient Mediterranean world and needs to be balanced with an appreciation of individual consciousness within collectivistically conditioned contexts. I have elsewhere complained about the one-sidedness of the old form-critical emphasis on the community,[25] and I am similarly puzzled by Dunn's consistent stress on the Christian community as a group that remembers corporately and thus establishes its identity.

Dunn has been much inspired by Kenneth Bailey's long experience of Middle East village life and the community's role of remembering and exercising control over the recitation of tradition at the so-called *haflat samar*.[26] He puts this "explanatory model for the Jesus

---

[23] M. Halbwachs, *Les cadres sociaux de la mémorie* (Bibliothèque de sociologie contemporaine; nouvelle édition; Paris: Presses Universitaires de France, 1952).

[24] Cf. the chapter titled "Mémoire collective et mémoire individuelle," in *La mémoire collective*, Bibliothèque de sociologie contemporaine (ed. J. Alexandre; Paris: Presses Universitaires de France, 1950), 1–34 (published posthumously).

[25] S. Byrskog, "Review Essay of Rudolf Bultmann, *The History of the Synoptic Tradition* (1963)," *JBL* 122 (2002): 549–55, esp. 551–52.

[26] K. E. Bailey, "Informal Controlled Oral Tradition and the Synoptic Gospels," *AJT* 5 (1991): 34–54; idem, "Middle Eastern Oral Tradition and the Synoptic Gospels," *ExpTim* 106 (1995): 363–67.

tradition"[27] at the heart of his new perspective, even raising it to the level of confirming "that the previous paradigms offered by Bultmann and Gerhardsson were inadequate."[28] Bailey himself had no such intention. He acknowledged that Bultmann's and Gerhardsson's views of oral tradition are both still very much alive in the Middle East and wished merely to introduce a third phenomenon that was unknown in New Testament circles at the time.[29] His model points to one phenomenon, but it does not exclude the existence of other settings of traditioning. In order to work as an "explanatory model" for the Jesus tradition, it needs to have some kind of link to texts that portray such practices in the ancient sociocultural setting. Moreover, it must account not only for the performance of a small village gathering but also for the urban setting of early Christian house meetings. It does neither of these things.

Oral history, with its attention to the individual person as part of a group or society and an informed view of how social memory actually works, might give a more helpful framework for how Jesus was remembered than the vague notion of corporate memory based on Bailey's model. Dunn, as I indicated previously, gives only little attention to oral history and fails to realize, first, that oral tradition overlaps with oral history and, second, that his own discussion of disciple-response locates the first traditioning in the oral histories of Jesus' followers.

Dunn is curious about theories of social memory and wishes to explore them further in a future publication.[30] In a recent article, he addresses them, only to conclude that they challenge his own focus on

---

[27] Dunn, *Jesus Remembered*, 210.

[28] Ibid., 209.

[29] "So informal uncontrolled oral tradition and formal controlled oral tradition are both still very much alive in the Middle East. The first results from natural human failings; the second is a carefully nurtured methodology of great antiquity that is still practiced and held in high regard by both Christians and Muslims in the Middle East today" (Bailey, "Informal Controlled Oral Tradition," 39). For further critique of Dunn's reading of Bailey, see R. Bauckham, *Jesus and the Eyewitnesses: The Gospels as Eyewitness Testimony* (Grand Rapids: Eerdmans, 2006), 252–63. Dunn now admits that he followed Bailey too closely in setting Bultmann and Gerhardsson in sharp antithesis ("Eyewitnesses and the Oral Jesus Tradition," 89). My point is that Bailey himself did not put them in such sharp antithesis.

[30] Dunn, "On History, Memory and Eyewitnesses," 481–82.

retentive memory.[31] All theories of social memory, however, are not opposed to the retentive aspect of memory. The memory may have an orientational function in the present *and* reflect past experiences. Mnemonic negotiation has to do with the past *and* the present, especially when the individual comes into view. Dunn does not mention that several of the social memory theories go hand in hand with the oral history approach and bring attention to the mnemonic negotiation of the individual as part of a group or society.[32] All too often, the social memory is seen as something that is totally separate from individual memory and confused with the presentist, collective memory of a group or society. Halbwachs himself distinguished among autobiographical memory, historical memory (the past to which we have no "organic" relation), and collective memory (the past forming our realities) and pointed out that individuals remember as members of groups,[33] but he made no further distinction in his use of the label "collective memory." In order not to neglect the individual aspects of mnemonic negotiations, it might be helpful to use "social memory" as a label distinct from "collective memory."[34] Although the latter is social in that it includes those recollections of a group or society that are shared by all of its members, being something else than the sum total of all the individual recollections, the former is social in that it deals with the social aspects of the mental act of remembering the past. Social memory is thus interested in the memory of individuals in social contexts that are larger than the individual and yet related to the individual.[35] It includes significant considerations of the individual memory and perceives memory in a way that is different from the collective memory of a group celebrating and performing its traditions.

That we do not have many texts from antiquity that portray the kind of corporate activity that Dunn envisions, whereas we have

---

[31] Dunn, "Social Memory and the Oral Jesus Tradition," 179–94.

[32] Cf. B. A. Misztal, *Theories of Social Remembering* (Philadelphia: Open University Press, 2003), 67–74. This chapter is titled "The Dynamics of Memory Approach: Memory as a Process of Negotiation" and presents an approach that differs from those that emphasize the invention of tradition and the confrontation of dominant ideology.

[33] M. Halbwachs, *La mémoire collective* (Paris: Presses Universitaires de France, 1950), 35–40.

[34] Cf. J. Fentress and C. Wickham, *Social Memory* (Oxford: Blackwell, 1992), ix.

[35] For further discussion, see Byrskog, "A New Quest," 319–36.

numerous texts picturing named individuals who within a communal setting seek out and try to remember and communicate persuasively information from other individuals, calls for a more nuanced view of the interplay between the collective memory of the group and the social memory of the individual in early Christian traditioning. The ancient historians, being most eager to find out things about the past, valued eyewitness testimony higher than other "sources." Heraclitus's saying, "Eyes are surer witnesses than ears," was the ideal.[36] This is also the impression that Papias gives in the quotations from Eusebius. It was, in his view, not the community as such but Mark who remembered (*[apo]mnēmoneuein* is used twice) things from the *chreiai* of a specifically named eyewitness, Peter (*Hist. eccl.* 3.39.15). Dunn mentions these texts only in passing.[37]

One could also visualize the remembering process by looking at Eusebius's quotation of how Ireneaus, in a letter to Florinus, relates that he carries in his memory traditions from Polycarp. Irenaeus remembers not what he learned about the Jesus tradition through the corporate celebration of it in a village gathering or the like but what he learned about it by meticulously observing Polycarp (the place where he taught, how he came in and out, his way of life, what he looked like, etc.) as well as by listening to and copying in his heart that which Polycarp retold from what he, in turn, had heard from eyewitnesses (*Hist. eccl.* 5.20.5–7). Dunn does not mention this text at all.

Should we dismiss Papias and Irenaeus as unreliable? Considering the widespread appreciation of individual memory and eyewitness testimony in Greek and Roman antiquity, it is likely that these two phenomena were of considerable significance also at a time when the churches existed and celebrated the tradition collectively. Dunn asserts, to be sure, that we should not "forget the continuing role of eyewitness tradents,"[38] but this assertion is of no importance as he summarizes his view.[39] It remains unclear how their "continuing role" is to be accounted in Dunn's picture of a group that identifies itself by the corporate remembering of tradition.

---

[36] References in Byrskog, *Story as History—History as Story*, 48–65.

[37] Dunn, *Jesus Remembered*, 179.

[38] Ibid., 242.

[39] Ibid., 253–54.

In response, Dunn has reiterated that he had no desire to downplay their importance but focused on the shared memory and the sharing of memories at the beginning of the traditioning process. He rejects the notion that Peter, Mary of Magdala, and the like stored up many memories of Jesus' mission, "which were only jerked into remembrance by 'oral history' inquiries of a Luke or a Matthew."[40] No one would of course claim that this is what happened, least of all those acquainted with the oral history approach. We seem to agree that the corporate activity of a group in no way should deter the attention from the role of specific persons behind the tradition or within the traditioning group. What I am asking for is a clearer vision of how the role of individuals and eyewitness testimonies interacted with the performance in the joint celebration of tradition precisely at the beginning, when these recollections were fresh, and as the tradition spread into various churches across the Mediterranean.[41]

The Role of Individuals

Let me develop my question further by discussing also the later development in the churches. In his book, Dunn occasionally points to the importance of individuals, but as with the eyewitnesses, it is difficult to estimate how he conceives concretely their relation to the churches. He stresses the importance of the early Christian teachers; he even thinks they were paid.[42] They served as "the congregation's repository of oral tradition,"[43] as a kind of walking reference library for the community.

---

[40] Dunn, "On History, Memory and Eyewitnesses," 483.

[41] The role of eyewitness testimony has been developed further by Bauckham, *Jesus and the Eyewitnesses*. In "Eyewitnesses and the Oral Jesus Tradition," 96–105, Dunn responds positively to Bauckham's emphasis on eyewitnesses to explain the beginning of the tradition process and clarifies several points, but he is skeptical to the idea that the tradition was consistently attributed to individuals. Here I agree with Dunn. Cf. my "The Eyewitnesses as Interpreters of the Past: Reflections on Richard Bauckham's *Jesus and the Eyewitnesses*," *JSHJ* 6 (2008): 157–68; and "A 'Truer' History: Reflections on Richard Bauckham, *Jesus and the Eyewitnesses: The Gospels as Eyewitness Testimony*," Nova et Vetera 6 (2008): 483–90.

[42] Dunn, *Jesus Remembered*, 176.

[43] Ibid.

I find it difficult to integrate this emphasis into Dunn's picture of the *haflat samar* for the initial period and his general notion of traditioning. Dunn might have misunderstood Bailey's model at this point when he disregards the role of eyewitnesses.[44] In any event, in response to my criticism, he maintains that "it is not really possible to speak of *tradition* except as community tradition."[45] Dunn does not address the old question if the traditioning activity of certain persons who took care of the Jesus tradition was entirely integrated into the larger group and its corporate activity or if they cared for its preservation and elaboration in a specific setting that was distinguished from the larger group. Performers often prepared themselves carefully.[46] As it seems, Dunn focuses on the former alternative. What these persons did, ultimately, was to reinforce "their church's corporate memory of Jesus tradition."[47] Is that all they did? In that case, what was the point of having specifically assigned and paid teachers who were responsible for the Jesus tradition? In what way did they reinforce their church's corporate memory? If one admits that teachers were assigned to do this task in the churches, one has to be more precise concerning the setting and function of their activity. In a recent article, Dunn puts the matter differently: "They *taught* the tradition for whose retention and transmission they would have had a primary responsibility in the early Christian communities."[48] This is clarifying and quite another thing than to say that they simply reinforced their church's corporate memory. It seems reasonable that they handled the tradition in mnemonic settings that were separate from the collective performance of the larger group and its worship. The performance in the church was rather a forum where they synchronized and celebrated the remembered tradition in joint acts of co-remembering.[49] In that case, we can integrate not only celebration and performance of tradition into

---

[44] Cf. Bauckham, *Jesus and the Eyewitnesses*, 260–61.

[45] Dunn, "On History, Memory and Eyewitnesses," 482.

[46] Cf. W. Shiner, *Proclaiming the Gospel: First-Century Performance of Mark* (Harrisburg, Pa.: Trinity Press International, 2003), 103–25.

[47] Dunn, *Jesus Remembered*, 186.

[48] Dunn, "Eyewitnesses and the Oral Jesus Tradition," 91 (Dunn's emphasis).

[49] For further discussion, see my article "A Century with the *Sitz im Leben*: From Form-Critical Setting to Gospel Community and Beyond," *ZNW* 98 (2007): 1–27.

our understanding of the traditioning process but also the deliberate transmission of tradition by specific didactic functionaries.

It is also not entirely clear how Dunn envisions the relationship between the authors of the Gospels and the Gospel communities. He criticizes Richard Bauckham and his colleagues by claiming that "particular communities were the Evangelist's *source* for the Jesus tradition."[50] How can a community that, in Dunn's own view, celebrates the oral tradition be a "source"?[51] That very term, as Dunn indicates elsewhere,[52] suggests that we think of the Jesus tradition in terms of sources that are being used in a rather scribal fashion.

This terminological issue reveals a more fundamental problem. What was the precise relationship between the authors of the Gospels and the communities? In what sense were the communities "sources"? Were not the authors themselves, in Dunn's view, part of the communities, and did they not have a leading role in the celebration of tradition, being their own point of reference within the community? Are the Gospels, in that case, a written outflow of the ongoing oral traditioning, or do they, after all, reflect the memories and theological profiles of single individuals who used the performances in order to communicate their own viewpoints, respectively? I understand Dunn to come closer to the former alternative. The Gospels, he maintains, are performances with oral features encoded into the text, eventually to become "frozen performances";[53] "hearings of the Gospel being read would be part of the oral/aural transmission . . . the written text was still fluid."[54] I share a similar view with regard to the text of the Gospels—they are "oral texts"—but this perspective needs to include insights that point to literary and theologically skilled authors. In response, Dunn fails to see that there is a problem here.[55] The alternative is of course not, as Dunn implies, that the evangelists only worked in isolation from the communities. It is their precise role *within* the community that

---

[50] Dunn, *Jesus Remembered*, 252.

[51] Ibid., 203.

[52] Elsewhere, Dunn criticizes Bauckham for speaking of eyewitness "source" ("Eyewitnesses and the Oral Jesus Tradition," 100n58).

[53] Dunn, *Jesus Remembered*, 884.

[54] Ibid., 250.

[55] Dunn, "On History, Memory and Eyewitnesses," 485.

is at stake and to what extent they, as individuals, influenced or were dependent on the oral traditioning of the group. The issue harks back to the well-known problem previously mentioned of how to relate the specific activities of certain persons who cared for the tradition and the composition of written Gospels to the worshipping group at large. In other words, how should we define the subtle relationship between the authors as part of an oral traditioning process and the authors as prolific individuals using the oral tradition as some kind of resource for their own literary and theological achievement?

Homeostasis and the Pastness of Tradition

A final point concerning the role of the community, according to Bailey's and Dunn's vision of the traditioning process, concerns its censoring function. Several decades ago, Jack Goody and Ian Watt presented the influential theory of *homeostasis*.[56] It is a functionalistic way of looking at oral tradition, today being endorsed by several scholars of orality. The nucleus of the theory is that societies and groups performing oral tradition censor the past and celebrate only those items of the tradition that are relevant to the present situation. It is a theory that takes seriously how groups function as they reconfigure the past. The present takes over. The present *is* the past; fact and fiction merge in an oral symbiosis. There surfaces a real sense of pastness only when writing and records of the past are introduced.

Dunn does not engage critically with this influential theory at all, not in his book and not in his subsequent articles, although it is implicit in Bailey's observation that the group at the *haflat samar* controls and censors the tradition. In the more recent articles, as he defends and clarifies his view, he does not, to my knowledge, comment at any length on the implication of his use of Bailey's model. This neglect is all the more surprising as it appears to be essential for Dunn that the oral Jesus tradition has an intrinsic diachronic dimension. On what basis is it possible to argue for a genuinely diachronic dimension of oral tradition and, at the same time, hold on to Bailey's model, as

---

[56] J. Goody and I. Watt, "The Consequences of Literacy," in *Literacy in Traditional Societies* (ed. J. Goody; Cambridge: Cambridge University Press, 1968), 27–68.

Dunn understands it? I agree with Dunn that oral tradition might have a diachronic dimension, but I fail to see how he integrates it into his general idea of performance and celebration. He stresses the corporate memory and endorses the act of performance and celebration more than the act of transmission, even if he has modified his view in later publications.

Scholars such as Jan Vansina and Paul Thompson, who have both studied various oralities closely, are critical of the theory.[57] For biblical scholars it clashes partly with the much-used criterion of dissimilarity. As will be evident from what has been said earlier, Dunn does not really show on what basis he assumes (a) that oral groups might have a real notion of the past, (b) that the individual memory does not disappear entirely through the censoring activity of the group and its collective memory, and (c) that the transmission and the performance of the oral tradition are intrinsically related. A discussion of these points would not only have clarified the pastness of the oral tradition but also—perhaps—modified Dunn's perspective in a way that distances the oral tradition somewhat from the overarching importance and mnemonic power of the celebrating community.

A fourth point is the presence of writing. One uses different labels to describe its interaction with orality. Dunn prefers the most common one, secondary orality. Perhaps there is the need for a more sophisticated classification. Orality comes in many different shapes and sounds. Also, the manner in which oral messages reflect historical events differs. One must take seriously that in the first century, oral conventions had been influenced by the written word, which created an element of abstract thinking and reflection about the past. Even if the literacy level in first-century Israel was not as high as we used to think, it is evident that the early Christian teachers and authors were well educated. There is no such thing as pure orality in early Christianity but various "oralities" and interactions with scribal practices. I have no problem with Dunn's use of the epithet "oral" for ancient Israel,[58]

---

[57] J. Vansina, *Oral Tradition as History* (London and Nairobi: James Currey and Heinemann, 1985), 120–23; Thompson, *The Voice of the Past*, 170.

[58] Cf. his recent discussion with Gerhardsson on whether ancient Israel was an oral society in "Eyewitnesses and the Oral Jesus Tradition," 94–96. That debate would benefit from a more varied terminology for "oral" phenomena.

for the Jesus tradition or for early Christianity, but I am looking for a more varied and precise terminology of expressing what is meant by that label. Dunn must clarify, it seems, the persisting question: If the individual memory played a subordinate role and if actual transmission of the Jesus tradition was closely related to performance and celebration of tradition, what kind of corporate and performed orality depended in such a significant and profound way on the past? What kind of orality are we envisioning when we speak of the oral Jesus tradition? Future research will have to put more work into differentiating between different kinds of "oralities" and "homeostatic fictionalities," both in antiquity generally and in early Christianity specifically.

Performance and Rhetoric

A possible avenue of further reflection is perhaps for scholars of orality to join hands with scholars of ancient rhetoric. It has been suggested that early Christianity represented a rhetorical rather than an oral culture.[59] The two are certainly not to be set over against each other. In a rhetorical culture, the spoken word imitates speech and writing, and writing imitates the spoken and the written word. Just as scholars pursuing rhetorical criticism need to remember that rhetoric is an outgrowth of a culture dominated by oral communication and avoid structuring their analyses in strictly scribal fashion, it is also vital that scholars with an interest in orality and the performance of oral tradition take seriously that performance is rhetorical *actio* aimed to persuade.[60]

Dunn writes frequently of performance but never of *rhetorical* performance. He thus cuts short the traditioning process by not taking into account the delivery and aural reception of tradition. To this critique, he readily admits that he did not give sufficient attention to the

---

[59] V. K. Robbins, "Writing as a Rhetorical Act in Plutarch and the Gospels," in *Persuasive Artistry: Studies in New Testament Rhetoric in Honor of George A. Kennedy* (JSNTSup 50; ed. D. F. Watson; Sheffield: Sheffield Academic Press, 1991), 142–68; idem, "Oral, Rhetorical, and Literary Cultures: A Response," *Semeia* 65 (1994): 75–91.

[60] I have tried to combine studies of orality, memory, and rhetoric in "The Early Church as a Narrative Fellowship: An Exploratory Study of the Performance of the *Chreia*," *Tidsskrift for Teologi og Kirke* 78 (2007): 207–26.

rhetoric of oral performance and will deal with it in a future study.[61] Indeed, he stands in a long line of scholars who have similarly preferred not to integrate considerations from ancient rhetoric into their study of tradition and transmission. Dunn has brought us a little bit forward by emphasizing generally the performance of tradition and introducing the more flexible term "traditioning." More is to be done. The all-important point of the performance was to make a lasting emotional impact. It included therefore many subtle ways to persuade, by voice, by gestures, with the eyes, and so on, creating for the audience an embodied vision of the tradition. The performer visualized what he delivered orally. "Granted the things you read make a point, what is affixed by delivery, expression, appearance and gestures of a speaker resides deeper in the soul," Pliny the Younger asserts (2.3.9), knowing that Nepos must hear the famous Isaios by seeing him perform his speeches.

If oral traditions were performed with rhetorical finesse, it is likely that skilled persons had deliberately worked them over in order to persuade others by argumentation.[62] A successful performance depended on the proper invention of arguments. The Christian teachers probably had considerable training in how to elaborate a *chreia* argumentatively. Again, the performance is not ad hoc, in that case, despite all the influences of the present situation at the collective moment of performance but prepared in a transmission that preserves and elaborates in order to convince the audience about Jesus of the past. This rhetorical view of transmission and performance is, it seems, somewhat different from Dunn's use of the concept of performance as the corporate celebration of oral tradition.

Points of Debate

Dunn's book has triggered a fruitful debate not only about Jesus of history but also concerning the role and characteristics of oral tradition in early Christianity. My own reading some years ago raised, in

---

[61] Dunn, "On History, Memory and Eyewitnesses," 486.

[62] Cf. B. L. Mack and V. K. Robbins, *Patterns of Persuasion in the Gospels* (Sonoma, Calif.: Polebridge Press, 1989).

brief, six basic points for further discussion. Dunn has responded to some of them. They remain to be fully addressed in future research:

1. How should the relationship between intention and impact be conceived in an environment dominated by oral/aural modes of communication? When Jesus seeks to intentionally communicate to the disciples, He uses, as Dunn recognizes, didactic techniques, but the life-shaping impact of Jesus' ministry and death goes far beyond his didactic intentions.
2. What conceptual framework is to be elaborated in order to distinguish between or integrate the remembering and the interpretative processes in the oral Jesus tradition?
3. How should the interplay between the collective and the individual memory and, more generally, the role of individuals within collectivistic settings be accounted for in early Christianity?
4. What kind of texts and literature do the Gospels represent in view of the authors' close reliance on the oral traditioning process on the one hand and their literary and theological profiles on the other hand?
5. What degrees of "homeostatic fictionality" are we to identify within the different "oralities" of the various strands of the oral Jesus tradition?
6. What is the rhetorical implication of the orally performed and aurally received Jesus tradition?

5

ORALITY AND THE PARABLES

WITH SPECIAL REFERENCE TO JAMES D. G. DUNN'S *JESUS REMEMBERED*

CRAIG L. BLOMBERG

The last century of synoptic scholarship has spawned a series of critical methods for the study of the first three Gospels: source, form, redaction, literary, and now social-scientific criticisms. Supporters have touted each, in turn, as the latest advance and ultimate key for unlocking these documents' mysteries. After a period of time with each new approach, most scholars have recognized that they all have their roles to play so that declarations about entire paradigm shifts exaggerate the contributions that each new criticism can make. At the same time, while reasoned eclecticism—to borrow a term from textual criticism—may characterize a large amount of synoptic study, a distressing amount of fragmentation has afflicted our discipline. Too many scholars still pitch their tents in one main camp, whether it be narrative or reader-response criticism, deconstruction, sociological or cultural anthropological analysis, rhetorical criticism, discourse analysis, semiotics or textlinguistics, intertextuality, liberationism, feminism, postcolonialism, cultural criticism, or gay, lesbian, bisexual, and transgendered readings of texts.[1]

Not surprisingly, then, the recent history of more specialized branches of synoptic criticism has undergone parallel developments. Take the parables, for example. After centuries of largely allegorizing interpretations, Jülicher's iconoclastic work vigorously argued for a thoroughgoing rejection of allegory and a "one-main-point" approach to every passage. Dodd and Jeremias returned the parables to their original eschatological settings but largely reaffirmed Jülicher's twin theses. In the 1970s, the new literary criticisms all shed valuable insights on the "world-subverting" nature of many of the parables, and the last third of the twentieth century likewise saw a variety of attempts to rehabilitate intended allegory (to be distinguished from illegitimate, subsequent allegor*izing*). Social-scientific analysis of the parables followed literary criticism, and again, today we can find approaches representing every one of the disparate methods into which our discipline has fragmented.[2]

The Gospels and Oral Tradition

Now turn to the study of oral tradition. For years, the classical form-critical model of Schmidt, Dibelius, and Bultmann held sway, particularly indebted to Axel Olrik's study of the prevailing principles of the transmission of oral folklore. For the composition and transmission of parables, most relevant were the observations that normally only two characters ever appeared "onstage" at the same time, that

[1] For overviews, see, for example, D. A. Black and D. S. Dockery, eds., *Interpreting the New Testament* (Nashville: B&H, 2001); J. B. Green, ed., *Hearing the New Testament* (Grand Rapids: Eerdmans, 1995); S. E. Porter and D. Tombs, eds., *Approaches to New Testament Study* (Sheffield: Sheffield Academic Press, 1995); and S. E. Porter, ed., *Handbook to the Exegesis of the New Testament* (rev. ed.; Leiden and Boston: Brill, 2002).

[2] For overviews, see C. L. Blomberg, *Interpreting the Parables* (Leicester and Downers Grove: IVP, 1990), 13–167; idem, "The Parables of Jesus: Current Trends and Needs in Research," in *Studying the Historical Jesus: Evaluation of the State of Current Research* (ed. B. Chilton and C. A. Evans; Leiden: Brill, 1994), 231–54; idem, "Poetic Fiction, Subversive Speech, and Proportional Analogy in the Parables," *HBT* 18 (1996): 115–32; and idem, *Preaching the Parables: From Responsible Interpretation to Powerful Proclamation* (Grand Rapids: Baker, 2004), 13–23.

each story contained no more than three main characters or groups of characters overall, that successive episodes often depicted close parallels or sharp contrasts, that the narratives built to a climactic ending, and that superfluous details were omitted so that the plots are single-stranded and tightly unified.[3] Largely from the study of the Synoptics themselves, Jeremias postulated 10 supposed "laws" of the transmission of the oral, parabolic tradition: (1) translation from Aramaic into Greek, (2) representational changes that transformed certain imagery from what was familiar in rural Palestine to what was appropriate for a more urban Greco-Roman milieu, (3) embellishment of detail, (4) addition of details under the influence of Old Testament or folk-story themes, (5) changes in the audiences to which the parables were addressed (most notably by applying to the disciples what Jesus originally intended for his opponents), (6) changes in emphasis from warning to exhortation, (7) modification of details in light of new situations in which the early church found itself, (8) allegorization, (9) formation of collections of parables that were originally independent or combinations of parts of two parables to form a new single story, and (10) changes in setting, primarily through alterations in the parables' introductions and conclusions.[4]

In the 1960s, an important voice of protest challenged the general form-critical emphasis on the fluidity of the oral tradition. Birger Gerhardsson's *Memory and Manuscript* argued that the best analogy for the transmission of the synoptic tradition in general and of the *meshalim* of Jesus in particular was the rabbinic model of careful memorization of sacred tradition.[5] Right from the start, Gerhardsson observed that until such tradition was placed on an exactly equivalent

---

[3] A. Olrik, "Epic Laws of Folk Narrative," in *The Study of Folklore* (ed. A. Dundes; Englewood Cliffs, N.J.: Prentice Hall, 1965; Germ. orig. 1909), 129–41. See my survey and critique in Blomberg, *Interpreting the Parables*, 72–78.

[4] J. Jeremias, *The Parables of Jesus* (3d ed.; London and Philadelphia: SCM and Westminster, 1972), 23–114. See my survey and critique in Blomberg, *Interpreting the Parables*, 79–94.

[5] B. Gerhardsson, *Memory and Manuscript: Oral Tradition and Written Transmission in Rabbinic Judaism and Early Christianity* (Uppsala and Lund: Gleerup; Copenhagen: Munksgaard, 1961); building on and expanding the seminal study of H. Riesenfeld, "The Gospel Tradition and Its Beginnings," in *The Gospel Tradition* (Philadelphia: Fortress, 1970; repr. 1959), 1–29.

level with the Hebrew Scriptures, "memorization" allowed for some flexibility in the inclusion or omission, expansion or abridgment, explanation and application of various details, particularly for haggadic material like the *meshalim*, but his critics tended not to notice or just ignored these caveats so that in more recent studies, he has emphasized these nuances more.[6] Those who rejected Gerhardsson's model also regularly stressed the differences between pre– and post– AD 70 Judaism, though again usually without interacting with his reply to this already anticipated criticism: although the content of Jewish thought demonstrably changed in important ways after the reconstruction of Judaism in the wake of Jerusalem's destruction, there is no evidence to suggest that the *forms* of Jewish teaching likewise changed.[7] Indeed, given the conservatism of educational methods in the ancient Mediterranean world more generally, it is prima facie unlikely that they would have been altered.

At the same time as Gerhardsson began publishing, Albert Lord and Jan Vansina were reporting on their extensive studies of the transmission of oral traditions in preliterate societies in Eastern Europe and Africa, respectively. In varying ways, these two scholars depicted a model of what might be called flexible tradition within fixed limits, freer than Gerhardsson's descriptions of "loose" memorization but still considerably more "guarded" than the classic form-critical approach.[8] Lord thought he could explain *all* the differences among the Synoptics via independent developments of the Jesus tradition,[9] but few scholars agreed with him. Two decades later, Werner Kelber

---

[6] Gerhardsson, *Memory and Manuscript*, 146–47, 329; idem, *The Origins of the Gospel Traditions* (Philadelphia: Fortress, 1979), 41; idem, "Illuminating the Kingdom: Narrative Meshalim in the Synoptic Parables," in *Jesus and the Oral Gospel Tradition* (ed. Henry Wansbrough; Sheffield: JSOT Press, 1991), 293–94; idem, "The Secret of the Transmission of the Unwritten Jesus Tradition," *NTS* 51 (2005): 6.

[7] B. Gerhardsson, *Tradition and Transmission in Early Christianity* (Lund and Copenhagen: Gleerup and Munksgaard, 1964).

[8] A. B. Lord, *The Singer of Tales* (Cambridge, Mass.: Harvard, 1960); J. Vansina, *Oral Tradition: A Study in Historical Methodology* (London: Routledge and Kegan Paul; Chicago: Aldine, 1965); idem, *Oral Tradition as History* (2d ed.; Madison, Wis.: University of Wisconsin Press, 1985).

[9] A. B. Lord, "The Gospels as Oral Traditional Literature," in *The Relationships among the Gospels: An Interdisciplinary Dialogue* (ed. William O. Walker Jr.; San Antonio: Trinity University Press, 1978), 33–91.

dropped a bombshell on the landscape of *Traditionsgeschichte* by postulating a large disjunction between the effects of the Gospel narratives circulating via oral tradition and of the written forms of those narratives, beginning with the production of the Gospel of Mark.[10] Kelber appears to have backed away from the most extreme forms of his early claims,[11] just as numerous scholars have stressed the ongoing importance of oral tradition, well into the mid-second century, even as more and more written accounts of the life and teachings of Jesus were appearing.[12]

Although he wrote only two short articles on the topic, Kenneth Bailey has garnered significant notice with his identification of the synoptic tradition as akin to what he calls "informal, controlled oral tradition." Bailey contrasts this approach with both "formal, controlled tradition" such as the memorization of the Hebrew Bible and "informal, uncontrolled tradition" found in preliterate communities that transmit comparatively unimportant traditions.[13] Bailey, however, generalizes from a fairly small database of comparative material; it is not clear that all of that (twentieth-century) material is sufficiently comparable to the ancient Mediterranean world of the first century, and it appears that he has not always accurately reported even what he has observed in the twentieth century.[14]

Where then do we stand today? Clearly, we have multiple, competing models. An astonishing number of scholars, particularly in America, especially associated in the 1990s with the Jesus Seminar, have managed to ignore virtually all of the study of oral tradition since

---

[10] W. H. Kelber, *The Oral and the Written Gospel* (Philadelphia: Fortress, 1983).

[11] W. H. Kelber, "Jesus and Tradition: Words in Time, Words in Space," *Semeia* 65 (1994): 139–67.

[12] J. Halverson, "Oral and Written Gospel: A Critique of Werner Kelber," *NTS* 40 (1994): 180–95; D. E. Aune, "Oral Tradition and the Aphorisms of Jesus," in *Jesus and the Oral Gospel Tradition* (ed. Henry Wansbrough; Sheffield: JSOT Press, 1991), 211–41; V. K. Robbins, "Oral, Rhetorical, and Literary Cultures: A Response," *Semeia* 65 (1994): 75–91; D. L. Balch, "The Canon: Adaptable and Stable, Oral and Written: Critical Questions for Kelber and Riesner," *Forum* 7 (1991): 183–205.

[13] K. E. Bailey, "Informal Controlled Oral Tradition and the Synoptic Gospels," *AJT* 5 (1991): 34–54; idem, "Middle Eastern Oral Tradition and the Synoptic Gospels," *ExpTim* 106 (1995): 563–67.

[14] T. J. Weeden Sr., "Theories of Tradition: A Critique of Kenneth Bailey" (Unpublished seminar paper, Santa Rosa, Calif., 2004), kindly shared with me by the author.

the 1960s and still adopt an old, free-flowing form-critical model. Bart Ehrman, in no less than an Oxford publication as recent as 2000, can still liken the transmission of synoptic tradition to the children's game of telephone, in which a fairly detailed message is whispered into one child's ear. They must then repeat what they think they heard in another quiet whisper to a second child, and the process continues throughout the room. Even with only a couple dozen "tradents," the message becomes hopelessly garbled and usually hilarious by the time the last person repeats aloud what was whispered to them.[15] But, of course, the first-century transmitters of the Gospel tradition were not children, were not whispering, had numerous checks and balances within the communities as they passed on the tradition, had countless reasons for valuing the tradition and its careful preservation highly, had authorized leaders who periodically traveled to ensure that the traditions were still being reported accurately, had living eyewitnesses to consult, and had the practice of taking notes for private reference on which to fall back.[16] Most important of all, they came from cultures in which education was dominated by rote learning, in which prodigious feats of memorization were cultivated, and in which traditions deemed sacred or from greatly revered teachers were hardly treated with the cavalier attitude of a children's party game.[17] Those who have replicated this contemporary game even among Middle Eastern students today have discovered that it does not work—people remember accurately what they are told and do not even understand the point of the exercise.[18]

A significant minority of scholars have followed Gerhardsson to one degree or another. Particularly important in bolstering and nuancing

---

[15] B. D. Ehrman, *Jesus: Apocalyptic Prophet of the New Millennium* (Oxford: Oxford University Press, 1999), 51–52.

[16] See especially A. F. Zimmermann, *Die urchristlichen Lehrer* (Tübingen: J. C. B. Mohr, 1984); and P.-G. Müller, *Der Traditionsprozess im Neuen Testament: Kommunikationsanalytische Studien zur Versprachlichung des Jesusphänomens* (Freiburg: Herder, 1981). Cf. also Ø. Anderson, "Oral Tradition," in *Jesus and the Oral Gospel Tradition* (ed. Henry Wansbrough; Sheffield: JSOT Press, 1991), 17–58; and P. S. Alexander, "Orality in Pharisaic-Rabbinic Judaism at the Turn of the Eras," in ibid., 159–84.

[17] See, for example, W. Shiner, *Proclaiming the Gospel: First-Century Performance of Mark* (Harrisburg, Pa.: Trinity Press International, 2003), 104–7.

[18] Bailey, "Middle Eastern Oral Tradition and the Synoptic Gospels," 366.

his arguments have been Rainer Riesner and Samuel Byrskog, particularly with their emphases on the need to revise upward the amount of literacy generally attributed to first-century adult Jewish men, given the proliferation of synagogue schools for boys from roughly ages 5 to 12 or 13, the importance of recognizing first-century Israel as a complex hybrid of oral and written cultures, and the tendencies to even more careful preservation of *oral* tradition once a part of it had been put into *writing*.[19] The most telling points against accounting for *all* the synoptic phenomena by means of oral processes remain those that most support Markan priority as a key part of the solution to the Synoptic Problem more generally—those texts in which extensive verbatim parallelism occurs in features not likely preserved by oral tradition at all but almost certainly due to the final Gospel writers—narrative asides, literary seams, thematic rearrangement, minor (but only minor) agreements of Matthew and Luke against Mark, and the like.[20] The most crucial counterargument to seeing the differences among the Synoptics as due to conscious redaction of written sources is the lack of access to written material (not least due to the prohibitive costs) even among the majority of the literate. Thus the culture remained oral/aural even for the dissemination and preservation of written texts.[21]

Ian Henderson could write almost 20 years ago that the agreed-on criteria for assessing orality in prose were increasingly clustering around (a) "syntactic and argumentative additivity," exhibited particularly in paratactic style; (b) "tolerance for logical and narrative inconsistency," discernible in digressions, ornaments, accumulative arguments, illustrative asides, and the like; (c) "relatively dense redundancy," with repetition, parallelism (both synonymous and antithetical) and linkage

---

[19] R. Riesner, *Jesus als Lehrer* (2d ed.; Tübingen: J. C. B. Mohr, 1988); idem, "Jesus as Preacher and Teacher," in *Jesus and the Oral Gospel Tradition* (ed. Henry Wansbrough; Sheffield: JSOT Press, 1991), 17–58; S. Byrskog, *Jesus the Only Teacher: Didactic Authority and Transmission in Ancient Israel, Ancient Judaism and the Matthean Community* (Stockholm: Almqvist & Wiksell, 1994); idem, *Story as History—History as Story: The Gospel Tradition in the Context of Ancient Oral History* (WUNT 123; Tübingen: Mohr Siebeck, 2000).

[20] See, for example, R. H. Stein, *Studying the Synoptic Gospels: Origin and Interpretation* (2d ed.; Grand Rapids: Baker, 2001), 49–96.

[21] H. Koester, "Written Gospels or Oral Tradition?" *JBL* 113 (1994): 293–97; J. D. Harvey, "Orality and Its Implications for Biblical Studies: Recapturing an Ancient Paradigm," *JETS* 45 (2002): 101.

by catchwords; and (d) "conceptual concreteness that prefers symbol" and imagery over abstractions.[22] Ten years later, John Harvey would sum up the tendencies of oral expression as additive, not subordinating; aggregative, not analytical; redundant, not concise; conservative, not creative; and acoustically oriented, not visually oriented.[23] A number of studies have applied criteria like these to Mark or Q, arguing that the presence of traditional oral forms even in the final versions of their documents demonstrate the probability that their authors composed in ways designed to facilitate multiple oral performances.[24]

A quite new subdiscipline within the guild of Gospel scholarship is what applies analyses of "social memory" to the New Testament narratives. Rather than focusing on the ways in which individual performers of a given oral tradition consciously or unconsciously alter it from one retelling to the next, the emphases here rest with issues important for the identity of the entire community or social group that the performer represents. This branch of study also focuses on various purposes for the selective and ideologically based preservation of tradition that have little or nothing to do with recording history or enabling people to remember what happened. Central among these is the exercise of power. Even in traditional cultures with a significant minority of literate people, inscriptions, publicly posted declarations, official documents, and the like would not have communicated information to the majority of the populace but would have indicated who held control or jurisdiction over a certain area of

---

[22] I. H. Henderson, "*Didache* and Orality in Synoptic Comparison," *JBL* 111 (1992): 283–306.

[23] Harvey, "Orality and Its Implications for Biblical Studies," 99–109. C.-B. Amphoux wants to make the approach of Marcel Jousse in his classic work on oral mnemonic devices from 1924 better known, which focused on rhythmic units, balance, catchwords, and formulas as signs of oral tradition. Amphoux provides brief illustrations of each in "Le style oral dans le nouveau testament," *ETR* 63 (1988): 379–84.

[24] See J. Dewey, "The Survival of Mark's Gospel: A Good Story," *JBL* 123 (2004): 495–507; V. K. Robbins, "Interfaces of Orality and Literature in the Gospel of Mark," in *Performing the Gospel: Orality, Memory, and Mark* (ed. R. A. Horsley, J. A. Draper, and J. M. Foley; Minneapolis: Fortress, 2006), 125–46; W. Shiner, "Memory Technology and the Composition of Mark," in ibid., 147–65; and R. A. Horsley, "A Prophet Like Moses and Elijah: Popular Memory and Cultural Patterns in Mark," in ibid., 166–90; and the entire anthology edited by R. A. Horsley with J. A. Draper, *Whoever Hears You Hears Me: Prophets, Performance and Tradition in Q* (Harrisburg, Pa.: Trinity Press International, 1999).

life. Tom Thatcher has written an entire book on the Gospel of John, applying principles from the study of social memory,[25] whereas two anthologies in the SBL's *Semeia Studies* series, edited by Thatcher and Alan Kirk and by Jonathan Draper, have demonstrated potential applications of this field to New Testament and cognate literature and tradition.[26] Several of the essays in a collection on *Performing the Gospel: Orality, Memory, and Mark* apply aspects of social memory to the Gospel tradition as well.[27]

Oral Tradition in *Jesus Remembered*

James D. G. Dunn is conversant with all these developments. In his magisterial *Jesus Remembered*, volume 1 of a projected three-volume series on *Christianity in the Making*, Dunn draws on elements from these numerous branches of Gospel criticism to fashion an appeal for taking the role of the oral tradition more seriously in accounting for the precise combination of similarities and differences that we encounter when comparing synoptic parallels. He helpfully prints the synoptic parallels, in English translation, with verbatim parallelism underlined.[28] His SNTS presidential address of 2002, subsequently published in *New Testament Studies* in 2003 and slightly revised for inclusion as an appendix in the printed form of his 2003 Acadia lectures, includes a number of the same examples but some different

---

[25] T. Thatcher, *Why John Wrote a Gospel: Jesus—Memory—History* (Louisville: Westminster John Knox, 2006). For applications to selected texts from Mark, Q, and *Thomas*, see J. Schröter, *Erinnerung an Jesu Worte* (Neukirchen-Vluyn: Neukirchener, 1997).

[26] A. Kirk and T. Thatcher, eds., *Memory, Tradition, and Text: Uses of the Past in Early Christianity* (Atlanta: SBL, 2005); J. A. Draper, ed., *Orality, Literacy, and Colonialism in Antiquity* (Atlanta: SBL, 2004). Cf. already, idem, "'Less Literate Are Safer': The Politics of Orality and Literacy in Biblical Interpretation," *ATR* 84 (2002): 340–57.

[27] R. A. Horsley, J. A. Draper, and J. M. Foley, eds., *Performing the Gospel: Orality, Memory, and Mark* (Minneapolis: Fortress, 2006). See especially H. E. Hearon, "The Implications of Orality for Studies of the Biblical Text," 3–21; J. Assmann, "Form as a Mnemonic Device; Cultural Texts and Cultural Memory," 67–82; and J. Schröter, "Jesus and the Canon: The Early Jesus Traditions in the Context of the Origins of the New Testament Canon," 104–22.

[28] J. D. G. Dunn, *Jesus Remembered* (vol. 1 of *Christianity in the Making*; Grand Rapids: Eerdmans, 2003).

ones as well.[29] The same is true of his article on Q in the Graham Stanton *Festschrift*.[30]

Assessments of Dunn's Case

Dunn's work on the Jesus tradition has already received some sustained scrutiny, eliciting, as one would expect, both affirmation and criticism.[31] It is arguable that his call for "altering the default setting" of how we think about first-century remembering of Jesus from literary to oral models is his most distinctive and important contribution in all this work. Repeatedly, one sees why the nature of the similarities and dissimilarities among the Gospel parallels move him in this direction—enough verbatim parallelism in numerous places so that he does not want to jettison either Markan priority or some form of a Q hypothesis but enough theologically and stylistically unmotivated changes, often scattered somewhat unpredictably about a lengthier pericope so that it is hard to retain confidence in any purely editorial model to account for the later changes in the tradition.

But how does one, if at all, quantify these results? Put differently, how does one determine when there is enough variety among the incidental details of a passage's parallel to suggest the influence of oral tradition and not just literary editing on the account? Dunn's doctoral student Terence Mournet devised one scheme by which he thought he could answer these questions. It is not enough to compute the overall percentage of verbatim parallelism between two different writers' accounts of the same teaching or episode from Jesus' life. One must subdivide the pericopae according to natural units of thought

---

[29] J. D. G. Dunn, "Altering the Default Setting: Re-envisaging the Early Transmission of the Jesus Tradition," *NTS* 49 (2003): 139–75; and idem, *A New Perspective on Jesus: What the Quest for the Historical Jesus Missed* (Grand Rapids: Baker Academic, 2005), 79–125.

[30] J. D. G. Dunn, "Q¹ as Oral Tradition," in *The Written Gospel* (ed. M. Bockmuehl and D. A. Hagner; Cambridge: Cambridge University Press, 2005), 45–69.

[31] B. Holmberg, "Questions of Method in James Dunn's *Jesus Remembered*," *JSNT* 26 (2004): 445–57; S. Byrskog, "A New Perspective on the Jesus Tradition: Reflections on James D. G. Dunn's *Jesus Remembered*," *JSNT* 26 (2004): 459–71; R. Morgan, "James Dunn's Jesus Remembered," *ExpTim* 116 (2004): 1–6; A. Gregory, "An Oral and Written Gospel? Reflections on Remembering Jesus," *ExpTim* 116 (2005): 7–12; and Gerhardsson, "The Secret of the Transmission."

and form and see how the variations between the parallels are distributed throughout the passage. Skewed conclusions could result, for
example, if two texts were compared, in which the first third of the
one was exactly parallel to the other, but the second two-thirds of the
first had no parallel at all in the other. A 33.3 percent level of parallelism would match the percentage obtained from two texts of the
same length with one-third of the words parallel but scattered evenly
throughout the passage. Yet the latter would be a much more natural
candidate for influence by oral tradition than the former. For all we
know, the former might just as easily reflect the conflation of two written sources, one of them not used by the other Gospel writer at that
juncture at all.[32]

Mournet also considers what *kind* of material reflects verbatim
parallelism and what does not. One would expect the pronouncement
in a pronouncement story to contain the greatest amount of parallelism to its synoptic counterparts, and that is exactly what one finds.
The moderate amount of diversity discernible among the parallels for
the rest of a given pericope is likewise just what one would expect the
tendencies of oral transmission to produce. But the same percentage of
less central words that reappear in identical form in parallel accounts
could tip the scales in the direction of literary dependence throughout
more or all of the passage. So, too, the *order* of parallel words must
be taken into account. Two texts that exhibit the identical amount
of verbatim parallelism as two other texts may be more likely to have
been influenced by the oral tradition if a significant number of those
paralleled words, phrases, or sentences recur in different places within
the overall pericopae.[33]

Mournet compiles, diagrams, and assesses his select passages
under three headings: those Dunn has labeled likely to reflect significant influence from the oral tradition, those Dunn sees as largely or
entirely the product of literary processes, and a "control group" of additional passages with a variety of percentages of parallel words. Mournet
believes that the statistics largely bear out Dunn's hypotheses. With

---

[32] T. C. Mournet, *Oral Tradition and Literary Dependency: Variability and Stability in the Synoptic Tradition and Q* (WUNT 2.195; Tübingen: Mohr Siebeck, 2005), esp. 204–12.

[33] Ibid., esp. 201–4.

just a few exceptions, he has rightly intuited which passages more likely represent the impact of the tendencies of the oral tradition.[34]

I have neither time nor space to replicate Mournet's exercise with the sophistication he used. But one important question could vitiate at least some of his results. Barry Henaut has argued that one does not need to resort to the oral tradition to explain the differences among the synoptic parallels, particularly in the Markan parable chapter (4:1–34), because all of the differences can be plausibly explained as due to conscious theological or stylistic redaction.[35] But what constitutes plausibility? Compare the works on the Synoptic Problem by Michael Goulder and his supporters and discover how it is possible to imagine that every passage in Luke found its current location in that Gospel because the author kept reading Mark and Matthew from start to finish sequentially (or perhaps backward), choosing different pericopae to include for reconstructible reasons, often related to catchwords or topics, each time.[36] But, of course, a moment's consideration reminds us that the order of *any* text with substantial parallels in one or more other documents can be explained by this method if one allows an indefinite number of passes through the supposed source texts. Not every procedure that is theoretically possible proves at all plausible.[37]

Against Henaut, then, it makes more sense to begin with Dunn's oral "default setting" and attribute to literary editing only those distinctives of a later Gospel that are demonstrably theological or stylistic predilections of the evangelists in question. Most of the passages scrutinized by Dunn and Mournet and assigned a fair measure of influence from the oral tradition do not contain such features. At the same time, it is not fair to skew the statistics *in favor of* one's hypothesis to such a degree that one excludes other credible options by one's very methodology. Here I think lies the biggest weakness of Mournet's methodology.

---

[34] Ibid., 212–86.

[35] B. W. Henaut, *Oral Tradition and the Gospels: The Problem of Mark 4* (Sheffield: JSOT Press, 1993).

[36] M. D. Goulder, *Luke: A New Paradigm* (2 vols.; Sheffield: JSOT Press, 1989); A. J. McNicol, with D. L. Dungan and D. B. Peabody, *Beyond the Q Impasse: Luke's Use of Matthew* (Valley Forge, Pa.: Trinity Press International, 1996).

[37] See further C. L. Blomberg, "The Synoptic Problem: Where We Stand at the Start of a New Century," in *Rethinking the Synoptic Problem* (ed. D. A. Black and D. Beck; Grand Rapids: Baker, 2001), 33–34, and the literature there cited.

Further Evaluation

More than 25 years ago, I published my findings from a comparison of the Lukan parables with all of their parallels in either Mark or Matthew. Instead of computing just the number of words in a given pericope that were paralleled in verbatim form in the Gospel to which I was comparing it, I calculated three percentages from the text of Aland's *Synopsis*: one involving verbatim parallels, one that also included words from the same Greek lexical root even if in different morphological form, and one that added in synonyms, too. Unless one can assume that all of the committee's choices of textual variants are unerring, that all of the oral tradition that influenced the evangelists' writing was in Greek and never still in Aramaic, and that all of the Synoptists' dependence on earlier Gospels or Gospel sources implied that they had copies of those documents in front of them as they dictated their works, one must allow for the likelihood that different morphological forms of the same root words and clear Greek synonyms would have frequently found their way into the later writers' versions of paralleled accounts *without* indicating changes bequeathed to them by the oral tradition. The small sample space of 14 parables that my study examined demonstrated that the difference between percentages of verbatim parallelism and parallelism when one counted identical words, identical roots, and synonyms all together could vary from as little as 8.4 percent to as much as 41.2 percent, with 8 of the 14 passages exhibiting between 15 percent and 25 percent variation between these two statistics.[38]

The issue I was interested in back then was the question of when an apparent parallel is indeed a genuine parallel. No one doubted that the multiple synoptic accounts of 8 of the 14 parables analyzed were genuine parallels: the parables of the householder and thief, leaven, children in the marketplace, faithful and unfaithful servants, sower, asking son, mustard seed, and wicked husbandmen. The amount of parallelism when all three of my categories were added together ranged from 100 percent to 67.5 percent, and the percentages were comparatively

---

[38] C. L. Blomberg, "When Is a Parallel Really a Parallel? A Test Case: The Lucan Parables," *WTJ* 46 (1984): 78–103.

evenly distributed over this range. To be specific, the passages, in the order previously listed, exhibited percentages of parallelism of 100.0, 100.0, 93.8, 90.2, 81.5, 79.2, 73.7, and 67.5 percent. A group of four parables constituted a second discrete cluster: the animals in the well, two builders, lost sheep, and pounds/talents, with percentages of parallelism of 52.9, 48.2, 44.6, and 41.5 percent, respectively. Finally, two parables—the great supper/wedding banquet and watchful servants/ doorkeeper—formed a third category, disclosing only 17.6 and 13.6 percent parallelism, respectively. I concluded that the combination of such low percentages of agreement, combined with the different contexts in which Luke and Mark or Matthew placed each pair, supported the identification of this last group of passages as separate teachings from different contexts in the life of Jesus and not as true parallels at all. The middle category reflected pairings where at least a handful of scholars had questioned whether the parallelism was genuine, but the percentages of agreement by themselves scarcely proved decisive. Contextual locations needed to be factored in as well.[39]

If one reexamines these data with the question of the possible influence of oral tradition in mind, one could easily hypothesize that the middle category of passages exhibited as little agreement as it did (between 41 and 53 percent) due largely to such oral processes. The talents/pounds might prove to be the one exception, since most of Luke's distinctive traits cohere into what has often been viewed as a separate, original parable of a throne claimant, which Luke has conflated with a parable very much like Matthew's talents.[40] Indeed, as we will see later, the wicked husbandmen (67 percent agreement) also proves to be a good candidate for variations due to tendencies of oral transmission. The mustard seed (74 percent agreement) again reflects conflation, at least in its Matthean form.[41] The remaining six parables (79 to 100 percent agreement) do not disclose the kinds of divergences that one can attribute with any confidence to the oral tradition. Mournet thinks that more than 70 percent agreement makes oral influence difficult to

---

[39] See the chart summarizing my findings in ibid., 81.

[40] See, classically, in Jeremias, *Parables*, 59.

[41] A. J. Hultgren, *The Parables of Jesus: A Commentary* (Grand Rapids: Eerdmans, 2000), 393.

demonstrate;[42] with our higher percentages based on a broader definition of parallelism, 80 percent seems like a reasonable cutoff figure.
The examples Dunn offers of passages in which literary dependence
appears sufficient to explain the phenomena all likewise demonstrate
more than 80 percent parallelism.

What happens to Dunn's other passages when one uses the more
generous statistic of possible parallelism due to literary dependence,
broadly conceived? Will his claims still be borne out as consistently
as they did with Mournet's narrower statistical comparisons? If they
are, then even more powerful support for his conclusions will have
emerged, since, by definition, the amount of parallelism will never
decrease but always increase or at least stay the same so that the
amount of variation left to attribute to oral tradition will almost always
shrink when moving from his analysis to ours. For the same reason, it
seems appropriate to divide the total number of paralleled words (in
any of the three categories) by the number of words in the shorter of
the two passages being compared. In lieu of the more detailed, sec-
tion-by-section breakdown that Mournet pursues, this process best
prevents two passages of noticeably disparate length from presenting
misleading statistics. Of course, there will be no parallelism under any
of our three headings for that material in a given pericope that has
no counterpart of any kind in the parallel passage. Because scholarly
confidence in Luke's and Matthew's uses of Mark is greater than that
behind any given form of the Q hypothesis, it also makes sense to look
at Dunn's Markan and "Q" examples separately to see if any distinct
trends emerge.

In the three aforementioned writings, in which he prints the
underlined replicas of an English synopsis, Dunn considers eight passages from Mark paralleled in either Matthew or Luke or both. I have
compiled my comparisons in tabular form below, with (a) referring to
the number of words exactly paralleled in the Aland Greek text, (b)
identifying the number of words with identical roots, and (c) specifying
the number of words I deem to be synonyms. The figure represented

---

[42] Mournet, *Oral Tradition and Literary Dependency*, 201–2; following T. Bergemann,
Q auf dem Prüfstand: Die Zuordnung des Mt/Lk-Stoffes zu Q am Beispiel der Bergpredigt (Göttingen: Vandenhoeck & Ruprecht, 1993), 56.

by (d), then, refers to the total number of words in the shorter of the two passages compared. When the text appears in the triple tradition, I have computed the percentages separately for Matthew versus Mark and for Luke versus both Matthew and Mark. I have adopted the latter approach as a concession to the greater amount of disagreement among scholars as to whether Luke used Mark and Matthew or Mark and Q, as compared with the large consensus that affirms that Matthew used Mark and Q (rather than Mark and Luke).[43] Again, if the results skew the research, it will be in the direction of limiting how much can be ascribed to oral tradition, not in the direction of attributing an overly generous amount to that factor. Thus, if the results still remain statistically significant, the case for the influence of oral tradition will have only been enhanced.

Passages	(Matt vs. Mark) $\dfrac{(a) + (b) + (c)}{(d)}$		(Luke vs. Mark & Matt) $\dfrac{(a) + (b) + (c)}{(d)}$	
Mark 12:41–44 par.	$\dfrac{34 + 5 + 9 = 48}{58}$	= 82.8%		
Mark 14:66–72 pars.	$\dfrac{51 + 14 + 9 = 74}{116}$	= 63.7%	$\dfrac{10 + 44 + 12 = 66}{111}$	= 59.4%
Mark 9:14–27 pars.	$\dfrac{40 + 7 + 14 = 61}{109}$	= 56.0%	$\dfrac{44 + 7 + 7 = 58}{92}$	= 63.0%
Mark 4:35–41 pars.	$\dfrac{25 + 13 + 5 = 43}{73}$	= 58.9%	$\dfrac{34 + 5 + 9 = 48}{94}$	= 51.1%
Mark 9:33–37 pars.	$\dfrac{19 + 4 + 1 = 24}{78}$	= 30.8%	$\dfrac{22 + 5 + 1 = 28}{61}$	= 45.9%
Mark 7:24–30 par.	$\dfrac{29 + 3 + 12 = 44}{129}$	= 34.1%		
Mark 16:1–8 pars.	$\dfrac{33 + 10 + 6 = 49}{136}$	= 36.0 %	$\dfrac{17 + 6 + 6 = 29}{122}$	= 23.8 %

---

[43] For all these generalizations, see again Blomberg, "The Synoptic Problem," 20–35.

The only example out of these seven that seems an unlikely candidate for demonstrating the influence of oral tradition is the first— the Markan and Lukan accounts of the widow's mite. Dunn admits that "with such a brief pericope the scope for explanation in terms of Luke's editing of Mark is stronger" but thinks that "even so, the flexibility of detail in the build-up to the climactic saying bespeaks more of oral than of literary tradition."[44] But this is where older form- and redaction-critical wisdom still proves valuable. The introductions to passages are where the evangelists are most likely to have inserted their editorial material, linking texts together,[45] and about half of all the differences between Mark and Luke can be accounted for by their distinctive introductions. The amount of parallelism also goes up when one uses the number of words in the shorter, Lukan text as the divisor. Without any comparable material at all to Matthew's unique segments, it is almost impossible to argue that either oral tradition or the evangelist's redaction was more likely to have been responsible.

The remaining six texts all exhibit sufficient parallelism to suggest that they are true parallels while containing sufficient divergence to point to the influence of oral tradition. The one passage that gives one pause is the stilling of the storm. Since Bornkamm's groundbreaking study, one is accustomed to thinking of at least some of the changes in wording as due to Matthew's desire to portray the disciples in a slightly less negative light than Mark.[46] But it is not obvious that even factoring in these differences would significantly decrease the percentage of unmotivated changes. The Markan resurrection account and its parallels provide the clearest example in which, even factoring in possible redactional changes, the amount of unmotivated change remains the greatest. In between, we find precisely the kinds of changes that informal controlled tradition or flexible tradition with fixed limits would be expected to exhibit—divergence in the descriptions of the

---

[44] Dunn, *Jesus Remembered*, 221.

[45] Cf. an otherwise rare agreement between R. Bultmann, *The History of the Synoptic Tradition* (trans. J. Marsh; Oxford: Basil Blackwell, 1963), 322–67; and Stein, *Studying the Synoptic Gospels*, 49–96.

[46] G. Bornkamm, "The Stilling of the Storm in Matthew," in *Tradition and Interpretation in Matthew* (ed. G. Bornkamm, G. Barth, and H.-J. Held; London: SCM; Philadelphia: Westminster, 1963), 52–57.

people who accused Peter of having been with Jesus, details about the affliction of the demon-possessed boy, details about the background and behavior of the Syrophoenician woman, varying ways of narrating Jesus' central teaching about servanthood and becoming like little children, and so on.

The eighth Markan passage proves different, in that Dunn appeals to the *four* accounts of the Lord's Supper, highlighting in particular Mark 14:66–72 and parallels. As has often been observed, Mark's and Matthew's accounts closely resemble one another ([55 + 2 + 3 = 60]/69 = 87.0% parallelism), whereas Luke's and 1 Corinthians' versions likewise show noticeable "family resemblances" ([34 + 1 + 2 = 37]/49 = 75.5% parallelism). Literary dependence is almost certainly at work in both of these pairings.[47] But what of the differences between the two pairs of traditions? The numbers yielded from a comparison of Luke and Mark, for example, are (32 + 5 + 3 = 40)/67 = 59.7%, well within the range of parallels noticeably influenced by oral tradition. Against Dunn, the liturgical use of these texts in and of itself does not necessarily favor variation due to oral transmission;[48] Paul in 1 Cor 11:23, with his language of passing on what he has received, uses technical terminology for *memorized* oral tradition, so we should expect "formal, controlled" transmission to be at work here.[49] Thus the relationships among the four forms might well be *more* complicated than with other kinds of Jesus material.

Twelve of Dunn's examples, however, come from the so-called Q material. Here we need to compute just a single percentage, because we are comparing only Matthew and Luke in each instance. Here are the results in tabular form:

---

[47] The evidence is nicely discussed, for example, in I. H. Marshall, *Last Supper and Lord's Supper* (Exeter: Paternoster; Grand Rapids: Eerdmans, 1980), 31–56.

[48] For Dunn's view, see *Jesus Remembered*, 229–31.

[49] Cf. A. C. Thiselton, *The First Epistle to the Corinthians* (Carlisle: Paternoster; Grand Rapids: Eerdmans, 2000), 867–68, and the literature there cited.

Passages	(Matt vs. Luke)
	$\dfrac{(a) + (b) + (c)}{(d)}$
Q 11:2–4	$\dfrac{26 + 4 + 3 = 33}{38}$ = 86.8%
Q 12:33–34	$\dfrac{13 + 5 + 1 = 19}{34}$ = 67.9%
Q 7:1–10	$\dfrac{91 + 11 + 10 = 112}{166}$ = 67.5%
Q 12:57–59	$\dfrac{21 + 5 + 2 + 28}{43}$ = 65.1%
Q 14:26–27	$\dfrac{11 + 5 + 6 = 22}{38}$ = 58.0%
Q 6:29–30	$\dfrac{15 + 1 + 3 = 19}{34}$ = 55.9%
Q 17:3–4	$\dfrac{9 + 5 + 2 = 16}{31}$ = 51.6%
Q 6:47–49	$\dfrac{21 + 16 + 3 = 40}{83}$ = 48.2%
Q 12:51–53	$\dfrac{5 + 7 + 7 = 19}{40}$ = 47.5%
Q 13:23–24	$\dfrac{4 + 1 + 2 = 7}{15}$ = 46.7%
Q 14:34–35	$\dfrac{8 + 2 + 0 = 10}{24}$ = 41.7%
Q 14:16–24	$\dfrac{10 + 14 + 4 = 28}{159}$ = 17.6%

Tellingly, 10 of these 12 texts display parallelism that ranges between 42 and 68 percent. Of course, one might suspect that Dunn looked for parallels that appeared, even without precise measurement, to be about half the same and half different. Still, he included the Lord's Prayer in its two versions, which displays far higher parallelism, when the distinctively Matthean and Lukan framing narratives are removed, again thinking that liturgical use demonstrated oral modifications[50] (but see previous text). And he included the two parables of the wedding banquet and great supper, which probably reflect Jesus' own reuse of the same general theme on two separate occasions.[51] The other 10 pairings, however, appear to support Dunn's suspicions.

The complicating factor that the wedding banquet and great supper present may, however, afflict a number of the other examples from Q. Given the frequency of these double-tradition passages appearing in entirely different contexts in the two Gospels that contain them, how are we to differentiate between one originating tradition and Jesus' own repeated use of similar sayings, especially since so much of Q is sayings material? If Dunn can legitimately argue that the "default setting" has inappropriately almost always favored literary dependence over oral influence, one may similarly complain that an even more unchanging default setting with Q sayings has been the assumption that Jesus could have been responsible, at most, for only one originating form, with all other variations due to *either* oral *or* written modification. If we should have learned anything from the studies of oral performances, though, it is that oral traditions do not usually have solitary originating exemplars, not least because the revered teachers who often initiated those traditions regularly reused the same contents and structures in multiple settings with variation. As Michael Bird sums up contributions from Wright, Kelber, and Gerhardsson, "That Jesus taught and said things in multiple instances in various locations means that acts of remembering Jesus in a communal setting already began at a pre-Easter stage by his closest followers and audience."[52]

---

[50] Dunn, *Jesus Remembered*, 227–28.

[51] Blomberg, *Interpreting the Parables*, 237–39. Cf. Hultgren, *The Parables of Jesus*, 333–35; D. L. Bock, *Luke 9:51–24:53* (Grand Rapids: Baker, 1996), 1269–70.

[52] M. F. Bird, "The Formation of the Gospels in the Setting of Early Christianity: The Jesus Tradition as Corporate Memory," *WTJ* 67 (2005): 133.

Again, "Jesus' itinerant ministry would require that much of the same thing be said from place to place as he urgently broadcast the message of the kingdom to the string of villages he entered."[53]

The Synoptic Parables

If we want the most helpful material to test for signs of oral tradition from Jesus' *sayings*, we will turn to his parables, regardless of the synoptic stratum in which any given passage appears. With a few exceptions, they are long enough so that if *any* of Jesus' teachings can give us an adequate sample size, they can. Plus there are enough of them to test for consistency of trends within a single pedagogical form. Audience analysis has demonstrated that, Jeremias' speculation notwithstanding, if one limits oneself to what the Synoptists explicitly state, there is an extraordinarily high level of agreement as to which parables were addressed to which audiences and on what occasions.[54] It makes sense, therefore, to analyze the non-Lukan parables to supplement our 25-year-old analysis of the Lukan parables and see what it obtains. The charts below represent the results of these efforts, using the same previous calculations.

	Markan Texts	
Passages	**(Matt vs. Mark)** $\dfrac{(a) + (b) + (c)}{(d)}$	**(Luke vs. Mark & Matt)** $\dfrac{(a) + (b) + (c)}{(d)}$
Mark 4:3–9 pars.	$\dfrac{56 + 12 + 6 = 74}{81} = 91.4\%$	$\dfrac{49 + 6 + 8 = 63}{76} = 82.9\%$
Mark 12:1–9 pars.	$\dfrac{67 + 18 + 1 = 86}{136} = 63.2\%$	$\dfrac{72 + 9 + 12 = 93}{130} = 71.5\%$

[53] Ibid. Cf. N. T. Wright, *The New Testament and the People of God* (Minneapolis: Fortress, 1992), 422–24; Kelber, *The Oral and the Written Gospel*, 30; Gerhardsson, *Memory and Manuscript*, 334–35.

[54] J. A. Baird, *Audience Criticism and the Historical Jesus* (Philadelphia: Westminster, 1969), esp. 49 and 73; P. B. Payne, "Metaphor as a Model for Interpretation of the Parables of Jesus with Special Reference to the Parable of the Sower" (PhD diss.: Cambridge, 1976), 239.

Mark 4:30–32 pars. $\dfrac{16 + 8 + 5 = 29}{50}$ = 58.0% $\dfrac{21 + 2 + 1 + 24}{38}$ = 63.2%

Mark 13:33–37 par. $\dfrac{2 + 4 + 3 = 9}{66}$ = 13.6%

Three kinds of "parallels" emerge within the four Markan parables that seem to reappear in Matthew or Luke. First, the parable of the sower remains above 80 percent in its parallelism when Luke is compared with Mark and Matthew and above 90 percent when Matthew is compared with Mark. This will not be a promising place to look for variation due to oral tradition. The second and third examples, on the other hand, do prove promising. As we will see later, when we return to the wicked husbandmen, even Luke's 71 percent agreement with either Mark or Matthew leaves several places where the oral tradition probably accounts for changes; the same will prove true all the more with Matthew's smaller degree of parallelism (63 percent). The example of the mustard seed is complicated, however, by the observation that Matthew appears to have conflated Mark with a Q form of the parable (see following text). Finally, the parallelism between the watchful servants in Luke and the doorkeeper in Mark is so small that these are more likely independent stories that Jesus told on separate occasions.[55]

	Q Texts		
Passages	**(Matt vs. Luke)**		
	$\dfrac{(a) + (b) + (c)}{(d)}$		
Q 12:39–40	$\dfrac{29 + 2 + 3 = 34}{34}$	= 100.0%	
Q 13:20–21	$\dfrac{15 + 3 + 1 = 19}{19}$	= 100.0%	
Q 11:16–19	$\dfrac{45 + 14 + 2 = 61}{65}$	= 93.8%	

[55] Though see D. Wenham, *The Rediscovery of Jesus' Eschatological Discourse* (Sheffield: JSOT Press 1984), 15–49. Wenham builds a case for all three Synoptic Gospels excerpting from an original discourse longer than the versions found in any current Gospel.

Q 12:42–46	$\dfrac{83 + 5 + 4 = 92}{102}$	= 90.2%
Q 11:11–13	$\dfrac{34 + 2 + 2 = 38}{48}$	= 79.2%
Q 14:5	$\dfrac{2 + 6 + 1 = 9}{17}$	= 52.9%
Q 6:47–49	$\dfrac{21 + 16 + 3 = 40}{83}$	= 48.2%
Q 15:4–7	$\dfrac{15 + 12 + 2 = 29}{65}$	= 44.6%
Q 19:12–27	$\dfrac{54 + 23 + 28 = 105}{253}$	= 41.5%
Q 14:16–24	$\dfrac{10 + 14 + 4 = 28}{151}$	= 18.5%

Intriguingly, the passages again cluster into three groups. The first five exhibit roughly 80 to 100 percent parallelism and can probably be accounted for entirely by theories of literary dependence and redaction. The last pair of passages (the great supper and wedding banquet), with under 20 percent parallelism (as already noted), probably represent separate originating forms. The remaining four parables all appear to be good candidates for the presence of oral influence, though (again, as already noted) the possible explanation of Luke 19:12–27 as the conflation of Matthew's talents with a separate throne claimant parable makes this a more complex and less clear-cut test case.

Elements of Orality

If we now return to our four most promising examples (the wicked husbandmen, the two builders, the lost sheep, and the animals in the well), what do we discover? The wicked husbandmen is by far the longest of the four, thus giving us the most material to work with. Matt 21:43, unique to Matthew, about the giving of the kingdom to a nation producing the fruit of it, is clearly a redactional emphasis, given

Matthew's narrative development from Jewish particularism to Jew-Gentile universalism.[56] But this verse does not form part of the parable proper. Luke's addition of "for a long while" to the landlord's initial trip away (Luke 20:9) has often been understood as reflecting his less imminent eschatology.[57] Many scholars think that Matthew and Luke have each independently reversed the order of the killing and casting of the son out of the vineyard to reflect Christ's actual crucifixion outside the city walls of Jerusalem, though this change may reflect simple stylistic improvement.[58]

Beyond these points, however, there is little among Matthew's and Luke's variations from Mark that is demonstrably redactional. None of the three accounts agrees on the precise details about the mistreatment or the exact number or nature of the various servants sent to collect the fruit of the vineyard. Matthew's account generalizes: "The tenants took his servants and beat one, killed another, and stoned another. Again he sent other servants, more than the first; and they did the same to them" (Matt 21:35–36). Luke's, on the other hand, organizes and enumerates: "He sent a servant. . . . And he sent another. . . . And he sent yet a third" (Luke 20:10–12). Both modifications of Mark's helter-skelter account of the harm inflicted reflect standard oral streamlining processes. Luke's unique addition of "perhaps" to the landowner's pronouncement, "they will respect him [the beloved son]" (v. 13), likely emerged in the oral performance of the tradition as well. Luke would hardly have been the first person to have thought of the need to forestall the possible misunderstanding of the landlord's prediction as failed prophecy, not appropriately attributed to a god figure in a parable.[59] The three distinct endings of the parable proper likewise remind one of the incidental changes regularly introduced in oral storytelling. In Matt 21:40–41, Jesus asks the crowd what the landlord will do to the wicked tenants, and the people predict coming punishment. In Mark 12:9, Jesus asks and answers his own

---

[56] Cf., for example, R. Schnackenburg, *The Gospel of Matthew* (Grand Rapids: Eerdmans, 2002), 212.

[57] See, classically, H. Conzelmann, *The Theology of St. Luke* (trans. G. Buswell; New York: Harper & Row, 1960), 98–136.

[58] M. Hubaut, *La parabole des vignerons homicides* (Paris: Gabalda, 1976), 52.

[59] Cf. J. Nolland, *Luke 18:35–24:53* (Dallas: Word, 1993), 951.

question. In Luke, he asks and answers his query, to which the crowd replies, "God forbid!" Unless one imagines Jesus questioning a crowd that responds like a choir in unison, it is very historically probable that different people shouted out different, even contradictory answers and that he had to affirm the answer with which he agreed. The divergent details can all be plausibly harmonized. But no single Gospel writer chose to tell the story that way. The distinctives seem to have no theological significance but read like the kinds of variation one finds in multiple oral performances.[60]

The accounts of the contrast parable of the two builders offer a classic illustration of what Jeremias called representational change.[61] The picture in Matthew (7:24–27) seems closer to Jesus' original and could have been inspired by the rare but dangerous flash floods that swept down through the desert wadis and into the Jordan River, washing away all but the most permanent of structures built into solid rock. The portrait in Luke (6:47–49) depicts instead houses constructed with or without foundations, like those of wise or foolish builders on the banks of the Orontes River in Syrian Antioch, where floodwaters simply overflowed the river's banks and little by little undermined homes with inadequate substructures.[62] Again, Luke *could* have been the first person responsible for this change, but as soon as the parable left Israelite soil for less rugged terrain, any tradent could have easily made the pictorial changes, precisely so that the main points of the story would *remain* intelligible.[63]

The two versions of the lost sheep are complicated by the fact that they appear in two quite different settings in Matthew and Luke. In Matt 18:10–14, Jesus is addressing the disciples in a discourse about humility and forgiveness. In Luke 15:3–7, he is presenting the first

---

[60] Cf. A. D. Baum, "Oral Poetry und synoptische Frage: Analogien zu Umfang, Variation und Art der synoptischen Wortlautidentität," *TZ* 59 (2003): 17–34.

[61] Jeremias, *Parables*, 26–27.

[62] J. A. Fitzmyer, *The Good News according to Luke I–IX* (Garden City, N.Y.: Doubleday, 1981), 644.

[63] Cf. C. H. Kraft, with M. G. Kraft, *Christianity in Culture: A Study in Biblical Theologizing in Cross-Cultural Perspective* (rev. ed.; Maryknoll: Orbis, 2005), 216–27. J. Nolland (*The Gospel of Matthew: A Commentary on the Greek Text* [NIGTC; Grand Rapids: Eerdmans, 2005], 343) comments more elliptically, "It is unlikely that the differences between [the two versions of the parable] are to be attributed entirely to intervention by the Evangelists."

in his triad of parables defending his association with tax collectors and other notorious sinners, against the complaints of his critics. If these are two versions of the same originating form (and this premise is not nearly as assured as many scholars allege it to be[64]), then many of the Matthean distinctives can be seen to mesh with a desire to portray the lost sheep as the wandering disciple, whereas in Luke it represents the completely despised outsider.[65] But not all the divergent details naturally line up with such designs. Luke's version assumes the lost sheep *will* be found, whereas Matthew has a conditional clause ("*if* he finds it"). Yet Luke scarcely believes that Jesus' mission to seek and save the lost (19:10) will eventually rescue all humans (contrast 19:11–27), whereas Matthew contains texts that suggest (borrowing Reformation-era terminology) that true saints will persevere, because Jesus says he *never* knew those who do not remain faithful (Matt 7:23; cf. 25:1–13). Even Matt 18:14 appends God's desire that no one will be lost (though of course some are) to the parable of the lost sheep. So perhaps these variations owe more to the oral tradition than to deliberate redaction. The same may be true of Luke's unique reference to the shepherd carrying the sheep home on his shoulders and to his calling his neighbors together to celebrate (Luke 15:5–6).

The animals in the well (Matt 12:11; Luke 14:5) is so short a passage, set in two different contexts and without the typical narrative form that produces the parabolic label, that it may seem a poor choice for a final illustration. Still, the *tis ex humōn* introduction matches that of longer, full-fledged parables couched as rhetorical questions, and whether the variations are due to Jesus' reuse of similar imagery or varying oral performances during the later transmission of the tradition, oral influences seem to have been at work. Luke's "son or ox" is a "sheep" in Matthew. Matthew's "pit" becomes a "well" in Luke. Matthew's "lay hold of and lift out" shrinks in Luke, with a different verb, just to "pulls out." Only Luke, however, adds "immediately," not using his favorite term *parachrēma*, but *eutheōs*, a word more

---

[64] See Blomberg, *Interpreting the Parables*, 179–84, and the literature there cited. Cf. Nolland, *Matthew*, 740.

[65] Hultgren, *The Parables of Jesus*, 48–62, is representative and detailed in his treatment.

characteristic of Matthew.[66] Varieties of oral performance could readily account for all of these differences.

Of course, just as the lack of parallel texts has not prevented synoptic scholarship from speculating in great detail about written sources underneath material distinctive to any given evangelist, so too it is possible to envision where oral tradition has left its mark on singly attested parables. The streamlined triad, "first the blade, then the ear, then the full grain in the ear" (*prōton . . . eita . . . eita*) in the seed growing secretly (Mark 4:28) fits the predilection of oral tradition for series of threes and reminds us of the improvements in Luke's wicked husbandmen of Mark's far less organized version of that parable. Matthew's wheat and tares includes a pair of rhetorical questions by the servants, who are not among the parable's central foci and are strictly speaking unnecessary to the furtherance of the plot (Matt 13:27–28). There is pleonasm in the command concerning the wheat—"and bind it into bindings" (*kai dēsate auta eis desmas*—v. 30), which could also reflect the common "untidiness" of oral performances.

The parables of the hidden treasure and pearl of great price (Matt 13:44–46) are worded in closely parallel fashion as if they belonged in the tradition together from the outset. Each begins with *homoia estin hē basileia tōn ouranōn* followed by a dative noun of comparison, modified by a second dative substantive. But in the second parable (of the pearl), the reference to the "man" is not repeated, whereas a subordinate participle and two finite verbs replace the less elegant parataxis of the four indicative verbs all joined by "and" in the first parable (of the hidden treasure). The historical present tense, represented by those four verbs, another feature otherwise much more common in Mark than in either Matthew or Luke,[67] does not reappear at all in the second parable nor does the superfluous reference to the item bought recur after the man makes his sale but is replaced simply with "it." Together these features could suggest that the oral tradition had streamlined or smoothed out the second parable a little; conceivably Jesus' twin originals matched each other almost verbatim.

---

[66] *parachrēma*—Matt. 2X, Luke 10X, Acts 6X, rest of NT 0X. *eutheōs*—Matt. 13X, Luke 6X.

[67] D. B. Wallace, *Greek Grammar Beyond the Basics* (Grand Rapids: Zondervan, 1996), 528.

The parable of the unforgiving servant contains a handful of touches potentially explicable via the processes of oral performance. A bit of Markan-like parataxis[68] appears in Matt 18:25: "He ordered him to be sold *and* his wife *and* his children *and* everything which he had, *and* [for it] to be paid back." Verses 32 through 34 repeat some of the information already provided at the outset of the parable, some of it this time in direct discourse on the lips of the king. Both patterns often feature in oral transmission. In the antithetical parallelism of the contrast parable of the two sons, the second diptych clearly abbreviates and leaves out elements readily understood to carry over from the first (Matt 21:28–30). Instead of repeating the father's command to go and work in the vineyard, Matthew reads, "He went to the second and said likewise." Neither does any reference to the second son changing his mind from his initial promise appear; we are told simply that, after saying he was going, he did not. Similar abbreviation of unnecessary repetition occurs in the parable of the 10 bridesmaids, when we read "five of them were foolish" and "five wise" (Matt 25:2). The quasi-parable of the sheep and the goats has numerous instances of slight abbreviation in what is otherwise very close parallelism between the actions of the faithful and the inaction of the wicked (25:31–46).

The predilection of characters in the peculiarly Lukan parables for soliloquy or monologue, sometimes heralded as a distinctive of an L-source (or of some otherwise undocumented Lukan redactional preference),[69] could just as easily be explained by its popularity in oral performances. One can see this in the rich fool (Luke 12:16–21), along with various redundancies; for example, "What will I do? . . . this I will do" (vv. 17–18); "He will say to his soul, 'Soul . . .'" (v. 19). Repetition by direct discourse of already provided information by the narrator recurs in the parable of the barren fig tree (13:7). The entire parable of the lost coin (15:8–10) is closely parallel in meaning and sense to its predecessor in Luke 15:4–7 (the lost sheep) but with many features omitted or abbreviated. Was it once the same length and structure as its "companion"? Needless repetition, on the other hand, occurs in the

---

[68] J. Marcus, *Mark 1–8* (New York: Doubleday, 1999), 80.

[69] K. Paffenroth, *The Story of Jesus according to L* (Sheffield: Sheffield Academic Press, 1997), 98–99.

direct discourse of the judge who we have already been told feared neither God nor humanity, when he speaks to himself out loud, conceding "though I fear neither God nor humanity" (Luke 18:2,4). Our examples could be multiplied.

Roadblocks and a Way Forward

The Achilles' heel for all these suggestions, however, as has been repeatedly pointed out, is that there is no single criterion for identifying the influence of oral processes that at times does not also explain the motivation of an editor making changes to written sources.[70] At best, we may speak of very general and rough indicators of some slight probability of oral factors at work behind a given text. There is, however, one overall tendency that has proven fairly consistent, on which we have not yet formally commented. Despite the claims of the early form critics to discern a "law of increasing distinctness," as dominical traditions developed,[71] later studies found that this "law" was contradicted as often as it was upheld.[72] Leslie Keylock, focusing just on the Synoptic Gospels, even argued for a tendency of *decreasing* distinctness.[73] At the risk, again, of oversimplification (but this *is* just a paper and not a book), if we focus solely on the issue of length (via word count), Luke very consistently presents abbreviated versions of his Markan material. In 71 out of 92 pericopae common to Mark and Luke, Luke has the shorter version (77.2 percent of the time). In the main body of Mark's Gospel, from 1:14 to 10:52, Mark exceeds Luke in length in 42 out of 48 pericopae (an 87.5 percent frequency). In one long stretch of this section, from Mark 3:7 to 9:29, Luke abbreviates his Markan parallels

---

[70] Gerhardsson, *The Reliability of the Gospel Tradition*, 117; idem, "Illuminating the Kingdom," 307; D. E. Aune, "Prolegomena to the Study of Oral Tradition in the Hellenistic World," in *Jesus and the Oral Gospel Tradition* (ed. Henry Wansbrough; Sheffield: JSOT Press, 1991), 62.

[71] See especially R. Bultmann, "The New Approach to the Synoptic Problem," in *Existence and Faith* (ed. S. M. Ogden; New York: Meridian, 1960; London: Hodder & Stoughton, 1961; Germ. orig. 1926), 41–42.

[72] See especially E. P. Sanders, *The Tendencies of the Synoptic Tradition* (Cambridge: Cambridge University Press, 1969).

[73] L. R. Keylock, "Bultmann's Law of Increasing Distinctness," in *Current Issues in Biblical and Patristic Interpretation* (ed. Gerald F. Hawthorne; Grand Rapids: Eerdmans, 1975), 193–210.

25 consecutive times. Matthew also reflects a tendency to abbreviate Mark more often than not, in 63 out of 102 pericopae (61.8 percent of the time).[74] That this majority is not as pronounced as in Luke may suggest a more complex relationship between Matthew and Mark than between Luke and Mark.

This tendency to abbreviate may be clearly discerned with the synoptic parables, but the sample space of passages to examine is not large. On the assumption of Markan priority, if we compare total word counts of the parallel versions of parables found in the triple tradition, the resulting data are as follows:

Parable	# of words in Matt	# of words in Mark	# of words in Luke
Sower	112	138	76
Mustard seed	50	57	38
Wicked husbandmen	148	136	130

Of the six instances of accounts in Matthew or Luke paralleled in Mark, the only time the later account is not shorter is with Matthew's version of the wicked husbandmen.

A larger sample space emerges if we examine the Q parables, but then the difficulty becomes in determining the version closer to the original, if indeed we may speak of an original. For, as already noted, the whole discipline of oral performance casts doubt in certain instances on the legitimacy as well as the manageability of trying to recover an originating form. Plus, if an initial storyteller, like Jesus himself, reused the same basic plot with variations on more than one occasion, then each form could have been preserved with the same degree of precision (or lack thereof), but the resulting accounts would still vary. Nevertheless, if one does adopt the consensus views of those who see Q as a fairly fixed literary document relied on by both Matthew and Luke and then notes which evangelist is generally believed to have

---

[74] For full details, see C. L. Blomberg, "The Tradition History of the Parables Peculiar to Luke's Central Section" (PhD diss.: Aberdeen, 1982), 25–27.

better preserved the more original form (via arguments unrelated to length or detail), we may again compare word counts of paralleled parables with the following results:

Parable	# of words in earlier form	# of words in later form
Two builders	95 (Matthew)	83 (Luke)
Asking son	50 (Matthew)	45 (Luke)
Children in marketplace	76 (Luke)	65 (Matthew)
Leaven	21 (Luke)	19 (Matthew)
Animals in well	22 (Matthew)	22 (Luke)
Lost sheep	81 (Luke)	65 (Matthew)
Householder and thief	39 (Matthew)	34 (Luke)
Faithful/unfaithful servants	111 (Matthew)	102 (Luke)
Talents/pounds	302 (Matthew)	253 (Luke)
Great supper/wedding banquet	159 (Luke)	151 (Matthew)

In every case, following the reconstructions of the Hermeneia commentary on Q, which for the most part is not paying attention to pericope length at all, the version to which its reconstruction of the Q form most closely approximates is found in the Gospel that, in its final form, can be seen as having the same-sized or longer account. With respect to the animals in the well, the commentary actually does not take a stand, questioning whether the passages even appeared in Q. But if it did, and given the deeper embedding of Luke 14:5 than Matthew 12:11 in its current context, presumably the Matthean version would win the claim to greater originality. There are, of course, two other pairs of passages where we have argued that it is not at all clear if they should be treated as genuine parallels (the talents/pounds and the great supper/wedding banquet). But if we do so treat them, they conform to the pattern discernible elsewhere.[75]

---

[75] See J. M. Robinson, P. Hoffmann, and J. S. Kloppenborg, *The Critical Edition of Q* (Minneapolis: Fortress; Leuven: Peeters, 2000), ad loc.

Rabbinic Parables

Where else can we turn to investigate the phenomenon of orality and the parables further? A logical place to look would be the large corpus of rabbinic parables. Robert Johnston isolated 325 *meshalim*, noticeably similar in form and structure to many of the parables of Jesus, just in the Tannaitic literature alone (or attributed to Tannaitic rabbis even if not found until the later Amoraic literature).[76] Twenty-eight of these parables occur more than once in this corpus of *meshalim*. Here Gerhardsson's convictions seem largely borne out. Particularly because we are working with the same language (i.e., Hebrew) for the originating performance(s), the transmission of the tradition, and the recording of the narratives in such texts as the early *midrashim*, the Mishnah, Tosefta and Talmuds, paralleled texts do contain large percentages of verbatim parallelism. When wording does differ, it often involves more trivial differences than what one finds in the Gospels. Still, there are interesting changes of imagery, omission or addition of detail, and rewording that could well be due to the oral tradition. As for abbreviation, most of the paralleled parables for which the later version still appears within the tannaitic literature recur in abbreviated form in the later accounts, whereas most of the paralleled parables for which the later version does not occur until amoraic times appear in expanded or longer forms.[77] Whatever the reason for this shift, at least during the time period closest to that of Jesus and the Gospel writers, the trend supports what we have already observed in the New Testament.[78]

The *Gospel of Thomas*

But there is another important corpus of parables noticeably closer in time and in contents to the parables of the Gospels. I speak, of course,

---

[76] R. M. Johnston, "Parabolic Interpretations Attributed to Tannaim" (PhD diss.: Hartford Seminary Foundation, 1978); for a representative sampling of just over 100 of these, cf. R. M. Johnston and H. K. McArthur, *They Also Taught in Parables* (Grand Rapids: Zondervan, 1990).

[77] For details, see Blomberg, "The Tradition History of the Parables Peculiar to Luke's Central Section," 420–43.

[78] More recently, cf. P. Höffken, "Gleichnisse in der rabbinischen Tradition," *TZ* 51 (1995): 326–39.

of the 13 parables in the *Gospel of Thomas*, most notably the 11 that have canonical parallels. What signs of influence from oral tradition might we detect there?

Relationship to the Canonical Gospels

Before we can proceed, we must tackle the controversial and convoluted question of the dating of *Thomas* and the relationship of this "fifth Gospel" to its canonical counterparts. One can detect three major phases in the scholarly investigation of these problems. From roughly 1950 through the mid-1960s, initial euphoria over the discovery of the Nag Hammadi literature led to unguarded claims, whereas even cautious scholars investigating in detail small portions of *Thomas* vis-à-vis Matthew, Mark, Luke, and John often argued for independent traditions at work behind *Thomas*, even though the finished form of this new Gospel was seldom dated to before the early or mid-second century.[79] With the publication of Schrage's monumental analysis of and commentary on the entire document, especially in light of the Coptic translations of the canonical Gospels,[80] the pendulum swung noticeably in the direction of dependence on the Synoptics and a later date, well into the second half of the second century, when other Christian documents regularly began to quote and not just vaguely allude to canonical texts. This approach tended to command the assent of the majority of scholars until the late 1980s or early 1990s.[81] Since then, a flurry of studies, most of them American, many of them under the influence of scholars like Helmut Koester or James Robinson,[82]

---

[79] Perhaps G. Quispel is as representative as anyone of this period, at least among the more cautious critics. In addition to a couple dozen articles on Thomas, see his two monographs, *Makarius, das Thomasevangelium, und das Lied von der Perle* (Leiden: Brill, 1967); and idem, *Tatian and the Gospel of Thomas* (Leiden: Brill, 1975).

[80] W. Schrage, *Das Verhältnis des Thomas-Evangeliums zur synoptischen Tradition und zu den koptischen Evangelienübersetzungen* (Berlin: Töpelmann, 1964).

[81] See my summaries as of 1986 in C. L. Blomberg, "Tradition and Redaction in the Parables of the *Gospel of Thomas*," in *Gospel Perspectives* (ed. D. Wenham; vol. 5; Sheffield: JSOT Press, 1985), 177–205.

[82] Both scholars have published voluminously on Thomas, but the writings most commonly cited as influential on this topic early on are H. Koester, "GNOMAI DIAPHOROI: The Origin and Nature of Diversification in the History of Early Christianity," in *Trajectories through Early Christianity* (ed. H. Koester and J. M. Robinson; Philadelphia: Fortress, 1971),

have argued again for *Thomas*'s independence from canonical traditions and even for his paralleled sayings regularly predating their equivalent versions in the New Testament.[83] Meanwhile, none of the data have actually changed.

The Jesus Seminar even *presupposed* a date for *Thomas* in the mid-first century as one of its givens, making no attempt to argue for it.[84] Scholars who do defend (rather than merely affirming) an early independent *Thomas* frequently point to the shorter, less detailed and less allegorical forms in its collection of 114 sayings attributed to Jesus, as key reasons for their beliefs.[85] But this flies in the face of everything we have discussed thus far. Even if abbreviation of a passage in its oral transmission or written redaction does not uniformly occur, it certainly takes place often enough that it can hardly be used as a reason for merely *assuming* a shorter text to be *earlier* than a longer parallel. And those who still argue that Jesus' parables could have contained no allegorical elements or that a nonallegorical form must necessarily be older than an allegorical form have managed to ignore about 35 years of parable scholarship that likewise has demonstrated that no such generalizations are possible.[86]

I have elsewhere compiled a detailed list of arguments for *Thomas*'s independence and then responded to them.[87] Here I would like merely to highlight one well-known and one fairly new argument that convinces me of *Thomas*'s *dependence* on the canonical Gospel and of a date no earlier than the last decades of the second century. The

---

114–57; J. M. Robinson, "ΛΟΓΟΙ ΣΟΦΩΝ: Zur Gattung der Spruchquelle," in *Zeit und Geschichte* (ed. E. Dinkler; Tübingen: J. C. B. Mohr, 1964), 77–96.

[83] One thinks especially of R. Cameron, S. Patterson, and M. Meyer, each in a number of publications.

[84] R. W. Funk, R. W. Hoover, and the Jesus Seminar, *The Five Gospels: The Search for the Authentic Words of Jesus* (New York: Macmillan, 1993), 15–19.

[85] See especially T. Zöckler, *Jesu Lehren in Thomasevangelium* (Leiden and Boston: Brill, 1999), 47–53.

[86] See especially H.-J. Klauck, *Allegorie und Allegorese in synoptischen Gleichnistexten* (Münster: Aschendorff, 1978). Closely related but adding important nuancing are the approaches that understand Jesus' parables as metonymy (see especially R. Etchells, *A Reading of the Parables of Jesus* [London: Darton, Longman & Todd, 1998]) or synecdoche (see especially S. I. Wright, *The Voice of Jesus: Studies in the Interpretation of Six Gospel Parables* [Carlisle: Paternoster, 2000]).

[87] Blomberg, "Tradition and Redaction in the Parables of the *Gospel of Thomas*," 177–81.

better known argument, though still often neglected, is that *Thomas* contains parallels to every postulated stratum of the most common source-critical partitioning of the New Testament Gospels—the triple tradition, the double (or Q) tradition, uniquely Matthean material, uniquely Lukan material, plus redactional overlay from Matthew, from Luke, along with the Johannine Signs-Source texts, in addition to distinctively Johannine redaction. Even uniquely Markan material (a rare commodity indeed) appears, with the use of Mark 4:29 and the parable of the seed growing secretly at the end of *Thomas* 21. The odds would appear microscopic that the compilers (or oral tradents) of every one of these sources would have drawn on an existing heterodox source like *Thomas*, much less without themselves moving in a similarly heterodox direction. But, if the compiler of *Thomas* knew and drew widely from all portions of the canonical Gospels, then this distribution of parallels would not prove nearly so surprising.[88] Of course, one can argue that whatever is postulated to have existed in the first century, superior in pedigree to the New Testament Gospels, did not contain the most obviously gnostic sayings; perhaps it contained little more than roughly half of the document that can be readily harmonizable with orthodox theology. But, of course, that is not what any of *Thomas*'s recent proponents want to allege because most of them want to endorse at least some tenets of Gnosticism themselves as part of their revivification of Walter Bauer's repeatedly debunked argument that "heresy" preceded "orthodoxy."[89] Moreover, the odds of every one of these different source-critical layers of the canonical Gospels drawing on a sayings-source only half as long as our present *Thomas* becomes even less probable. Each would have had less material to attract their attention, from which to choose, and from which

---

[88]   Cf. R. McL. Wilson, *Studies in the Gospel of Thomas* (London: Mowbray, 1960), 73; J.-M. Sevrin, "L'interpretation de *l'Évangile selon Thomas*, entre tradition et redaction," in *The Nag Hammadi Library After Fifty Years* (ed. J. D. Turner and A. McGuire; Leiden: Brill, 1997), 347–60.

[89]   Noticeable particularly in E. Pagels, *Beyond Belief: The Secret Gospel of Thomas* (New York: Vintage, 2003); and B. D. Ehrman, *Lost Christianities: The Battles for Scripture and the Faiths We Never Knew* (Oxford: Oxford University Press, 2003). For debunking, see especially L. W. Hurtado, *Lord Jesus Christ: Devotion to Jesus in Earliest Christianity* (Grand Rapids: Eerdmans, 2003); D. L. Bock, *The Missing Gospels: Unearthing the Truth Behind Alternative Christianities* (Nashville: Nelson, 2006).

to have established itself as something significant enough on which to draw in the first place.

The second argument summarizes the recent thesis of Nicholas Perrin. Using the vocabulary from the Syriac Gospels and related materials, along with the most standard translations for other words, Perrin reconstructs a Syriac translation of *Thomas*. Already known in the Coptic and Greek for using catchwords to link about half of all the juxtaposed sayings, *Thomas*, when translated into Syriac, discloses catchwords (and, more often than not, multiple catchwords) linking *every* saying in the Gospel to every preceding and subsequent saying. At last, we have a plausible explanation for the seemingly random order of much of this collection. But this suggests that Syriac, not Greek, was the original language of *Thomas*, a plausible hypothesis anyway since a reasonable consensus of scholars believes *Thomas* originated in Syria. But on what Syriac sources would Thomas have relied for his traditional or paralleled material, complete, on occasion, with built-in catchwords linking consecutive pericopae in the same sequence as the canonical Gospels? The Gospels had not yet been translated into Syriac, as far as we know. Indeed, the only known Syriac compilation of the Gospel traditions by the end of the second century was Tatian's Diatessaron. From early on in Thomasine research, parallels between distinctive forms of sayings in *Thomas* and the Diatessaron have been noted, but usually the assumption was that the Diatessaron influenced Thomas. Perrin convincingly reverses these lines of dependence, arguing that it is much more likely that Thomas depended on Tatian, which also means that *Thomas* cannot predate AD 180.[90]

Once again, it is completely plausible to suggest that isolated traditions, not yet compiled in a *Thomas*-like collection, may go back to a much earlier date. There is wisdom in the approach of a number of mediating studies, which argue that one must examine each logion

---

[90] N. Perrin, *Thomas and Tatian: The Relationship between the Gospel of Thomas and the Diatessaron* (Atlanta: SBL, 2002). A. D. DeConick's dismissal of Perrin's hypothesis, *Recovering the Original Gospel of Thomas: A History of the Gospel and Its Growth* (New York and London: T & T Clark, 2005), 48–49, astonishingly alleges that Perrin has no explanation for *Thomas*'s structure (but the catchwords provide precisely that) and ignores his point that we know of no other source in Syriac in the second century but the Diatessaron to account for the distinctive parallels in wording that we find.

on a case-by-case basis.[91] April DeConick has developed in greatest detail the hypothesis that there was a core collection of *Thomas* sayings that formed a first edition of this document. She believes she can then trace events and times at which various layers of additional sayings or additions to sayings expanded the document until it reached its present form in the early second century.[92] But she relies on numerous improbable assumptions in the process: (a) that the original core sayings existed largely without subordinate clauses, which would have been added later as explanatory supplements (but how many people ever issue dicta and commands wholly without explanation?); (b) that the time of composition of supplementary material matched the time of cultural events for which they would be particularly relevant (but what about prophylactic teachings?); and (c) that it is more likely that an ancient sayings collection of this nature would grow in this multilayered fashion rather than being composed by a single editor or compiler all at once (what happened to two generations of insights from redaction and literary criticism that chastened the original form critics?). Indeed, all three of these problems to one degree or another bedevil Q research as well, spawning the renewed interest in oral tradition that Dunn's research reflects.

Thomas's *Parables*

What, then, can be said about the corpus of 11 paralleled parables in *Thomas*? Intriguingly, even with this small database, parallels to all the aforementioned synoptic strata appear, although the parallel to the end of Mark's unique parable of the seed growing secretly is tacked on to the end of an otherwise nonparabolic logion. It would seem the most reasonable approach to begin with the assumption, at least with the paralleled parables, that *Thomas's* forms are later than and largely dependent on their synoptic counterparts.[93] Detailed analysis

---

[91] T. Baarda, *Essays on the Diatessaron* (Kampen: Kok, 1994); M. Lelyveld, *Les logia de la vie dans l'Évangile selon Thomas* (Leiden: Brill, 1987); R. Uro, *Thomas: Seeking the Historical Context of the Gospel of Thomas* (London and New York: T & T Clark, 2003).

[92] DeConick, *Recovering the Original Gospel of Thomas*. Cf. already idem, "The Original Gospel of Thomas," *VC* 56 (2002): 167–99.

[93] Similarly, M. Fieger, *Das Thomasevangelium: Einleitung, Kommentar und Systematik* (Münster: Aschendorff, 1991), 3–8, 290–94; K. R. Snodgrass, "The *Gospel of Thomas*: A

may overturn this assumption, but the burden of proof must be on the one who would argue at any point for independence or an earlier date. To be consistent in our quest for the possible contribution of the oral tradition, we must also exclude anything that is most likely gnostic and redactional in origin. But we need to recognize that there is a fair amount of material scattered about *Thomas* that, while amenable to Gnostic interpretation, could have originated at an earlier point and been interpreted in a less heterodox fashion.[94] Let us, therefore, consider each of these 11 parables briefly.

The parable of *the net* (log. 8) no longer snares fish of all kinds, which are then sorted into good and bad, but captures one large fish along with many smaller ones, with only the large one kept. This almost certainly reflects the gnostic elitism that flies directly in the face of the historical Jesus' concern for the least and the lowliest. That the fisherman is called "wise" is probably also a redactional change, since *Thomas*'s community centered on the quest for wisdom. The most noteworthy change attributable to oral tradition, thus, is the overall noticeable abbreviation of the parable so that numerous canonical elements are simply missing.[95]

The parable of *the sower* (log. 9) is likewise noticeably abbreviated, at least compared to the Markan and Matthean forms. The most prominent alterations (rather than just omissions) include (a) the sower *filling his hand* to scatter the seed, (b) the first seed falling *on* the road, (c) the second seed *not producing ears*, (d) the third seed being *eaten by worms*, and (e) the final seed bearing *120-fold*. I am not as convinced as I was 20 years ago that any or all of these must reflect explicit gnostic redaction, though plausible explanations remain for how each could do so. But neither do any of these details show signs of inherent primitivity, so they could easily be the natural, minor variations

Secondary Gospel," *SecCent* 7 (1989–90): 19–38; C. M. Tuckett, "Thomas and the Synoptics," *NovT* 30 (1988): 132–57.

[94] See, again, throughout Uro, *Thomas*; and cf. idem, ed., *Thomas at the Crossroads: Essays on the Gospel of Thomas* (Edinburgh: T & T Clark, 1998).

[95] J.-M. Sevrin, "La redaction des paraboles dans l'Évangile de Thomas," in *Actes du IVe Congrés Copte* (ed. M. Rassart-Debergh and J. Ries; Louvain-la-neuve: Institut orientaliste, 1992), 348–49. Cf. T. Baarda, "'Chose' or 'Collected': Concerning an Aramaism in Logion 8 of the *Gospel of Thomas* and the Question of Independence," *HTR* 84 (1991): 373–97.

that multiple oral performances produced during the tradition's transmission.[96] *Thomas*'s agreements, in different places, with each of the Synoptics against the others, seem to confirm the secondary nature of his version of this parable overall.[97]

The parable of *the mustard seed* (log. 20) offers yet a third example of abbreviation. Although some have wondered if this simple simile could represent a version underlying both Mark and Q, *Thomas*'s rare use of "kingdom of heaven" rather than his characteristic "kingdom of the Father" suggest knowledge of Matthean redaction and thus of the latest canonical form, which conflated Mark and Q.[98] That the disciples pose in question form the issue of the kingdom fits *Thomas*'s practice elsewhere while never occurring in the New Testament Gospels. The *tilled* earth probably suggests those people who do have the spark of divinity in them are thus prepared to receive Gnostic revelation. The remaining foci—the small seed that becomes a great plant and the shelter it provides for the "birds of the sky"—match canonical emphases. The most likely contribution of the period of ongoing oral tradition lies simply in the streamlining of the contents.[99]

The parable of *the wheat and tares* (log. 57) is the most abbreviated of all of *Thomas*'s parables. If a shorter, less allegorical form proves primitivity, then here appears *Thomas*'s showcase example. But there are telltale signs that details are missing from this passage that must be presupposed to make it intelligible.[100] The farmer who illustrates the kingdom of the Father must not only have *had* good seed, but he must have sown it in his field. Otherwise, an enemy sowing weeds at night could scarcely threaten his crop. An antecedent must be supplied for

---

[96] Cf. H. Koester, "Three Thomas Parables," in *The New Testament and Gnosis* (ed. A. H. B. Logan and A. J. M. Wedderburn; Edinburgh: T & T Clark, 1983), 196–97; P. Sellew, "Oral and Written Sources in Mark 4.1–34," *NTS* 36 (1990): 241–45.

[97] Schrage, *Das Verhältnis des Thomas-Evangeliums zur synoptischen Tradition*, 44.

[98] Ibid., 65; A. Lindemann, "Zur Gleichnisinterpretation im Thomas-Evangelium," *ZNW* 71 (1980): 225.

[99] R. A. Guelich, *Mark 1:1–8:26* (Waco: Word, 1989), 247. Cf. H. Fleddermann, "The Mustard Seed and the Leaven in Q, the Synoptics, and Thomas," *SBLSP* 28 (1989): 219–23.

[100] W. R. Schoedel, "Parables in the *Gospel of Thomas*: Oral Tradition or Gnostic Exegesis?" *CTM* 43 (1972): 554. H.-M. Schenke (*On the Compositional History of the Gospel of Thomas* [Claremont: The Institute for Antiquity and Christianity, 1998], 20) views this text as one of several in *Thomas* that are so shortened that their meanings are "deformed."

the "them" to whom the farmer next speaks and who are prevented from pulling up the crop. The canonical form, of course, provides precisely such individuals—the farmer's servants who come asking if they should start weeding the field. The parable ends depicting only the fate of the weeds, not the success of the good seed, which again must be assumed from the fact that the good seed produced something worth harvesting. Finally, without any preparation earlier in the account, Thomas suddenly tells us that this good seed was "wheat." A few details could represent incidental changes during oral transmission—referring to the time the farmer was sleeping as "night," the reference to the reapers' intentions, and the time when the weeds will become "plainly visible." But the dramatically condensed form may well be the most important contribution of the oral stage of the parable's history.

The second most abbreviated parable in *Thomas* is the next one we encounter as we read sequentially through the Gospel. *The rich fool* (log. 63) has also been put forward as an example of a pristine parabolic form. It, at least, *is* intelligible on its own.[101] But, in fact, it has been recast and streamlined so that it is less about the farmer's "greed," as in the New Testament, and more about the *inherent* dangers of money or material possessions, a common theme in *Thomas* and in Gnosticism more generally.[102] The man is said to have a lot of money, and his bumper crop results from his putting his money to work. Diverging from Luke's account, Thomas makes this man's wealth the result of intentional effort, not a surprisingly good harvest. Then the two accounts agree with their conclusion that the man dies the same day he is making his plans. Still, most of the details Thomas has omitted could support the points he wants to make, so it seems probable that the abbreviation occurred before the final redaction of the passage—that is, during its oral transmission.

The parable of *the great dinner* (log. 64) forms the second of three consecutive parables that Thomas has arranged to create a miniseries

[101] R. Valantasis, *The Gospel of Thomas* (London and New York: Routledge, 1997), 141–42.
[102] Lindemann, "Zur Gleichnisinterpretation im Thomas-Evangelium," 228.

on the dangers of wealth. The triad itself is a sign of later redaction.[103] Scholars have often observed that if an original, nonallegorical parable had underlain both Matthew's wedding banquet and Luke's great dinner, it could well have appeared quite similar to *Thomas*'s version—that is, minus the king's destruction of the city and the appended account of the guest without a wedding garment in Matthew and minus the extra sending of the servant to round up more (Gentile?) guests in Luke. Nevertheless, there are signs that even in this drastically shortened form, elements of Thomasine redaction intrude. The irony of the guests' refusal to come is less intelligible without the background of the initial invitation (which presumably would have been accepted), followed by their later reneging on their promises. Three of the four reasons for refusing the invitation relate explicitly to monetary concerns; the fourth, preparing the wedding banquet for a friend, conflicts with gnostic asceticism and dislike of marriage.[104] The shift from the invitee being the one getting married to the one preparing the dinner also makes him more directly involved in the purchase of the goods needed for that meal. Thus, the final line in *Thomas*'s account, acknowledged by almost all as a gnostic intrusion, far from being a later tack-on to the pristine form of the parable, fits well with the imagery of the story throughout. "Businessmen and merchants will not enter the Places of my Father."[105] Whether Jesus spoke one or two originating forms, it appears clear that Thomas has conflated the two. But it is easy to suppose that once both canonical forms were widely known, the continuing oral tradition would begin this conflation, just as multiple forms of most Gospel traditions have been combined together in popular preaching and teaching throughout church history, thus blurring the distinctives of the original evangelists. That such conflation could simultaneously result in the overall abbreviation of the story conflicts with standard intuition, though, so perhaps each story was being abbreviated orally and it was only Thomas who then conflated the two already abbreviated forms.

---

[103] Fieger, *Das Thomasevangelium*, 186–87.

[104] Lindemann, "Zur Gleichnisinterpretation im Thomas-Evangelium," 230–31; E. Haenchen, *Die Botschaft des Thomas-Evangeliums* (Berlin: Töpelmann, 1961), 56.

[105] Valantasis, *The Gospel of Thomas*, 142–43.

The parable of *the wicked husbandmen* follows the parable of the wedding banquet in both Matthew and *Thomas* (log. 65). Here appears one of several places where Thomas betrays knowledge of the canonical sequence of passages, especially with the cornerstone passage immediately following in logion 66 as well. Again, *Thomas*'s shorter, less allegorical form has spawned speculation that it might reflect the most original version of this parable. But careful reading discloses that Thomas shares with Lukan redaction the insertion of "perhaps" into the soliloquies of the landowner, especially to avoid the notion that God (behind the symbol of the landowner) was mistaken when he thought the tenants would respect his son. Perhaps this "problem" with Jesus' parable was anticipated well before Luke got a hold of it and stems from the clarifying concerns of an oral tradent and that *Thomas*'s additional "*perhaps* they did not recognize [one of the servants]" likewise flows from the oral tradition in the period between Luke and Thomas. So, too, the streamlining of the disparate synoptic forms into a simple series of three messengers—two servants and the son—fits what one would expect of continuing oral tradition. (As previously noted, Luke, or the tradition he inherited, had already smoothed out Mark's version into *three* servants and the Son.) The noticeably abbreviated version in Thomas is thus much more likely due to postsynoptic oral tradition than to an independent, presynoptic process.[106]

The parable of *the pearl* (log. 76) is the first one we encounter in Thomas that is not shorter than its canonical counterpart(s). But it *would* have been slightly shorter were it not for the appending of a sentence that seems to have been taken from Matt 6:19–20: "You, too, seek his unfailing and enduring treasure where no moth comes near to devour and no worm destroys." This conflation of two Matthean texts points to the secondary nature of *Thomas*'s form.[107] Thomasine redaction most likely intrudes in the remaining alterations. The pearl probably represents *gnōsis* (wisdom), and the selling of the man's consignment of merchandise suggests that he is giving

---

[106] Snodgrass, "The *Gospel of Thomas*," 28–31; C. A. Evans, *Mark 8:27–16:20* (WBC 34b; Nashville: Nelson, 2001), 218.

[107] R. Kasser, *L'Évangile selon Thomas* (Neuchâtel: Delachaux & Niestlé, 1961), 98–99.

up his evil vocation as a businessperson in favor of the true spiritual knowledge that the pearl represents. This explains the addition of the previously unconnected teaching of Jesus about seeking spiritual rather than worldly treasure.[108]

The parable of *the leaven* (log. 96) is about as short as a parable could be and still form a full-fledged narrative with a beginning, a middle, and an end. It was already this short in Matthew and Luke, and it remains so in Thomas. There is a woman who takes leaven (the beginning), hides (or places) it in some dough (the middle), and makes large loaves (the end). Thomas makes explicit what is implicit in the New Testament: Jeremias estimates that three seahs of flour would have produced enough bread to feed more than 100 people.[109] Perhaps the inclusion of "large" is meant to parallel the large fish in logion 8[110] and portray the elect gnostic, or perhaps it represents an understandable clarification introduced in the oral tradition. Otherwise, there is little alteration on which to comment. If oral tradition naturally expanded succinct logia, one would have surely expected this tiny parable to grow over time and appear embellished in whichever source was latest. But we discover no such expansion.

The parable of *the lost sheep* (log. 107) once again displays a shorter form than either of its canonical parallels. Assuming Matthew and Luke both reflect one originating performance (which they may well not), one could easily imagine *Thomas*'s more succinct, less allegorical form as closest to the original. Careful scrutiny, however, again betrays his knowledge of both Matthew's and Luke's versions, thus suggesting his secondary nature. Like Matthew's version, the missing sheep "went astray"; that is, it wandered off on its own. Like Luke's account, however, the shepherd searches "until" he finds it.[111] The most obvious redactional touches involve identifying the missing sheep as the largest (recall *Thomas*'s unique forms of the parables of the net and the

---

[108] On the "almost certain" dependence of both logia 76 and 109 on Matthew, see D. A. Hagner, *Matthew 1–14* (Dallas: Word, 1993), 190.

[109] Jeremias, *Parables*, 147.

[110] S. J. Patterson, *The Gospel of Thomas and Jesus* (Sonoma, Calif.: Polebridge, 1993), 144.

[111] Schoedel, "Parables in the *Gospel of Thomas*," 555–57; cf. I. H. Marshall, *The Gospel of Luke* (Exeter: Paternoster; Grand Rapids: Eerdmans, 1978), 521.

pearl) and the shepherd's declaration that he loved the one *more* than the 99.[112] A partly parallel contrast appears in the New Testament with the greater rejoicing in heaven over the salvation of one unrighteous soul than over 99 who need no repentance (Luke 15:7), but that is not quite the same. Presumably, the 99 all received their moment of special attention and rejoicing, too, when they first became believers. In Thomas, there is nothing to suggest any good tidings at all for the 99 left behind. Except for abbreviation, little exists here to credit to the continuing oral tradition.

Finally, we come to the parable of *the hidden treasure* (log. 109). Here unfolds the sole parable in Thomas that is noticeably longer than its synoptic partner but not by virtue of any conflation. The law of "three" may well have influenced its form in the oral tradition—two generations of field owners who do not know about the treasure and sell the field to others prior to the one who discovers the treasure. It is these owners' lack of recognition of the treasure in their midst that makes *Thomas*'s form distinctive and very naturally fits the emphasis on secret knowledge in gnostic thought.[113] Surprisingly, the end of the parable uses moneylending as an apparently positive metaphor to stress what the *nouveau riche* can do with their wealth before temptations to use it sinfully overwhelm them. Presumably, the interest they earn is entirely spiritual.[114]

A Statistical Summary

Is there any way to quantify the abbreviating trend we have observed in *Thomas* in order to compare it with the statistical tables already compiled? At first glance, that the full form of *Thomas* exists only in Coptic, whereas the New Testament was written in Greek, would appear to thwart our efforts. Of course, we can still compare general length, but how can we determine precise numbers of words and whether they were parallel? Our two options would be to match Coptic with Coptic or Greek with Greek. Later Coptic Gospels of course exist, but they

---

[112] Valantasis, *The Gospel of Thomas*, 187.

[113] J.-É. Ménard, *L'Évangile selon Thomas* (Leiden: Brill, 1975), 207–8.

[11] Fieger, *Das Thomasevangelium*, 272.

are not early enough to help us with the Greek or Syriac *Thomas* of the second century. The Oxyrhynchus papyri do not help us with the parables of *Thomas*, but they do remind us that a Greek *Thomas* existed in the second century. Rodolphe Kasser, who has returned to the scholarly limelight for his role in deciphering, translating, and publishing the Gospel of Judas in English for the National Geographic Society,[115] provides one partial solution via his 1961 commentary on *Thomas*. In it, he translates Coptic *Thomas* back into Greek, deliberately choosing the wording of the Greek New Testament whenever *Thomas* incorporates paralleled material and whenever Kasser believes the Coptic could well have been a rendering of the same word(s) or expression(s) found in the canonical texts.[116] What this means is that our statistics are likely to err on the side of indicating too *much* parallelism, because in some instances *Thomas*'s Greek *Vorlage* may not have used the same words or forms that Kasser has chosen. But if it should turn out that the amount of variety among paralleled forms is sufficient to resemble what we have identified as probably correlating with oral tradition, then to the extent that Kasser has exaggerated the amount of parallelism, the case for influence via oral performance will only be enhanced. Here then is my count of the number of words exactly parallel, from the same root, or synonyms, in Kasser's reconstructed Greek *Thomas*, when compared with its synoptic parallel(s), with percentages again based on division by the number of words in the shortest pericope, just as before.

Parables	(Thomas vs. Synoptics) $\dfrac{(a) + (b) + (c)}{(d)}$	Words in shortest parallel to Gospel represented by (d)
Mustard seed	$\dfrac{18 + 5 + 0 = 23}{36}$ = 63.9%	38 (Luke)
Leaven	$\dfrac{7 + 4 + 0 = 11}{18}$ = 61.1%	19 (Matt)

---

[115] R. Kasser, M. Meyer, and G. Wurst, with additional commentary by B. D. Ehrman, *The Gospel of Judas* (Washington, D.C.: National Geographic, 2006).

[116] Kasser, *L'Évangile selon Thomas*, 23.

Sower	$\dfrac{39 + 2 + 3 = 44}{76}$ = 58%	76 (Luke)
Lost sheep	$\dfrac{16 + 3 + 1 = 20}{36}$ = 55.6%	65 (Matt)
Wicked husbandmen	$\dfrac{28 + 12 + 5 = 45}{84}$ = 53.6%	120 (Luke)
Wheat and tares	$\dfrac{22 + 7 + 1 = 30}{59}$ = 50.8%	132 (Matt)
Pearl	$\dfrac{8 + 3 + 0 = 11}{23}$ = 47.8%	25 (Matt)
Hidden treasure	$\dfrac{4 + 5 + 0 = 9}{31}$ = 29.0%	50 (Thomas)
Rich fool	$\dfrac{5 + 4 + 2 = 11}{39}$ = 28.2%	88 (Luke)
Great dinner	$\dfrac{28 + 8 + 1 = 37}{138}$ = 26.8%	151 (Matt)
Net	$\dfrac{5 + 5 + 1 = 11}{46}$ = 23.9%	71 (Matt)

If Dunn and Mournet are right that 70 percent verbatim parallelism still leaves enough room for influence by the oral tradition (recall previous figure), then not one of these parables even borders on the threshold of having too much parallelism to preclude significant oral influence. Indeed, when one compares the percentages of parallelism, listed in decreasing order, with the percentages we have compiled for the parables paralleled *within* the Synoptics, one is struck by the considerably greater room for the oral tradition to have been responsible for introducing changes in both wording and content. In both the synoptic and Thomasine parables, allowance must be made as well for the final redactors to have introduced their own changes, particularly when distinctive features accord with their theological emphases and stylistic tendencies elsewhere. But, in both corpora, even after factoring in these probabilities, otherwise unmotivated changes abound that most likely derived from varying oral performances of the material at hand.

At least if Dunn is right about our "default setting," then that is the conclusion to which we should come. Nothing in this study would suggest otherwise. But the most striking contribution of the oral tradition, both between the historical Jesus and the composition of the Synoptics as well as between the Synoptics and the final form of Thomas, would appear to be a very consistent and occasionally dramatic tendency to abbreviate, especially the longer parabolic narratives.[117]

Conclusion

Bultmann's law of increasing distinctness should be laid to rest once and for all. So should Jeremias' tendencies of embellishment and addition of detail. Dunn is undoubtedly correct that we must change the default setting from literary to oral models. But he is also correct in not trying to deny literary dependence with respect to either Markan priority or some form of a Q hypothesis. Rather, we must begin with a presumption of orality but then shift back to literary models as soon as the parallelism is great enough to demand the influence of written sources on later written texts, and that in fact regularly happens. But the default setting remains oral.

I have never understood the appeal of Ockham's razor in most arenas of *historical* research. How often is the simplest hypothesis really the most probable with respect to the causes and effects of multifaceted historical events? The Synoptic Problem affords an excellent example. E. P. Sanders and Margaret Davies, in their introduction to the topic, plausibly suggest that a complete solution to the relationship among the first three Gospels will be *more* complex than most standard hypotheses, not less.[118] If one takes seriously (1) the likelihood of eyewitnesses to the life of Christ passing on information about their social and personal memories of him; (2) the prevalence of oral tradition in first-century Mediterranean culture on a spectrum from Gerhardsson's, Riesner's, and Byrskog's more formal and fixed (yet still flexible) memorizations to Lord's, Vansina's, and Bailey's

---

[117] Cf. Snodgrass, "*Gospel of Thomas*," 21, citing Kelber, *The Oral and the Written Gospel*, 29.
[118] E. P. Sanders and M. Davies, *Studying the Synoptic Gospels* (London: SCM; Valley Forge, Pa.: Trinity Press International, 1989), 112–19.

informal (yet still controlled) retellings; (3) Alan Millard's emphasis on the probability of disciples and others taking private written notes of various kinds, some of which may have been worked up into short written sources;[119] and if we recognize (4) that Q itself, to say nothing of M or L, probably represents some combination of oral and written traditions, perhaps in more than one recension, then we can see why a complete solution to the Synoptic Problem will probably always evade us. Whatever models we do suggest as at least *reasonably* complete should be sufficiently complex to allow for the combination of all of the previous influences. And that includes permitting portions of paralleled pericopae to vary because they were modified in oral transmission, even those pericopae in which demonstrably literary dependence also occurs.

A few of Dunn's proposed examples of the influence of oral tradition seem implausible. Most, however, appear to reflect keen intuition. Although sometimes intuition and statistical evidence contradict each other, it is hoped that this short study has provided at least some quantificational support for Dunn's convictions. Their findings may even complement and reinforce Mournet's far more nuanced study, which appears to suffer at times from *overly* mechanical analysis. At any rate, we may confidently declare that the approach to oral tradition of Dunn's *Jesus Remembered* remains far more likely to approximate historical realities than those of Funk, the Jesus Seminar, and others who promote the model of informal, *un*controlled tradition. What is most significant is not that the oral tradition regularly introduced a raft of minor changes to a given pericope but that the main contours of a majority of those passages remained as solidly intact as they did. When more major changes occurred, as in some of *Thomas*'s parables, they always aligned themselves with key redactional emphases of the final compiler, not the natural incidental variations produced by multiple oral performances. The *first-century* oral tradition may not have been quite as guarded as Riesenfeld and the early Gerhardsson suggested, though at times it seems to have come close. But in the cross-sections of the Gospel tradition that we have sampled, it never comes

---

[119] A. Millard, *Reading and Writing in the Time of Jesus* (Sheffield: Sheffield Academic Press, 2000), 202–4.

even remotely close to the old form-critical model of Bultmann and his kin. Ehrman and others may continue to make contrary claims, with sensationalizing titles for books, like *Misquoting Jesus*,[120] but, if they do, it will be *they* who will be misrepresenting history and, specifically, the oral traditions of Jesus' life and teachings.[121]

---

[120] B. D. Ehrman, *Misquoting Jesus: The Story Behind Who Changed the Bible and Why* (San Francisco: HarperSanFrancisco, 2005), mostly referring to textual criticism but stressing the parallels between patterns of scribal modification and variations in the oral tradition and misleading in representing how much of each occurred.

[121] This chapter is a nominally revised version of a paper that was delivered at a seminar of the annual meetings of the SNTS in Aberdeen, Scotland, August 2006.

6

REMARKS ON JAMES D. G. DUNN'S APPROACH TO JESUS RESEARCH

JENS SCHRÖTER

In the following chapter, I will enter into a discussion with James D. G. Dunn's contribution to the "Third Quest" of the historical Jesus in his important book, *Jesus Remembered*.[1] Thereby, I will also refer to his article "Jesus Tradition in Paul."[2] I will concentrate on some of those aspects that are, from my perspective, most relevant and fruitful for further discussion. In the second part of the chapter, I will formulate some critical questions in order to stimulate our debate on topics worthy of closer analysis or perhaps reexamination.

At the beginning, I would like to refer to an outstanding feature of *Jesus Remembered*: The volume is not just a book on Jesus. It is the first part of a projected three-volume project of which the second volume just appeared.[3] This broad perspective is a remarkable characteristic of Dunn's approach. From the many books and articles that flow from his pen, I just mention the monumental study "The Theology of Paul," his commentaries on Galatians and Acts, and his investigation

---

[1] J. D. G. Dunn, *Jesus Remembered* (vol. 1 of *Christianity in the Making*; Grand Rapids: Eerdmans, 2003).

[2] J. D. G. Dunn, "Jesus Tradition in Paul," in *Studying the Historical Jesus. Evaluations of the State of Current Research* (vol. 19 of *New Testament Tools and Studies*, ed. B. Chilton and C. A. Evans; Leiden: Brill, 1994), 155–78.

[3] J. D. G. Dunn, *Beginning from Jerusalem* (vol. 2 of *Christianity in the Making*; Grand Rapids: Eerdmans, 2009).

of the development of early Christology, "Christology in the Making."
These and many other studies have prepared the ground for a comprehensive history of early Christianity that, according to Dunn, begins
with Jesus' activity, not with a post-Easter kerygma.

With regard to the so-called quest for the historical Jesus, a child
of historical criticism, such an approach is by no means self-evident.
Instead, the hypothesis of a decisive break between Jesus' life and fate
on the one hand and the Christology of the early church on the other,
formulated for the first time by Hermann Samuel Reimarus, is still
very influential in contemporary scholarship. In this perspective, the
aim of historical Jesus research is to recover the historical facts or events
behind the texts in order to overcome the constraints of the Christian
dogma. In critical discussion with such approaches, Dunn seeks for a
model, which explains the relationship between the historical Jesus
and the emergence of Christianity with more historical plausibility. In
the remarkable chapter 6 on "History, Hermeneutics and Faith" Dunn
places the quest of the "historical Jesus" into a broad epistemological
and hermeneutical perspective.[4] The two "flights" from dogma to history and from history to faith form the characteristic tension of the
search for a historical Jesus from its very beginning. The quest for the
"historical Jesus," as it originated in the eighteenth century, presupposes
a specific understanding of history as a fixed reality behind the sources.
The Enlightenment and the historical consciousness of the nineteenth
century developed this perspective further. A logical consequence was
the identification of historical fact and truth: the results of historical
inquiry are regarded as scientifically proven and therefore independent
of dogmatic ideas and of time restrictions.

It is this approach, and especially its understanding of history,
that Dunn calls into question. Relying on more recent developments
in theory of historiography, he refers to a distinction of data, event, and
fact (102): the historical event is lost with the past, all what the historian has at hand are the data—that is, the historical material. From
these data, he has to reconstruct the facts. History, I would continue,
therefore neither gives an image of the past as it "really" was but as it
appears under the circumstances of the present. Consequently, the idea

---

[4]	Dunn, *Jesus Remembered*, 99–136.

of recovering "real" events of the past should be replaced by a model of history as "remembered past." Consequently, the idea of recovering "real" events of bygone times should be replaced by an understanding of history as remembered past. To put it in my own words, history, as image of the past, is always due to revisions and modifications. When the image of the past changes, so does our perception. It is therefore possible to transform or to correct the historian's pictures of Jesus by referring to sources, not noticed or not known so far, or to confront the familiar material with new insights. The idea of getting behind the texts to reality itself would, however, not be convincing. There is simply no reality, which could be stripped off from the sources because there are no data without interpretation. Trying to come closer to Jesus by figuring out his "real" words or deeds, and arranging them with colors according to their historical probability, neglects that doing history is always a hermeneutical enterprise that can reach a certain degree of probability but that will never recreate the past. Instead, it creates an image of it. History is always a hypothesis about how it *could have been.* Consequently, there is no invulnerable point of departure, neither for Christian faith nor for an approach, that seeks to recover (or to excavate) Jesus apart from the perspective of the historian. His image of the past cannot but be made on the basis of sources; most of them are memories that were remembered from the perspective of Christian faith.

As a consequence, Dunn argues, the alternative between a dogmatic Jesus of the Christian tradition and an approach that seeks to replace the "theological" perspective by purely historical perception might be misleading. Instead, in a (re)construction of the history of early Christianity, it has to be explained why Jesus—in Dunn's words, "the founder of Christianity"[5]—made an impact on his first followers, which eventually led to the emergence of Christianity. According to Dunn, "historical faith" as response to Jesus' activity was present already at the root of the Jesus tradition. This is not to deny that reinterpretation of that tradition from a post-Easter perspective was an important development in the formation of Christian faith. Following Dunn, the Jesus tradition does not lead us back to Jesus himself but

---

[5] Dunn, *Jesus Remembered,* 174.

only to the memory of his earliest followers. Hence, he concludes, "The character of the tradition as shared memory means that we do not know precisely what Jesus did or said" (241). This is an important hermeneutical insight and, at the same time, a corrective of the form-critical perspective. Dunn is not prepared to pick up the differentiation between a reality behind the texts still untouched by what he calls "faith" on the one hand and its later "kergymatic" interpretation on the other. Instead, he argues that "historical faith," as response to Jesus' activity, is present already at the root of the Jesus tradition. This is not to deny that post-Easter elaboration and reinterpretation of the tradition was an important development in the formation of Christian faith. But Dunn emphasizes that there was continuity between pre-Easter memory and post-Easter proclamation (133). Consequently, already the earliest memories of Jesus have to be regarded as "faith." Christian faith as disciple-response, therefore, has it roots in pre-Easter response, not in post-Easter kerygma.

The importance of this argument is that it links not Jesus himself but the earliest recollections about Jesus to the origins of Christianity by arguing that already the earliest memories have to be regarded as "faith." Christian faith as disciple-response, therefore, began as pre-Easter response, not as post-Easter kerygma. One might agree in principle, although it should be mentioned in passing at this point that Dunn deals with a rather vague definition of "faith." I will return to this issue later.

To develop this hermeneutical perspective a step further, I quote a passage of Johann Gustav Droysen, the founder of modern theory of historiography in the nineteenth century. In his book *Principles of History*, Droysen wrote,

> The outcome of criticism is not "the exact historical fact." It is the placing of the material in such a condition as renders possible a relatively safe and correct view. The conscientiousness which refuses to go beyond the immediate results of criticism, makes the mistake of resigning all further work with these results to fancy, instead of going on to find such rules for this further work as shall assure its correctness.[6]

---

[6] J. G. Droysen, *Principles of History* (3d ed.; trans. E. B. Andrews; Boston: Ginn & Company, 1897), 25–26.

Accordingly, dealing with the past is only possible by using what Collingwood has called "constructive imagination." Already Droysen referred to the necessity of interpretation as part of the work of the historian, which has to accomplish the critical evaluation of the historical material. It is always the historian himself who composes historical narrative on the basis of the remains from the past. There is no meaning in the remains themselves without such an interpretation.

Dunn's approach, therefore, leads to two consequences. First, it reminds us that the old hypothesis of an incisive difference between the pre-Easter Jesus and the post-Easter Christ might be a false dichotomy and should, therefore, be reassessed. This is not to give up the insights of historical criticism and to retransform exegesis into a dogmatic discipline. But it means that the epistemological presuppositions of historical criticism are themselves in need of reflection. Second, the long-standing debate on how to relate Jesus to a theology of the New Testament with Dunn transformed into the thesis that *the remembered Jesus*, not the "earthly Jesus," and certainly not the "historical Jesus," belongs to the formative components of Christianity.

Let me now turn to some critical questions. First, in chapter 8, "The Tradition," Dunn argues that the Jesus tradition does not lead us back to Jesus himself but only to the memory of his earliest followers. Hence, he concludes, "The character of the tradition as shared memory means that in many instances we do not know precisely what it was that Jesus did or said" (241). Instead, what we have in the Jesus tradition are the features of the impact made by Jesus' deeds and words.

I want to link this remark to the observation that in several early Christian writings (e.g., in Paul, 1 Peter, James, and the Didache), we have analogies to the synoptic tradition that are not ascribed to Jesus but to another authority (e.g., James or the 12 apostles) or quoted as anonymous tradition. In his article "Jesus Tradition in Paul," from 1998, Dunn explains this evidence with regard to Paul as follows: "In communities of shared discourse allusions can be all the more effective because they trigger off wider associations and communal memories."[7] Accordingly, the Jesus tradition, as it is quoted by Paul, "was not yet

---

[7] J. D. G. Dunn, "Jesus Tradition in Paul," in *The Christ and the Spirit: Collected Essays of James D. G. Dunn* (vol. 1 of *Christology*; Grand Rapids: Eerdmans, 1998), 189.

finally fixed." But by the same time, Dunn argues that it would be an "odd conclusion" to think that "the Synoptic-like traditions used in the early churches were not remembered as stemming from Jesus, or at least that the early churches did not think it necessary to retain the attribution of them to Jesus in their corporate memory."[8] I would explain the evidence otherwise and argue that there was a form of early Christian catechesis to which Jesus' teachings belonged together with quotations from Scripture and Jewish traditions. Let me explain this by referring to some examples.

First, there is no quotation either in 1 Cor 7:10–11 or 1 Cor 9:14; instead, Paul himself formulates the advice in the Lord's authority. It is further characteristic of both passages that Paul combines the words of the Lord with his own remarks on divorce and on the apostle's right to support in such a way that they constitute one argument among others.

Second, in 1 Cor 7:8–12, he gives advice to the unmarried and widows, as well as "the rest," on his own authority and explicitly differentiates this teaching from that of the Lord. In 7:25, he contrasts the "command of the Lord" (*epitagēn kyriou*) with his own opinion (*gnōmen*) in introducing the teaching about virgins. At the end of the whole section, he grounds the assertion that his own opinion also has a claim to authority by saying that he, too, has the Holy Spirit.

Third, in chapter 9, Paul founds his right to support from the Corinthian community on a word of the Lord (*ho kyrios dietaxen*), but he regards his own decision not to claim such support as a valid stance in terms of his service to the gospel.

Fourth, in 1 Thess 4:15, Paul uses "a word of the Lord" to formulate his teaching about the living and the dead at the Lord's Parousia. Here again he is quite obviously not citing the earthly Jesus; rather, Paul places his own teaching under the Lord's authority.

Fifth, in 1 Cor 11:23–25, Paul introduces the account of the institution of the Lord's Supper with the remark that he received it from the Lord and was handing it on to the Corinthians. It is quite obvious that he is referring not to words of the earthly Jesus but to a Christian tradition and is thus placing it within a traditional context.

---

[8] Ibid., 185.

This is apparent from the very fact that the quoted tradition is introduced by the characteristic terms for handing on tradition, "received" (*paralambanō*) and "handed on" (*paradidōmi*), showing that Paul is here quoting an early Christian tradition about the Last Supper (see also 1 Cor 15:3). The same is evident also from the fact that shortly before this, Paul had introduced a different interpretation of the early Christian meal (1 Cor 10:16).

When Paul, in these passages, always refers to the Lord (*kyrios*) but never speaks of a "word of Jesus," it shows that he understands the "words of the Lord" to be a teaching legitimated by the Risen and Exalted One that is made concrete in various situations through the apostles and prophets. His intention is thus not to hand on, word for word, what was spoken by the earthly Jesus but to connect to a tradition grounded in the authority of the Lord as the basis of early Christian teaching. In instances involving words that originated with the earthly Jesus, Paul is interested in the fact they are Jesus' words only insofar as the earthly Jesus is also the one raised and exalted by God.

This is underscored by the fact that beyond the explicit references to the Lord, we find an abundance of analogies to traditions in other early Christian writings, including the Synoptic Gospels, which nonetheless are not described by Paul or other writings as words of the Lord. The saying about the thief in the night in 1 Thess 5:2 appears also in 2 Pet 3:10 and has analogies in Rev 3:3; 16:15. In Luke 12:39 // Matt 24:43, and *Gos. Thom.* 21:5–7, the metaphor of the thief is transformed into an image used by Jesus. In every case, the context is an urging to alertness because the time when Jesus will come for judgment is unknown. The call to be peaceful in 1 Thess 5:13 (cf. Rom 12:18) is introduced in Mark 9:50 (cf. Matt 5:9) as a command of Jesus.

Analogies to the appeal in 1 Thess 5:15 and Rom 12:17 not to repay evil with evil as well as to the related admonition in Rom 12:14 to bless persecutors and not to curse them appear in the Sermon on the Plain and the Sermon on the Mount (Luke 6:28; Matt 5:44) and also in 1 Pet 3:9. This is a *topos* of early Christian paraenesis that was received both in the Synoptic Gospels and in the epistolary literature.

The saying about kindness to enemies in Rom 12:20, which Paul cites from Prov 25:21, appears in the synoptic tradition as Jesus' commandment of love of enemies (Luke 6:27,35; Matt 5:44). Compare the *topos* in Rom 14:14, that nothing is of itself unclean, with Jesus' words in Mark 7:15 and Matt 15:11: "There is nothing outside a person that by going in can defile." The saying about the faith that moves mountains in 1 Cor 13:2 has analogies in Mark 11:22–23 and Matt 17:20 (cf. Luke 17:6 and *Gospel of Thomas* 48 and 106).

These findings show that even before the origins of the Gospels, there was a sphere of tradition made up of words of Jesus, early Christian teaching authorized by the Lord, *topoi* from Jewish-Hellenistic ethics, and citations from scripture. Within this sphere, out of which primitive Christianity created its own tradition and associated it historically with the phenomenon called "the teaching of the apostles" (Acts 2:42), the distinction between "genuine" words of Jesus and other traditions played no part at all. What was decisive, rather, was that early Christian teaching as a whole was regarded as resting on the authority of the Lord. This is also the reason Paul and also 1 Peter, James, and the Didache sometimes use formulations without referring to Jesus that are very close to traditions that appear in the Synoptic Gospels as Jesus sayings.

If the analogies of the Synoptics with Paul, James, 1 Peter, and the Didache are interpreted in that way, a slightly different picture than that of "Jesus remembered" could emerge. The impulses of the earthly Jesus, which are so important for Dunn's approach, were probably enriched very early with motifs from the Hellenistic Jewish tradition and transmitted as paraenesis and catechesis of the early communities. This could also explain why we do not find biographical information about Jesus in the letters of the New Testament. This tradition was later combined in the Synoptic Gospels and Q with biographical material and ascribed to Jesus' authority. Given this development, the remembered Jesus could somewhat fade away, because parts of the tradition were ascribed to him only at a later stage in the history of early Christianity.

Consequently, the evangelists probably ascribed a bulk of sayings to Jesus that formerly were handed down as anonymous catechetic tradition of the early communities. To this tradition belonged, without doubt, sayings not only from Jesus but also from other sources (e.g., from the Scriptures). Therefore, for the early communities, the teaching of Jesus had its authority only because he was by the same time the exalted Lord but also because it was—at least in some cases—not of primary importance to distinguish between "authentic" Jesus sayings and other catechetical material. Consequently, the Synoptics compiled their portraits of Jesus by using material that only partly goes back to Jesus himself. This also explains why "authentic" Jesus sayings appear side by side with material that otherwise is quoted as anonymous traditions or under another authority as "Jesus traditions." Every portrait of Jesus therefore inevitably relies on the memories of the early communities. This leads to the methodological consequence that one has to distinguish even more distinctly than *Jesus Remembered* does between the early memories of Jesus and the words and deeds of Jesus himself. The category "impact" that plays an important role in *Jesus Remembered* for linking the early Jesus tradition with Jesus himself should perhaps be reassessed in the light of these observations.

My second point concerns Dunn's dictum that it would be an allusion to think of a Jesus who did not inspire "faith." In agreement with Martin Kähler, Dunn argues instead that in the early sources, we meet only a Jesus who inspired faith, whereas reconstructions that neglect this faith perspective would appear as illusions. A very serious problem in this regard is that nowhere in the book is it precisely described what the term "faith" precisely means. Is it something like a black box that consists of all kind of positive reactions to Jesus? Is there not a difference between pre-Easter reactions and post-Easter faith—although there might be continuity? Is there only one kind of "faith," or should we not think of a multitude of confessions, better described as different kinds of faith for which Jesus is of different importance (e.g., in pre-Pauline tradition, in Paul, in Mark, in the Johannine writings, in Hebrews, etc.)? Is it appropriate in light of this diversity to speak of "Christian faith" as a phenomenon that began in Jesus' own time?

This may be illustrated a bit further. First, we do not only have *positive* reactions to Jesus. Besides a few echoes in non-Christian sources, which Dunn mentions in passing, there are also traces of serious conflicts about Jesus in the Gospels themselves that point to reactions other than faith. I mention just two examples.

In the Beelzebul controversy, a common tradition of Mark and Q and therefore probably a very early tradition, some of Jesus' contemporaries are mentioned who are not convinced that he is the Son of God and the bearer of God's spirit. First, there are those who attribute Jesus' power over the demons to Beelzebul (whether these are scribes, Pharisees, or other Jews can be left aside here). Moreover, Mark mentions Jesus' family who wants to restrain him because, in their opinion, he has gone out of his mind. This story reflects that Jesus' exorcistic activity obviously did not by itself cause positive reactions—or even "faith"—but rather was an irritating phenomenon and led to different reactions.

Second, more than once within the Jesus tradition we are confronted with Jesus' failure to convince his addressees to repent and to accept his message of God's kingdom drawing near. In Mark 6:6, Jesus is amazed at the unbelief (*apistia*) of the Nazarenes; in Q 10:13–15, he exclaims the woes about the Galilean villages Chorazin, Bethsaida, and Capernaum because of their unwillingness to repent; and in Mark 4:10–12, an inner circle of the disciples who are instructed about the secret of the Kingdom of God is separated from the crowds. These texts reflect the rejection or the indifference that Jesus' followers faced during their mission. But it is very probable that they also preserve traces of pre-Easter constellations where the majority of his Jewish contemporaries refused Jesus himself. Accordingly, there are indications of reactions to Jesus other than acceptance, sympathy, or even faith in the Gospels themselves. From a historical point of view, these reactions must be explained as historically plausible reactions as well. To follow Jesus was obviously only *one* possible reaction, a reaction that most of his contemporaries obviously were not prepared to give. Consequently, it would *not* be an allusion to think of a Jesus who did not inspire "faith," because there was certainly *not* only a Jesus who "inspired faith." Dunn's dictum "There is no such Jesus"[9] is therefore perhaps in need of reassessment.

In this regard, it might also be worthy to look at some of the non-canonical texts—not as sources that lead us back to the "real Jesus" but as witnesses for Christianity in the first and second century as a quite diverse phenomenon. Even if one agrees that, for example, the *Gospel of Thomas* belongs to a postsynoptic stage in the history of the Jesus tradition, it nevertheless shows diversity within the Jesus tradition,

---

[9] Dunn, *Jesus Remembered*, 126.

which should not be set aside too quickly by referring to "the developed form of a Gnostic redeemer myth,"[10] especially because it is doubtful whether such a myth is really presupposed in the *Gospel of Thomas*. Particularly in an approach that favors the concept of a "remembered Jesus," sources like the *Gospel of Thomas* cannot be excluded so easily from the relevant "Christian" sources. At least some the noncanonical writings belong to the Christian memory of Jesus as well. Therefore, *Jesus Remembered* might be in danger of depicting a portrait of Jesus that relies more on the canonical writings than the evidence of the early sources allows.

My third point concerns the question of how the Jesus tradition was transmitted in the first decades after his death. First, a remark on this enigmatic source called "Q." I do not want to challenge the Q hypothesis in general, not at least because I have myself written many pages about Q during the last years. Nevertheless, I agree with Dunn that we should take into account the difference between non-Markan material common to Matthew and Luke on the one hand and a document from which this material was drawn on the other. The blurring of these two definitions of Q—common material or a certain document—is a problem in Q research from its beginning up to very recent contributions. The confusion is already present in the work of Christian Hermann Weisse, who was the first scholar to formulate the assumption of two sources at the beginning of the Jesus tradition. The puzzle returns in a somewhat different manner in those approaches, which seek to solve the question by postulating different strata or literary redactions of Q. The difficulty one faces here is that the non-Markan material is quite diverse in verbal agreement as well as in literary character. It is by no means proved that all of it was ever joined together in one and the same document. Dunn's proposal of a distinction between "Q" and "q" is therefore worthy of serious consideration.

A more problematic aspect is the question of how the Jesus tradition was transmitted in the first decades after his death. Dunn obviously thinks of a process characterized by personal and material continuity in which the basic contents of Jesus' preaching were preserved. Referring to research on oral tradition since Johann Gottfried

---

[10] Ibid., 164.

Herder as well as to the approach of an "informed controlled tradition" (Kenneth Bailey), Dunn argues that the synoptic tradition cannot adequately be explained with a model of literary redaction(s). Instead, behind the different versions of an episode from the synoptic tradition, he often assumes an oral tradition that was not preserved verbally but in which can be distinguished between "fixed elements and constant themes on the one hand, and the flexible and variable elements on the other."[11]

There is certainly much truth in this assumption. Most of us would agree that a strictly literary model would fail to explain the process of transmission of the early Jesus tradition. Moreover, for example, as Werner Kelber has pointed out time and again, oral tradition is characterized by different performances of a tradition, not by an "original" that was subsequently expanded and altered. Hence, the form-critical approach that seeks to separate "tradition" from "redaction" might be misleading, because it works with the model of different layers that in a reversal process can be uncovered (or, as we have learned more recently, "excavated").

Nevertheless, this does not yet explain the role of the Jesus tradition in early Christianity. From my perspective, Dunn is less successful in describing how that tradition was transmitted and used. He speaks of the three Jerusalem "pillars"—Peter, James, and John—as "apostolic custodians" who guaranteed a personal continuity from pre-Easter times to the Jerusalem church;[12] he cites examples from Paul's letters, as well as from James and 1 Peter, to show that the Jesus tradition was widely remembered and used in different strands of primitive Christianity, and he can refer to the biographical interest of the Gospel writers who preserved the memory of Jesus.

I touched on my difficulties with this scenario already in my first point. Here I want to add that the development of the first decades of Christianity, as it is described in *Jesus Remembered*, is much in common with the model of Acts: continuity between the earthly Jesus and the Jerusalem community, Paul's incorporation into the circle of trustworthy witnesses of the Jesus tradition, and not at least the continuation of

---

[11] Ibid., 253.
[12] Ibid., 180–81.

the story of Jesus by the development of the early church, guided by the apostles, are distinctive facets of Luke's picture of early Christianity.

Certainly, Acts is one of the most important sources—often the only one—for information about persons, events, and developments in primitive Christianity. But no one doubts that Luke's story has to be read critically if it is used as a historical source. Whether Acts describes the relationship between Jesus' pre-Easter activity and the post-Easter preaching of the apostles in a way that stands to critical scrutiny may be questioned. I feel a little ill at ease when Dunn quickly moves from the late perspective of Acts to a supposed continuity, which was allegedly "important from the first."[13] A critical reading of Acts would probably lead to a more diverse picture of the beginnings of Christianity with, for example, the Hellenists, Barnabas, Peter, Paul, James, and Apollos as leading figures with different access to the Jesus tradition and distinctive views on the meaning of it, not to mention persons and communities that Luke does not even mention. It might be a little dangerous, therefore, to refer to Acts as a witness for a remembered Jesus. Dunn's rather uniform picture of the development from Jesus to Paul might consequently be in need of some revision.

My last point: Toward the end of his study, Dunn deals with Jesus' self-understanding as well as with possible expectations and interpretations of his suffering and death by Jesus himself. According to Dunn, for Jesus, the proclamation of God's kingdom was important, whereas the identity of the proclaimer was secondary.[14] Jesus saw his death as the fulfillment of God's will and interpreted it in the first place against the background of Jewish martyrological tradition. Moreover, because he was convinced that God was about to make a new covenant with his people through his own mission, he spoke of his death as a "covenant sacrifice."

In the light of this interpretation, two questions arise. First, if Jesus used the Aramaic "bar nasha" at least partly in a self-referential way, perhaps alluding to Dan 7:13, as Dunn convincingly argues, it may be questioned whether the proclaimer of God's kingdom for Jesus was in fact only secondary. Although there may be indications of a use of

---

[13] Ibid., 180.
[14] Ibid., 762.

the "Son of Man" phrase in a more general sense, there are certainly also sayings that indicate an exclusive self-understanding of Jesus as the representative of God's kingdom, for example, as Q 7:34; 9:58; 12:8–9; Mark 2:10,28. Here I am inclined to strengthen Dunn's overall perspective of continuity between Jesus' activity and the origins of early Christology. If Jesus thought of himself as the decisive messenger of God's kingdom and as mediator between God and Israel and if he used the expression "bar nasha" in that sense as a self-referential phrase, the application of other designations like "Messiah" or "Son of God," as well as the "high" Christology that speaks of Jesus as God's word or image, would become explicable as interpretations and elaborations of an impulse originating with Jesus himself.

Concerning the interpretations of Jesus' death, we enter one of the thorniest areas of Jesus research. Dunn is well advised to be very careful at this point not to switch too hastily from early Christian interpretations to Jesus himself. But at some points, I hesitate to agree with his conclusions. I completely agree that it would be difficult to find evidence that Isaiah 53 influenced Jesus in the interpretation of his fate. But I am not so certain whether Isaiah 53 was "very influential in earliest Christian reflection on Jesus' death" at all.[15] The only explicit quotation of Isaiah 53 in connection with Jesus' death as an "effective death" is in 1 Peter, whereas a link to Mark 10:45 could be questioned. Perhaps, then, one has to go further and to concede that the idea of a vicarious suffering and death was not stimulated by Isaiah 53 at all but was only later linked to that text.

The hypothesis that Jesus spoke of his death in terms of a covenant sacrifice is likewise not without problems. The covenant terminology is absent from the Jesus tradition with the Last Supper being the only exception. Whether the idea of a new covenant can be linked to Jesus himself, therefore, remains uncertain. Perhaps we are left with Jesus' expectation that God will complete his kingdom very soon and that he himself will play a decisive role in God's reign, as it is expressed (e.g., in Mark 9:1 and 14:25).

I want to conclude with a more skeptical remark concerning the project "historical Jesus" or "Jesus remembered" in general. Perhaps we

---

[15] Ibid., 811.

are too eager in looking for the one impulse behind the texts (and, by analogy, for the one text behind the different manuscript versions). Perhaps it would be more adequate to the early sources to allow for a plurality of recollections (or "performances") from the beginning and not to reduce them to one "original" version of a text behind the manuscripts, to one Jesus behind the varied memories, and to one origin of multiple Christianities. Of course, historically speaking, there was one Jesus behind the different stories of a "remembered Jesus." But it is by no means certain that reduction automatically comes closer to the origin or the "truth." Perhaps the search for one Jesus behind the diverse Jesus stories—for a "Jesus" behind the memories—is a replacement of the New Testament canon as a document of divine inspiration by a "historical" or "remembered" Jesus who secures the Christian identity. My suggestion would be to rethink the project of a "historical Jesus" in this direction. *Jesus Remembered* is without a doubt an important step in that direction.

7

Jesus' Dissimilarity from Second Temple Judaism and the Early Church

Craig A. Evans

Any discussion of Jesus' *dissimilarity* from Second Temple Judaism and the early Christian community, especially in reference to a criterion for determining what authentically derives from Jesus, will these days prompt objections and calls for qualification. And so it should. As the influence of Bultmann and his following waned in the 1960s and beyond, several scholars have rightly called into question this dubious criterion, especially when it has been applied negatively, insisting that only material that is dissimilar from early Judaism and Christianity may be regarded as authentic.[1] In his magisterial *Jesus Remembered*, James D. G. Dunn on occasion refers to this criterion and the way it is sometimes misused and misapplied. I find his comments judicious

---

[1] For a recent critical assessment of the dissimilarity criterion, see T. Holmén, "Doubts about Double Dissimilarity: Restructuring the Main Criterion of Jesus-of-History Research," in *Authenticating the Words of Jesus* (NTTS 28/1; ed. B. D. Chilton and C. A. Evans; Leiden: Brill, 1999), 47–80. Of interest are these older studies: D. L. Mealand, "The Dissimilarity Test," *SJT* 31 (1978): 41–50; M. D. Hooker, "On Using the Wrong Tool," *Th* 75 (1972): 570–81; R. H. Fuller, "The Criterion of Dissimilarity: The Wrong Tool?" in *Christological Perspectives: Essays in Honor of Harvey K. McArthur* (ed. R. F. Berkey and S. A. Edwards; New York: Pilgrim Press, 1982), 42–48, 264–66.

and reasonable.[2] My comments that follow take Dunn's insights into account, though I often go my own way.

Of course, the criterion of dissimilarity does have some usefulness when applied positively. That is, when material does not align itself with emphases and assumptions in Second Temple Judaism and, moreover, when it stands somewhat in tension with emerging Christian beliefs, we may well suspect that the tradition is indeed rooted in Jesus. The logic here is that it is not likely that early Christians invented sayings and activities that do not square with Christian beliefs and practices. And if the saying does not exactly match Jewish teaching in late antiquity, it is less likely that it is no more than a saying of a rabbi that entered the dominical tradition and came to be thought of as a saying of Jesus. If its difference with Jewish thinking cannot be explained as the result of Christian teaching, then the probability of it deriving from Jesus is increased. So go the arguments, in varying shades and nuances.

The task before me is not to assess the strengths and weaknesses of the criterion of dissimilarity but to address in what ways the teaching and activities of Jesus may well have been dissimilar *from* or out of step *with* traditions and emphases common among his contemporaries—before and after Easter.

I will review a few passages in which I find material that presupposes ground common to Second Temple Judaism but then at its climax introduces something new and unexpected. I find that these novel features do not always fit comfortably with the ideas of Jesus' disciples—before Easter and after.

I will look at Jesus' use of Isa 5:1–7 in his parable of the Vineyard, his appeal to Hos 6:2 in his word of assurance to his disciples that he will be raised up in three days, his interpretation of Dan 7:14 in the ransom saying, his allusion to Daniel's prayer in his own prayer of thanksgiving for God's revelation, his interpretation of Ps 110:1 in his challenge of the scribal habit of referring to the Messiah as "son of David," and his remarkable acceptance of the exorcist not among his following who makes use of his name. In all of these examples, which I shall treat very briefly, we find important coherence with Jewish

---

[2] For examples, see J. D. G. Dunn, *Jesus Remembered* (vol. 1 of *Christianity in the Making*; Grand Rapids: Eerdmans, 2003), 81–84, 191–92.

traditions and interpretation of Scripture, and yet we encounter surprising, unexpected, and perhaps even unique elements, elements that do not necessarily sit well with the early Christian community's theology.

Isaiah 5:1–7 and Israel as the Lord's Vineyard

Set in the context of controversy with the temple authorities, Jesus utters his well-known parable of the Vineyard (Mark 12:1–12) in which the tenant vinedressers refuse to respect the vineyard owner's servants, finally killing his son in a bid to take possession of the vineyard. Although some scholars, notably numbered among the Jesus Seminar, have argued that the Markan form of the parable is secondary to the form found in the *Gospel of Thomas*,[3] most now recognize that *Thomas* is in fact based loosely on Luke's trimmed version and is edited in keeping with *Thomas*'s ascetic, eastern Christian perspective that came to expression in the second century.[4]

Given the exegetical complexity and subtlety of the role played by Isa 5:1–7 at the beginning of the parable and a similar complexity and subtlety in the role played by Ps 118:22–23 at the conclusion of the parable, it is more prudent to view the Markan form of the parable as deriving from Jesus than as a product of interpretive evolution in the hands of an allegorizing church.[5]

---

[3] For the ablest interpretation of the parable from this perspective, see J. S. Kloppenborg, *The Tenants in the Vineyard* (WUNT 195; Tübingen: Mohr Siebeck, 2006). For a critical challenge, see K. R. Snodgrass, *Stories with Intent: A Comprehensive Guide to the Parables of Jesus* (Grand Rapids: Eerdmans, 2007), 276–99.

[4] The anticommercial bias of *Thomas* is seen in the saying that immediately precedes the parable (i.e., logion §64: "Businessmen and merchants will not enter the places of my Father") and in the editing of the parable itself: "There was a businessman who owned a vineyard" (logion §65). Some have misread and mistranslated the opening line to read, "There was a good man who owned a vineyard." The Coptic text reads *chrestes* (money lender or businessman) not *chrestos* (good man). The misreading obscured the anticommercial bias of *Thomas* and thus obscured the secondary nature of this version of the parable.

[5] As is rightly argued by G. J. Brooke, "4Q500 1 and the Use of Scripture in the Parable of the Vineyard," *DSD* 2 (1995): 268–94; reprinted in idem, *The Dead Sea Scrolls and the New Testament* (Minneapolis: Fortress Press, 2005), 235–60. See also C. A. Evans, "God's Vineyard and Its Caretakers," in *Jesus and His Contemporaries: Comparative Studies* (AGJU 25, ed. C. A. Evans; Leiden: Brill, 1995), 381–406; idem, "How Septuagintal Is Isa. 5:1–7 in Mark 12:1–9?" *NovT* 45 (2003): 105–10.

Isaiah's Song of the Vineyard is an allegorical parable that describes God's establishment and loving care for Israel on his holy hill, Jerusalem. Israel is likened to a choice vine planted in soil that has been cleared of stones and is surrounded by a hedge, protected by a tower, and equipped with a wine vat for collecting the juice. Indeed, God will even command favorable weather. Nevertheless, despite these many advantages, the vineyard fails to produce satisfactory fruit. In frustration, God abandons his vineyard to destruction. Lest the meaning of the allegory escape some, the prophet Isaiah declares in literal language, "For the vineyard of the LORD of hosts is the house of Israel, and the men of Judah are his pleasant planting; and he looked for justice, but behold, bloodshed; for righteousness, but behold, a cry!" (Isa 5:7).

Jewish interpretation of this passage of Scripture is interesting. Early on, the focus of the allegory narrowed to that of the temple establishment itself. This is seen in the fragments of 4Q500, where in fragment 1 we can make out references to "your winepress, built among stones," "gate of the holy height," "channels of glory," and, with restoration, "your vineyard." The words "winepress, built among stones" constitute an unmistakable allusion to Isa 5:2 and the words "gate of the holy height" and "channels of glory" make it clear that the vineyard is understood in reference to the Temple Mount. This perspective is made explicit in rabbinic interpretation, where, in two passages in Tosefta, the tower and wine vat of Isa 5:2 are identified as the sanctuary and altar, respectively; and by means of clever midrash, the wine vat is also understood to allude to the fructifying channels that issue forth from the altar (cf. *t. Me'ilah* 1.16; *Sukkah* 3.15).[6]

The exegesis in these examples is positive. But the interpretive orientation found in the Targum, the Aramaic paraphrase of Scripture, is wholly negative, as indeed the full context of Isaiah 5 requires. Here again we have identification of the tower and wine vat with sanctuary and altar (cf. v. 2: "I built my sanctuary in their midst, and I even gave my altar to atone for their sins"), but this time we have an explicit

---

[6] As was rightly observed by J. M. Baumgarten, "4Q500 and the Ancient Conception of the Lord's Vineyard," *JJS* 40 (1989): 1–6. The imagery of fructifying rivers of water is seen in Rev 22:1–2, though in somewhat different form.

threat of the judgment and destruction of the temple establishment. Verse 5 in the Aramaic is paraphrased to read, "I will take up my Shekinah from among them. . . . I will break down the place of their sanctuaries."[7]

There can be little doubt that in the crafting of the parable of the Vineyard Jesus had in mind the temple interpretation of Isaiah 5. But Jesus' interpretation goes beyond merely identifying the vineyard of the prophet's song with the temple establishment. Jesus introduces a new set of characters in the drama: the vinedressers, who play the role of the ruling priests.

In doing this, Jesus exculpates the vineyard itself, which is Israel. Thus, it is not the people of Israel who are guilty in the eyes of the Lord; it is her religious leadership. To buttress this point, Jesus appends a quotation of Ps 118:22–23, which, in the Aramaic, understands the builders who reject the stone as the ruling priests and the rejected stone itself as David, who is worthy of his appointment as king and ruler.[8] The Markan evangelist is surely correct in stating that the ruling priests understood that the parable had been directed against them (and not against the whole of Israel).

That this parable, as we find it in Mark, derives from Jesus seems almost certain. Keeping the theme of dissimilarity in mind we may ask, Where in Christian interpretation does the Church liken itself to the Lord's vineyard? Why would the Church appeal to this passage? After all, in both the Greek and the Hebrew the vineyard is hardly exculpated—it is fruitless and stands under God's judgment. So would the Church identify itself with the vineyard? It seems unlikely.

---

[7] Translation by Chilton. For translation and brief discussion, see B. D. Chilton, *The Isaiah Targum* (ArBib 11; Wilmington, Del.: Glazier, 1987), 10–11.

[8] For translation, see D. M. Stec, *The Targum of Psalms: Translated, with a Critical Introduction, Apparatus, and Notes* (ArBib 16; Collegeville, Minn.: Liturgical Press, 2004), 210: "The architects forsook the youth among the sons of Jesse, but he was worthy to be appointed king and ruler." Here the Hebrew's "stone" rejected by the builders is none other than David, who becomes king. David is identified by name in *Tg.* Ps 118:26, 28. The Aramaic version of Psalm 118 incorporates elements of the story of David's selection as Israel's king (1 Sam 16:1–13). For interpretation of *Tg.* Ps 118:19–29, see C. A. Evans, "The Aramaic Psalter and the New Testament: Praising the Lord in History and Prophecy," in *From Prophecy to Testament: The Function of the Old Testament in the New* (ed. C. A. Evans; Peabody, Mass.: Hendrickson, 2004), 44–91, here 81–85.

In Mark 12 and parallels, we do not have *ecclesiastical* allegory; it is a prophetic allegory that was extended and adapted in various ways in Jewish interpretive traditions. In turn, Jesus gave it his own application, focusing the prophetic complaint on the religious leaders themselves, not on Israel. His exegetical strategy, so far as I can tell, was unique among the range of interpretive strategies attested in Jewish circles and, at the same time, was not coherent with a post-Easter understanding of the Christian community as an entity distinct from Israel. Accordingly, the parable of the Vineyard, as seen in its synoptic context (and not in the context of the *Gospel of Thomas*), is dissimilar to aspects of Jewish tradition on the one hand and Christian theology on the other. The most plausible explanation of the parable is that Jesus uttered it.

Hosea 6:2 and the Hope of Resurrection after Three Days

After startling his disciples with his prediction of suffering and death, Jesus attempts to encourage them with a confident prediction that "after three days," the Son of Man will rise again (Mark 8:31; cf. 9:31; 10:34). In the Matthean parallels, it is "on the third day" (Matt 16:21; 17:23; 20:19); so also in Luke and Paul (Luke 9:22; 18:33; 24:7; Acts 10:40; 1 Cor 15:4). Hope of resurrection *on* the third day or *after* three days is almost certainly an allusion to Hos 6:2, which, according to the Hebrew, reads, "After two days he will revive us; on the third day he will raise us up, that we may live before him." Not only we do find the verb "raise up" (Hebrew, *qum*; Greek, *anistēmi*), but we also have the two prepositions reflected in the two forms of the resurrection predictions in the New Testament: "after" and "on." That Hos 6:2 is very probably alluded to in Jesus' saying is seen in the Aramaic paraphrase, which reads, "He will give us life in the days of consolations that will come; on the day of the resurrection of the dead he will raise us up and we shall live before him."[9]

---

[9] For translation and notes, including important rabbinic parallels, see K. J. Cathcart and R. P. Gordon, *The Targum of the Minor Prophets* (ArBib 14; Wilmington, Del.: Glazier, 1989), 41. For discussion of the original meaning of Hos 6:2, as well as related ideas of resurrection, see H. W. Wolff, *Hosea* (Hermeneia; Philadelphia: Fortress, 1974), 117–19.

Once again, Jesus' interpretation and application of Scripture are distinctive. Consistent with the original meaning of the prophecy, Jewish interpretation understood Hos 6:2 as promising national renewal. After exile, God was going to rise up and renew the nation. In keeping with this orientation but enhancing the eschatological potential, the Aramaic tradition came to understand the prophecy as referring to resurrection. But it was the resurrection of the nation, of the many, not of one individual and not of the Messiah himself. Here is where Jesus goes his own way. He finds in this passage assurance that he will be raised up, after suffering and after being put to death. Apart from the passion and resurrection predictions themselves, there is no evidence that the early Christian community exploited Hos 6:2.

Had Jesus not appealed to this Scripture, would early Christians have done so? Why not appeal to the more obvious Dan 12:2 or Isa 26:19, whose resurrection interpretation would have been more readily recognized and whose application to the righteous, as opposed to the ungodly, would have made either text (especially Dan 12:2) more suitable? Accordingly, in my view, it seems best to see the somewhat novel interpretation of Hos 6:2 originating in Jesus, not in the early Church.[10]

Daniel 7:14 and the Son of Man Who Came Not to Be Served

Perhaps one of the most startling interpretations of Scripture in the dominical tradition is found in Jesus' allusion to Dan 7:14. That Jesus alluded to the mysterious "Son of Man" figure of Dan 7:13 is widely recognized and increasingly is being accepted as originating in Jesus and not in some sort of post-Easter Christology. Jesus understood himself as the human figure (the meaning of the Aramaic idiom "Son of Man") who stood before God and received authority and kingdom from God. Accordingly, as Son of Man, with "authority on earth to forgive sins"

---

[10] For further discussion, see C. A. Evans, "Did Jesus Predict His Death and Resurrection?" in *Resurrection* (JSNTSup 186; RILP 5; ed. S. E. Porter, M. A. Hayes, and D. Tombs; Sheffield: Sheffield Academic Press, 1999), 82–97.

(Mark 2:10) and to make Sabbath pronouncements (Mark 2:28), Jesus proclaims the kingdom, or rule, of God. And, although rejected and put to death, he will return in power as Son of Man, seated at the right hand of God, coming with the clouds of heaven, and will sit in judgment on his judges (Mark 14:62).

The surprise comes in Mark 10:45, where Jesus tells his disputing disciples, "The Son of man also came not to be served but to serve, and to give his life as a ransom for many." This utterance not only alludes to Dan 7:14 but also inverts it. The passage in Daniel reads, "And to him [i.e., the Son of Man] was given dominion and glory and kingdom, that all peoples, nations, and languages should serve him" (Dan 7:14a). According to Daniel, the nations serve the Son of Man; according to Jesus, the Son of Man did not come to be served but to serve.[11]

To be sure, the early Christian community searched the scriptures for prophecies that shed light on the life, teaching, death, and resurrection of Jesus. We immediately think of the proof-texting of Matthew and John. Sometimes Scripture is understood in creative ways, and sometimes an understanding is dependent on a variant reading. But where do we have evidence of anyone subverting Dan 7:14 so that the Son of Man is not served but does the serving himself?

Jesus appears to have found in Isaiah 53 (whose servant in the Aramaic is understood to be the Messiah), as well as in the broader context of Daniel 7, which describes the struggle of the saints against the forces of evil, the grounds for his remarkable inversion of Dan 7:14. Of course, his bold affirmation before the high priest, as well as prophecies made to his disciples (in Mark 13 and elsewhere), suggests that Jesus foresaw a time when the nations would in fact honor and serve the Son of Man. But the idea that the Son of Man figure of Daniel 7 would himself *first serve* is truly remarkable and is not easily explained as deriving from either Jewish exegesis or early Christian apologetics or Christology.

---

[11] For discussion, see P. Stuhlmacher, "Vicariously Giving His Life for Many, Mark 10:45 (Matt. 20:28)," in *Reconciliation, Law, and Righteousness* (Philadelphia: Fortress, 1986), 16–29; C. A. Evans, *Mark 8:27–16:20* (WBC 34b; Nashville: Nelson, 2001), 113–25.

Daniel 2 and Revelation Given to the Innocent

Another remarkable inversion of Scripture is seen in yet another allusion to Daniel. In a prayer attributed to Jesus, found in Q, we read, "I thank you, Father, Lord of heaven and earth, that you have hidden these things from the wise and understanding and revealed them to babes; yes, Father, for such was your gracious will" (Matt 11:25–26; Luke 10:21). The basic structure and contents of this prayer allude to Daniel's prayer in Dan 2:20–23. If I may be allowed to cite two parts of this prayer, transposed, the parallels to the prayer of Jesus will be very apparent: "To you, O God of my fathers, I give thanks and praise, for you have given me wisdom and strength . . . he gives wisdom to the wise and knowledge to those who have understanding" (vv. 23a, 21b).

What is fascinating is that although Jesus apparently has alluded to Daniel's prayer, he has thanked God for acting in precisely the opposite manner. In Daniel's prayer, God is thanked for having given "wisdom to the wise and knowledge to those who have understanding." God has granted wisdom to the professional wise men—that is, to Daniel, a wise man in the king's court. But in Jesus' prayer, God is thanked for having "hidden these things from the wise and understanding." God has withheld his revelation from the professionals of Jesus' time—that is, from the priests and scribes. Instead, God has revealed his truths to "babes"—that is, to those who lack professional training (as in Acts 4:13, where the disciples of Jesus are referred to as "unlettered and unlearned").[12]

It is unlikely that this is a post-Easter community formulation, for it puts the earliest followers of Jesus at a disadvantage. One could argue that the dominical prayer perhaps reflects the very tradition cited in Acts, in which the lack of professional training of the disciples is acknowledged and perhaps even turned to advantage (i.e., despite the lack of training, they, having been with Jesus, are more than a match for the priests and scribes). But this sits uncomfortably with the Matthean evangelist, who emphasizes the knowledge

---

[12] For a detailed study of the allusion to Daniel 2 in Jesus' prayer of thanksgiving, see W. Grimm, *Jesus und das Danielbuch. Band I: Jesus Einspruch gegen das Offenbarungssystem Daniels (Mt 11,25–27; Lk 17, 20–21)* (ANTJ 6/1; Frankfurt am Main: Peter Lang, 1984), 1–111.

and understanding of the disciples and, indeed, may well understand himself as the "scribe trained for the kingdom of heaven" (Matt 13:52). The tradition does not sit too comfortably within the Lukan context either, in which there is marked reluctance to be too disrespectful of the scribes and religious experts. Although the perspectives of the Matthean and Lukan evangelists cannot guarantee the authenticity of the dominical prayer, the preservation of this prayer in both, despite its awkward aspects, argues that the tradition was recognized as early, authoritative, and almost certainly deriving from Jesus.

Psalm 110:1 and Messiah as "Lord"

Set in the context of controversy with temple scribes and religious authorities, Jesus asks, "How can the scribes say that the Christ is the son of David?" (Mark 12:35–37). Evidently, Jesus is dissatisfied with the messianic epithet "son of David." Perhaps he believes that it is inadequate for expressing the true essence of the Messiah. In any case, Jesus appeals to Psalm 110, in which David (it is understood) declares, "The Lord said to my Lord, 'Sit at my right hand, till I put thy enemies under thy feet'" (Ps 110:1). Jesus wonders on what basis the Messiah can be called "son of David" (in which "son" implies inferiority to the ancestor) when David himself addresses his descendant as "lord" (implying one superior). If David himself, inspired by the Holy Spirit, spoke this way, then who are the scribes to speak differently? So goes the argument.[13]

In my view, we have good reasons for tracing this interesting exegesis back to Jesus. We must ask, once again, Who would have developed this line of interpretation? On the one hand, it seems impossible to trace it to Jewish interpreters who were searching the scriptures for messianic insights. Jewish interpretation seems perfectly comfortable with "David" and "son of David" as epithets for the Messiah. On the other hand, would early Christians, who know the messianic and Davidic value of Psalm 110 (see especially Hebrews), have generated a dominical tradition that could leave an impression that Jesus

---

[13] For further discussion, see Evans, *Mark 8:27–16:20*, 270–76.

called into question either the value of Psalm 110 or the correctness of the Davidic descent of the Messiah? Paul acknowledges the Davidic descent of Jesus, even if almost dismissively (Rom 1:3–4), and the Matthean and Lukan evangelists believe that it is important to trace Jesus' lineage to the famous king. Accordingly, it seems most unlikely that the exegesis of Ps 110:1 that we find in Mark 12:35–37 derives either from non-Christian interpretation or from Christian interpretation. The best explanation is that it derives from Jesus himself.

If so, this may then lend important support to the authenticity of Jesus' remarkable reply to the high priest in Mark 14:62, already mentioned, in which Jesus combines elements from Dan 7:13 and Ps 110:1. When Jesus is asked if he is the Messiah, the Son of God, he affirms, "I am; and you will see the Son of Man seated at the right hand of Power, and coming with the clouds of heaven" (Mark 14:62). Here we may well have the reason Jesus is dissatisfied with the scribal messianic epithet "son of David." The Messiah is not simply, or primarily, the son *of David*; he is the Son *of God*, the being (or "Son of Man") who stood before the very throne of God and received kingly authority. This David foretold but did not experience. Therefore, David acknowledges the superiority of this person, referring to his descendant as "lord" and not as his "son."

One can readily understand why early Christian interpreters found Psalm 110 so important.[14] It is therefore hardly a surprise that it is quoted and alluded to in many places and plays an important role in emerging Christology. But even so, the exegesis found in Mark 12:35–37 does not fit too comfortably with this emerging Christology and its usage of Psalm 110. The best explanation is that the challenge to scribal custom derives from Jesus, not from post-Easter Christian tradition.

Casting Out Demons in the Name of Jesus

One of the most fascinating episodes to take place in the public ministry of Jesus is the report of an exorcist who casts out demons in the name of Jesus (Mark 9:38–40). The disciples tell Jesus that they forbade

---

[14] See D. M. Hay, *Glory at the Right Hand: Psalm 110 in Early Christianity* (SBLMS 18; Nashville: Abingdon, 1973).

the exorcist "because he was not following us." To their surprise—and, I suspect, to the lasting surprise of many Christians—Jesus replies, "Do not forbid him; for no one who does a mighty work in my name will be able soon after to speak evil of me. For he that is not against us is for us" (vv. 39–40).

The position that Jesus takes in response to the report of the exorcist outside his following is surprising because that evidently is not the disposition of the early community, if the stories in Acts are anything to go on. In at least two stories, it is clear that spiritual power and activity outside the bounds of Christian faith are not sanctioned.

The first story concerns the slave girl who had a spirit of divination (or "python spirit"). Following Paul and his companions, she cried out, "These men are servants of the Most High God, who proclaim to you the way of salvation" (Acts 16:17). From a Christian point of view, everything she said was true. There is no hint that her utterances or the spirit that gave rise to them were unorthodox or threatening in any way. She spoke the truth; Paul and his companions were indeed servants of the Most High God and were indeed proclaiming the way of salvation. One might think that given the pagan setting in which they found themselves, Paul and his companions would have welcomed this ecumenical endorsement, but that is not so. Paul is annoyed and rebukes the spirit: "I charge you in the name of Jesus Christ to come out of her" (Acts 16:18).

The tenor of this story stands in noticeable tension with the attitude of Jesus expressed in Mark 9. One could easily imagine Jesus saying something to this effect in response to Paul's reaction to the girl in Acts: "Do not forbid her; for no one who proclaims you and your message will be able soon after to speak evil of me. For she that is not against us is for us."

Even more startling is the strange story of the seven sons of Sceva, a Jewish high priest (Acts 19:11–17). Impressed by the miracles that God performed at the hands of Paul, the itinerant exorcists undertook to pronounce the name of Jesus over those possessed by evil spirits: we "adjure you by the Jesus whom Paul preaches" (v. 13). The outcome is hardly what the professional exorcists expected. We hear of no apostolic rebuke. None is needed, for the evil spirit undertakes this task itself, retorting, "Jesus I know, and Paul I know; but who are you?" (v. 15). The spirit overpowers all seven of these men utterly and completely (v. 16) with the result that fear fell on both Jews and Greeks "and the name of the Lord Jesus was extolled" (v. 17).

These two episodes stand in sharp contrast to the position that Jesus himself takes in Mark 9. It is probable that the man observed by the disciples was himself a professional exorcist (perhaps like Eleazar, the exorcist described by Josephus),[15] who made use of incantations and the names of powerful authorities, including the name of Solomon, the master of incantations, herbs, and remedies. Learning of the efficacy of the name of Jesus, he now uses it too. That the disciples rebuke him is not surprising. Yet Jesus does not agree with the disciples, admonishing them not to forbid him.

Nor is there any hint that the exorcist outside Jesus' circle was unsuccessful or encountered any mishap approaching the disaster that befell the seven sons of Sceva. Although we know nothing of the man mentioned in Mark 9, in the case of the sons of Sceva we know much. They are sons of a Jewish high priest, which implies religious knowledge and expertise on their part and perhaps also a measure of protection through holiness. They are seven in number, which adds strength to their presence, in the face of the evil spirit. Reference to them fleeing while naked would probably have been understood as the loss of their robes adorned with special symbols, phylacteries, sacred names, and magical words.

But even with all of these advantages and protective armament, the sons of Sceva are defeated. They flee naked and wounded (i.e., their robes and phylacteries were of no use and could not protect them). In contrast to this unmitigated failure stands the man in Mark 9, who for all the reader knows has been successful in invoking the name of Jesus.[16]

Here again we see elements of dissimilarity in play, which encourages us to view the tradition in question—in this instance, Mark 9—as

---

[15] See Josephus, *Antiquities*, 8.46–49.

[16] There is evidence that long after the ministry of Jesus and the founding of the Church, Jews and pagans continued to invoke the name of Jesus. A dramatic example is seen in the Magical Papyri: "I conjure you by the God of the Hebrews, Jesus . . . !" (*PGM* IV. 3019–20). See also Origen, *Contra Celsum* 1.6; 6.40. Origen mentions pagan exorcists in his time who invoke the name of Jesus.

deriving from the historical Jesus and not from the early Christian community.

Conclusion

In view of the examples considered—and I am sure that many others can be adduced—I conclude that the concept of dissimilarity from Second Temple Judaism and the early Church in assessing the teaching and activities of Jesus remains not only valid but also very important. If used positively and with proper nuance, this criterion can assist us in identifying elements distinctive to Jesus. Of course, it is less helpful in identifying elements that Jesus held in common with the Judaism of his day or identifying elements that his early followers took over without change. Nevertheless, it is important to assess the development and transmission of the dominical tradition with great care, for points of tension and shifts in nuance may well provide important clues of the presence of the creative mind of Jesus.

8

THE TRANSMISSION OF
THE REMEMBERED JESUS

INSIGHTS FROM TEXTUAL CRITICISM

BILL WARREN

In his *Jesus Remembered* volume, James D. G. Dunn has highlighted the tremendous impact that oral culture had on the transmission of the memories about Jesus.[1] Dunn notes that the transmission of the Jesus story in oral culture most likely followed the "informal controlled tradition" model as presented by Kenneth Bailey rather than the literary-culture model that has dominated prior historical Jesus studies. In essence, Dunn posits that the content that was related to the identity of the community was passed along faithfully under the control of the leaders of the community, even if some details were at times shifted in the telling of the stories.

So what does this have to do with textual criticism? The two fields are quite intertwined since they both relate to the texts that provide our earliest data for talking about the remembered Jesus. But dialogue between the two fields has been sorely lacking. In light of this lack of integration, the goal of this article will be to highlight some of

---

[1] See J. D. G. Dunn, *Jesus Remembered* (vol. 1 of *Christianity in the Making*; Grand Rapids: Eerdmans, 2003), 205–10.

the insights that can be gained from textual criticism on the topic of *Jesus Remembered*.[2]

Oral Tradition and Textual Criticism

Before proceeding, a word of appreciation needs to be expressed to Dunn not only for a magnificent volume but also for a needed high-lighting of this key oral tradition factor that needs to enter into the discussion more. With regard to textual criticism, Dunn's empha-sis on oral traditions in the early church resonates well as a healthy reminder for understanding the history of the transmission of the New Testament (NT) text. Namely, the origins of some of the early expansions to the text of the NT are to be found in the impact of the "informal controlled tradition" on the transmission of the text. To be more specific, the expansions and alterations in the earliest stages to the Gospels would be both anticipated and expected since the oral traditions about Jesus would have remained central to the life of the church in which the texts were being copied. This scenario seems to be exactly what is indicated in the well-known statement by Papias that he preferred the oral traditions to the written text: "For I did not think that what was to be gotten from the books would profit me as much as what came from the living and abiding voice."[3] Dunn indeed high-lights this when he refers to David Parker's work, *The Living Text of the Gospels*, in making the point that the oral performances even of the early written text would have caused the written text to remain fluid as an oral tradition.[4] Gratitude is due to Dunn for putting the spotlight

---

[2] Introductions to the field of NT textual criticism give full discussions of the general issues and data associated with the field. See B. Metzger and B. Ehrman, *The Text of the New Testament: Its Transmission, Corruption, and Restoration* (4th ed.; New York: Oxford University Press, 2005); K. Aland and B. Aland, *The Text of the New Testament: An Introduction to the Critical Editions and to the Theory and Practice of Modern Textual Criticism* (2d rev. ed.; Grand Rapids: Eerdmans, 1995); H. Greenlee, *Introduction to New Testament Textual Criticism* (rev. ed.; Peabody, Mass.: Hendrickson Publishers, 1995); and B. D. Ehrman and M. Holmes, eds., *The Text of the New Testament in Contemporary Research: Essays on the Status Quaestionis* (Grand Rapids: Eerdmans, 1995).

[3] Eusebius, *Hist. eccl.* 3.39.4, citing Papias.

[4] Dunn, *Jesus Remembered*, 250n306. See also D. Parker, *The Living Text of the Gospels* (Cambridge: Cambridge University Press, 1997).

on the role of oral tradition in such a way that it can serve to spur more consideration of this aspect by reminding textual critics again of this type of influence in the life of the early church.

As to how these phenomena are viewed in textual criticism, a good example of the impact of oral tradition is seen in the "D-text," a term derived from the letter "D" used for codices Bezae and Claromontanus (Dp). This name is a more accurate description for what formerly (and even today, in some circles) was called the "Western" form of the text, since this enigmatic form of the text, although found in the Old Latin manuscripts, did not originate in the Western part of the Roman Empire but rather should be traced to the eastern shores of the Mediterranean, as seen in the early Syriac support for many of its readings as well as the probable origin of Codex Bezae in the Lebanon area, as highlighted by Parker.[5] As is well known, the D-text includes a large number of expansions to the text when compared to the Alexandrian and Byzantine forms of the text. But sometimes we forget that some of these expansions are traced back to the second century based on the presence of this text in many of the early church fathers. This fact, which is a standard view for most textual critics, has been known for some time, as seen in Westcott and Hort's discussion of the origins of some of the D-text readings:

> In the second century oral traditions of the apostolic age were still alive; that at least one written Gospel closely related to one or more of the four primary Gospels, together with various forms of legendary Christian literature concerning our Lord and the Apostles, was then current in some churches; and that neither definition of the Canon of the New Testament nor veneration for the letter as distinguished from the substance of its sacred records had advanced far enough to forbid what might well seem their temperate enrichment from such sources as these.[6]

---

[5] D. Parker, *Codex Bezae: An Early Christian Manuscript and Its Text* (Cambridge: Cambridge University Press, 1992). See pp. 266–78 for Parker's arguments in favor of Berytus (Beirut) as the place of writing for Bezae.

[6] B. F. Westcott and F. J. A. Hort, *Introduction to the New Testament in the Original Greek* (New York: Harper and Brothers, 1882; repr. Peabody, Mass.: Hendrickson Publishers, 1988), 174. See their discussion of the characteristics of the Western text on pp. 120–26 where they give their conclusion that the readings in this form of the text date back to the second century.

They clearly situate the origin of many of the D-text reading in the period when oral traditions were still circulating, so at least some of the D-text readings are likely to incorporate oral traditions current in the late first and early second centuries.

To clarify this situation a bit, although the vast majority of these D-text readings most likely do not belong to the earliest form of the writings in which they are found, the idea that they may represent authentic oral traditions about Jesus is often expressed by textual critics. For example, after stating that John 7:53 to 8:11 is not original to John, Bruce Metzger notes, "At the same time, the account has all the earmarks of historical veracity. It is obviously a piece of oral tradition which circulated in certain parts of the Western church and which was subsequently incorporated into various manuscripts at various places."[7] Such textual variants provide further evidence of Dunn's proposal that the oral stories of the remembered Jesus would have been passed along even after some of the written sources appeared, with some interaction between the two inevitable.

To elaborate a bit more on this, the primary use of the written texts in the first stages of the church (and afterward as well, for that matter) was for public reading in the worship services. These would be the same settings in which the oral traditions would have circulated, so in such settings, the addition of other sayings or accounts from the Jesus traditions would be natural to mention, with a few of these even making their way into the written texts. This trajectory seems to be very much in keeping with the attitude behind what Papias said about having the written documents but treasuring the oral stories even more.[8] Namely, the oral traditions were still circulating alongside the written texts and were still highly valued, with most textual critics convinced that such traditions were valued so much that they impacted the written text, with the D-text witnesses especially preserving that impact. This is to be somewhat expected since the early geographic settings for the D-text in the Lebanon and Syria regions,

---

[7] B. Metzger, *A Textual Commentary on the Greek New Testament* (2d ed.; Stuttgart: German Bible Society, 1994), 188.

[8] For the Papias quotation, as noted earlier, see Eusebius, *Hist. eccl.* 3.39: "For the things from the books I did not think would aid me as much as the things received from the living and still remaining voice."

both not far from Palestine, are so close to the settings from the life of Jesus and the foundations of the early church. These settings would have provided ample access to substantial oral traditions that came to be treasured and ultimately preserved at times via the textual variants that are found in the text of the Gospels.

Insights from the Variants

The actual state of affairs, however, is that most involved in historical Jesus studies do not consider the evidence from textual criticism in their work, which is unfortunate. Dunn and others engaged in the search for the historical Jesus use data from the Synoptic Gospels, Q, the *Gospel of Thomas*, John, and other literature from early Christianity and beyond, yet they virtually overlook the data from the textual variants and the manuscripts in which the variants are found.[9] To be fair, only a few voices have addressed the need for dialogue between these two areas of study from within the field of textual criticism. Earlier works from the text-critical side include those on the importance of textual criticism for the Synoptic Problem as well as the well-known work by Bart Ehrman on the theological importance of textual variants.[10]

One of the most recent discussions comes from Michael Bird, who has planted some solid ideas on this in his recent article titled "Textual Criticism and the Historical Jesus."[11] Bird notes three areas where textual criticism should be interacting with historical Jesus studies. First,

---

[9] While Stanley Porter and a few others have been exceptions to this, the general characterization holds. See S. E. Porter and M. O'Donnell's chapter titled "The Implications of Textual Variants for Authenticating the Words of Jesus," in *Authenticating the Word of Jesus* (New Testament Tools and Studies, ed. B. Chilton and C. Evans; Boston: Brill, 2002), 97–133, as a good example of Porter's work.

[10] See G. Fee, "Modern Textual Criticism and the Synoptic Problem," in *J. J. Griesbach: Synoptic and Text-Critical Studies 1776–1976* (SNTSMS 34; ed. B. Orchard and T. R. W. Long-staff; Cambridge: Cambridge University Press, 1978), 154–69, and idem, "A Text-Critical Look at the Synoptic Problem," *NovT* 22 (1980): 12–28; B. D. Ehrman, *The Orthodox Corruption of Scripture: The Effect of Early Christological Controversies on the Text of the New Testament* (New York: Oxford University Press, 1993); and W. Kannaday, *Apologetic Discourse and the Scribal Tradition: Evidence of the Influence of Apologetic Interests* (vol. 5 of *Text-Critical Studies*; Leiden: Brill, 2005).

[11] M. F. Bird, "Textual Criticism and the Historical Jesus," *JSHJ* 6 (2008): 133–56.

the issue of the integrity of the NT text needs more attention since most scholars are too quickly assuming the United Bible Societies (UBS) *Greek New Testament* (GNT) or the Nestle-Aland (NA) *Novum Testamentum* text as being solid without addressing the questions being debated in the text-critical field. If an unbridgeable chasm exists between the original writings of the NT and the forms of text in the extant manuscripts, then using the Gospels as reliable sources would be impossible. Second, the sayings of Jesus found outside of the text of the four NT Gospels merit more consideration. Some of these sayings are found in the textual variants of the NT but never discussed by historical Jesus scholars. Third, certain NT texts warrant deeper text-critical analyses in order to ascertain the importance of the various textual readings for the overall meaning of the passage and reconstruction of the life of Jesus. Bird's work is a solid step in the right direction from the textual criticism side of the discussion.

Returning specifically to Dunn's work, obviously not all textual variants will be helpful for getting back to the remembered Jesus since the vast majority of textual variants are rather mundane and not at all anchored in early oral tradition. And even some of the variants that likely reflect early oral traditions may not add content that is significant for the historical Jesus search. So what should be the criteria for isolating the textual variants most likely to contain early oral traditions of the remembered Jesus? Here are a few suggested guiding principles for identifying the variant readings most likely to interface with Dunn's emphasis on oral tradition:

1. For text marked with single brackets and readings given a "D" or "C" rating, proper consideration should be given to the alternative variant readings.
2. Especially in the Gospels, variant readings that include the "addition" of material such as historical clarifications may retain remnants of solid oral traditions.
3. Variant readings that circulated independently from the NT as "self-contained" statements or content are more likely to derive from oral tradition.
4. Variant readings that contain "Christological misfits" may be based on early oral traditions.

Now let us look at each of these in more detail to see how they relate to Dunn's emphasis on the remembered Jesus.

For text marked with single brackets and readings given a "D" or "C" rating, proper consideration should be given to the alternative variant readings. A relatively easy way to isolate possible early readings is to look where brackets are used in the printed GNT (both GNT and NA editions have these). Those readings are regarded as difficult to determine, so de facto the variant readings might be correct instead of the printed reading, or minimally the variant reading is likely early in origin and attestation. Too many who use the NT fail to pay attention to these places where uncertainty exists as to the correct reading for the text. To be sure, Dunn notes a number of these places, so he has done better than most historical Jesus scholars in this regard, but even so, he overlooks a large number of places where the text is difficult to determine. One example involves the wording at the end of Mark 1:1: should the words "Son of God" be included or not? Dunn does not include these words when he cites this passage but neither does he address the textual issue on this passage, so the citation may not have reflected a decision about the textual problem at all.[12] The lack of certainty about the correct readings for such texts minimally should warrant some attention so that reliable oral traditions are not suppressed by overlooking the textual variants.

Likewise, most "D"- and many "C"-rated readings in the UBS GNT are worthy of considerable examination. In light of the insights of Kent Clarke, perhaps the third edition of the UBS GNT would be more helpful than the subsequent editions. Clarke noted that the 144 "D" ratings in the third edition of the UBS text were reduced to only nine such readings in the fourth edition.[13] As Clarke highlighted, such textual optimism is unwarranted. By definition, a "C" or "D" rating for a variant reading is a weak enough verdict so as to merit further review as well as consideration of the readings determined to be nonoriginal, for those readings most likely originated very early.

---

[12] Dunn, *Jesus Remembered*, 352.

[13] K. Clarke, "Textual Certainty in the United Bible Societies' *Greek New Testament*," *NovT* 44.2 (2002): 2, 113. Textual critics rightfully should cringe at the thought of only nine true "D" readings being noted in the text.

*Especially in the Gospels, variant readings that include the "addition"
of material such as historical clarifications may retain remnants of solid oral
traditions.* Since Dunn's emphasis is on the oral traditions about Jesus
that were passed along, the variants that will help in accessing those
oral traditions are most likely going to be found in the Gospels where
the life and ministry of Jesus are discussed. Or to state this another
way, oral Jesus traditions were more likely to enter the text where they
could "fit" into a context that would be somewhat natural for the reading, which means that the Gospels are the primary texts for finding
these types of readings. On the other hand, sometimes other NT writings mention sayings or actions of Jesus, as in 1 Cor 11:23–26, for
example, so those settings also might be places where oral traditions
about Jesus could become attached to the text.

But which of these readings are "early" in origin? The witnesses to
the reading have to be evaluated as well as the content of the reading to
determine if the reading itself is early. When variants are well attested
by (a) church fathers, (b) some of the earlier NT manuscripts and versions, or are known through (c) other early sources, the likelihood that
such readings represent remnants of oral tradition is greatly enhanced.
While Dunn's emphasis on Bailey's "informal controlled tradition" is
helpful for weighing the information found in the earliest forms of
the NT writings and other sources, it is not as easily applied to textual variants. The impact of reliable oral traditions on the text would
have become less and less as the generations passed and Christianity
increasingly shifted away both from its place of origin (following the
destruction of Jerusalem in the Jewish-Roman war) and from its original ethnographic Jewish base (as non-Jews became the majority in the
church). The numerous examples of fantastic tales in the Christian traditions of the second and third centuries where Jesus becomes less and
less a human figure and more and more of a walking miracle worker
who does whatever he wants, such as stretching beams and causing
clay pigeons to fly away, show how the earlier oral traditions were
being replaced with speculative fiction stories.[14] Due to this reasonably

---

[14] E. Hennecke, *New Testament Apocrypha* (ed. Wilhelm Schneemelcher; trans. R.
McLachlan Wilson; 2 vols.; Philadelphia: Westminster Press, 1963, 1965), 1:393, 396. The
two examples both come from the *Infancy Story of Thomas*.

clear tendency toward the exaggeration of details and creation of fictional stories, the earlier a variant's likely date of origin, the more likely it is that the reading might contain material that is worth examining as possibly reflecting remnants of reliable oral traditions. Perhaps by the late second century and surely by the third century and later, the chance of this happening would have diminished substantially.

This is in large part why the D-text readings are of particular interest since the origin of that form of the text is generally traced to the early second century, as noted previously. For example, the secondary reading that gives a clarification in John 5:3–4 about the angel descending, stirring up the water, and then healing the first one to enter the water may be authentic Jewish tradition from the time before or not long after the fall of Jerusalem. In other words, although not a part of John's original text, this addition may come from the late first or early second century, as indicated by its presence in D-text witnesses such as some of the Old Latin and Old Syriac witnesses and Tertullian. This tradition might be helpful as a commentary that further locates the site of this miracle in Jerusalem, thereby giving even more pause to Crossan's idea referenced by Dunn that the miracle in "John 5:1–7, 14 is a variant tradition of Mark 2:1–12."[15] The writer of the Gospel of John and some in the early church seem to have remembered a tradition that related to the pool in Jerusalem. The addition of these oral tradition details about that setting became known quite early as seen in the witnesses for the variant reading.

Since the goal is to find early oral traditions about Jesus, obviously the addition of material in a variant reading is of primary interest versus word order changes, omissions, and word substitutions. Of course, one scribe's "addition" could be another's "omission," but since the most common critical editions of the GNT normally form the basis for speaking about the text in Dunn's work as well as that of others who have written on the historical Jesus, "additions" as used here means versus the text as represented in the UBS GNT and the NA *Novum Testamentum Graece*.[16] An example of this type of variant

---

[15]   Dunn, *Jesus Remembered*, 678n300.

[16]   Increasingly in the field of NT textual criticism, the concept is that of addition or omission since the decision about the earliest form of the text defines what is an addition or

reading is found in Luke 23:48. In this passage after the statement that those witnessing the crucifixion were beating their chests, Codex Bezae adds, "and their foreheads," whereas some of the Old Syriac and Old Latin manuscripts have longer additions that may very well come from oral tradition in the earlier period following the fall of Jerusalem. As Metzger notes, the Old Sinaitic and Curetonian Syriac manuscripts state that "all they who *happened to be there and saw* that which came to pass were beating on their breasts and saying, '*Woe to us! What has befallen us? Woe to us for our sins!*'"[17] One Old Latin manuscript is even more direct, adding, "Woe to us on account of our sins that we have committed this day! For the desolation of Jerusalem has drawn near." Also the *Gospel of Peter* and *Ephraim's Commentary on the Diatessaron* have somewhat similar statements about judgment on Jerusalem due to what was happening to Jesus.[18] The variety of witnesses and antiquity of the readings show that these additions almost certainly originated from an oral tradition that was well known and that perhaps became more popular due to the anti-Jewish backlash of the early second century. Regardless, the links between the death of Jesus and destruction of Jerusalem in AD 70 are already well represented in the Synoptics, so the oral tradition represented in these readings in Luke 23:48 and in other sources could reasonably have come from the second half of the first century. This would seem to be a case of an early oral tradition entering into the text via a variant reading so as to give an interpretation of the significance of the death of the historical Jesus.

In another example, Dunn does not discuss the variant in Matt 27:16–17 where the Greek text included "Jesus" as the name for Barabbas in brackets, thus indicating that the words are considered original to the text but with some doubts about their authenticity.[19]

---

omission. While the exact reading for the earliest attainable form of the text is not always certain, the most broadly accepted, closest overall approximation at this time is the text as printed by the UBS. See B. Aland, K. Aland, J. Karavidopoulos, C. Martini, and B. Metzger, eds., *Novum Testamentum Graece* (27th rev. ed.; Stuttgart: Deutsche Bibelgesellschaft, 2001), and idem, *The Greek New Testament* (4th rev. ed.; Stuttgart: UBS, 1994).

[17] Metzger, *Textual Commentary*, 155–56.

[18] Ibid.

[19] See Dunn's comments on this in Dunn, *Jesus Remembered*, 775n67.

The reading in some textual witnesses has the name "Jesus" being used for Barabbas as his actual name in both v. 16 and v. 17. "Jesus" was a common Jewish name that any Jew would have been proud to bear since it represented "Joshua" in the Old Testament, but in the church it became revered and fell out of use among most Christians except in reference to Jesus the Christ. Even in Col 4:11, Justus likely changed his name so as not to be called "Jesus." As another example of this outlook, Origen noted the existence of the name "Jesus" for Barabbas but disapproved of the reading due to the negative light it would cast on "Jesus" as the name for Jesus Christ.[20] While the textual evidence is not decisive for including the name "Jesus" for Barabbas in the text, minimally this reading represents an early tradition.[21] If "Jesus" is taken as the original reading, then the omission shows an early church emphasis on revering the name itself by not allowing others and especially not a negative character to bear the name. If "Jesus" is taken as not original, it still very likely represents an authentic oral tradition about Barabbas.

Variant readings that circulated independently from the NT as "self-contained" statements or content are more likely to derive from oral tradition. Readings that are transmitted independently in other writings from the early church may be oral traditions that are known outside of the variants found within the NT text itself. Those readings designated by double brackets in the text, namely Mark 16:9–20, Luke 22:43–44, Luke 23:34, and John 7:53–8:11, are solid candidates for attention in this category, with three having a higher potential for helping access early oral traditions, namely Luke 22:43–44, Luke 23:34, and John 7:53 to 8:11.

Mark 16:9–20 is a bit of a different case since the ending of Mark almost begs for a longer ending after 16:8, especially after the publication of the other Gospels, and so invites what is likely an early second-century attempt to round out Mark in light of the other three Gospels

---

[20] See Metzger, *Textual Commentary*, 56, for a good overview of the evidence on this variant.

[21] Metzger's *Textual Commentary* remains the best available overview of the major textual variants in the GNT. A more recent work that is also very helpful is by T. Omanson, *A Textual Guide to the Greek New Testament: An Adaptation of Bruce M. Metzger's Textual Commentary for the Needs of Translators* (Stuttgart: German Bible Society, 2006).

by adding 16:9–20. While some authentic oral tradition might have been preserved in this passage (the unbelief at the report of Mary Magdalene in v. 11 and the repetition of the Great Commission in vv. 15 and 16), most of what is found is secondary and based on the other Gospels rather than being founded on an independent tradition.

On the other hand, the variant readings in Luke 22:43–44 and 23:34 both seem to contain independent details not related elsewhere in the Gospels. These seem to be traditions that were especially esteemed in the church but that were not in any of the Gospels, and so these traditions either needed to be inserted into the text of one of the Gospels or fall by the wayside. The variant reading that includes Luke 22:43–44, although not likely to be original to Luke's Gospel since so many early manuscripts from a variety of textual traditions omit these verses, is known as early as the middle of the second century by Justin Martyr.[22] With such early attestation, this variant reading most likely originates from early oral tradition about Jesus, whether judged reliable or not is another matter. Dunn, however, passes over this variant reading without evaluating it even though he mentions the larger Lucan passage briefly.[23]

For the statement of Jesus in Luke 23:34, "Now Jesus was saying, 'Father, forgive them, for they don't know what they are doing,'" Dunn gives a cursory mention of the content but does not consider that perhaps the statement is authentic oral tradition.[24] This saying of Jesus, which was known by the second half of the second century by Irenaeus, is likely another case of oral tradition looking for a home in the text.[25]

The *pericope adulterae* noted as John 7:53 to 8:11, besides being omitted entirely in a number of manuscripts, is sometimes found at the end of John, after John 7:36, or in Luke. This is a clear example of a story that has a circulation life of its own! Since Gospels were canonized, not stories, this tradition needed to be inserted into a book and so was inserted most often after John 7:52, even though it was not

---

[22] J. Martyr, *Dialogue with Trypho*, 103.
[23] See Dunn, *Jesus Remembered*, 713.
[24] See ibid., 779–80, esp. n86.
[25] Irenaeus, *Haer.*, 18.

original to John's Gospel (the "floating" nature of the story shows that it was "searching for a home" in the text). Witnesses such as Codex Bezae, the Apostolic Constitutions, early manuscripts mentioned by Jerome and Didymus as containing the passage, and the inclusion of this passage by some Old Latin manuscripts support the idea of this story at least being early second-century tradition if not earlier than that.[26] While Dunn mentions this story in support of the presence of women in the Jesus tradition, he does not deal with the content of the passage.[27] The emphasis on forgiveness in this story in conjunction with the forgiveness statement in the variant reading in Luke 23:34 is noteworthy. The textual tradition seems to be affected by attempts to insert material related to Jesus forgiving others. And the content as seen in Luke 23:34 and John 7:53 to 8:11 both seem to originate at least in the early second century if not before. Here the textual variants would seem to deserve more attention as possible bearers of reliable oral tradition.

Variant readings that contain "Christological misfits" may be based on early oral traditions. Bart Ehrman has highlighted a number of variant readings that might reflect early Christological battles in the early church, and Wayne Kannaday has spotlighted some of the texts where apologetic battles had impacts on the text.[28] In light of these two studies and others on the same general topics, some of the text may need to be reconsidered versus the NA and UBS texts. For example, Kannaday presents a compelling case for "anger" being the correct reading in Mark 1:41 instead of "compassion," the word that Dunn cites based apparently on Meier's reasoning.[29] Those engaged in historical Jesus studies should also consider some of the variant readings noted and at times favored by Ehrman due to their early attestation and probable point of origin. These "Christological misfits" that seem so out of sync with the somewhat normal ways of portraying Jesus merit special consideration as possible remnants of valid oral traditions.

---

[26] See the critical apparatus in the UBS GNT 4th ed. for more information on the textual witnesses for this variant reading.

[27] Dunn, *Jesus Remembered*, 536.

[28] See Ehrman, *The Orthodox Corruption of Scripture*.

[29] Dunn, *Jesus Remembered*, 681. In n309, Dunn references Meier's discussion of this variant.

Conclusion

The point of this discussion is not that all variant readings necessarily contain reliable oral traditions but that some of the variant readings offer yet another source of possible information as we seek to uncover the remembered Jesus. Dunn has mentioned these readings more than many engaged in historical Jesus studies, but even so there is more work to be done in this venue. Textual critics routinely say that most of the variants originated during the first three centuries, a period that includes some overlapping with oral traditions that still circulated about the historical Jesus. Most historical Jesus scholars, however, have by and large ignored the potentially valuable information found in the textual variants that are not original to the text itself. The time has come for more dialogue among those in the fields of textual criticism and historical Jesus studies so that together we can discern and understand the remembered Jesus better.

9

Why Not "Beginning from Bethlehem"?

A Critique of James D. G. Dunn's Treatment of the Synoptic Birth Narratives

CHARLES L. QUARLES

In his *Jesus Remembered*, James D. G. Dunn begins his treatment of Jesus' life with Jesus' baptism by John the Baptist, an event that he regarded as commanding "almost universal assent."[1] Dunn prefaced his treatment of Jesus' baptism with a section titled "Why Not 'Beginning from Bethlehem'?" in which he listed several reasons for rejecting the synoptic birth narratives as a starting point for his research and dismissed the historical reliability of those narratives. This chapter will examine Dunn's arguments against the reliability of the synoptic birth narratives and suggest that the evidence that the birth narratives preserve historical facts is considerably stronger than Dunn's work acknowledges.[2]

---

[1] J. D. G. Dunn, *Jesus Remembered* (vol. 1 of *Christianity in the Making*; Grand Rapids: Eerdmans, 2003), 339.

[2] Since this chapter will be generally critical of one aspect of Dunn's work, it is important for readers to be aware of the author's appreciation for many of the other contributions of *Jesus Remembered*, some aspects of which are expressed in C. L. Quarles, "Dunn, James D. G.," in *Encyclopedia of the Historical Jesus* (ed. C. A. Evans; New York: Routledge, 2008).

Baby Jesus Remembered

Dunn's first rationale for rejecting the birth narratives relates to his proposed historical method that seeks to trace the earliest disciples' memories of Jesus. Dunn wrote, "Our whole procedure is based on the recognition that Jesus made an impact on those who became his disciples, an impact which is still evident in the traditions which have come down to us."[3] Dunn argued that no evidence suggests that the magi or the shepherds became disciples and transmitted to others memories of the events surrounding Jesus' birth. More importantly, although he conceded that Luke's statement that Mary "kept all these things in her heart" (Luke 2:19; cf. 2:51) suggested that the events had an impact on Mary that made them memorable, he denied that these references suggested that Luke was appealing to a carefully preserved tradition since the birth narrative was hardly a "tradition told and retold in the thirty years before Jesus' mission began."[4]

This dismissal is puzzling for several reasons. First, the Lucan Prologue indicates that Luke depended primarily on those who were "the original eyewitnesses and servants of the word" (Luke 1:2) as the sources for his Gospel.[5] To require that a tradition undergo an extensive period of oral transmission—that is, be "told and retold" before accepting the tradition—seems to prefer the testimony of later tradents to the testimony of original eyewitnesses to which Luke as a responsible historian normally sought to appeal.[6]

Several evidences suggest that Luke relied on the testimony of Mary, perhaps mediated through James, as the primary, if not exclusive,

---

[3] Dunn, *Jesus Remembered*, 340.

[4] Ibid.

[5] For important implications of the Prologue, see L. Alexander, *The Preface to Luke's Gospel: Literary Convention and Social Context in Luke 1.1–4 and Acts 1.1* (SNTSMS 78; Cambridge: Cambridge University Press, 1993); and idem, "The Preface to Acts and the Historians," in *History, Literature, and Society in the Book of Acts* (ed. B. Witherington III; Cambridge: Cambridge University Press, 1996), 73–108.

[6] For the argument that eyewitnesses played a greater role in the transmission and preservation of the Jesus tradition recorded in the Gospels, see especially R. Bauckham, *Jesus and the Eyewitnesses: The Gospels as Eyewitness Testimony* (Grand Rapids: Eerdmans, 2006). For the excellent treatment of Luke's Prologue, see especially pp. 116–24. Although Dunn's work appeared before Bauckham's, Dunn was aware of the earlier work by S. Byrskog, *Story as History—History as Story: The Gospel Tradition in the Context of Ancient Oral History* (WUNT 123; Tübingen: Mohr Siebeck, 2000). See, for example, Dunn, *Jesus Remembered*, 178n28.

source of his birth narrative. Only Mary is the common denominator in the various portions of the birth narrative. She alone was in
the position to know the very private and personal experience related
in Luke 1:26–38. Due to her familial relationship to Elizabeth, she
had access to the information regarding the circumstances surrounding John's birth related in Luke 1:5–25 and 1:57–80. Assuming that
Dunn is correct that the shepherds did not become Jesus' disciples and
transmit the tradition in Luke 2:1–20, only Mary or Joseph could have
been the ultimate source of the account. Finally, only Mary or Joseph
is likely to have preserved the memory of the encounters with Simeon
and Anna. Since Mary is the single common denominator in the narratives of Luke 1–2, she is likely the ultimate source of information
for Luke.

Luke seems to signal this through the statements in Luke 2:19
("But Mary was treasuring up all these things in her heart and medi-
tating on them") and 2:51 ("His mother kept all these things in her
heart").[7] Luke 2:19 is positioned at the conclusion of the narrative of
the births of John and Jesus that extends from 1:5 to 2:20. Luke 2:51 is
likewise positioned at the end of the narrative of Jesus' childhood that
extends from 2:21 to 2:52. The positioning of the references to Mary's
reminiscences at precisely the same point in the two major sections
of the narratives seems hardly coincidental. The references seem to
be Luke's means of indicating the ultimate source of his information
regarding Jesus' birth and early life.

Luke appears to use a somewhat similar device to highlight the
identity of his primary eyewitness sources elsewhere in the Gospel.
Richard Bauckham has argued convincingly that a literary *inclusio* (4:38
and 24:34) identifies Peter as the primary source for the Gospel. A secondary literary *inclusio* (8:2–3 and 24:10) identifies Mary Magdalene,
Joanna, and Susanna as the sources of some of Luke's special traditions.
In light of these other Lucan features, Luke 1:19 and 2:51 should be
regarded as Luke's identification of Mary as the primary source of information for the birth narrative. Since Acts 1:21–22 clearly identifies the

---

[7] E. E. Ellis, *The Gospel of Luke* (New Century Bible; Grand Rapids: Eerdmans, 1974),
38; I. H. Marshall, *The Gospel of Luke* (Exeter: Paternoster; Grand Rapids: Eerdmans, 1978),
144; D. Bock, *Luke 1:1–9:50* (BECNT; Grand Rapids: Baker, 1994), 223.

original eyewitnesses and ministers of the word on which his Gospel was dependent as the Twelve, Luke may have felt that the identification of the source of the birth narrative was important since none of the Twelve witnessed these events that occurred outside of the temporal limits "beginning with the baptism of John until the day he was taken up from us" (Acts 1:22).

The likelihood that Mary no longer lived at the time that Luke wrote his Gospel does not preclude the implication of the concluding statements. Mary's testimony regarding the circumstances of Jesus' birth could easily have been mediated through James, the brother of Jesus, to Luke. The first-person plural pronoun in Acts 21:18 includes the author of Luke–Acts in at least one visit to James in which the inquisitive evangelist might have gleaned this information.[8]

This theory of composition fits well with the linguistic character of the Lucan birth narrative. R. Laurentin has shown that the language of this section is strongly Semitic.[9] Although some scholars have suggested that this phenomenon is simply the result of Luke's intentional imitation of Septuagintal style throughout his two-volume work, this is unlikely since the first two chapters of Luke are more markedly Semitic than any other section of Luke's work. Furthermore, P. Winter has demonstrated that some of the linguistic features, particularly those in 1:17, 37, and 2:24 cannot be explained by Septuagintal influence alone.[10] Perhaps most importantly, when Luke formally cites

---

[8] The traditional view pertaining to the "we" passages of Acts regards the author of Luke–Acts to have included his own eyewitness narrative in Acts. See J. Fitzmyer, *Gospel According to Luke I–IX* (AB 28; New York: Doubleday, 1982), 1:35–53; M. Hengel, *Acts and the History of Earliest Christianity* (trans. J. Bowden; London: SCM, 1979), 66. For other views, including especially the view that the "we" passages record the testimony of another source that was used by the author of Acts, see S. E. Porter, *Paul in Acts* (Library of Pauline Studies; Peabody, Mass.: Hendrickson, 2001), 19–46. The view that Luke interviewed James to glean information about Jesus' birth has been suggested also by C. S. Keener, *A Commentary on the Gospel of Matthew* (Grand Rapids: Eerdmans, 1999), 85.

[9] R. Laurentin, "Traces d'Allusions Étymologiques en Luc 1–2, I," *Bib* 35 (1956): 449–56. See also S. C. Farris, "On Discerning Semitic Sources in Luke 1–2," in *Gospel Perspectives 2: Studies of History and Tradition in the Four Gospels* (ed. R. T. France and D. Wenham; Sheffield: JSOT Press, 1981), 201–37.

[10] P. Winter, "Some Observations on the Language in the Birth and Infancy Stories of the Third Gospel," *NTS* 1 (1954–55): 111–21; idem, "On Luke and Lucan Sources," *ZNW* 47 (1956): 217–42.

the Old Testament (OT) in 2:23–24 (Exod 13:2,12,15; Lev 12:8), he does not follow the LXX.[11] Thus one may reasonably concur with I. H. Marshall's conclusion: "It appears most probable that Luke had sources at his disposal, and that these came from Palestinian Jewish Christian circles which had links with the family of Jesus."[12]

Although this reconstruction admittedly involves some speculation, it seems more probable than the claim that the Lucan birth narrative is largely, if not exclusively, fictional. Luke's Prologue claims that the Gospel was based on the careful research of eyewitness testimony, and Acts 1:21–22 reconfirms the importance of eyewitness testimony. Assuming the two-source hypothesis, Luke's handling of Mark in Luke 3–24 demonstrates his responsible handling of sources that he deemed reliable and apostolic. To view the Lucan birth narrative as fictional is to claim that Luke 1:5 to 2:52 bears a character or belongs to a genre that is at odds with the claims of the immediately preceding prologue and disparate from the remainder of the Gospel. It is far more probable that the narratives are of a consistent character throughout Luke.

Efforts to trace Matthew's sources for his birth narratives are much more subjective since he has not left the clear clues of mentioning his sources at the conclusion of major sections like Luke. The focus on Joseph, who is not mentioned by name in the Gospel after 2:19 (see, however, 13:55) and does not appear again in Matthew's lengthy narrative, may imply that Matthew intended to identify Joseph as the ultimate source of the birth narratives. After examining Matthean redactional features, internal tensions within a passage that suggest that material from two different sources were joined, and parallels to other material, scholars generally conclude that a fairly large portion of the Matthean birth narrative is pre-Matthean.[13] Davies and Allison suggested that the first stage in the history of the Matthean birth

---

[11] T. Holtz, *Untersuchungen über die alttestamentlichen Zitate bei Lukas* (Texte und Untersuchungen 104; Berlin: Akademie-Verlag, 1968), 82–83.

[12] Marshall, *Luke*, 45–49, esp. 49.

[13] See the method suggested by R. Brown in *Birth of the Messiah* (New York: Doubleday, 1977), 104–19. Brown is largely followed by Davies and Allison. These scholars posit that Matthew merged two sources: one that described Jesus' birth in parallel to the Moses Haggadah and another that described Jesus' birth in Davidic terms. See W. D. Davies and D. Allison, *Introduction and Commentary on Matthew I–VII* (vol. 1 of *Matthew*; ICC; Edinburgh: T & T Clark, 1988), 190–95.

narrative "painted the picture of Jesus' nativity with Mosaic colours."[14] They further surmised, "This stage, whose core is roughly represented by 1.18–21, 24–5; 2.13–15, and 19–21, just may have originated in the same group responsible for the early traditions Luke has preserved in Acts 3 and 7."[15] This suggestion is based on the observation that these two chapters of Acts "draw a number of parallels between Jesus and Moses, and they show familiarity with the haggadic traditions about the infancy and young life of Moses."[16]

If this suggestion is correct, the origins of the bulk of the Matthean birth narrative must be traced to Palestine and must be quite early. Luke traces the Moses motif to the preaching of Peter and Stephen in Jerusalem in the years immediately following the death of Jesus. Nevertheless, James, the brother of the Lord (martyred in AD 62), was active in these years as the leader of the Jerusalem church. He was part of what Dunn has called the "Jerusalem triumvirate" together with Peter and John and served as both a "pillar" of the church (Gal 2:9) and an "apostolic custodian" of the Jesus tradition.[17] It is difficult to imagine a narrative of Jesus' birth that was largely or purely fictional circulating freely and with the church's approval under James's watch. Yet the Palestinian origins of the narrative seem clear, and a date of origin after James's death seems too late to allow for further development before inclusion in Matthew's Gospel. Given these circumstances, a connection of the narrative to Jesus' family is plausible.[18]

---

[14] Davies and Allison, *Matthew I–VII*, 194.

[15] Ibid.

[16] Ibid.

[17] Dunn, *Jesus Remembered*, 180–81.

[18] Brown calls the theory that Joseph was the source of the Matthean birth narrative and Mary the source of the Lucan narrative "just a pious deduction from the fact that Joseph dominates Matthew's account, and Mary dominates Luke's." However, the evidence is significantly stronger than this. One must also consider the Lucan Prologue's explanation of the evangelist's historical method, consider the references to Mary that conclude the major sections of the birth narrative, and seek to answer why the Gospels that place so little emphasis on Jesus' family elsewhere give them so much prominence here. Brown rejected the theory since he can imagine no reason Joseph would not have reported the annunciation to Mary or why Mary would not have reported the visit of the magi and the flight to Egypt. Reasonable explanations can be given, however, for the absence of these pericopes, not the least of which is concern for space. The evangelists clearly intend Jesus' adult life, ministry, death, and resurrection to dominate their accounts. If either recorded all of the details (even if they knew them), the birth narratives would have grown too lengthy to suit their purposes.

The Birth Narratives as Creative Historiography

Dunn's second objection to the historicity of the synoptic birth narratives is "that they have been in considerable measure contrived to bring out various significant allusions and theological emphases, not least by Matthew and Luke themselves."[19] Nevertheless, the theory that the birth narratives are a form of midrash that wove together narrative motifs of the OT to create a "theological tale" that has no real basis in history is plagued by several difficulties. First, no evidence exists that suggests that early Christians read Matthew or Luke in this fashion.[20] Second, scholars have not yet been able to identify other examples of such creative historiography from the first-century Jewish world.[21] Third, comparisons of the birth narratives to OT accounts often improperly analyze only the similarities between the narratives and overlook their profound differences. The differences between the accounts are often so significant as to make it doubtful that the evangelists simply created the narratives from the OT narrative motifs without any regard for history.[22] Fourth, it is unlikely that the birth narratives were created from OT prophecies since the most crucial OT citation (Isa 7:14) was apparently not regarded as messianic by first-century Jews and since some of the citations so awkwardly apply to the events of the narrative that it seems more likely that the evangelists started with history and sought a prophetic basis for the history than that they started with the prophecies and created the "history."[23] Raymond Brown's analysis of Isa 7:14 led him to conclude,

> It has been suggested that reflection on Isa. 7:14 and on its prediction that a virgin would give birth gave rise to Christian belief in the virginal conception of Jesus. I am maintaining that there was nothing

---

[19] Dunn, *Jesus Remembered*, 340.

[20] See C. L. Quarles, *Midrash Criticism: Introduction and Appraisal* (Lanham, Md.: University Press of America, 1998), 75–79, for a response to the claims of M. Goulder and R. Gundry that early Christians like Ignatius, Justin, and Papias recognized the Gospels as midrash and expanded on their midrashic themes.

[21] See ibid., 56–60, for a response to claims that the creative historiography of Matthew and Luke is paralleled by *Jubilees*, the *Genesis Apocryphon*, *Josephus*, or the *Liber antiquitatum biblicarum* (Pseudo-Philo).

[22] Ibid., 86–91.

[23] This observation has also been made in Keener, *Matthew*, 82.

in the Jewish understanding of Isa. 7:14 that would give rise to such a belief nor, a fortiori, to the idea of a begetting through the creative activity of the Holy Spirit, an idea found explicitly in both Matthew and Luke but not in Isa. 7:14. At most, reflection on Isa. 7:14 colored the expression of an already existing Christian belief in the virginal conception of Jesus.[24]

Dunn gives several alleged examples of the evangelists' contrivance of the accounts based on OT allusions. The limits of this essay allow treatment of only two of these examples. Dunn suggests that Matthew created the star of the magi from Num 24:17. He points out that Num 24:17, "A star will come forth out of Jacob, and a scepter shall arise out of Israel," was "a popular source of speculation and hope in Jewish thought of the time" and cites references from Qumran (CD 7.18–26; 4QTest 9–13; and 1QM 11.6) and *T. Levi* 18.3 as examples.

There are a few thematic links between Numbers 24 and Matthew 2. Balaam was regarded as a magus in later literature, though not in the OT. Num 24:17 does refer to a rising star. Dunn fails to note, however, that in Num 24:17 and the Qumran texts, the star is a title for the Messiah, not an astronomical phenomenon that marks the Messiah's birth. *T. Levi* 18.3 is the only known Jewish text to refer to a star as a sign of the Messiah's birth: "His star will rise in heaven as of a king." Furthermore, if Matthew developed his account from the OT or intended an allusion, it is odd that he used the term *astēr* rather than the Septuagintal *astron* to describe the star since Matthew tends to follow the LXX fairly closely in his other citations. The one clear lexical connection between the account of the magi and the Balaam narrative is Matthew's statement that the magi were "from the East" (*apo anatolōn*) and the description of Balaam in Num 23:7 as "from the mountains of the East" (*ex oreōn ap anatolōn*). The similarities between the two texts are simply not sufficient to suggest a literary dependence. When a single word or two is deemed to be sufficient evidence of a literary or compositional dependence, one may as easily suggest Joseph's star in Genesis 37 or statements in Isa 60:6 or Ps 72:10,15 as

---

[24] Brown, *Birth of the Messiah*, 149. In n50, Brown added, "As we shall see, it is not clear to what extent, if at all, Isa 7:14 entered into Luke's description of the virginal conception."

Matthew's source.[25] The wide variety of views held by midrash critics highlights the subjectivity of this type of approach.

Dunn also suggests that the description of Herod in Matthew 2, particularly the slaughter of the innocents, was created from Exodus 1–2. Matthew probably did intend for his description to evoke memories of the slaughter of the male infants of Israel at Pharaoh's command in order to highlight Jesus' identity as the new Moses. The question is whether Matthew created the event or is recording a historical incident using provocative language. Dunn reasons that Matthew created the incident since "the slaughter of the innocents is hardly out of character for Herod, but it is also unlikely to have escaped the notice of Josephus. And the whole Egyptian episode, including Joseph and Mary's return to settle in Nazareth, does seem somewhat contrived."[26]

Nevertheless, Josephus's silence regarding the slaughter is not at all surprising.[27] Josephus stated that in the last four years of his reign, Herod slew large groups of people on several occasions and, in one instance, executed an entire family.[28] The descriptions of Herod's character in Josephus's *Antiquities of the Jews* 15:6,7; 16:11; and 17:6 and *Wars of the Jews* 1:17 and 1:22 are perfectly consistent with Herod's involvement in the slaughter of the innocents. If Herod's slaughter of Israel's principal men at the time of his death warranted only the brief mention found in *Antiquities* 17:6.5, one would not expect Josephus to mention the slaughter of the innocents. Herod's many other crimes were so atrocious as to overshadow the slaughter of a few newborns in the region of Bethlehem and to explain the absence of an account of this event in both Luke and Josephus.

Furthermore, the *Assumption of Moses* 6:4 probably preserves reminiscences of the slaughter. The consensus of scholars recognizes that the early ruler who is described in this section of *Assumption* is Herod the Great since he ruled for precisely 34 years. Most date the book shortly after Herod's death in 4 BC. The text states,

---

[25] See, for example, M. D. Goulder, *Midrash and Lection in Matthew* (London: SPCK, 1974), 231–39.

[26] Dunn, *Jesus Remembered*, 344.

[27] W. F. Albright and C. S. Mann, *Matthew* (AB 27; Garden City, N.Y.: Doubleday, 1971), 18.

[28] Josephus, *Antiquities*, 15:284–90; 16:393–94; 17:42–44; 17:167; and *Wars* 1:655.

And a wanton king, who will not be of a priestly family, will follow them [Hasmonean priests]. He will be a man rash and perverse, and he will judge them as they deserve. He will shatter their leaders with the sword, and he will (exterminate them) in secret places so that no one will know where their bodies are. He will kill both old and young, showing mercy to none. The fear of him will be heaped upon them in their land, and for thirty-four years he will impose judgments upon them as did the Egyptians.[29]

Although the reference to Herod killing the young could refer to his murder of his own children rather than the infants of Bethlehem, the reference to the slaughter of the innocents is supported by the comparison of Herod's atrocities to those inflicted by the Egyptians. The text may well point to the parallel between Herod's actions and the murder of the male Hebrew children by Pharaoh in Exodus 1–2. The text appears to be independent of Matthew since most date the book in the late first century BC.[30] Although these factors do not prove the historicity of the slaughter of the innocents, they do make the affirmation of Matthew's historicity here more plausible than Dunn's own suggestion that "memories of the destruction of Sepphoris (or the surrounding villages) in consequence of the uprising which followed the death of Herod in 4 B.C.E." were the contributing factor to the Matthean episode.[31]

The Birth Narratives' Expression of Postresurrection Concepts

Dunn argues that the birth narratives did not develop until the post-Easter period since their core tradition is the double affirmation of Jesus' Davidic and divine sonship.[32] This conclusion is odd since this same double affirmation is implied by Jesus' statement in Mark

---

[29] See J. Priest, "Testament of Moses: A New Translation and Introduction," in *Apocalyptic Literature and Testaments* (vol. 1 of *The Old Testament Pseudepigrapha*; ed. James Charlesworth; Garden City, N.Y.: Doubleday, 1985), 920–21, 930.

[30] See also R. T. France, "Herod and the Children of Bethlehem," *NovT* 21 (1979): 116.

[31] See Dunn, *Jesus Remembered*, 340–41n7 and 309n253.

[32] Ibid., 342.

12:35–37. Dunn acknowledged that the passage is usually seen as a retrojection back into Jesus' mission since no evidence suggests that the Jews of the Second Temple period interpreted Psalm 110 as messianic. Nevertheless, Dunn countered,

> And the possibility cannot be excluded that Jesus himself was the first to suggest a messianic interpretation. Moreover, the format does not read much as a bold affirmation of either Jesus' Davidic sonship or of his lordship. It has more the character of a riddle, the sort of riddle which was once the delight of oral societies. In this case the riddle obviously plays on the presupposition of a patriarchal society that the son was by definition subservient to the father. So how could the anointed king be both David's son and David's lord? Perhaps, then, the tradition originated with the memory of Jesus posing the conundrum in a day when the possible messianic significance of Ps. 110.1 was beginning to be discussed.[33]

Dunn recognizes that the riddle of the text is not a denial of Jesus' Davidic descent. He critiques C. Burger's claim that Jesus' Davidic sonship was rejected in the pre-Markan pericope.[34] Nevertheless, Matthew correctly observed that Jesus' riddle implied more than a dual relationship to David as both descendant and lord. Matthew's question, "Whose son is he?" (Matt 22:42), indicated that Matthew saw Jesus' divine sonship as implied by the riddle; that is, Jesus is both son of David and the Son of God.

Mention of divine sonship and Davidic messiahship also appear together in both the Matthean ("Son of God") and Markan ("son of the Blessed") forms of the high priest's question during Jesus' trial (Mark 14:60–61). Dunn notes that 2 Sam 7:12–14 lay behind the priest's question since this OT text was "the primary root of Israel's ideology of Davidic kingship."[35] Betz had earlier noted that 4Q174 1.10–13

---

[33] Ibid., 634–35.

[34] After referring to C. Burger, *Jesus als Davidssohn* (FRLANT 98; Göttingen: Vandenhoeck & Ruprecht, 1970), 52–59, Dunn remarked, "But supporting evidence that Jesus' Davidic sonship was questioned within early Christianity is lacking." Dunn, *Jesus Remembered*, 635. He referred to p. 345n34 in which he favorably cited F. Hahn: "The Davidic descent of Jesus cannot be disputed."

[35] Dunn, *Jesus Remembered*, 633.

interpreted the Samuel passage as referring to the Davidic Messiah.[36] The promise to David was threefold: (1) a descendent of David (2) would build a house for God's name (the Temple) and (3) would be regarded by God as his son. Since the high priest's question merged the issues of Jesus' relationship to the temple, his messianic identity, and his divine sonship, Dunn regarded the question as an allusion to Nathan's prophecy to David. Dunn concluded, "The probability is strong, therefore, strong beyond plausible rebuttal, that the issue of messiahship was raised at the hearing before Caiaphas and that the outcome of the hearing turned on that issue."[37]

Dunn's historical reasoning would naturally suggest that the issue of divine sonship was also raised at the trial and would indicate that the question pertaining to Jesus' identity as the "son of the Blessed" is likewise historical. This element of Jesus' questioning should probably be traced back to the riddle of Mark 12:35–37. Thus Dunn's own claims seem to make the assertion that the conviction that Jesus is both David's son and God's son is necessarily a post-Easter development quite tenuous.

If Jesus intended to imply that he was both David's son and God's son in the manner that the riddle of Mark 12:35–37 and the questioning at his trial suggest, the question remains, "From whence did Jesus derive this self-understanding?" One may plausibly suggest that he initially derived this self-understanding from reflection on the circumstances of his birth as related to him by members of his family. Luke certainly intended to portray Jesus as recognizing himself as the Son of God in some sense very early in life (Luke 2:49) and includes this claim among Mary's reminiscences (Luke 2:51).

Other Means of Weighing Historical Plausibility

After raising the previously mentioned objections to the historical reliability of the birth narratives, Dunn asks, "Are there, then, no historical facts concerning Jesus' birth to be gleaned from the birth narratives?"

---

[36] O. Betz, "Die Frage nach dem messianischen Bewusstsein Jesu," *NovT* 6 (1963): 24–37.

[37] Dunn, *Jesus Remembered*, 633–34.

He answers, "The prospects are not good."[38] Dunn affirms that the conviction that Jesus' birth was from the Spirit "was arrived at very early in the disciple groups and first churches." Thus, "the birth narratives provide a valuable index of how earliest Christian thinking developed."[39] Nevertheless, Dunn rejects the historicity of birth in Bethlehem, the virginal conception, and every other detail of the birth narratives.

Although Dunn is certainly correct that the standard "criteria of authenticity" have their problems,[40] they may serve as a helpful supplement to Dunn's own method. This supplementation is necessary for evaluating the birth narratives since Dunn's method makes no provision for evaluating material from the period prior to the beginning of Jesus' adult ministry. An even-handed application of the criterion of multiple independent attestation, the criterion of coherence, and the criterion of embarrassment suggests that Dunn's reduction of the birth narratives to a core tradition that Jesus was born "from the Spirit" is unnecessarily minimalistic.

The majority of New Testament (NT) scholars today affirm the two-source hypothesis. A few are championing the solutions to the Synoptic Problem associated with Greisbach and Farrer-Goulder. Although the solutions are different in other ways, both of the solutions suggest that Luke depended on Matthew as one of his sources. Nevertheless, these solutions have failed to persuade most scholars. The two-source hypothesis remains the consensus view, even if this consensus shows some signs of weakening.[41] Thus most scholars insist that Matthew and Luke are literarily independent. Perhaps the most compelling evidence for the literary independence of Matthew and Luke is the number of differences between their narratives of Jesus' birth. The accounts can be harmonized. Nevertheless, one suspects that either evangelist would have made some attempt at harmonization if he were aware of the account of the other.[42]

---

[38] Ibid., 343.

[39] Ibid., 348.

[40] Ibid., 83.

[41] See A. Köstenberger, S. Kellum, and C. L. Quarles, "Introduction to Jesus and the Gospels," in *The Cradle, the Cross, and the Crown: An Introduction to the New Testament* (Nashville: B&H Academic, 2009), 158–77.

[42] This observation was also made by U. Luz, *Matthew 1–7* (Continental Commentary; trans. Wilhelm C. Linss; Minneapolis: Fortress, 1989), 103.

Despite the differences in their narratives, Matthew and Luke agree on the following details as noted by Raymond Brown:

a) The parents to be are Mary and Joseph who are legally engaged to be married, but have not yet come together to live or have sexual relations (Matt 1:18; Luke 1:27,34).

b) Joseph is of Davidic descent (Matt 1:16,20; Luke 1:27,32; 2:4)

c) There is an angelic announcement of the forthcoming birth of the child (Matt 1:20–23; Luke 1:30–35).

d) The conception of the child by Mary is not through intercourse with her husband (Matt 1:20,23,25; Luke 1:34).

e) The conception is through the Holy Spirit (Matt 1:18,20; Luke 1:35).

f) There is a directive from the angel that the child is to be named Jesus (Matt 1:21; Luke 1:31).

g) An angel states that Jesus is to be Savior (Matt 1:21; Luke 2:11).

h) The birth of the child takes place after the parents have come to live together (Matt 1:24–25; Luke 2:5–6).

i) The birth takes place at Bethlehem (Matt 2:1; Luke 2:4–6).

j) The birth is chronologically related to the reign (days) of Herod the Great (Matt 2:1; Luke 1:5).

k) The child is reared at Nazareth (Matt 2:23; Luke 2:39).[43]

Brown noted that some of the agreements are problematic due to differences between the two accounts. For example, one is hesitant to label the material in (c) as multiple independent attestation since Matthew's annunciation is to Joseph and Luke's is to Mary. Nevertheless, even after one subtracts such elements, attestation of Jesus' birth in Bethlehem to the virgin Mary by the Holy Spirit in the days of Herod the Great, Joseph's Davidic descent (and thus Jesus' legal ancestry), and relocation to Nazareth remain. Brown himself insisted that an "intelligent case" could be made for the historicity of some details of the birth narratives that have a close relationship to Christian doctrine including Jesus' Davidic descent, his birth in Bethlehem, and the virginal conception.[44]

---

[43] Brown, *Birth of the Messiah*, 34–35.

[44] Ibid., 37n26 and appendices 2, 3, and 4.

Birth in Bethlehem

Dunn affirms that Jesus' Davidic descent is "least vulnerable to historical skepticism" and elsewhere cites Rom 1:3; 2 Tim 3:8; Ign *Eph.* 18:2; 20:2; Ign *Symrn.* 1.1; and Rev 5:5 as evidence.[45] He suggests, however, that the notion of Jesus' birth in Bethlehem may simply be an elaboration of the claim of Jesus' Davidic descent, a "history" invented to support and express the church's theology. He appeals to Jesus' association with Nazareth in numerous texts, particularly the statement in Mark 6:1 that Nazareth and Galilee were his "native place" (*patris*), and John's failure to defend Jesus' Bethlehemite origin in John 7:41–42.

Certainly, the Gospels do portray Nazareth as the place where Jesus grew up. Nevertheless, the birth narratives also agree on this without any hint that this was inconsistent with birth in Bethlehem. The Greek word *patris* refers to one's hometown in the sense of "a relatively restricted area as locale of one's immediate family and ancestry."[46] Nevertheless, the term does not necessarily speak of one's own birthplace. Normally, in the LXX, one's birthplace is identified by the words "his city" (*polis autou*; 1 Sam 20:6; 2 Sam 15:12; 17:23). This is similar to the nomenclature that Luke used to describe Joseph's relationship to Bethlehem in Luke 2:3, although Luke strengthened the construction by replacing *autou* (his) with *heautou* (his own). Despite describing Bethlehem as Jesus' birthplace, Luke agrees with Mark in describing Nazareth as his "hometown" (*patris*) in Luke 4:23. This implies that "hometown" was not a perfect synonym for "birthplace" and might speak merely of the place where one's parents resided at the time or where one was raised. Thus the use of *patris* in the Gospels to describe Jesus' relationship to Nazareth is not a convincing argument against his birth in Bethlehem.

In John 7:41–42, some individuals in a crowd rejected Jesus' messiahship with the objection, "Surely the Messiah doesn't come from Galilee, does He? Doesn't the Scripture say that the Messiah comes from David's offspring and from the town of Bethlehem, where David once lived?" John does not follow up on the question by affirming

---

[45] Dunn, *Jesus Remembered*, 345.
[46] BDAG, 788.

Jesus' birth in Bethlehem, and Dunn sees this as evidence against Bethlehemite birth.

Brown has argued, however, that this text cannot be used as an argument either for or against Jesus' birth in Bethlehem since the text is an expression of Johannine irony in which John's readers know that Jesus came from God, from above, not from Galilee. Brown adds that a secondary irony may be that John's readers know that Jesus truly did come from Bethlehem in the sense necessary to fulfill OT prophecy.[47] This secondary irony seems necessary given John's concern for the fulfillment of prophecy elsewhere (e.g., John 1:23; 4:25–26; 13:18; 15:25; 19:24,36) as well as fulfillment of the messianic anticipations of the Jewish celebrations and symbols. It is unlikely that John would imply now that Jesus' failure to fulfill OT prophecy was irrelevant simply since he came from God. It is also unlikely that John or his readers rejected the messianic interpretation of Mic 5:2 that was well established in Second Temple Judaism as the Targum on Micah and the Targum of Pseudo-Jonathan on Gen 35:21 demonstrate. In the absence of any early contradictory evidence and with the possible corroboration of the irony of John 7, the double, independent attestation to Jesus' birth in Bethlehem should be accepted as historical.

Virginal Conception

The virginal conception of Jesus also received double, independent attestation. Dunn acknowledges that the core tradition (Matthew and Luke) affirms "that Jesus' birth was special—'from the Holy Spirit' (Matt. 1.20), by the power of the Holy Spirit (Luke 1.35)."[48] He suggests that the virginal conception is not a necessary implication of birth from the Holy Spirit but could have been "an elaboration of the basic affirmation."[49]

Dunn rejects the virginal conception on several grounds. First, he suggests the NT tradition should have appealed earlier and elsewhere

---

[47] Brown, *Birth of the Messiah*, 516n6.
[48] Dunn, *Jesus Remembered*, 347.
[49] Ibid.

to Isa 7:14 LXX as apologetic proof of the event. Instead, the tradition preserves only "two or three tantalizing allusions or possible allusions to some popular knowledge or a rumour regarding an irregularity in Jesus' birth."[50] Nevertheless, evidence exists in the NT that multiple sources attested to the virginal conception of Jesus well before the composition of Matthew and Luke. Although some scholars suggest that Matthew's birth narrative is simply his own creation, most scholars posit that Matthew drew his narrative from several sources. Davies and Allison affirm a position that is similar but not quite identical to Raymond Brown in suggesting that Matthew drew from a preexisting genealogy that "lies behind what is now Mt 1.6b–16." They affirmed that "Matthew's genealogy was composed by a believer in the virginal conception," despite the later redaction that associated the genealogy with Joseph. The feminine relative pronoun in v. 16 from Matthew's source identified a human mother but not a human father of Jesus in contrast to the emphasis on human fathers earlier in the genealogy.[51]

Many scholars also affirm that the narrative of the annunciation to Joseph was also partially derived from a pre-Matthew source.[52] Yet the narrative clearly emphasizes that Jesus' birth was the result of a virginal conception, not only in the fulfillment citation that is often regarded as Matthean redaction, but also in vv. 18 and 25.[53] Scholars also posit multiple sources for chapter 2 including a source related to Herod and the infants and another related to the magi and the star.[54] Nevertheless, the notion of virginal conception runs through at least one of these sources as well. Matthew 2 typically identifies Jesus, not in relationship to Joseph, but in relationship to Mary. When the angel instructed Joseph to take the holy family and flee to Egypt, one would expect, "Take your wife and son," but instead we read "Take the child and his mother" (2:13). The same construction appears in 2:14, 20, and 21. This construction implies that Joseph did not share with Jesus the same intimacy that Jesus shared with Mary; that is, Mary was Jesus'

---

50   Ibid., 345.
51   See Davies and Allison, *Matthew 1–7*, 166, 185.
52   Again, Davies and Allison are representative. See ibid., 196–97.
53   Ibid., 185.
54   Ibid., 194–95.

mother but Joseph was not his biological father. That allusion or affirmation of the virginal conception appears in multiple pre-Matthew sources should make one pause before dismissing it too lightly.[55]

Mark 6:3 records the question of the synagogue assembly in the account of Jesus' rejection in Nazareth: "Is not this the carpenter, the son of Mary and brother of James, Joses, Judas and Simon?"[56] Since Jesus' critics identified a human mother but made no reference to Jesus' father, the challenge seems to imply doubts about Jesus' paternity. Dunn correctly dismisses attempts to explain the absence of reference to a human father by suggesting that Joseph was long dead.[57] Paternity continued to be an important mark of a Jewish male's identity, even long after the father's death, as the very names of several NT figures attest (e.g., Simon, son of Jonah). Thus Dunn states, "The Markan tradition may be evidence of some popular rumour regarding an irregularity in Jesus' birth."[58] The jibe in John 8:41, "We (emphatic) weren't born from sexual immorality," has the same effect.[59] Although some scholars have inferred Jesus'

---

[55] If one speaks in terms of the "stages of composition" mentioned by Davies and Allison rather than individual sources, allusion to the virginal conception may appear in all three major stages, the Mosaic, Davidic, and redactional stages. For the view that Paul was aware of the virginal conception, see R. J. Cooke, *Did Paul Know of the Virgin Birth?* (New York: Macmillan, 1926); G. A. Danell, "Did St. Paul Know the Tradition about the Virgin Birth?" *ST* 4 (1951): 94–101; W. C. Robinson, "A Re-study of the Virgin Birth of Christ," *EvQ* 37 (1965): 198–211. For the opposing view, see Brown, *Birth of the Messiah*, 519.

[56] The issue is slightly complicated by the fact that the earliest manuscript of Mark, 𝔓45, identifies Jesus as the "son of the carpenter" rather than "the carpenter." However "the carpenter" is the more difficult (and thus preferred) reading since it disagrees with the parallel in Matt 13:55 (Luke 4:22), and since scribes were more likely to conform Mark to Matthew, the church's favorite Gospel, than to introduce a tension with Matthew. Matthew may have adapted the Markan question because he regarded it as an irreverent challenge to Jesus' legitimacy or an implicit denial of Joseph's legal paternity of Jesus that qualified him as a son of David.

[57] Brown suggested that this was the easiest way of explaining the designation of Jesus as "the son of Mary." See Brown, *Birth of the Messiah*, 540. However, Matthew seems aware of Joseph's death early in Jesus' life since Joseph disappears from the Gospel narratives after the birth narratives in which he was prominent. Yet Matthew still believed that the question required adaptation. This suggests that Matthew read the question as implying something other than Joseph's mere absence.

[58] Dunn, *Jesus Remembered*, 346.

[59] On the text-critical issues related to John 1:13 and whether this text originally affirmed the virginal conception, see especially J. W. Pryor, "Of the Virgin Birth or the Birth of Christians? The Text of John 1:13 Once More," *NovT* 27 (1985): 296–316.

illegitimacy or identity as a *mamzer* from these clues in the tradition, this is just what one would expect to arise in response to claims of a virginal conception.[60] Thus, although the Markan statement does not constitute independent attestation to the virginal conception of Jesus, it does satisfy the criterion of coherence.

Since the response of Jesus' and early Christians' opponents to the claim of virginal conception was naturally the charge of illegitimacy, the references in Matthew and Luke to the virginal conception of Jesus also satisfy, in at least some measure, the so-called criterion of embarrassment. Ultimately, only Mary and Joseph could have been sure of Mary's virginity at the time of Jesus' conception. This would have made the virginal conception difficult to defend. Thus it is doubtful that early Christians would have invented the doctrine for apologetic purposes as some scholars have suggested. It seems more likely that Matthew and Luke insisted on the doctrine because witnesses or tradition(s) that they deemed reliable insisted on the historicity of the event or because they viewed the virginal conception as a necessary correlation of core affirmations of the kerygma.

Dunn is willing to grant that Jesus' divine sonship together with the idea of conception of birth from the Spirit "was arrived at very early in the disciple groups and first churches" in part because it resonates with "a fundamental motif in earliest Christianity." That motif is that believers who experience the Spirit are brought into sonship with God. Dunn reasons that believers "will hardly have thought that Jesus' sonship was of a lesser kind."[61] At this point, Dunn seems to be applying a new criterion to the evaluation of the birth narratives. This criterion might be called the criterion of theological necessity. Affirmations that are necessary given the confirmed early testimony of the disciples are also very early.

Although Dunn sees the idea of Jesus' identity as the preexistent Son of God or as full deity as arising only late in the first century in

---

[60] For a response to Bruce Chilton's suggestion that Jesus was regarded as a *mamzer* (a view referenced by Dunn), see C. L. Quarles, "Jesus as *Mamzer*: A Response to Bruce Chilton's Reconstruction of the Circumstances Surrounding Jesus' Birth in *Rabbi Jesus*," *BBR* 14 (2004): 243–55.

[61] Dunn, *Jesus Remembered*, 348.

the Gospel of John,[62] a growing number of scholars are arguing that this high Christology is not the late by-product of an evolutionary or developmental process but is assumed in the very earliest Christian tradition.[63] Numerous lines of evidence support this conclusion. Perhaps most importantly, the use of texts about Yahweh to describe Jesus in early NT documents (e.g., Rom 10:9,13 [Joel 2:32]; Phil 2:10–11 [Isa 45:23]; Mark 1:2–3 [Mal 3:1; Isa 40:3]) affirms a very early and very high Christology. Karl Barth observed that a miraculous conception of Jesus seems to be a necessary corollary to this high Christology.[64] Barth suggested that the silence of the NT outside of Matthew and Luke regarding the virginal conception might only indicate that the doctrine was taken for granted.[65]

Some theologians have rejected the virginal conception on the grounds that it stands in tension with another NT affirmation, the true humanity of Jesus. Emil Brunner famously asked, "Is a man who is born without a human father a 'true man'?"[66] Frederick Dale Bruner has offered the obvious counterquestion: "Although our first parents in the biblical creation accounts are recorded as having had no human parents, do these accounts not intend that we read their stories as the stories of real human beings?"[67] Bruner admitted that the historical arguments for the virginal conception are "rather tenuous" since only Mary would know if Jesus were born of a virgin and since her testimony

[62] J. D. G. Dunn, *The Theology of Paul the Apostle* (Grand Rapids: Eerdmans, 1998), 274–75.

[63] See M. Hengel, *The Son of God: The Origin of Christology and the History of Jewish Hellenistic Religion* (Minneapolis: Fortress, 1977); R. Bauckham, *God Crucified: Monotheism and Christology in the New Testament* (Carlisle: Paternoster/Grand Rapids: Eerdmans, 1998); L. W. Hurtado, *Lord Jesus Christ: Devotion to Jesus in Earliest Christianity* (Grand Rapids: Eerdmans, 2003); and S. J. Gathercole, *The Preexistent Son: Recovering the Christologies of Matthew, Mark, and Luke* (Grand Rapids: Eerdmans, 2006).

[64] K. Barth, *Doctrine of the Word of God* (vol. 1, part 2 of *Church Dogmatics*; Edinburgh: T & T Clark, 1956), 202.

[65] Ibid., 175.

[66] E. Brunner, *The Mediator: A Study of the Central Doctrine of the Christian Faith* (Philadelphia: Westminster, 1947), 325. See also idem, *The Christian Doctrine of Creation and Redemption* (vol. 2 of *Dogmatics*; trans. Olive Wyon; Philadelphia: Westminster, 1952), 355; W. Pannenberg, *Jesus—God and Man* (Philadelphia: Westminster, 1961), 141–50.

[67] F. D. Bruner, *The Christbook: Matthew 1–12* (vol. 1 of *Matthew: A Commentary*; rev. ed.; Grand Rapids: Eerdmans, 2004), 39. See a similar dismissal of this objection in Brown, *Birth of the Messiah*, 531.

might not have been available to the evangelists. Nevertheless, as he explained why he regarded Barth's theological arguments as more persuasive than he had in his earlier edition, he commented, "I become increasingly convinced that we are all finally (or perhaps even primarily) driven to theological reasons for our final positions on the most hotly contested issues. For I think it verifiable that 'behind every historical method there is a hidden dogmatic' (Wilhelm Lütgert)."[68] Although many historians might be reticent to appeal to the theological necessity of Jesus' miraculous conception as evidence for its existence in the earliest traditions of the church, Dunn himself used a similar theological argument to demonstrate the great antiquity of the idea that Jesus was born of the Spirit. This line of evidence is appropriate to consider here.

Second, Dunn's rejection of the virginal conception seems to be influenced by a certain skepticism regarding the very possibility of the event. In a detailed note supporting his section treating the virginal conception, Dunn adds,

> Here we also need to be aware of the biological and theological corollaries of insisting that the virginal conception/birth was a historical fact. E.g. Arthur Peacocke concludes his brief study, "DNA of Our DNA," in G. J. Brooke, ed., *The Birth of Jesus: Biblical and Theological Reflections* (Edinburgh: T & T Clark, 2000), 59–67, with the blunt statement: "For Jesus to be fully human he had, for both biological and theological reasons, to have a human father as well as a human mother and the weight of the historical evidence strongly indicates that this was so—and that it was probably Joseph. Any theology for a scientific age which is concerned with the significance of Jesus of Nazareth now has to start at this point."[69]

Dunn does not clearly indicate whether he concurs with Peacocke's statement. Nevertheless, the statement reflects concerns that commonly drive debate over the historicity of the virginal conception and thus should be addressed. By "scientific age," Peacocke appears to mean an age in which people affirm the historical possibility

---

[68] Ibid., xix.
[69] Dunn, *Jesus Remembered*, 66.

only of events that are repeatable and can be observed by researchers today. This would, of course, preclude acceptance of the virginal conception of Jesus or any other genuinely unique historical event. Nevertheless, the objection to the possibility of a virginal conception on these grounds is generally guided more by philosophical presuppositions rather than scientific "facts." Naturalistic or deistic worldviews that deny the existence of a personal deity or disallow his activity in human history will naturally have no place for this or any other miracle. Nevertheless, a theistic worldview that affirms the existence of God and acknowledges the possibility of his intervention in history will be open to the possibility of the historicity of supernatural occurrences.[70] Unfortunately, it has become common for scholars who personally affirm theism to follow an approach to the historical study of the Gospels that is paramount to methodological naturalism.[71] Nevertheless, as Craig Keener has observed, "We must evaluate the function and reliability of the virgin birth story by tools more reliable than culturally and historically shaped philosophical positions."[72]

Dunn critiqued the automatic rejection of the supernatural by the liberal quest and affirmed the historical likelihood that Jesus performed what he and others of his day believed to be miracles.[73] Dunn also recognized that the traditions regarding the resurrection of Jesus were worthy of historical research and seems to affirm that Jesus was truly raised.[74] Openness to the possibility of resurrection would seem to require also an openness to the possibility of virginal conception and

---

[70] I agree with the position of Augustine, who argued, "Whatever marvel happens in this world, it is certainly less marvelous than this whole world itself—I mean the sky and the earth, and all that is in them—and these God certainly made" (*City of God*, X.12).

[71] See especially C. S. Evans, "Methodological Naturalism in Historical Biblical Research," in *Jesus and the Restoration of Israel* (ed. C. C. Newman; Downers Grove: InterVarsity, 1999), 180–205, 314–15.

[72] Keener, *Matthew*, 84. Of course, rejection of the virginal conception is not merely the result of a post-Enlightenment worldview. For a good history of the debate over the virginal conception, see J. P. Sweeney, "Modern and Ancient Controversies over the Virgin Birth of Jesus," *BSac* 160 (2003): 142–58.

[73] See especially his excellent treatment of the liberal quest in Dunn, *Jesus Remembered*, esp. 29–34, 670.

[74] Ibid., 861–62.

other miraculous elements of the birth narratives.[75] Once that possibility is acknowledged and seriously entertained, the general reliability of the Gospels as attested in Dunn's research, the double, independent attestation of the virginal conception in Matthew and Luke, the charge of illegitimacy that coheres with virginal conception, and the theological necessity of virginal conception for the church's early and high Christology should tip the balance in favor of the claim that Jesus was remembered by some of his earliest disciples as conceived by a virgin.

In his monumental study of the birth narratives, Brown reached a conclusion that was only slightly more cautious: "I think that both of them [Matthew and Luke] regarded the virginal conception as historical." He later added that "the scientifically controllable biblical evidence leaves the question of the historicity of the virginal conception unresolved."[76] Noting that this conclusion seemed "retrogressively conservative" to many scholars, he quipped, "I would shock them more by affirming that I think that it is easier to explain the NT evidence by positing historical basis than by positing pure theological creation."[77]

Conclusion

Evidence supports the historical reliability of several important features of the synoptic birth narratives. These features include Jesus'

---

[75] Despite Dunn's openness to the supernatural, at other times he seems dismissive of the miraculous. When he argues that no historical facts can be gleaned from the birth narratives, he remarked, "Matthew's moving star does not evoke a strong impression of historical credibility" (ibid., 343–44).

[76] For a philosophical evaluation of Brown's arguments and conclusions, see G. Labooy, "The Historicity of the Virginal Conception. A Study in Argumentation," *EuroJTh* 13 (2004): 91–101. In his "Epistemological Assessment," Labooy concludes that the historicity of the virginal conception should be ranked "between *probable* and *beyond reasonable doubt*."

[77] Brown, *Birth of the Messiah*, 528–29. See also J. Nolland, *The Gospel of Matthew: A Commentary on the Greek Text* (NIGTC; Grand Rapids: Eerdmans, 2005), 92. Although he accepts the influence of the Moses Haggadah on Matthew's account of Jesus' birth, he ultimately concludes, "While our present infancy narratives offer Christianised accounts of Jesus' origins, the idea of a virginal conception has not been borrowed either from pre-Christian Judaism or from the wider world of the early Christian period. It is not readily explicable as a theologoumenon, and it is unlikely to be simply a pious lie to cover the embarrassment of Mary's having fallen pregnant in the normal manner prior to her marriage to Joseph. Despite all critical reserve the traditional view continues to have much to commend it."

Davidic lineage, his birth in Bethlehem during the reign of Herod the Great, and the virginal conception. Other features of the narratives indicate that they have a connection to the testimony of original eyewitnesses either directly or indirectly. In light of this evidence, Dunn's conclusion that the "prospects are not good" for gleaning any "historical facts" from the birth narratives seems unduly skeptical. The evidence is sufficient to confirm the general reliability of the narratives and to shift the burden of proof to those who reject the Matthean and Lucan testimony.

10

"CHRISTIANITY IN THE MAKING"

ORAL MYSTERY OR EYEWITNESS HISTORY?

BEN WITHERINGTON III

*When Thou hast **done**, Thou hast **not done**, For I **have more**.*

—John Donne, "A Hymn to God the Father"

Dunn Remembered—Any Eyewitness Account

The very long and notable tradition at the University of Durham in England of having world-class New Testament (NT) scholars stretches back now some 150 years and includes the likes of J. B. Lightfoot, B. F. Westcott, Alfred Plummer, H. E. W. Turner, Charles Cranfield, C. K. Barrett, James D. G. Dunn, and now John Barclay, Francis Watson, Loren Stuckenbroeck, and others. It is a notable and rich heritage, and in the early 1980s, Dunn succeeded Kingsley Barrett (my own mentor) in the Lightfoot Chair there.

When we look back now at the body of work that Dunn has given us since he assumed the Lightfoot Chair, it is clear that whereas

197

his work before the early 1980s was important and noteworthy, it was but a harbinger of bigger things to come. Who could have foreseen two such massive and important works as his *Theology of Paul* and now *Jesus Remembered* when he first came to give the Lightfoot lecture at Durham in the late 1970s—on "glossolalia" no less? I remember well Barrett and Cranfield slowly walking home to North Hill animatedly chatting after that lecture, and the word "extraordinary" could be heard as they went.

The highest compliment I can give Dunn is that I believe Lightfoot himself (one of Dunn's heroes, and mine too) would have been impressed with what has come forth from his pen ever since he became a Lightfoot Professor at Durham. Clearly, the remark of that other Donne, John Donne the English cleric, is appropriate here: "When Thou hast done, Thou hast not done, For I have more." And indeed, Dunn has much more to do, judging from the fact that his *Christianity in the Making* series involves two more volumes beyond the 900 pages of *Jesus Remembered*!

I mention this eyewitness account of my own, from nearly 30 years ago, by way of saying that I still remember vividly the occasion, the subject discussed, some of the major points, and the reasons Cranfield and Barrett were thinking that some of the remarks made were "extraordinary." Though the memory has dulled some, the basic character of the event and what was said and the responses remain clear to me, lo these many years later. My esteemed professors were hoping for more of a lecture on Paul, but what they got was more of a lecture on some of the things Dunn was going on about in *Jesus and the Spirit*, including the modern phenomenon of glossolalia. If I can remember these kinds of details over a 30-year span, I can only imagine what those ancients with keen minds, raised in an oral culture in which memorization was a staple of education, could have remembered from Jesus' own era when they sat down to write the Gospels some 30 or more years after the death of Jesus.

Dunn has always had a lively mind that teases other minds into active thought. It is the mark of an excellent teacher and scholar, and Dunn is both. I have learned much from him over the years, including from *Jesus Remembered*, which I would consider a masterwork in so many ways. It takes considerable skill to make a technical work of this size both readable and continuingly interesting. I begin this chapter with an "homage" because I would not want any of the critique that follows to be seen outside of the larger appreciation I have for what has been accomplished in *Jesus Remembered*. It is a book I wish I could have written myself, though with some differences, of course.

It is precisely the issue of eyewitnesses, an issue largely neglected in Dunn's *Jesus Remembered* in favor of talking about the developments of oral traditions, that I want to raise in this chapter. In order to do so, however, it is important to lay out how Dunn differentiates the methodology of his project from the previous efforts to analyze the Jesus tradition largely on the basis of form and redaction criticism. It will be seen that I am in full agreement with much of his critique of the use of both of these tools in the study of Jesus and his words and deeds.

Oral Traditions or Redaction History?

The scope of Dunn's project is breathtaking, but equally impressive is the critical rigor applied to the data and the compelling sequential logic of his argument. It takes some 300-plus pages to actually get to the point of discussing "Jesus remembered," and unlike some books of this nature and length, the preliminary discussion is hardly pro forma or boring. Indeed, it is so well written and interesting that one forgets about being impatient to hear what Dunn will say about what was remembered about Jesus and simply enjoys the ground-clearing and stage-setting exercises done with the efficiency and panache of a well-seasoned, highly learned scholar. What becomes clear throughout the first 300 pages of this study is that Dunn actually wants to change some of the paradigm and the methodological assumptions by which we evaluate the Jesus tradition and the Gospels. No, he is not rejecting Markan priority or even the reality of the Q tradition, nor does he reject the concept of redactional activity of a literary sort being applied by Matthew or Luke on the earlier Markan and Q material and other sources.

What Dunn wants to argue long and hard for, however, is that such redactional activities do not account for a vast amount of what we find in the Jesus tradition—we need a more "oral" and less "literary" way of evaluating these things, including the way we evaluate what happened between the time Jesus actually spoke and acted and the time when the Gospels were written down. Let us consider some particulars of how he argues his case.

At the very beginning of his study, Dunn informs us that "the most distinctive feature of the present study will be to attempt to freshly assess the importance of the oral tradition of Jesus' mission and the suggestion that the Synoptic Gospels bear testimony to a pattern and technique of oral transmission which has endured a greater stability and continuity in the Jesus tradition than has thus far been generally appreciated."[1] This places him between the form critics of old and those who stress the close connection of the tradition with eyewitnesses. Drawing on recent studies of orality by Werner Kelber, and more importantly the now somewhat dated studies of Kenneth Bailey, Dunn finds fault with the attempts to treat the Gospels and their sources as literary texts in the modern sense rather than oral texts in the ancient sense. Dunn stresses that both Jesus and the Gospel writers lived in largely oral cultures, which he is certainly correct about, and therefore he pleads his case that what we need to be examining is how largely oral cultures pass on their sacred traditions and what the function of sacred texts would be in such a setting. This is exactly right in my judgment.

Dunn believes that various modern forms of literary criticism, including form, redaction, and indeed narrative criticism, approach the text in thoroughly modern, not to mention ahistorical ways. For example, read his critique of narrative criticism:

> Narrative criticism has attempted in effect to narrow the hermeneutical circle of the whole and parts, by limiting the whole to the text itself. In narrative criticism, in order to make sense of a part, verse, or passage of the Gospel, the hermeneutical circle need only take in the whole of the Gospel itself. . . . The reality is that the historical text draws on (and its communication potential depends on) wider linguistic usage of the time; it makes references and allusions to characters and customs which are not explained within "the closed universe"

---

[1] J. D. G. Dunn, *Jesus Remembered* (vol. 1 of *Christianity in the Making*; Grand Rapids: Eerdmans, 2003), 6.

of the text; it cannot be adequately understood without some aware-ness of the society of the time. For example, without knowledge of the extra-textual social tensions between Jews and Samaritans, a central thrust of the parable of the Good Samaritan (Luke 10) will be lost.[2]

Dunn is no ally to those who say, "All we have is texts." In other words, a more historical and less anachronistic approach to the Gospels is necessary if we are to properly understand them. In this, Dunn sounds much like a traditional historian or linguist. It is precisely for this same reason that Dunn will go on to caution against using models of tra-dition development that are entirely too modern, such as analyzing Balkan folklore, as a tool to explain the permutations and variations we find in the Gospel traditions.

He is not happy either with what can only be called the vicious circle of the hermeneutics of reader-response criticism, another form of modern literary criticism. There must be interplay between the text and the reader such that

> the text reacts back upon the pre-understanding, both sharpening it and requiring of it revision at one or another point, and thus enabling a fresh scrutiny of the text. . . . To conceive the hermeneutical process as an infinitely regressive intertexuality is a counsel of despair which quickly reduces all meaningful communication to impossibility and all communication to a game of trivial pursuit.[3]

Thus far, Dunn sounds both traditional in his use of the his-torical method and rather conservative. But he warns repeatedly that we do not have "the Jesus papers" in the Gospels. We do not have Jesus directly or the exact words of Jesus in the sayings collections. Jesus probably did not speak Greek to his disciples, much less King James English! We have then, as the subtitle of his book stresses, a mediated Jesus—Jesus as various disciples remembered him. This does not mean that Dunn thinks that we are not in touch with the historical Jesus through such material. What he is wanting to stress is the mediated character of the portraits, reflecting in his view oral

---

[2] Ibid., 119.
[3] Ibid., 121.

traditions passed down over a couple of generations orally before reaching a somewhat fixed written form.

What is interesting is that he does not apply a hermeneutic of suspicion to these traditions in the same way some (e.g., the Jesus Seminar) would. For example, he urges,

> The idea that a Jesus reconstructed from the Gospel traditions (the so-called historical Jesus), *yet significantly different from the Jesus of the Gospels*, is the Jesus who taught in Galilee (the historical Jesus!) is an illusion. The idea that we can see through the faith perspective of the NT writings to a Jesus who did *not* inspire faith or who inspired faith in a *different* way is an illusion.[4]

What is the original impetus and impulse behind the Gospel record? In Dunn's view, it is the sayings and deeds of Jesus himself as witnessed, heard and seen, and retained in the memory of his disciples. We have the impact crater, not the meteor, that made the impact in the Gospels, not Jesus in all his fullness but rather the remembered Jesus. For example, the sayings and deeds of Jesus reported are the ones remembered over the course of time and eventually recorded. As John 20:30 and 21:25 say, there were many other things Jesus said and did that were not remembered and not passed on orally or in writing for that matter.

In chronicling the process that led to the Gospels, Dunn goes on to stress that several of these Gospel traditions reflect the pre-Easter impact of Jesus creating faith even then. Peter and the other disciples did not first become disciples after Easter or did they first begin to learn, remember, think about, and appropriate in faith the words and deeds of Jesus only after Easter. The "actual Synoptic tradition, with its record of things Jesus did and said bears witness to a continuity between pre-Easter memory and post-Easter proclamation, a continuity of faith. However great the shock of Good Friday and Easter for the first disciples, it would be unjustified to assume that these events marked a discontinuity with their initial disciple-response."[5] Just so, and thus we might expect Dunn to elaborate at length as to whether

---

[4] Ibid., 126. The italics are his.
[5] Ibid., 133.

we have, at least in Mark and Q, eyewitness memory, but this he does not do. Rather, in a lengthy chapter 8, Dunn lays out his theories about oral Gospel tradition, oral texts, and their development over time. It is to this material that we need to pay especially close attention, and here especially Dunn's indebtedness to Bailey is very apparent indeed.

Let us start with the spectrum of possibilities he sets up for how the Jesus tradition was passed on: formally controlled tradition (a la Birger Gerhardsson); informal controlled tradition (a la Bailey); and informal uncontrolled tradition (a la various of the form critics, including recent ones in the Jesus Seminar: Robert Funk, John Dominic Crossan, et al.).

Against Rudolf Bultmann, Dunn thinks the handling of the Jesus tradition as a sacred tradition, whereas not like the latter rabbinic models of memorization and passing on of tradition, nonetheless was rather conservative. There was community control, of a pedagogical sort. Dunn is working then with a sociological model of community control and formation of the oral tradition.

Dunn is not convinced by the argument of Eugene Boring and others that new sayings of the risen Jesus were retrojected back into the Gospels alongside of the authentic sayings of the historical Jesus. Christian prophets are not depicted as speaking with the voice of Jesus or for Jesus in the Christian assemblies in Corinth and elsewhere, and so it is unlikely that they were the tradents shaping the tradition. According to Dunn, "Bultmann and Boring are overeager to find evidence of prophetic activity in the Synoptic tradition. The broader evidence suggests rather that such utterances were the exceptions rather than the rule."[6] He adds that any prophecy claiming to come from the exalted Lord would have been tested against what was already known of what Jesus said and did. Thus, in a surprising conclusion, he urges that "the less closely a saying or motif within the Jesus tradition coheres with the rest of the Jesus tradition, the more likely is it that the saying or motif goes back to Jesus himself!"[7] This is because an alleged prophetic saying of the exalted Jesus would be subject to a criterion of coherence with previous tradition.

---

[6] Ibid., 188.
[7] Ibid., 192.

Bultmann had wanted to suggest that there were "laws of style" that determined how traditions were transmitted, in what forms, and how they would be elaborated. Basically, he argued a "from the simple and pure, to the complex and prolix" sort of case, drawing on a literary model of accretions, additions, and editing. In Dunn's words, "The image is drawn from the literary process of editing, where each successive edition (layer) is an edited version (for Bultmann an elaborated and expanded version) of the previous edition (layer). But is such a conceptualisation really appropriate to a process of oral retellings of traditional material?"[8]

If you are going to dethrone a dominant theory, then one has to have something to put in its place. What Dunn draws on largely, as I have said, are the insights of Bailey. Dunn is right to find it amazing that the old form critics (Bultmann and Martin Dibelius) and even more recent ones never actually bothered to investigate, if possible, the original first-century techniques of oral transmission. Birger Gerhardsson tried to remedy this oversight by proposing formally controlled tradition along the lines of the later rabbinic model, with memorization being the basic technique of all such early Jewish education. Thus Gerhardsson, in reacting to Bultmann, insisted that Jesus taught his disciples to memorize his teachings by heart, and thus the Synoptic Gospel writers had a fixed tradition to work with when they wrote their Gospels.[9]

There were several objections to this sort of view: (a) the Gospels do not depict Jesus teaching his disciples to rehearse things by repetition; (b) the post–AD 70 situation in Israel and elsewhere changed how Jews handled tradition, and the later Mishnaic model of traditioning should not be retrojected back into Jesus' day; and (c) most importantly, all the variants we find in the parallel versions of Jesus' words and deeds suggest a less formal or rigid handling of the Gospel traditions. In other words, Gerhardsson is accused of anachronism, just in a less gross or remote form than Bultmann.

What then could be the bridge between Jesus and the Gospels, or the original disciples and the Gospel writers, and what sort of tradition transmission was there? Dunn opts for oral transmission

---

[8] Ibid., 194–95.
[9] See ibid., 198.

"mid-state between fixed and free." Oral transmission "exhibits 'an insistent conservative urge for preservation' of essential information, while it borders on carelessness in its predisposition to abandon features that are not met with social approval." "Variability and stability, conservatism and creativity, evanescence and unpredictability all mark the pattern of oral transmission"—the "oral principle of 'variation within the same.'"[10]

On this theory, variations on a story or a saying are more likely to reflect multiple tellings of the tradition, not redactional or other literary work at the juncture when Gospel writers were editing their sources.

Dunn is certainly right that ancient texts were meant to be heard and are, by nature, "oral texts."[11] They were not meant to be read silently, and they partake of all the oral and aural devices one would expect (rhythm, rhyme, alliteration, assonance, etc.). What Dunn does not say is that it is precisely these oral features that make the material memorable, indeed even memorizable, as Charles Fox Burney pointed out long ago.[12]

It is interesting that Dunn does not seriously engage with or pause to refute an alternate theory to his own by Samuel Byrskog (a student of Gerhardsson), namely, the theory of oral history. He only says this of Byrskog's model: "But this model assumes later historians (like Luke) seeking out and inquiring of those like Peter, the women at the cross and tomb, and the family of Jesus, who could remember the original events and exchanges (cf. Luke 1:1–4). Byrskog, in fact, has no real conception of or indeed role for oral transmission as itself the bridging process."[13] In other words, this theory is dismissed without refutation. And furthermore, this comment is buried in a footnote.

Dunn then does not bother to rebut the theory of oral history; he basically ignores it, practicing benign neglect in favor of the notion that there was a generation or more during which time there was oral transmission of this Gospel material that involved a good deal

---

[10] Ibid., 200. He is quoting and following Werner Kelber closely at this point.

[11] On this point, see my forthcoming volume *Shifting the Paradigms* (Waco: Baylor University Press, 2009).

[12] See C. F. Burney, *The Poetry of our Lord* (Oxford: Clarendon, 1925).

[13] Dunn, *Jesus Remembered*, 198–99n138.

of flexibility, except for the central features or sayings of a tradition. This is problematic not simply because a viable alternative theory is not dealt with, much less refuted. It is problematic because it does not explain some crucial things about the synoptic tradition. For example, Dunn's theory hardly explains why it is that 95 percent of Mark's material is found in Matthew, and of that material, it is 52 percent verbatim. This hardly seems like a case where there is considerable flux around the edges except when it comes to central motifs or crucial sayings or events. The differences in the shared material between Mark and Matthew, perhaps our two earliest Gospels, are much more easily explained on the whole in terms of Matthew's redactional tendencies than on the basis of oral variations on a theme. For example, where Mark tends to raise questions about the disciples having no faith, they are regularly called "you of little faith" in Matthew. Consistent tendencies of variation in Matthew compared to Mark seem purposeful and the result of a particular kind of editing of source material.

To his credit, Dunn does not deny there has been redaction of Gospel source material by later Gospel writers. He simply wants to stress that a good deal of the differences in the accounts can be best explained as reflecting orality and oral transmission. It is a shame that Dunn's masterwork came out prior to the publication of the equally masterful work of Richard Bauckham, titled *Jesus and the Eyewitnesses*, in which work Bauckham draws on and expands on the argument of Byrskog, dealing with the issue of eyewitnesses more seriously and in depth. We will have occasion to draw on Bauckham in critiquing Dunn's approach in the next section of this chapter.

Here, however, we need to get to the heart of the matter: the reliance on the suggestion of Bailey of "informal controlled tradition" in the Gospels based on an assumed analogy with what Bailey observed for many years in Middle Eastern villages in the earlier twentieth century. First of all, Bailey, unlike Gerhardsson, draws on illustrative situations that are hardly from antiquity. In this respect, Bailey could equally be accused of the same sort of anachronism that Bultmann is accused of. The assumption is that village life in the Middle East in the twentieth century must be much the same as village life in Jesus' day *when it comes to the matter or orality, oral tradition, and most importantly oral transmission of key or sacred traditions.*[14] Indeed, this is an enormous assumption that needs substantiation.

Dunn freely admits that Bailey's evidence is anecdotal and not the subject of systematic or scientific research.[15] We do not become more assured about Dunn's reliance on Bailey's observations when he adds "the character of oral tradition which it illustrates accords well with the findings of other investigations of oral tradition and *is self evidently far closer to the sort of oral traditioning which must be posited for the Jesus tradition.*"[16] Beware when scholars tell you something is self-evident or that a particular theory *must* be posited for the Jesus tradition. This last remark is all the more stunning when one turns to the next page and then reads, "We certainly do not know enough about oral traditioning in the ancient world to draw from that knowledge clear guidelines for our understanding of how the Jesus tradition was passed down in its oral stage."[17]

But if we do not know such things about antiquity, then we also *do not know* that the analogy with oral traditioning in twentieth-century village life in and around Palestine is apt. One needs knowledge on both sides of the comparison. Even more specifically, should we really assume that Palestinian nomads and their traditioning processes are a good point of analogy for what could be said about Jesus and his disciples and the processes they used?

It takes a considerable leap of faith, not to mention a leap over all sorts of cultural differences, to accept this analogy with much confidence. For example, Jesus and his disciples grew up in a Jewish culture or subculture as people of the Hebrew sacred scriptures. These nomads did not. Second, the issue is not how just any sort of oral traditions, stories, parables, and proverbs might be handled or handed down but how those considered "sacred traditions" were handled. But Bailey does not really make this sort of necessary distinction. He simply thinks

---

[14] The most important of Bailey's works that is relied on is, of course, his *Poet and Peasant* (Grand Rapids: Eerdmans, 1976). It should be noted that this is mainly a study of Luke's parables. It is not a systematic comparison between what we find in the Gospels and what Bailey observed in the Middle East.

[15] Dunn, *Jesus Remembered*, 209.

[16] Ibid., 209; emphasis added.

[17] Ibid., 210.

that orality works the same way regardless of what sort of stories and sayings one is relaying and retelling to others.

Dunn seeks to bolster his case by providing core samples from the NT, where oral transmission and retelling of stories seems best to explain things. Oddly, his first example is the threefold telling of Saul's conversion in Acts, not a part of the Gospel tradition at all. If we compare side by side the three accounts in Acts 9, 22, and 26 and also compare the way Dunn analyzes the data with the way, for example, Robert Tannehill analyzes the three accounts as examples where Luke cumulatively informs his audience about Saul's conversion by adding fresh and different details as the narrative goes on, then it must be said that Tannehill is more convincing in explaining the differences in the accounts. They are purposeful, and they reflect various Lukan tendencies in his editing and overall presentation of his material over his two volumes, not oral tendencies.[18] Luke is following the rhetorical rules about varying an account when it is repeated and amplifying or adding new details to the later accounts so we do not have simple redundancy. In other words, the variations here do not reflect multiple oral retellings by later Christians; they reflect in the first instance that Luke is drawing on both first-person accounts, one of which he heard, and then composing a third-person account, which we find in Acts 9, composing each with attention to the rhetorical rules about such speech material. I have dealt with this at length elsewhere and have shown how we can learn much about what is going on in Acts from the way Luke edits his Markan and Q source material in his Gospel.[19]

What is most surprising to me is that, despite all his emphasis on orality, Dunn does not discuss at all the issue of rhetoric, the oral art of persuasion in the Greco-Roman Empire, even though Luke has been shown at length, by numerous commentators, to be using rhetoric

---

[18] See R. Tannehill, *The Narrative Unity of Luke-Acts. The Acts of the Apostles* (Minneapolis: Fortress, 1994). Somehow the influential work of Tannehill does not even make it into Dunn's large bibliography. We do find a passing reference to the first of Tannehill's two volumes (Dunn, *Jesus Remembered*, 94n143), but Dunn does not seem to know his second volume and its significance.

[19] See B. Witherington III, "Editing the Good News: Some Synoptic Lessons from the Study of Acts," in *History, Literature and Society in the Book of Acts* (ed. B. Witherington III; Cambridge: Cambridge University Press, 1996), 324–47.

especially in the presentation of his speech material in Luke–Acts.[20] He does not talk about it even though we have long known there was a school of rhetoric in Jerusalem in Jesus' era and afterward, and even though Christianity was an evangelistic movement seeking to persuade others about Jesus.

If you are going to deal with the orality of early followers of Jesus, including the Gospel writers who wrote in Greek, Paul, and others, then you have to come to grips with the nature of a rhetoric-saturated culture and how oral traditions and sacred traditions function in a rhetorical culture. When you do assess the data in light of rhetorical conventions and tendencies, rhetorically purposeful variation rather than just flexible oral storytelling and traditioning better explains most of the data.

Dunn analyzes briefly the two accounts of the healing of the centurion's servant (Matt 8:5–13; Luke 7:1–10) and raises the point that the differences between these two versions of the story (and also from John 4:46–54) are better explained by the theory or oral transmission that has stability in the central saying and skeletal narrative elements but flexibility in the rest of the pericope than by positing two different editions of Q: one used by Matthew and one by Luke. I agree with this critique about Q, but is this explanation also more plausible than assuming consideration amplification of the story by Luke himself or recasting of the story by John? Dunn thinks so, and I must say that his argument seems stronger here. Whatever one makes of the differences in these three accounts, they need to be explained in some fashion, and they do not seem to easily submit to the theory of mere redactional change, augmentation, or recasting. It must be said, however, that since we obviously do not know what the oral tradition looked like independent of its frozen form in our actual Gospels, there is less control that can be exercised by positing this theory than when one explains the differences on the basis of redaction of earlier traditions, at least when we are dealing with a use of Mark, by Matthew and Luke. With Q, since we do not have it independently of its inclusion in Matthew and Luke, obviously there is much less certainty about earlier forms or redaction, despite the confidence of those who find multiple layers in a

---

[20] See B. Witherington III, *The Acts of the Apostles* (Grand Rapids: Eerdmans, 1996).

Q document we do not have on hand to examine. There is the further problem, of course, that in an oral culture, what we call Q may well have not been a document or documents but rather streams of memorized oral tradition, which both Matthew and Luke dip into from time to time in various ways and places.

Dunn also discusses the triple-tradition story of the stilling of the storm (Mark 4:35–41; Matt 8:23–27; Luke 8:22–25). He asserts at the outset, "Here again we have the characteristic features of different retellings of a single story about Jesus."[21] It would have been more reassuring if he had actually analyzed the details of the three accounts explaining why his theory works better here than a more literary theory.

What he does point to is that there are inconsequential variations of synonymous verbs, little varying details about Jesus sleeping and the like, and he thinks this is best explained by independent retellings of the story orally. This overlooks that there were specific rhetorical rules the Gospel writers could have followed when it comes to the matters of repetition and amplification of written or oral source material. One of the key rules was that you would deliberately use differing terms that convey the same meaning to make the material your own.[22] In any case, there are clear editorial tendencies evident when one compares the presentation of the disciples in Mark and in Matthew. In the former presentation, the disciples say, "Lord, don't you care we are perishing?" and Jesus responds, "Have you still no faith?" Both the phrase "Lord, don't you care?" and the reference to no faith that reflects badly on the disciples are missing in Matthew. Luke also ameliorates the harshness of the Markan account with Jesus simply asking, "Where is your faith?" which seems to suggest that Jesus thinks they have some faith but are not exhibiting it. Dunn wishes to argue for spontaneous, multiple variations on a theme rather than different versions of the story or different editing of a story.

After presenting several more examples, especially choosing those in which there is a wide degree of variation between the different forms of the story or passage, Dunn then stresses that we need to free

---

[21] Dunn, *Jesus Remembered*, 217.
[22] See, for example, my discussion on repetition and amplification in *Letters and Homilies for Hellenized Christians Volume One* (Downers Grove; Intervarsity, 2007).

ourselves from thinking of these traditions in a purely literary way, as if the differences could only be explained in terms of differing source texts or redaction of texts. I agree with this. Dunn also admits, however, that many of the differences can be explained on the basis of Luke or Matthew editing Mark or Q, and again, I must agree.

On more than one occasion, Dunn cites the material in Eusebius where he is quoting from the earlier writings by Bishop Papias of Hierapolis about the composition of Mark: "But Peter adapted/gave his teaching with a view to the *chreias* but not as making an orderly account of the Lord's sayings, so that Mark did no wrong in thus writing down some things as he recalled them" (*Hist. eccl.* 3.39.15). Here Dunn translates *chreia* in its mundane sense of needs (needs of whom?) and does not even consider the possibility that Papias is telling us that Mark composed his work following the rhetorical rules about forming *chreia*—short stories usually climaxing with a pithy memorable saying of the central figure. Elsewhere, I have demonstrated at length that this is precisely how Papias's quotation ought to be read and, indeed, is precisely what Mark was doing.[23] Mark follows the elementary rules for composing brief narratives in a rhetorically effective manner. Luke does the same thing as well. What is in play here is not mere oral flexibility or variation on a theme but a purposeful editing or modifying a tradition, whether oral or written, so that it adds to the persuasiveness of the material in Greek. It is only Matthew who seems to have other tendencies and aims in the way he handles the tradition, doing so in what I would call a far more Jewish, even halakhic or haggadic manner. Thus, although I agree that the variations in shared traditions do not at all reflect a cavalier attitude about history or a lack of historical interest, it is a shame that Dunn does not see that rhetoric is one of the keys to analyzing how the tradition was handled, shaped, and handed on, early and late. Nevertheless, he is right that these traditions are not traditions freely composed or, for that matter, traditions seen as inviolable and frozen into a sort of textual rigor mortis either.[24] The actual differences in the parallel accounts must be given their due and not be glossed over. The question is, How are the differences most adequately explained?

---

[23] See B. Witherington III, *The Gospel of Mark* (Grand Rapids: Eerdmans, 2001).

[24] Dunn, *Jesus Remembered*, 223, 238.

What Dunn wants to insist on in the end is the corporate or group formation of the tradition through repeated tellings rather than the theory of mainly key apostolic individuals shaping the tradition. Striving for some balance, he puts it this way after a long lobbying for the communal and oral nature of the tradition:

> Nor should we forget the continuing role of eyewitness tradents, of those recognized from the first as apostles or otherwise authoritative bearers of the Jesus tradition. . . . Such indications as there are from the pre-Pauline and early Pauline period suggest already fairly extensive outreach by such figures, both establishing and linking new churches, and a general concern to ensure that a foundation of authoritative tradition was well laid in each case. In focusing particular attention on the communal character of the early traditioning process we should not discount the more traditional emphasis on the individual figure of authority respected for his or her own association with Jesus during the days of his mission.[25]

And now we get to the real heart of the matter. Dunn thinks there is a need for a considerably long bridge between Jesus and the Gospel writers, and his theory of a rather lengthy oral stage in the process is the bridge he provides between A and B. This is why he rejects Byrskog's theory about oral history. That theory makes the eyewitnesses not some kind of supplement to the communal shaping of the tradition over considerable time but rather makes them much more central in positing a theory of how we get from Jesus to Gospels.[26]

In actuality, Dunn is looking for a middle way, a via media, between the theory of memorization and close contact of the Gospel writers with eyewitnesses on the one hand and free-flowing, freely amplified tradition in a literary mode based on little shards of historical information going back ultimately to Jesus on the other.[27] He is to be commended for this, but one must ask if in fact the evidence we have, not only from Papias, but also from Luke's preface in Luke 1:1–4 and from what Paul tells us about traditions handed down to him,

---

[25] Ibid., 243.
[26] Ibid., 244.
[27] Ibid., 249.

apparently by eyewitnesses, needs to be given a bit more credence and careful attention. One must ask whether Byrskog actually has the better of the argument on this point. At this juncture, we will take time to interact first with Byrskog and then with Bauckham and his use of Byrskog and see what further light this sheds on Dunn's approach.

Jesus, the Eyewitnesses, and Oral History: Byrskog's Model

It is to the credit of Byrskog that, despite the neglect in recent orality studies by Werner Kelber and others of the theory of oral history that is grounded in the actual examination of oral testimony and oral informants in antiquity, he has continued to pursue the matter. And it has borne good fruit in the recent masterful study of Bauckham. As Byrskog points out, the alleged polarity between orality and written texts, overplayed repeatedly by Kelber and his disciples, has skewed the discussion of the Gospel traditions in various ways and even led to a romanticizing of orality and oral performance as opposed to "textual rigor mortis."[28] The basis of Byrskog's study is the examination of the actual practices and also what is said by ancient historians ranging from Herodotus to Luke about the handling of eyewitness testimony. To his credit, Byrskog is aware of the way rhetoric and ancient philosophy affected these matters, and so he also takes into account what is to be learned from rhetoricians and philosophers about eyewitness testimony and oral history.

Byrskog focuses on the historians because they were the ones who systematically and consistently tried to search out the past.[29] "They are the prime representatives of ancient people who related in a more or less conscious way to past events. Their writings are most clearly reflective of the dynamics of story and history, present and past, in the socio-cultural setting of the gospel tradition."[30] Byrskog goes to some lengths to make clear that orality and writing should not be set over against one another, as if the latter was seen as a dead medium

---

[28] See S. Byrskog, *Story as History—History as Story* (Leiden: Brill, 2002), 33ff.
[29] Ibid., 45.
[30] Ibid.

and the former as a living, in some sort of dramatic contrast. It is true that there was a preference for the living voice over the written record in many contexts, but the texts we have in the NT are by and large "oral texts" that not merely come out of an oral environment but are meant to be read out loud and heard, even in various cases meant to be performed in a rhetorically effective manner. When texts are but surrogates for or transcripts of oral speech, there can be no hard and fast division between the oral and the written or a pitting of one as opposed to the other.

Byrskog is right on target in saying that in a culture of about 10 to 15 percent literacy, what is remarkable about the NT documents is the level of literacy, knowledge, and rhetorical skill reflected in them. He puts it this way:

> The majority of the authors of the New Testament, as we realize today, were highly literate, and not, it seems, all that reluctant to employ rather refined forms of the written medium as a means of communication. Not only the rich "bibliographical substructure" but also the advanced literary level of the New Testament contradict, on the face of it, our insistence that in antiquity writing was after all inferior to the oral medium.[31]

For our purposes, what the NT exclaims to us by its very features is that early Christianity was led to a large extent by a socially more elite group of persons than we are sometimes led to think, persons who not only could read and write but also who could write sophisticated biographies or historical monographs, sermons, or letters in ways that would be effective in a culture that was awash with rhetoric, both in the form of avid producers and consumers of rhetoric.

In his criticism of the old form critics and their views of orality and aurality, Byrskog makes some telling points: First, the critics assumed that it did not matter who passed on or who received the oral tradition "because the individuality of each informer and listener was entirely swallowed up by the collective identity and the common hearing of the larger community. The challenge of oral history to take

---

[31] Ibid., 109.

seriously the uniqueness as well as the representativeness of each narration is nowhere to be found in Bultmann's approach."[32] What is ironic about Dunn's study is that although he is very critical of the old form critical approach, he still ends up with a more collectivistic view of the formation and passing on of the oral tradition, and he stresses the oral dimension to the neglect of the eyewitness dimension of things. Second, yet there is an emphasis in the ancient tradition on actual seeing and being in contact with those who have seen the events and the oral performances of Jesus. In other words, the neglect of the "autopsy" factor is everywhere apparent not only in the old form critical approach but also in Dunn's work. "Discipleship was always the matrix of a double activity; it was a way of learning that included hearing as well as seeing."[33]

When we hear in the Gospel of John that "the man who saw it has given testimony and we know his testimony is true" (John 19:35), the connection between eyewitness and oral testimony becomes clear and is seen as very important even in the latest canonical Gospel to be produced. Or again, in the preface to 1 John when we read, "That which was from the beginning which he heard, which we have seen with our eyes, which we have looked at and our hands have touched" (1 John 1:1), we are not encouraged to think of a process of the passing on of tradition that was both strictly oral and anonymous. As Luke says, the tradition was handed down by "those who were from the first eyewitnesses and servants of the word" (Luke 1:2). We neglect these deliberate assertions about eyewitnesses to our peril if we want to understand the bridge between Jesus and the Gospels.

What we find in Byrskog, which is missing in Dunn, is a serious discussion of the eyewitnesses of Jesus' ministry. Byrskog puts it this way: "The historical Jesus event was experienced through their [i.e., the earliest disciples] eyes and their ears and soon became historic by entering into the present, oral currencies of observers such as Peter, the women, James, and Mary; it became their own oral history which they proclaimed to others. One needed their eyes as well as their ears."[34] This

---

[32] Ibid., 102–3.
[33] Ibid., 105.
[34] Ibid., 106.

is because, of course, that what Jesus did included what he said. Speaking was an action not divided from other deeds in the memory of the eyewitnesses. The narratives or stories told included words and deeds from the first, which should not be radically separated, as if we can only get back to the historical Jesus by treating him as a talking head.

Oral history is the testimony of eyewitnesses in the first place, and this is the bridge between past and present that is being actually mentioned in the NT itself, not an anonymous passing on of oral traditions in general through however many generations and voices. When the material is written down, it is written down for oral performance, what Byrskog calls reoralization, such that the Gospels are oral texts that are grounded in the testimony of eyewitnesses, not merely later ear-witnesses of the story. The ancient model was history and story in constant interaction, such that the story was corrected by the history and by the eyewitnesses, the retelling normed by those who were the original eyewitnesses and the faithful servants of the Word who heard them.

Byrskog stresses that we must not view the memory of ancient witnesses as a sort of fuzzy and entirely fluid collection of reminiscences. This is not only because memorization was an essential part of all education, especially the education of persons who learned to read and write—persons such as the Gospel writers themselves—but also because in oral cultures there were times, places, and rewards for recitation for what one had correctly stored in one's memory. The sophist Hipias tells us of how Plato was able to repeated 50 names after hearing them only once (*Hi. Maior* 285e), or Seneca tells us that as a youth not only could he repeat 2,000 names read to him but he also could recite back in reverse order 200 verses of some text read to him (*Contr.* 1, Vs. 2). Even allowing for rhetorical exaggeration here, you get the picture clearly that oral memory was cultivated and praised and prized in antiquity. What of course helped this process was the use of mnemonic and rhetorical devices to make things lodge in one's memory.

"The oral history approach takes very seriously the fact that accurate memory depends on social interest and need. A person involved remembers better than a disinterested observer."[35] This is not to say

---

[35] Ibid., 167.

that eyewitnesses did not have their biases and points of view. Of course they did. Yet ancient historians and biographers rightly preferred the testimonies of those actually and actively involved in the events for the very good reason that they were fully engaged mentally in what was happening and were more likely to remember substantial details of what was said and done, though undoubtedly their reports had to be carefully and critically sifted.

Notice again that Luke says that he observed and carefully investigated things over a period of time before he sat down to write out an orderly account for Theophilus (Luke 1:1–4). In this, he is not acting any differently from other ancient historians who placed a premium on eyewitness testimony. Ancient historians were wiser than many modern ones in understanding that "the historical reliability of an eyewitness has little or nothing to do with passive transmission or detachment from the event. Engaged interpretation is part of the process from the very beginning; to see is to interpret with one's own frame of mind; the present is always a part of the past; and this is an asset not a drawback, even insofar as we are concerned with historical reliability."[36] Byrskog then has presented a cogent and plausible case for seeing oral history and the way oral history was dealt with by the ancients as the proper model for viewing both the orality and literacy that lead to the Gospels we have. At this juncture, we need to turn to the application of the model by Bauckham in his recent book *Jesus and the Eyewitnesses*.

Bauckham and the Gospel Tradition

I was given the privilege of reading the proofs of *Jesus and the Eyewitnesses* while staying with the author in St. Andrews in the summer of 2006, and I realized at once that this was a landmark study, just as *Jesus Remembered* is. Bauckham stresses from the outset that the model for evaluating the Gospels properly is the model of testimony. They are the sort of historiography that the term testimony best describes.[37] Bauckham maintains, "Testimony offers us, I wish to suggest, both a

---

[36] Ibid., 175.
[37] R. Bauckham, *Jesus and the Eyewitnesses: The Gospels as Eyewitness Testimony* (Grand Rapids: Eerdmans, 2006), 5.

reputable historiographic category for reading the Gospels as history, and also a theological model for understanding the Gospels as the entirely appropriate means of access to the historical reality of Jesus."[38] What Bauckham is arguing, and I would also stress, is that the Gospels are not the result of a long process of anonymous oral transmission of traditions that went through umpteen permutations and combinations. To the contrary, the Gospels were all written while there was still living memory of eyewitnesses to be consulted about the events. Furthermore, those eyewitnesses did not suddenly retire to a nice beachside condo and never speak about the matter after they first told the tales. For "at least a generation they moved among the young Palestinian communities, and through preaching and fellowship their recollections were at the disposal of those who sought information."[39]

Thus Bauckham stresses that "the period between the 'historical' Jesus and the Gospels was actually spanned, not by anonymous community transmission, but by the continuing presence and testimony of the eyewitnesses, who remained the authoritative sources of their traditions until their deaths."[40] This does not mean of course that many others did not tell these tales in worship and fellowship meetings. What it does mean is that the ones on whom the Gospel writers relied for their information were the eyewitness, not later tradents. What prompted the writing of the Gospels was precisely that the eyewitnesses were dying out and that their testimonies needed to be preserved, in this case, in writing. The method that the Gospel writers used when it came to collecting and editing their source material was to seek out the eyewitnesses and those who were in contact with the eyewitnesses and listen closely to their testimonies. Oral testimony from such persons was much preferred over anonymous written records. These ancient writers heard and responded to the cry "*ad fonts*," which was the preferred and indeed normal modus operandi of ancient historians and biographers of the age.

---

[38] Ibid., 5.

[39] This is actually part of a memorable quote from V. Taylor, *The Formation of the Gospel Tradition* (London: Macmillan, 1935), 42.

[40] Bauckham, *Jesus and the Eyewitnesses*, 8.

Bauckham is well aware of some of the criticisms leveled against the work of Byrskog, and sees it as his task to answer them or fill in the gaps where Byrskog did not adequately deal with possible objections. In order to do so, Bauckham turns to the report of that early second-century bishop, Papias of Hierapolis, and what he says about the origins of the Gospel tradition. Besides the internal data of the Gospels themselves, this account, coming from the early second century from someone who was actually in touch with at least one eyewitness and another person or two who seems to have known some eyewitnesses, is extremely valuable indeed, and unfortunately Dunn is only one of the most recent in a long line of scholars who neglects to interact seriously and in detail with the Papias traditions. Bauckham makes up for such an oversight in the balance of his study that goes on for some 500 more pages. Here I can only give a précis of some of the crucial highlights.

Bauckham points out that we should not simply derive from Papias the preference for the living voice over the written book, for what Papias is mainly saying in Eusebius's account in *Hist. eccl.* 3.39.3–4 is that he wanted to hear from the eyewitnesses or those who were in contact with them.[41] As Bauckham stresses, this passage calls Aristion and John the Elder disciples of the Lord, which is to say that they are eyewitnesses of Jesus. Papias apparently claims to have had personal conversation with them, which means probably no later than in the AD 80s.[42] The text may, however, mean he had personally met those who had had personal contact with these two men. Papias also seems to have been in direct contact with the prophesying daughters of Philip mentioned in Acts 21:9 (*Hist. eccl.* 3.39.9). In any case, this testimony must be put alongside what Luke 1:1–4 says both of which seem to be commenting on a period in the 80s when eyewitnesses were still alive and could be consulted, during the time when all the Synoptic Gospels seem to have been written.

What is important about this portion of Papias's testimony, as Bauckham stresses, is that Papias is speaking about oral testimony that is connected to specifically named eyewitnesses, not an anonymous community. Furthermore, what Papias means when he refers to his

---

[41] Ibid., 15–16.
[42] Ibid., 19.

preference for "the living voice" is not merely a preference for oral over written but, as he says, for the "living *and surviving voice*." He is referring to "the voice of an informant—someone who has personal memories of the words and deeds of Jesus and who is still alive." The "saying about the superiority of the 'living voice' to books refers not to oral tradition as superior to books, but to direct experience of an instructor, informant, or orator as superior to written sources."[43] Bauckham profitably compares this to 1 Cor 15:6, where Paul refers to numerous witnesses of the risen Lord "who are still alive, though some have died."[44] The point is simple: whether we begin with Paul, Luke, the Fourth Gospel, or finally Papias, all these writers are concerned with being in touch with not merely the oral tradition but with the autopsy of eyewitnesses. The distinction between oral history and oral tradition becomes clear—the former necessarily involves the testimony of eyewitnesses that the latter does not. Oral tradition may have passed from mouth to ear many times and is typically collective and anonymous. Oral history is not. Papias had no interest in simply reflecting on the collective memory of early Christian communities. He wanted to hear preferably directly from the eyewitnesses, and in failing to do so, he relied on those who had heard the eyewitnesses.

In an article that appeared after Dunn's *Jesus Remembered*, Dunn quite specifically and more directly critiques Byrskog. Here his tone is more strident:

> I simply do not believe that Peter, Mary of Magdala and the like stored up many memories of Jesus' mission, which were only jerked into remembrance by "oral history" inquiries of a Luke or a Matthew. They had already fed those memories into the living tradition of the churches, as major contributory elements in the forming and shaping of that tradition. No doubt other memories were brought to the surface by inquiries of a Luke or a Matthew, but these would be supplementary to what was already known and performed in the various assemblies week by week. I guess the same was true of Papias and Irenaeus.[45]

---

[43] Ibid., 27.
[44] Ibid., 28.
[45] J. D. G. Dunn, "On History, Memory and Eyewitnesses: In Response to Bengt Holmberg and Samuel Byrskog," *JSNT* 26 (2004): 483–84.

As Bauckham laments, Dunn simply assumes here that the Gospels are the product of community tradition, but this is not at all that Luke says in Luke 1:2 about his modus operandi and who he consulted. Bauckham further complains, rightly, that it was not a case of prying information out of eyewitnesses who heretofore had remained silent. Of course, they had shared, probably many times, their testimonies, and of course, those testimonies had become common coin in various communities. This is not the point. The issue is, *who did the Gospel writers consult when they wrote their Gospels?* Luke tells us he consulted eyewitnesses, and he implies he knows previous attempts to write an account of the Gospel events. Similarly, Paul tells us in Galatians 1 that he went up to Jerusalem to learn the *historia* from Peter, James, and John, and we may be sure that they did not spend two weeks discussing the weather on Zion's heights. Thus, when he tells us that he passed on what he had received in 1 Corinthians 11 or 15, we should take this to mean he got it from the horse's mouth. He consulted the eyewitnesses when he was able to do so. We should also take seriously what was said in Acts 1 about the criteria for who could become the replacement for Judas among the Twelve, namely, someone who had been a participant in the ministry of Jesus from the baptism of John onward. Why this criteria? Because they wanted eyewitnesses of as much of the story as possible if the Twelve were to continue to be the agents for and representatives of Jesus in Israel.

What about the Gospel of Mark? After pointing out the interesting *inclusio* in Mark 1 and 16, where Peter is the first-named disciple of Jesus, and then hearing in Mark 16:7 that the women must go tell the disciples and Peter that Jesus is going before them into Galilee, and after noting that Mark's Gospel has the highest frequency of mentions of Peter of any canonical Gospel (Matthew included), Bauckham turns once more to the tradition of Papias about the composition of Mark's Gospel, our earliest and, in some ways, most important Gospel for the purposes of this discussion.[46] I will say here that the explanation as to why Luke or the First Evangelist would have used Mark so extensively, especially when it was known that Mark

---

46 Bauckham, *Jesus and the Eyewitnesses*, 125.

was not an eyewitness and Luke professes to consult such people, will become less of a mystery in a moment. In short, it is because it is the testimony of Peter.

Here is the crucial passage from Papias, as translated, helpfully clarified, and amplified by Bauckham:

> The Elder used to say: Mark, in his capacity as Peter's *hermēneutēs*, wrote down accurately as many things as he [Peter?] recalled from memory—though not in an order form—of the things either said or done by the Lord. For he [Mark] never heard the Lord nor accompanied him but later, as I said, [he heard and accompanied] Peter, who used to give his teachings in the form of *chreiai* but had no intention of providing an orderly arrangement of the *logia* of the Lord. Consequently Mark did nothing wrong when he wrote down some individual items just as he [Peter?] related them from memory. For he made it his one concern not to omit anything or falsify anything (Eusebius, *Hist. eccl.* 3.39.14–16).

This passage, whose historical significance is too often dismissed or ignored, Bauckham elaborates at length. Here are some of the key points. Although *hermēneutēs* could certainly mean interpreter here, it can also mean translator. As Bauckham says, what Papias goes on to add suggests that he means translator by the use of this term. Mark's job was to omit nothing and add nothing, so as to avoid falsifying Peter's eyewitness testimony. Thus Mark does not even assume the authority to arrange the material in a best order; he simply reproduces exactly what he heard from Peter just as he recalled it. In other words, this is not about Mark being Peter's interpreter when the oral word was shared by Peter. This is a reference to how the Gospel of Mark came to be composed as it was. And it may also explain why Luke stresses that he (unlike his Markan source) will indeed offer up a rhetorically and historically effective ordering of the material.

This brings us to a third important point. At various junctures in Mark, we have brief quotations of Aramaic from Jesus that are then rendered telegraphically into Greek. This, of course, presupposes that Mark's audience does not know Aramaic, but it shows that the evangelist is bilingual, at a minimum (he may know some Latin as well). Maurice Casey has shown at great length that a considerable portion of our earliest Gospel is quite readily retrojected back into Aramaic.[47] He suggests that some of the awkwardness we find in Mark's Greek is due to translation issues, which is more than just the issue of Semitic interference (a person thinking first in a Semitic language and then attempting to compose in Greek but often still carrying over the structures or earmarks of the primary language).

This brings us to an important point. Casey's insights favor the suggestion of Bauckham that Mark translated Peter's Aramaic recollections into his Gospel. Peter spoke in Aramaic and perhaps some wooden Greek, remembering various things Jesus did and said, and Mark wrote it down in better Greek. As Bauckham stresses, the second verb for memory in the passage from Papias means "relate or record from memory." But this verb is much more naturally applied to Peter, whose testimony Papias is, after all, interested in than to Mark. Thus we see Mark as the scribe for Peter, taking down what Peter recalled and then related from memory. And as Bauckham goes on to stress, this very language is the language used in Greek of *Memoirs* by Xenephon and, more importantly, by Justin Martyr to refer to the Gospels as the "memoirs of the Apostles" (1 *Apol.* 66.3; 67.3; *Dial.* 107–17).[48]

Bauckham goes on to stress that the translation of *chreia* here as "according to needs," which Dunn favors, has largely been abandoned by Markan scholars and rightly so.[49] As a rhetorical term, it makes very good sense in terms of what we find in our earliest Gospel—short narratives contain actions and sayings, or actions or sayings often climaxing with a pithy memorable remark. The English word anecdote is perhaps the closest parallel. *Chreia* was a form of rhetorical composition found at every level of education and was used to teach reading and writing. To say that Peter related and Mark composed these tales in the form of *chreia* is not to claim a sophisticated knowledge of rhetoric like the one we find in Paul or the author of Hebrews, only an elementary knowledge of it.

---

[47] M. Casey, *Aramaic Sources of Mark's Gospel* (Cambridge: Cambridge University Press, 2007).

[48] Bauckham, *Jesus and the Eyewitnesses*, 211–12.

[49] See the discussion in Witherington, *Gospel of Mark*, 9–36.

But if indeed this Gospel was written for an audience in Rome, such a form of composition would have been not merely helpful but almost required, for Rome was rhetoric central in the mid-first century AD and no persuasion was likely to happen particularly of any educated persons without the use of it. What the use of *chreia* implies is the evangelistic intentions of Peter, Mark, or both. They wanted the relaying of the Jesus tradition to convince people about "the Good News of Jesus the Christ, the Son of God." There is much more in Bauckham's rich treatment of Byrskog's theory and his amplification and justification of the approach of oral history to the formation of the Gospel tradition, but this must suffice for now; he seems to have shored up all the gaps and weaknesses in Byrskog's presentation and made a compelling case for this sort of approach to our canonical Gospels. It is now time for us to draw this discussion to a close and assess what all of this means for evaluating Dunn's *Jesus Remembered*.

And So?

What are the implications of the previous discussion for this study on Dunn's work? The actual historical evidence both in the Gospels and elsewhere in the NT, and in the testimony of Papias, strongly "suggest" that the proper model for evaluating the Gospel traditions is the model of oral history, not the model proposed by Dunn of informally controlled oral tradition that percolated for a long time in communities and was subject to anonymous collective control from one Christian community to another. This does not mean Dunn is wrong and I am right. He may well be right. But he must demonstrate why the case laid out in full by Bauckham is in error at crucial junctures. This he has not yet done, and so his work is not done.

In the crucial sections of Dunn's work in which he deals with sources and traditions, one could have wished for a much more detailed justification for the view that the Gospel traditions, especially when there are notable differences in the parallels, support the view of considerable flexibility in the oral tradition, only an informal control at most, rather than supporting the view of editing and amplification by the Gospel writers themselves. The flexibility itself speaks against the view of a more formal control as envisioned by Byrskog's mentor, Gerhardsson. Dunn is right that the evidence for some sort of strict, formal control like later Mishnaic practice is lacking in the actual data we have in the Gospels themselves when closely examined.

It is the great merit of Dunn's methodological discussion that he shows the fatal weaknesses in the old form critical approaches to the Gospel data, which were not based on well-known ancient analogies as to how oral tradition was handled. As we have seen in this chapter, however, I am doubtful that the modern materials produced and drawn on by Bailey are much more helpful in allowing us to deal with this material. But the detailed work of Byrskog and Bauckham on ancient historians, rhetoricians, and biographers helps remedy this problem with the proper sort of ancient Greek analogies.

But here is the irony in all of this discussion. The parallel accounts in the Synoptics say what they say, whatever our theories about the origins and transmission of these traditions. Any theory of origins and transmission must make sense of and allow for the actual differences we find there. As Dunn stresses, they cannot be ignored, they cannot be finessed, they cannot be dismissed, and they must be dealt with. Even if one was only sure that Matthew used quite a lot of Mark and that Luke used some of it and we claim nothing else, it is quite clear that there was some flexibility in the handling of even the sayings of Jesus, though they were more conservatively passed on than some of the narrative material, it would appear.

It appears to me that while this flexibility may, in a minority of incidences, reflect a flexibility at the oral stage of things, the repeated patterns of Matthew's and Luke's uses of Mark (and perhaps of Q) suggest that most of the differences we find are purposeful and important and are the result of the evangelists' handling of the material themselves. Indeed, most of them can be explained in terms of the evangelists' following either their own agendas and interests or following the guidance of the rhetorical rules of how to make a narrative an effective act of persuasion and keep the audience interested, even when one is sometimes repeating material.

Let me stress once more, the evidence both internal in and external about the Gospels suggests to me that the theory of oral history—rather than somewhat flexible, informally controlled oral transmission—better explains what we find in the canonical Gospels. We have here in these Gospels "Jesus remembered" not just by "anyone" or "everyman," but rather by those who knew him best, those who were eyewitnesses or in touch with the eyewitnesses and original heralds of the Word.[50] The communities did not create these traditions; the eyewitnesses did.

What the communities did do was validate the tradition's veracity and use their contents mightily to lead many to become followers of Jesus. The final words of the Fourth Gospel encapsulate very well the role of both community and eyewitnesses. The community said, pointing beyond itself, "This is the disciple who testifies to these things and has written them down. We know his testimony is true" (John 21:25). Herein lies the roles of both laid bare and they explain why, as Dunn so rightly stresses, the historical Jesus is indeed the Jesus of the Gospels, the Jesus lodged in the minds and hearts of his earliest disciples and eyewitnesses and enshrined in our canonical Gospels.

---

[50] See at length B. Witherington III, *What Have They Done with Jesus?* (San Francisco: Harper, 2006).

11

REMEMBERING JESUS' SELF-UNDERSTANDING

JAMES D. G. DUNN ON JESUS' SENSE OF ROLE AND IDENTITY

PAUL RHODES EDDY

With the 2003 publication of his *Jesus Remembered*, James D. G. Dunn has joined the ranks of the likes of John Dominic Crossan, John Meier, E. P. Sanders, and N. T. Wright—the ranks of those contemporary New Testament (NT) scholars whose work on the historical Jesus all future studies will have to reckon with if they wish to be taken seriously.[1] The purpose of this chapter is to reflect on Dunn's conclusions to the question, How did Jesus see his own role? or, more simply, Who did Jesus think he was? What was Jesus' essential self-understanding?[2]

---

[1] J. D. G. Dunn, *Jesus Remembered* (vol. 1 of *Christianity in the Making*; Grand Rapids: Eerdmans, 2003). For further clarity on Dunn's distinct methodological approach, see his *A New Perspective on Jesus: What the Quest for the Historical Jesus Missed* (Grand Rapids: Baker Academic, 2005); and his "Remembering Jesus: How the Quest of the Historical Jesus Lost Its Way," in *The Historical Jesus: Five Views* (ed. J. Beilby and P. R. Eddy; Downers Grove: InterVarsity, 2009), 199–225.

[2] By "self-understanding," I do not mean to suggest that we are embarking on anything like psychoanalysis or mind reading with respect to Jesus. Historiographically speaking, the self-understanding of Jesus is accessible to the degree that there is enough evidence to answer the question, "What beliefs about himself would Jesus have held in order to most plausibly

For reasons that will become clear in this chapter, I will focus most of my time on Dunn's assessment of the controversial question of Jesus' messianic self-consciousness.

Dunn's Assessment of Jesus' Self-Understanding

Dunn's consideration of Jesus' self-understanding is laid out in chapters 15 and 16 of *Jesus Remembered*. Given his methodological conviction that the only Jesus we have access to is the "remembered Jesus"—that is, the impact of Jesus left on the memories of his earliest disciples[3]— one might suspect that Dunn would stop short of asking the question of Jesus' own self-understanding. But such is not the case. Dunn explicitly addresses this question: "My own emphasis on the impact made by Jesus also does not necessarily close off the road to Jesus' self-understanding. For the clearer the impression made, the clearer the object making the impression."[4] Still, Dunn is most comfortable beginning with the prior question, a question he explores in chapter 15: "Who did *others* think Jesus was?"[5] As he notes, the question is quite appropriate in that it is posed numerous times within the Jesus tradition itself (e.g., Mark 1:27; Luke 4:36; Mark 6:2–3 pars.; Mark 6:14–16 pars.; 8:27–28 pars.; Mark 14:61 pars.; John 7:40–52; John 9:16–17,29–30; 10:19–21). In chapter 16, Dunn finally turns to the thornier question of Jesus' self-understanding.

---

explain what he said and did?" On this matter, see N. T. Wright, "Jesus' Self-Understanding," in *The Incarnation: An Interdisciplinary Symposium on the Incarnation of the Son of God* (ed. S. Davis, D. Kendall, and G. O'Collins; New York: Oxford University Press, 2002), 53.

[3] Dunn, *Jesus Remembered*, 130–31; see also idem, *A New Perspective on Jesus*, chap. 1.

[4] Dunn, *Jesus Remembered*, 616. Dunn's caveat aside, it is not clear that a simple appeal to the metaphor of an object leaving a clear "impression" in some moldable material answers the question of how Dunn's modest critical realism along with his corollary of the "remembered Jesus" as the only available object of historical pursuit can—on methodological grounds—lead one to anything like confident conclusions about Jesus' self-understanding. In a recent interchange, Samuel Byrskog has pressed this question ("A New Perspective on the Jesus Tradition: Reflections on James D. G. Dunn's *Jesus Remembered*," *JSNT* 26 [2004]: 461–63) and Dunn has responded to him ("On History, Memory and Eyewitnesses: In Response to Bengt Holmberg and Samuel Byrskog," *JSNT* 26 [2004]: 480). In this piece, Dunn admits that his attempt to "inquire into Jesus' own intention . . . seems to be at odds with my insistence that we cannot get back to Jesus himself, only the remembered Jesus." His response does little more than restate what he has already said in *Jesus Remembered*.

[5] Dunn, *Jesus Remembered*, 616.

In the end, Dunn concludes that Jesus was quite comfortable identifying with several of the roles that are attributed to him within the Jesus tradition. The following is a summary of his conclusions:

1. *Prophet.* With respect to the category of "prophet," Dunn notes that others clearly regarded Jesus as a prophet. What of Jesus himself? Although he sees the evidence as "patchy," he concludes that it is most likely the case that Jesus saw himself as a prophet. Although "there is no suggestion that Jesus saw himself as 'the prophet,'"[6] it seems that the "programmatic prophecy" of Isa 61:1–3 was paradigmatic for his own sense of mission, that he evidenced a sense of prophetic commissioning, and that he was remembered for engaging in various prophetic actions (e.g., choosing the Twelve, eating with sinners, healing and exorcistic activity, the final entry into Jerusalem, the Temple action, and the Last Supper), some of which suggest that Jesus saw his own ministry as in continuity with the classical prophetic tradition.[7] Finally, Dunn raises the question of whether Jesus saw himself as "more than a prophet." He concludes that there are "several hints that Jesus may have seen his mission in terms transcending the category of prophet"—more specifically, that Jesus recognized an "eschatological significance" for his mission, and thus for himself, that transcended the standard Jewish category of prophet.[8] This additional "eschatological significance" is expressed in rather vague terms by Dunn. This vagueness is, to some degree, I suspect, tied to Dunn's conclusion that Jesus' notion of "the kingdom of God"—that central, eschatological concept of his mission and teaching—is, in the end, an irreducible, evocative metaphor: a concept that, whereas having reference, had "no precision of 'meaning.'"[9]

2. *"Doer of Extraordinary Deeds": Jesus as healer and exorcist.* Dunn aligns himself with the majority of Jesus scholars today when he concludes that Jesus' reputation as a healer and exorcist is "one of the most widely attested and firmly established of the historical facts with which we have to deal."[10] It is within the context of his recognition of Jesus as healer and exorcist that Dunn explicitly

---

[6] Ibid., 661.

[7] Ibid., 657, 660–64.

[8] Ibid., 664, 666.

[9] Ibid., 487.

[10] Ibid., 670. Although Dunn prefers to avoid the "still problematic category of miracle," he decisively sides with those who conclude that Jesus was known as a "doer of extraordinary

rejects the application of the category of "magician" to Jesus.[11] In exploring the question of Jesus' self-understanding of his healings and exorcisms, Dunn once again resorts to the phrase "eschatological significance." He writes, "We are unlikely to appreciate Jesus' kingdom teaching and his mission as a whole unless we are willing to recognize that Jesus claimed (was remembered as claiming) a distinctive, and distinctly eschatological, empowering for his mission, as evidenced particularly in his healings and exorcisms."[12] In fleshing this out, Dunn writes, "Most striking is the fact that Jesus seems to have regarded his successful exorcisms as the defeat (or evidence of the defeat) of Satan, as the plundering of his Satan's [sic] possessions."[13] Dunn's observation of the distinctive interpretation that Jesus explicitly gave of his exorcisms is an important one, and one to which we shall return.

3. *Teacher*. Next, Dunn explores the category of "teacher" as it related to Jesus. He begins by noting both that " teacher" is the most common title given to Jesus in the tradition and that "in many ways this is the most obvious category for audience and onlookers to 'fit' Jesus into."[14] The tradition clearly reflects the memory of a teacher known both for his memorable style and content. Nevertheless, the impact of Jesus' teaching does not stop here: Jesus was also remembered for the "surprising authority" with which he taught, an authority that evoked mixed reactions, including both surprise and hostility.[15] Not surprisingly, this leads Dunn to raise the question, Did Jesus see himself as "something greater" than a teacher with a God-given authority?[16] For example, might Jesus have seen himself not merely as a "teacher of wisdom," but rather as "the eschatological spokesman for Wisdom, acting in God's stead?"[17]

---

deeds" (ibid., 667). Although at one point he claims that he has "little to add" to J. P. Meier's (*A Marginal Jew: Rethinking the Historical Jesus* [vol. 2 of *Mentor, Message, and Miracles*; New York: Doubleday, 1994]) in-depth analysis of Jesus' "extraordinary deeds" (Dunn, *Jesus Remembered*, 671), Dunn actually takes a more optimistic stance than Meier on the question of whether the nature miracles of Jesus have any basis in actual historical events (e.g., ibid., 688). Here, he appears closer to G. Twelftree (*Jesus the Miracle Worker: A Historical and Theological Study* [Downers Grove: InterVarsity, 1999], 317–22) than Meier.

[11] Dunn, *Jesus Remembered*, 689–94.

[12] Ibid., 696.

[13] Ibid., 696.

[14] Ibid., 696, 697.

[15] Ibid., 698.

[16] Ibid., 702.

[17] Ibid., 703.

Dunn is tentative in his conclusion:

> It may be that such a line of exposition pushes the data too
> hard. [It could be that] the voices of post-Easter reflection
> may well have begun to drown out the pre-Easter reminis-
> cences and the voice of Jesus himself. . . . [Nevertheless, we
> are left with the] tantalizing possibility that Jesus deliberately
> claimed a degree of distinctiveness for his mission, for all its
> thoroughly Jewish character, which left both hearers and dis-
> ciples struggling for words to express the significance of what
> they were seeing and hearing—and remembering.[18]

4. *God's eschatological agent.* In turning to chapter 16—and the focused
question of "How did Jesus see his own role?"—Dunn begins by
reiterating the likelihood that Jesus understood himself as prophet,
healer and exorcist, and teacher. He goes on to suggest two important senses in which Jesus' exemplification of these three categories find common ground. First, each of these roles was "not so
clearly or fully defined." Thus, Jesus was willing to embrace each of
these roles, since "they could be acknowledged by Jesus . . . without causing his mission to be misunderstood. . . . Their function
was subsidiary to his main kingdom objectives. And no single one
of them provided a complete or sufficient description of his mission"[19] Second, the tradition bears witness to the impression left
by Jesus that he understood his exemplification of each of these
threes roles—prophet, healer and exorcist, and teacher—as including what Dunn calls an "eschatological plus." Thus, Dunn begins
his explicit discussion of Jesus' self-understanding with the claim
that a central category by which Jesus understood his role within
God's kingdom is that of "eschatological agent." Dunn writes,

> The Jesus tradition strongly suggests that at the very least
> Jesus claimed for his mission an extraordinary significance, of
> eschatological fulfillment in the present and of final import
> for his hearers. At the very least we overhear in the words of
> the remembered Jesus a claim for the divine significance of his
> mission, as the (not just an) eschatological emissary of God.
> How much more can be said is less clear. In particular, how
> much the claim for the significance of his *mission* was also a
> claim for the significance of *himself* remains an open question.[20]

---

[18] Ibid., 704.
[19] Ibid., 706.
[20] Ibid., 707; emphasis in original.

5. *Son of God.* Dunn begins his consideration of whether Jesus thought of himself as "God's son" by noting that, within Jewish tradition, the title "Son of God" could have a variety of referents, including angelic beings/heavenly council, collective Israel, Israel's king, and the expected royal Messiah.[21] Generally speaking, the "common denominator" in each of these uses is that the phrase "Son of God" denotes "someone specially related to or favored by God."[22] In turning to the question of whether Jesus consciously identified himself as God's son, Dunn roots his response in an analysis of Jesus' Abba prayer. He argues that although the evidence is "not substantial," it is nonetheless "probably sufficient" to conclude that Jesus' Abba prayer was a distinctive feature of his prayer life and that it expressed Jesus' "profound sense of and confidence in his relationship with God as his father." Dunn goes on to further deduce that Jesus' sense of sonship was central to his own self-identity and that it served as "the source of the immediacy of authority with which he proclaimed the kingdom of God."[23]

6. *Son of Man.* Next, Dunn explores the "Son of Man" designation, with the perennial conundrums that surround it. In the end—after almost 40 pages of analysis—Dunn overcomes the long-standing debate of whether to understand the phrase as merely an idiomatic circumlocution for oneself or as an apocalyptically oriented reference to the "one like a Son of Man" who comes to the Ancient of Days in Daniel 7, by arguing for a both-and approach. He concludes (a) that Jesus did use the phrase "Son of Man" in Aramaic, (b) that he was remembered as using this phrase in "*a general and self-referential way*"—that is, as something parallel to the English phrase "a man like me"—a phrase whose humble self-designation could easily signal the frailty of humanity, and yet (c) that, at times, he used it as an allusion to the Danielic "Son of Man," an image that "may have encouraged him in hope of being welcomed by the Most High on the completion of his mission."[24]

Just as important to Dunn's vision of Jesus' self-understanding are several lines of argument concerning roles or titles that Jesus did *not* exemplify or embrace. Four such concepts deserve mention here:

---

[21] Ibid., 709.

[22] Ibid., 711.

[23] Ibid., 724.

[24] Ibid., 761. Along the way, Dunn does argue that, in its context, the "direction of travel" of the Danielic Son of Man clearly is that of a coming before the Most High in the heavenly realm—not a coming (i.e., return) of Jesus to earth (ibid., 757–58, 761).

1. *Cynic philosopher.* Dunn decisively rejects the image, recently popular in some post-Bultmannian circles, of Jesus as something akin to a Cynic philosopher. Once the thoroughly "Jewish" (i.e., Torah-true, etc.) nature of first-century Galilee and its Judaism is properly understood, anything like a plausible context for a Diogenes-like Jesus is called into question.[25]

2. *Magician.* In the course of addressing Jesus' "extraordinary deeds," Dunn considers the claim—one made famous by Morton Smith—that Jesus is best understood as an itinerant, first-century wonder-worker or "magician." Dunn notes that, even once the problematic of defining "magic" in the ancient world is set aside, the relative lack of ancient magical techniques in the Jesus tradition and the eschatological context in which his miraculous deeds are always understood naturally leads one to conclude that "Jesus did not 'come across' as a typical magician. Even Josephus, when he writes of Jesus' extraordinary deeds, does not resort to the polemical label of 'magician.'"[26]

3. *Political revolutionary.* Dunn also considers the claim, one made popular by such Jesus scholars as S. G. F. Brandon and Reimarus himself, that Jesus should be understood as a military-political revolutionary with aspirations of freeing Israel from Rome's iron grip and thus fully restoring the promised land to God's people. Dunn understandably dispatches with this view rather quickly. As he notes, this thesis "has won little scholarly support" over the years.[27] In terms of evidence, it runs headlong into one of the most fundamental messages of Jesus, namely, the centrality of agape (love) to his kingdom message. More specifically, as Dunn observes, "if Jesus did indeed teach that love of neighbor included love of enemies, as most agree, then that alone knocks a large hole in any thesis that Jesus sought a military solution."[28]

4. *Messiah.* We arrive, finally, at the last major concept that Dunn considers—and rejects—as part of Jesus' self-understanding. Dunn spends almost 40 pages considering whether Jesus understood himself to be the royal Messiah—the "Christ." He concludes that, even though during his own lifetime a variety of people were led to suspect he was the Davidic Messiah (i.e., Dunn rejects Wrede's

---

[25] Dunn's analysis of Jesus and his context serves to call into question the Cynic Jesus thesis at several points; see ibid., 61–62, 298–300; 593–99.

[26] Ibid., 693.

[27] Ibid., 623.

[28] Ibid., 623–24. On this question, see M. Hengel, *Victory Over Violence and Was Jesus a Revolutionist?* (trans. D. E. Green and W. Klassen; Eugene, Oreg.: Wipf & Stock, 2003).

"messianic secret" thesis, which claims that the declaration of Jesus as Messiah is purely a piece of post-Easter theological reflection), it seems most likely that *Jesus himself explicitly rejected the role*. Dunn concludes his deliberations on this matter thus:

> Did he claim to be the long-hoped-for David's royal son? In the light of our findings above, the answer must be a qualified No!
>
> The answer is No because Jesus is never once recalled as using the title Messiah of himself or as unequivocally welcoming its application to him by others (Mark 14:62 is the sole exception). The qualification is necessary, however, because there is a legitimate query as to whether the then current understanding of the royal Messiah's role was the only one possible from Israel's prophetic texts.[29]

Dunn acknowledges that an important piece of data is the fact that Jesus' earliest followers, in light of Good Friday, quickly and decisively applied the title "Messiah" to Jesus. In doing so, they "in effect emptied the title of its traditional content and filled it with new content provided by the law and the prophets and the psalms." Nevertheless, in Dunn's eyes, "that does not quite validate the corollary that Jesus believed and taught his role to be that of a suffering royal Messiah."[30]

Dunn concludes his assessment of Jesus' self-understanding by nothing that at a certain level, "our findings thus far are disappointing."[31] Specifically, he concludes that Jesus "made no attempt to lay claim to any title as such." In fact, according to Dunn,

> Jesus saw it as no part of his mission to make specific claims for his own status. . . . Allusion to his own role comes out more as a by-product of his proclamation of God's kingdom; his role was a role in relation to that, rather than an assertion of his own status as such. Evidently, it was his proclamation of the kingdom which was important; the identity of the proclaimer was a secondary matter.[32]

---

[29] Dunn, *Jesus Remembered*, 652–53.
[30] Ibid., 653.
[31] Ibid., 761.
[32] Ibid., 761–62.

And yet, Dunn sees the evidence as suggesting that Jesus did see himself as taking on the role of "eschatological spokesman for God." A role that includes "the conviction of being God's eschatological agent at the climax of God's purposes for Israel, his sense of intimate sonship before God and of the dependence of his disciples on him, and his probably strong hope for final acknowledgement as the man who was playing the decisive role in bringing the kingdom to fulfillment and consummation."[33] Dunn asks, "At a responsible historical level, can we say more?" His implicit answer is "No."

Reflections on Dunn's Assessment of Jesus' Self-Understanding

Much of Dunn's work on Jesus' self-understanding parallels solidly established findings in the field today. The idiosyncratic views of Jesus as most analogous to a Cynic philosopher or wandering magician are, as Dunn rightly concludes, best laid to rest once and for all.[34] Likewise, the claim that Jesus' mission ever included military-political aspirations is also best left in the category of "curious cul-de-sacs within the history of the Quest."

Dunn's claim that Jesus would have comfortably embraced the roles and titles of prophet, teacher, and healer and exorcist are, historically speaking, well founded and largely undebated by those within the mainstream of Jesus scholarship today.[35] Nevertheless, that many scholars

---

[33] Ibid., 762.

[34] For a survey and critique of the Cynic Jesus thesis, see my "Jesus as Diogenes? Reflections on the Cynic Jesus Thesis," *JBL* 115 (1996): 449–69.

[35] Those who find room for the rubric "prophet" in their assessment of Jesus include Marcus Borg, Maurice Casey, Bruce Chilton, Craig Evans, William Herzog, Morna Hooker, Richard Horsley, John Meier, E. P. Sanders, Gerd Theissen, N. T. Wright, and Adela Yarbro Collins. For two extensive investigations of Jesus as prophet, see Meier, *Marginal Jew*, 2:1043–47; N. T. Wright, *Jesus and the Victory of God* (vol. 2 of *Christian Origins and the Question of God*; Minneapolis: Fortress, 1996), part 2. (One point at which some will take issue with Dunn's reading of Jesus' prophetic self-consciousness is at the point where he denies any sign that Jesus saw himself as "the [eschatological] prophet"; see, for example, S. McKnight, "Jesus and Prophetic Action," *BBR* 10 [2000]: 197–232.) That Jesus enacted the role of a Jewish "teacher" among his followers is equally well represented in the field today—even R. Funk and the Jesus

today affirm each of these roles as part of Jesus' self-consciousness and yet go on to propose startlingly different portraits of Jesus raises an important issue. It is not simply the identification of the various roles that Jesus embraced that determine one's historical reconstruction of Jesus. It is the precise manner in which Jesus is understood as having fleshed out each role, as well as the manner in which each role is understood to have qualified and complexified the others within Jesus' mind, that largely shapes one's final conception of Jesus.

Thus it is as Dunn fleshes out the precise manner in which Jesus self-consciously embraced each of these roles that one might take issue at certain points. For example, Dunn claims that teacher is "the least overtly messianic and eschatological of the categories" under consideration.[36] And, considered abstractly and in isolation, no doubt it is. Nevertheless, this claim might be qualified if one considers the manner in which Jesus acted as a teacher within the context of his equal embrace of the role of prophet, particularly if one thinks his prophetic consciousness included an "eschatological" dimension (which Dunn does) and if one goes on to nuance the category of prophet by identifying Jesus as an example (though not exclusively so) of a "popular" prophet—that is, a prophetic figure that is a movement builder or leader.[37] Once Jesus is understood as acting as a popular prophet-teacher of a fledgling movement with a distinctively eschatological orientation, and I would argue that he was,[38] then the fact that he was also consistently remembered as a teacher whose words were both centered on the *kingdom* of God and known for their unusual *authority*

Seminar (*The Acts of Jesus: The Search for the Authentic Deeds of Jesus* [San Francisco: HarperSanFrancisco, 1998], 566) voted "red" on the statement, "Jesus was an itinerant teacher in Galilee." See also Meier, *Marginal Jew*, vol. 2, part 2; W. Herzog, *Prophet and Teacher: An Introduction to the Historical Jesus* (Louisville: Westminster John Knox, 2005). Finally, from evangelical circles to the Jesus Seminar, it is widely recognized that Jesus functioned as a healer-exorcist. See, for example, G. H. Twelftree, *Jesus the Exorcist: A Contribution to the Study of the Historical Jesus* (Tübingen: Mohr Siebeck, 1993); Funk and Jesus Seminar, *Acts of Jesus*, 566.

[36] Dunn, *Jesus Remembered*, 696.

[37] On the important categories of "oracular" and "popular" prophet types, see R. L. Webb, *John the Baptizer and Prophet: A Socio-Historical Study* (Sheffield: Sheffield Academic Press, 1991).

[38] See P. R. Eddy, "The (W)right Jesus: Eschatological Prophet, Israel's Messiah, Yahweh Embodied," in C. C. Newman, ed., *Jesus and the Restoration of Israel: A Critical Assessment of N. T. Wright's 'Jesus and the Victory of God'* (Downers Grove: InterVarsity, 1999), 43.

strongly suggests an eschatological—even a "messianic"—significance for his teaching activity. Likewise, Dunn's conclusion that Jesus' distinctive self-understanding of his exorcistic activity was bound up with the defeat of the cosmic enemy, Satan, has, I believe, important ramifications for our understanding of other aspects of Jesus' self-consciousness—particularly the vexed question of whether Jesus considered himself to be the Messiah (a point we shall return to shortly).

Several of Dunn's conclusions will elicit discussion and debate at a more fundamental level. At times, Dunn's arguments lead to conclusions that place him as something of a third quotient between more standard minimalist views, on one hand, and commonly argued conservative views, on the other. Some will herald his moves here as signaling a properly balanced via media. Others, however, may suspect that, with regard to certain controversies, Dunn offers little more than the cramped quarters of an imaginary no-man's-land. When it comes to his assessment of Jesus' sense of being God's son, those of a more minimalist bent will wonder whether Dunn has not retrojected a good amount of post-Easter reflection onto the earthly Jesus, whereas those toward the other end of the spectrum may ask whether he has given Jesus' sense of divine sonship—and the attendant implications—their full due. Similarly, his "both-and" conclusion on the perennial "Son of Man" debate will leave those who have embraced Vermes's analysis concerned about his (from their perspective) inappropriate and undue weight given to the Danielic image, whereas those who strongly gravitate to Daniel 7 as the primary key to this moniker may well see Dunn's appreciation of it as a clear example of underappreciation.[39]

Nevertheless, it may be that Dunn's discussion and conclusions surrounding the question of Jesus' messianic self-consciousness will engender even more debate.[40] For, on one hand, Dunn concludes

---

[39] For a helpful review of the history of the "Son of Man" debate, see D. Burkett, *The Son of Man Debate: A History and Evaluation* (New York: Cambridge University Press, 1999).

[40] Several reviews of Dunn's book have highlighted this question. See, for example, L. W. Hurtado, review of J. D. G. Dunn, *Jesus Remembered*, *ThTo* 62 (2006): 104; D. McCartney, review of J. D. G. Dunn, *Jesus Remembered*, *WTJ* 67 (2005): 432; D. Wenham, review of J. D. G. Dunn, *Jesus Remembered*, *EvQ* 77 (2005): 174. For a number of scholars, another area of question will involve Dunn's complete elimination from the self-consciousness of Jesus any sense of a more personal identification with Yahweh. No doubt, for Dunn, this is linked with his views on the relatively late rise of a high Christology in the early church. In his earlier

that Jesus most likely rejected the title "Messiah." Yet, ironically, it strikes me that some of the very seeds necessary for a robust historical argument for Jesus' messianic self-consciousness are ready at hand in Dunn's own work. For example, Dunn argues for the following points:

1. Although he acknowledges the diversity of views regarding Messiah in Second Temple Judaism, Dunn notes two broad themes that, generally speaking, characterize Jewish thought at this time: (1) a "lively hope for the restoration of the Davidic kingly line" and (2) that the Davidic Messiah would be a "warrior king who would destroy the enemies of Israel."[41] Dunn rightly avoids adopting too monolithic a conception of Messiah in the Second Temple period. Nevertheless, I would want to press him a bit more on the implications of a trend that appears to have been coalescing by the first century, namely, the convergence of the (Danielic-inspired) "Son of Man" concept with that of the Messiah concept, as evidenced (beyond the NT) by the Old Greek (LXX) version of Daniel 7, 4Q246; *Similitudes of Enoch* 48:10; 52:4; *4 Ezra* 13; and, into the

---

work, Dunn has concluded that even the apostle Paul did not express a high Christology similar to what would eventually emerge in, for example, second-generation Gentile Christian circles. Dunn's presupposition of a (relatively) rigid first-century Jewish monotheism essentially precludes for him the developments necessary for a high Christology among Jesus' early Jewish followers or, not surprisingly, within Jesus' own self-understanding. Along with a growing number of scholars within what some are calling the "new history-of-religions school," I would want to take issue with Dunn's reading of these things. More helpful are the following assessments of the nature of first-century Jewish monotheism and Jesus' self-understanding within that context: R. Bauckham, *God Crucified: Monotheism and Christology in the New Testament* (Carlisle: Paternoster/Grand Rapids: Eerdmans, 1998); L. W. Hurtado, *One God, One Lord: Early Christian Devotion and Ancient Jewish Monotheism* (Philadelphia: Fortress, 1988); idem, *Lord Jesus Christ: Devotion to Jesus in Earliest Christianity* (Grand Rapids: Eerdmans, 2003). I have offered a summary discussion of this issue in P. R. Eddy and G. Boyd, *The Jesus Legend: A Case for the Historical Reliability of the Synoptic Jesus Tradition* (Grand Rapids: Baker Academic, 2007), chap. 2, esp. 92–101, 128–30.

[41] Dunn, *Jesus Remembered*, 621. Recognition of these two broadly shared messianic themes in Second Temple Judaism is a healthy corrective to the more extreme tendency in recent decades to deny any significant—let alone common—messianic conception among the Jews of this time. This more extreme view, which was a reaction against the likewise problematic "traditional" view of a single, standard notion of the Messiah among virtually all ancient Jews, widely impacted the field with the publication of J. Neusner et al., *Judaisms and Their Messiahs at the Turn of the Christian Era* (New York: Cambridge University Press, 1987). Dunn represents those who have settled on a more plausible via media.

second century, *Sibylline Oracles* 5.[42] As John Collins has noted, this convergence naturally led to a qualification of the Messiah concept.[43] In light of the fact that this convergence was under way in the first century and given Dunn's positive conclusions regarding both Jesus' use of the "Son of Man" title and Jesus' sense of being God's "eschatological agent," one wonders if the early Jesus tradition—with its ubiquitous presence of the "Jesus as Messiah" theme—is not better explained by positing that Jesus embraced the Son of Man designation with its (qualified) first-century messianic connotations intact.[44]

2. Dunn acknowledges that Jesus' lowly birth would not, in and of itself, have precluded the idea that he could be Messiah, and he may well have been known as a descendant of David.[45]

3. Dunn argues that the question of whether Jesus might be Messiah was raised at least during the latter part of his mission, as evidenced by historically likely cores to the following narratives of the Jesus tradition: the feeding of 5,000; Peter's confession of Jesus' messiahship; Bartimaeus's identification of Jesus as "son of David"; Jesus'

---

[42] On the Old Greek rendering of the Danielic "one like a Son of Man" figure as displaying a clear messianic character, see B. E. Reynolds, "The 'One Like a Son of Man' According to the Old Greek of Daniel 7,13–14," *Biblica* 89 (2008): 70–80. While this fusion of these concepts within 4Q246 has been debated, John Collins's assessment has provided an appropriately nuanced defense of the claim; see J. J. Collins, "The Messiah as the Son of God," in *The Scepter and the Star: The Messiahs of the Dead Sea Scrolls and Other Ancient Literature* (New York: Doubleday, 1995), 154–72. Regarding the dating of the *Similitudes*, while the question has been a matter of significant debate, they are best understood as written prior to the fall of Jerusalem in 70. (For further discussion and relevant sources on this matter, see n78.) Although *4 Ezra* is best dated after 70, it appears to have no literary connection to the *Similitudes*. Together, with the NT documents, they plausibly signal the existence of a first-century trend (just how wide we cannot say) in Jewish thought. For a helpful overview, see J. J. Collins, "The Son of Man in First-Century Judaism," *NTS* 38 (1992): 448–66.

[43] Collins, "The Son of Man in First-Century Judaism," 465.

[44] This line of argument is strengthened all the more when one recognizes that the broader section of Daniel within which this passage is set supplies two of the most characteristic features of Jesus' message and ministry, namely, the themes of (1) satanic opposition and its ensuing struggle with God's people and (2) the triumph of the kingdom of God. For an insightful reflection on these Danielic themes and their implications for Jesus research, see C. A. Evans, "Defeating Satan and Liberating Israel: Jesus and Daniel's Visions," *JSHJ* 1 (2003): 161–70.

[45] Dunn, *Jesus Remembered*, 627–28. John Meier has presented a plausible case for the claim that Jesus may well have been known to be of Davidic stock; see Meier, *A Marginal Jew*, 2:216–19.

entry into Jerusalem, the Temple Act; Jesus' "Render to Caesar" saying; and, finally, various events connected with the Jesus' death, including reminiscences about the Caiaphas's questioning at the trial and, most concretely, the fact that Jesus was eventually crucified, under Roman authority, seemingly as a messianic pretender—as "King of the Jews."[46]

4. Dunn admits that the "Son of God" concept—a concept that he includes within Jesus' self-understanding—"would have been seen as an appropriate corollary to any identification of Jesus as royal Messiah, son of David."[47]

In addition, several of Dunn's methodological convictions, when applied to the textual data just reviewed, seem to me to offer further possibilities in this direction. First, if Dunn is correct that what historical research can recover in the end is "not Jesus himself, but the remembered Jesus"—the "impact" of Jesus left on the memories of his earliest followers—and if he is correct in his proposal regarding the relative reliability of the oral Jesus tradition that flowed from the original memories to and around the written texts themselves (and I would argue that he certainly is),[48] then how is one to explain the ubiquitous (i.e., multiply attested in the most dramatic of ways) and exceedingly comfortable "memory" of a Jesus who was, in fact, the royal Messiah? From whence this pervasive "memory," this thoroughgoing and decidedly countercultural "impact," if not from Jesus himself? Even more pressing, How is this seeming impactful memory to be explained if, as Dunn surmises, Jesus explicitly declined the title of "Messiah"? In light of both the textual evidence (which Dunn admits could very well be seen as relating to messianic themes) and these methodological considerations, one may wonder what could ever lead Dunn to conclude against a royal messianic self-consciousness for the earthly Jesus.

Dunn's answer is clear: In significant ways, Jesus' teaching and ministry stand in counterpoint to the Second Temple concept of Messiah as a militarily and politically oriented warrior-king who would

---

[46] For Dunn's discussion on these matters, see Dunn, *Jesus Remembered*, 627–47.

[47] Ibid., 710.

[48] I, with Gregory Boyd, have offered a defense of the generally reliable nature of the early oral Jesus tradition that is quite compatible with Dunn's; see our *Jesus Legend*, chaps. 6–7.

free Israel from its enemies. For Dunn, claiming that Jesus rejected the title "Messiah" seems almost to be as sensible—and uncontroversial—as claiming that Jesus was no military-political revolutionary, as suggested by the marginal scholarly tradition of Reimarus and Brandon.[49] His explains the ubiquitous presence of the "Jesus as Messiah" theme in the tradition thus:

> The only plausible option remaining is that they had in fact been convinced that Jesus was Messiah, son of David, during his mission, but that their conception of his messiahship was radically transformed by the events of Good Friday. In that light they in effect emptied the title of its traditional content and filled it with new content provided by the law and the prophets and the psalms.[50]

Although he does acknowledge that, in transforming the concept of Messiah, they were "taking up pointers Jesus had provided in his talk of eschatological reversal and suffering," Dunn decisively stops short of attributing this fundamental reenvisioning and transformation of the role and title of Messiah to Jesus himself.[51] Rather, Jesus is read as consistently avoiding, dodging, and, at times, explicitly "declining" this role and title throughout his ministry.

Building on these observations, I find Dunn's conclusion at this point to be less than plausible for these reasons. First, it strikes me that most of the exegetical arguments that Dunn offers as evidence of the memory of Jesus declining the title "Messiah" are less than persuasive and, in fact, can often be read in a more plausible counterfashion. The following are examples:

1. *Peter's messianic confession.* Dunn admits there is no indication that Jesus denied the confession. But he goes on to state that there is no indication Jesus "accepted or welcomed it."[52] In fact, Dunn

---

[49] I say "almost" here because Dunn is quite cognizant that his claim must come with a "qualification"—that is, the fact that Jesus was suspected of being Messiah during his ministry and was decisively proclaimed as such by his post-Easter followers leaves something significant to be explained (see again Dunn, *Jesus Remembered*, 652–53).

[50] Ibid., 653.

[51] Ibid., 653.

[52] Ibid., 648.

concludes that Jesus' command to silence "functions more to indicate a messianic misunderstanding than a messianic secret."[53] To this I want to say, "yes" and "no." Yes, we can agree that the Messianic Confession at Philippi tradition was meant to correct a messianic misunderstanding. But there is no indication, as Dunn suggests, that the misunderstanding was that his followers thought he was Messiah. Rather, it was that they thought he was Messiah *as popularly understood.* A straightforward reading of the passage, especially when augmented by the Matthean version of the tradition, suggests Jesus affirmed Peter's confession and thus tacitly accepts the title, and then, in the next breath, sets about redefining significant aspects of the popular understanding. Adela Yarbro Collins nicely captures the force of the report: "The response of Jesus makes it clear that the acclamation is accepted; the immediate response is not to reject or reinterpret, but to command the disciples to keep the identity of Jesus secret."[54]

2. *Bartimaeus's "Son of David" confession.* Here Dunn argues that nothing is made of the messianic significance of the title "son of David," and "Jesus neither rebukes nor acknowledges the title."[55] True, Jesus does not rebuke—or even dodge—the title, which seems odd if Dunn is correct that Jesus "declined" it. The question left hanging is, Where in the tradition is Jesus *ever* remembered as explicitly declining the title "Messiah," as one might expect if Dunn's theory were correct?

3. *Entry into Jerusalem and Temple Action.* Dunn emphasizes the ambiguity of the entry in the Markan account and notes that an explicit military coup is ruled out vis-à-vis the Temple Action. Furthermore, he suggests that since the Temple Act per se is not mentioned in the Trial accounts, this fact "may indicate that it was not reckoned as particularly serious, either politically or prophetically."[56] Although Dunn grants that, in this episode, Jesus is "possibly a self-conscious actor in the eschatological drama already beginning to unfold," he nonetheless concludes that "how the episode contributes to the question of whether Jesus saw his role in messianic terms is hard to say."[57] Nevertheless, a more persuasive

---

[53] Ibid., 649.

[54] A. Y. Collins, "The Messiah as Son of God in the Synoptic Gospels," in *The Messiah in Early Judaism and Christianity* (ed. M. Zetterholm; Minneapolis: Fortress, 2007), 24.

[55] Dunn, *Jesus Remembered*, 649.

[56] Ibid., 650.

[57] Ibid., 650.

line of argument is that which recognizes in his last journey to Jerusalem a display of several well-crafted *prophetic symbolic acts*—most clearly seen in the entry into Jerusalem and the Temple incident—that reveal in explicit (though nonverbal) terms Jesus' sense of (redefined) messianic consciousness. It is in this light, as Wright effectively argues (and he is far from alone), that the entry is seen as "clearly messianic."[58] This conclusion is further warranted by the fact that, unlike Matthew's and John's later accounts, Mark's original report is not presented in a stylized prophetic-fulfillment fashion—in fact, it does not even cite the messianic key to this event found in Zech 9:9. Rather, it reads as if Mark is reporting an event that, in hindsight and in context, is readily explainable only on the assumption that Jesus had the Zechariah passage (with its messianic connotations) implicitly guiding his behavior.[59]

In turning to consider the Temple Action, we encounter what potentially is "the most obvious act of messianic praxis within the gospel narratives."[60] These twin symbolic actions are reminiscent of the Maccabean paradigm and are further illuminated by a series of "royal riddles" within the sayings tradition. The evidence does suggest, against Dunn, that given the role that Jesus' prophecy against the Temple played at his trial (e.g., Mark 14:57) and given a plausible connection between prophetic warning of destruction and the symbolic Temple Act itself, the Temple Action indeed was viewed as a particularly serious incident—if not in an overt political sense, at least prophetically. Dunn's vague and ambiguous

---

[58] Wright, *Jesus and the Victory of God*, 491. See also A. Chester, "The Nature and Scope of Messianism," in *Messiah and Exaltation: Jewish Messianic and Visionary Traditions and New Testament Christology* (Tübingen: Mohr Siebeck, 2007), 315–19; M. D. Hooker, *The Signs of a Prophet: The Prophetic Actions of Jesus* (Harrisburg, Pa.: Trinity Press International, 1997), 43–44; J. P. Meier, "From Elijah-like Prophet to Royal Davidic Messiah," in *Jesus: A Colloquium in the Holy Land* (ed. Doris Donnelly; New York: Continuum, 2001), 67–71.

[59] As many have noted. See for example, Chester, "Nature and Scope of Messianism," 312–13. A. Laato has offered a compelling argument that Zechariah 9–14 was a much more fundamental textual key to unlocking Jesus' own interpretation of the actions and events of his last week than most scholars have recognized. Given that this text seems (at least in part) to have supplied the scripts for the entry (9:9–10) and the Temple Action (14:21), he raises the intriguing question of whether it might not have also offered the script for Jesus' sense of the necessity of his rejection and impending death (11:4–14; 12:10; 13:7–19). See A. Laato, *A Star is Rising: The Historical Development of the Old Testament Royal Ideology and the Rise of the Jewish Messianic Expectations* (Atlanta: Scholars Press, 1997), 344–48.

[60] Wright, *Jesus and the Victory of God*, 490; see pp. 493–510 for Wright's line of argument here.

suggestion that in the Temple Act we see Jesus as a "self-conscious actor in eschatological drama" is appropriately fleshed out by recognizing the (redefined) messianic consciousness of Jesus implicit in this prophetic, symbolic act.

4. *Jesus' trial and condemnation.* Dunn emphasizes the "ambivalence" of Jesus' reply to the questions of Caiaphas and Pilate about his messianic status. Apart from Mark's account of Jesus before Caiaphas—where, in answer to the messianic interrogation, Jesus responds, "I am" (Mark 14:62)—all the other passages report a response from Jesus of something akin to "You say so." He thus argues that Mark's version is a secondary gloss on the original and more ambiguous response. In this light, he concludes that Jesus showed "an unwillingness to accept the title of Messiah/king, or, to be more precise, an unwillingness to accept the role which the title indicated to the questioner. . . . [And thus] 'Messiah' was a term Jesus preferred *not* to use for his own role."[61]

Once again, I am in general agreement with Dunn—up to the point of Jesus' rejection of the title per se. Although the evidence substantiates his "more precise" point that Jesus refused the common version of the messianic role popularly assumed to come with the title, there is nothing in the trial tradition to suggest that Jesus refused the title. Interestingly, Dunn is forced (on the assumption of the two-source theory) to regard the earlier report of Mark as "secondary" and inauthentic and the later reports of Matthew and Luke as more reflective of Jesus' actual ambiguous response. I wonder, however, if a more historically plausible account does not run in the opposite direction. It appears that there was a stream within Second Temple Judaism (as evidenced by *Psalms of Solomon* 17, *4 Ezra* 13:52; 1QS) that believed no one could be the Messiah if he openly and explicitly claimed the role, since the Messiah could only be declared as such by God himself. In light of this conviction, it may well be that the later Gospel writers are "taming" Mark's record of Jesus' blatant affirmation, which could be seen as embarrassingly inappropriate for the (preenthroned) Messiah himself to utter. Thus, by the criterion of embarrassment, Mark's report can plausibly be seen as the most authentic.[62]

---

[61] Dunn, *Jesus Remembered*, 652.

[62] Another text worthy of consideration (one that Dunn does not consider in detail in terms of its messianic significance) is the woman's anointing of Jesus (Mark 14:3–9 pars.).

In addition—and a point I believe Dunn's thesis never adequately addresses—if Jesus did decline the title explicitly and completely, what then is the plausible historical explanation for why he was condemned and crucified as a would-be Messiah? If Jesus rejected the title of Messiah, why was he executed as King of the Jews? Dunn rightly acknowledges (along with N. A. Dahl) that the fact of the resurrection alone would have never been enough for the early disciples to conclude Jesus was Messiah—"messiahship was not an obvious, far less necessary, corollary of resurrection."[63] Against the Bultmannian tradition, Dunn also rightly concludes for the authenticity of the *titulus*—Jesus was, in fact, crucified by Rome as a messianic pretender. But as Dahl himself has stated, "The crucifixion of Jesus as 'King of the Jews' is a necessary condition but not a sufficient cause of the faith in Jesus as the Christ."[64] Dunn himself, in contradistinction to Wrede, arrives at what would seem to be the very doorstep of Jesus' messianic self-consciousness when he concludes that the resurrected Jesus was proclaimed Messiah by his earliest followers because "that

---

In the course of arguing for its historicity, R. Bauckham has recently observed that, in light of the location of this event during Jesus' last days in Jerusalem (i.e., after the messianically charged entry and Temple Action) and the likely political implications of the event given the "protective anonymity" strategy that appears to be at work in the tradition, this anointing was probably intended as "the anointing entailed by the term messiah. . . . The woman was acknowledging or even designating Jesus as the Messiah ben David." Following his common pattern, "Jesus recognizes the messianic significance of the anointing but interprets it according to his own [redefined] messianic vocation as entailing suffering and death." R. Bauckham, "The Bethany Family in John 11–12: History or Fiction?" in *The Testimony of the Beloved Disciple: Narrative, History, and Theology in the Gospel of John* (Grand Rapids: Baker Academic, 2007), 185, 186.

[63] Dunn, *Jesus Remembered*, 627. Dahl makes this point in several essays; see, for example, N. A. Dahl, "Messianic Ideas and the Crucifixion of Jesus," in *The Messiah: Developments in Earliest Judaism and Christianity* (ed. J. H. Charlesworth; Minneapolis: Fortress, 1992), 390–91. A. Schweitzer made a similar observation a century ago in *The Quest of the Historical Jesus* (trans. W. Montgomery; New York: Macmillan, 1948), 343.

[64] Dahl, "Messianic Ideas," 403. This is not to say that Dahl concludes for Jesus' messianic self-consciousness during his ministry years. He is known for the theory that it was the apparently regal status conferred upon him by Pilate, as recorded on the *titulus*, that led the early disciples to the postcrucifixion recognition of him as Messiah (see idem, "The Crucified Messiah," in *The Crucified Messiah and Other Essays* [Minneapolis: Augsburg, 1974], 10–36), although even here he qualifies his rejection of the idea (e.g., see pp. 32, 33). Elsewhere (idem, "Messianic Ideas," 403), he judges that the question of Jesus' messianic self-understanding "will, of necessity, elude the historian" (ibid.). While complex to be sure, I find no inherent "necessity" to its seeming elusiveness.

resurrection was seen as a vindication of a claim which had been in play *before* Jesus' crucifixion and resurrection."[65] Unfortunately, once Dunn embraces the view that Jesus himself consistently rejected this title, there is little left to account for its central role in the crucifixion or the later tradition than the overzealous—but, with respect to Jesus' own intentions, deeply mistaken—notion of some of his more ambitious disciples. And many will find this to be too unlikely a cause for such a historically robust effect.[66]

Second, a related question for Dunn's thesis is, If in fact Jesus *had* internally embraced the title of Messiah—though always in conjunction with a redefined role—*how would the data we possess look any different?* All of the data Dunn points to as evidence that Jesus rejected the title can just as easily—I would argue more easily—be explained as the memory of Jesus' acceptance of a *redefined* messianic role, with the always-attendant memory of Jesus' vigilant negotiation of where, when, how, to whom, and to what degree he was willing to reveal this self-understanding, given what must have been his constant awareness of just how easy it would be for his hearers to misunderstand and recast him in terms of the popular conception. Related to this, once the ubiquitous presence of the theme of Jesus as a redefined, paradoxical Messiah within the tradition is recognized as the wide-ranging impact left by the memory of Jesus' own carefully shaped and strategically shared self-understanding, the relatively well-attested "'messianic secret" theme makes good historical sense. In this vein, I applaud Dunn's

---

[65] Dunn, *Jesus Remembered*, 627; emphasis in original.

[66] In light of the preceding observations on the texts in question, I find myself far more persuaded by the line of argument offered by Dunn in a 1970 essay on the same question. After analyzing several of these same passages—including Peter's confession, the entry into Jerusalem, and Jesus' trial—Dunn concluded, "Jesus was crucified as a messianic pretender because of the political connotations of the title King of the Jews. But this implies that there was some basis for the charge and the condemnation—that there were substantial grounds for applying it to Jesus—that, indeed, the title was in some sense accepted by him. . . . [I conclude that] Jesus believed himself to be Messiah, but that his conception of the messianic role was an unexpected and unpopular one. . . . He did not take what might appear the easiest course—that of completely renouncing the title. . . . These conclusions follow directly from [these] passages we examined. But I believe that they hold true for the whole of the Markan tradition." J. D. G. Dunn, "The Messianic Secret in Mark," in *The Christ and the Spirit: Collected Essays of James D. G. Dunn* (vol. 1 of *Christology*; Grand Rapids: Eerdmans, 1998), 70, 73. Originally published in *TynBul* 21 (1970): 92–117.

critique of Wrede's skeptical "'messianic secret" thesis, as far as it goes.[67] Nevertheless, what I am suggesting here is the need for an even more thoroughgoing "de-Wrede-fication" of this aspect of the tradition.[68]

Third, moving beyond exegetical specifics, although it is doubtless that Jesus rejected the role of the popular conception of Messiah (i.e., as a military-political warrior-king, an observation that goes hand in hand with the recognition that Jesus was no aspiring political revolutionary), the ubiquity of the title within the early Jesus tradition and its early use (e.g., Paul) in such a way that it becomes virtually a proper name for Jesus is difficult to explain on Dunn's terms alone.[69] It forces the conclusion that his closest followers unrepentantly crowned Jesus with a title and role that he himself had decisively rejected during his ministry, a title that, to say the least, would be exceedingly difficult for traditional Jews to apply to Jesus in light of his crucifixion. What forces could ever have pushed them to such a seemingly mistaken (i.e., vis-à-vis their Lord's own self-understanding, on Dunn's account) and culturally nonsensical conclusion? Martin Hengel has pressed this line of thought. To those who reject the notion of the messianic self-consciousness of Jesus, and in light of the fact that Jesus' earliest followers should have retained distinct memories of his rejection of the title, he poses this question:

> Why do we nowhere find a protest against this "messianic" falsification of Jesus [within the tradition]? . . . A pious veneration of a suffering righteous Jesus, who now (as with all the righteous) resided with God, would have given less offense among their own compatriots, and the impending separation from Judaism could have been avoided. . . . But such a protest in favor of the true, unmesssianic intention of Jesus is nowhere attested or even alluded to in early Christianity.[70]

---

[67] Dunn took issue with Wrede's "messianic secret" thesis as far back as 1970; see Dunn, "Messianic Secret in Mark."

[68] It is worth remembering that, ironically enough, Wrede himself began this process when, in a 1905 letter to Harnack, he states that he is increasingly inclined to believe that Jesus had seen himself as Messiah. See H. Rollmann and W. Zager, "Unveröffentliche Briefe William Wredes zur Problematisierung des messianischen Selbstverständnisses Jesu," *ZFT* 8 (2001): 317.

[69] On this important point, see M. Hengel, "Jesus, the Messiah of Israel," in *Studies in Early Christology* (Edinburgh: T & T Clark, 1995), 1, 7–9.

[70] Ibid., 15. Hengel has been a major voice in recent years among those seeking to revive the notion of Jesus' messianic self-understanding.

Given his strong emphasis on the centrality and general reliability of the impact made by Jesus on the memories of his early, pre-Easter followers and the respective impression of these memories on the Jesus tradition itself, this question seems to me to be a troubling one for Dunn.

Fourth, related to this, Dunn claims that although Jesus declined the role and title of Messiah, "no wonder, then, that when the first Christians used it of Jesus, *as use it they must*, they did so by transforming its current significance completely."[71] But this begs the question of why Dunn would think they felt compelled to use it—and thus transform it—in the first place. Given its popular meaning, *why would the earliest Christians feel the need to reinterpret and apply the title "Messiah" to a crucified prophet who himself refused the designation while he was alive?* To my mind, Dunn's thesis cannot adequately answer this question.

Fifth, when it comes to the common first-century concepts of prophet, exorcist, and teacher, Jesus tends to (a) in some fashion modify their more popular conceptions (often by the transformation or even subtraction of familiar aspects), (b) adds to each of them (to use Dunn's phrase) an "eschatological plus," and (c) finally, in these transformed modes, embraces them himself. Now, Dunn rightly argues that the concept of royal Messiah "was a category full of eschatological significance."[72] As noted earlier, he also, and again rightly, argues that one of the chief categories by which Jesus understood his own role was that of God's "eschatological agent." Given Jesus' pattern with other roles and titles and in light of the clear eschatological significance of the Messiah concept, is it not more plausible that it was Jesus himself who similarly modified the role of Messiah and, in this transformed sense, embraced it as a component of his multifaceted self-understanding? This possibility is further enhanced in light of what appears to be a trend within Second Temple Judaism (again, just how widely we do not know) that, inspired by the image of Isa 61:1–3, embraced a merger of the messianic and prophetic roles.[73] An important witness here is

---

[71] Dunn, *Jesus Remembered*, 706; emphasis added.

[72] Ibid., 705.

[73] In light of this merger, some have come to interpret Jesus as embracing the role of a "prophetic Messiah," in contrast to that of a royal-Davidic (i.e., warrior) Messiah. See, for example, J. J. Collins, "Jesus and the Messiahs of Israel," in *Geschichte—Tradition—Reflexion:*

4Q521 (known as "On Resurrection" or "Messianic Apocalypse"). This text begins with the affirmation that the "heavens and earth will obey his Messiah." It goes on to, in some fashion, implicate this Messiah figure with God's liberating activity that leads to "free[ing] the captives, open[ing] the eyes of the blind, straighten[ing] those bent double." Interestingly, the description of this liberating activity continues with "heal[ing] the wounded, resurrect[ing] the dead, proclaim[ing] glad tidings to the poor." Moreover, God or this Messiah figure will also "lead the Holy Ones, he will shepherd them."[74] This text appears to reveal a type of messianic prophet, one inspired by the key text of Isa 61:1–3. And (as Dunn himself argues), it is this very Isaianic text that undergirded Jesus' own sense of calling as an eschatological prophet.[75] This very amalgam of a miracle-working prophet-king who meets the needs of the poor is explicitly mentioned by John as a conceptual synthesis by which people were interpreting Jesus during his ministry (John 6:12–16).[76]

At this point, Dunn would ask for—and rightly deserves—a clear response to the question of just what plausible historical account could flesh out and adequately explain this alternative thesis, that this redefined role of Jesus as Messiah most likely originated within his own

---

Festschrift für Martin Hengel zum 70. Geburtstag (ed. Hubert Cancik et al.; 3 vols.; Tübingen: Mohr Siebeck, 1996), 3:287–302; see also the similar argument of M. de Jonge, *Jesus, The Servant-Messiah* (New Haven: Yale University Press, 1991), 68–72. However, as I suggest later, there is good reason to think Jesus did not bifurcate these messianic roles but rather self-identified with *both* the prophetic and the royal-Davidic-warrior images—though (particularly with regard to the latter) in a decidedly redefined fashion. Broadly speaking, Hengel ("Jesus, the Messiah of Israel," 69) has argued in a similar fashion.

[74] The text is taken from J. D. Tabor and M. O. Wise, "4Q521 'On Resurrection' and the Synoptic Gospel Tradition: A Preliminary Study," *JSP* 10 (1992): 151.

[75] Dunn, *Jesus Remembered*, 662, 664, 706.

[76] Also of possible relevance here is the targumic tradition at Mic 4:6–8. In the Aramaic rendering, the Hebrew "lame" becomes the "exiled" whom God will gather and restore in the eschaton, with the "Anointed One of Israel" being given the "kingdom." As Craig Evans has noted, this interpretation "coheres with Jesus' ministry to the lame, a ministry characterized by a proclamation of the Kingdom of God. . . . This paraphrase heightens the latent messianic dimension of the text"; C. A. Evans, "A Note on Targum 2 Samuel 5.8 and Jesus' Ministry to the 'Maimed, Halt, and Blind,'" *JSP* 15 (1997): 82. For further reflections on the "messianic" character of certain passages in the Targums and their possible relevance for early Christian and historical Jesus studies, see M. B. Shepherd, "Targums, the New Testament, and Biblical Theology of the Messiah," *JETS* 51 (2008): 45–58.

self-understanding. I begin my response to this question by resetting the context. Although "consensus" is almost always a dangerous term in Jesus studies today, it seems to me that we are close to such with regard to the concept of "Messiah" within late Second Temple (and just beyond) Jewish apocalyptic thought. On one hand, the concept was far from monolithic, with a range of perspectives on both the nature and function of God's anointed eschatological agent. Nevertheless, within this diversity (e.g., as witnessed by the relevant passages in *Psalms of Solomon* 17–18; *Similitudes of Enoch*; *4 Ezra* 7; *2 Baruch* 29, 30, 39, 40, 70, and 72) a broadly shared minimal sketch emerges.[77] Loren Stuckenbruck has accurately summarized this image: "an eschatological ruler, chosen by God to act decisively against the wicked on behalf of the righteous of God's people Israel." Beyond this "very broad profile," Stuckenbruck reminds us, "diversity takes over."[78] This diversity is, nonetheless, fueled by a similar broad methodological approach, namely, creative reflection on a discernable pool of biblical themes or texts (e.g., Psalm 2, Daniel 7, Isaiah 11). It seems to me that the most plausible thesis regarding the genesis of the "Jesus as Messiah" motif is that this concept represents Jesus' own creative theological synthesis within the wider ferment of Jewish apocalyptic speculation on the Messiah question.[79]

---

[77] Perhaps partly in reaction to prior inappropriately uncritical uses of the *Similitudes of Enoch* to explain early Christian messianism, some, going to the other extreme, have unjustifiably dismissed the *Similitudes* as relevant to the question. For two properly balanced assessments—including the defense of a pre-70 date—see M. Black, "The Messianism of the Parables of Enoch: Their Date and Contribution to Christological Origins," in *The Messiah: Developments in Earliest Judaism and Christianity* (ed. J. H. Charlesworth; Minneapolis: Fortress, 1992), esp. 161–68; J. H. Charlesworth, "Can We Discern the Composition Date of the Parables of Enoch?" in *Enoch and the Messiah Son of Man: Revisiting the Book of Parables* (ed. Gabriele Boccaccini; Grand Rapids: Eerdmans, 2007), 450–68.

[78] L. Stuckenbruck, "Messianic Ideas in the Apocalyptic and Related Literature of Early Judaism," in *The Messiah in the Old and New Testaments* (ed. S. E. Porter; Grand Rapids: Eerdmans, 2007), 112.

[79] There has been a persistent and seriously flawed tendency in critical Jesus studies to trace all real theological innovation within the Jesus tradition to the post-Easter community rather than to Jesus himself. Often, this tendency appears to have operated as a liberal Protestant apologetic strategy to distance—and thus render more credible to the "modern" mind—Jesus from the supposedly later "mythological" theological constructs of the early church. G. B. Caird perceptively pointed out the problem with this tendency decades ago; see G. B. Caird, *The Apostolic Age* (London: Duckworth, 1955), 81–82. At times, Dunn is willing to

Now, Dunn's thesis is primarily driven by his conviction that Jesus resisted the role associated with the popular conception of Messiah as a militarily or politically oriented warrior-king. In one important sense, of course, Dunn is absolutely correct: Jesus was no political aspirant or revolutionary upstart. Nevertheless, in another sense, even this claim must be qualified, for although Jesus certainly declined the popular conception of Messiah as militarily victorious warlord, his redefining and embracing of the role did not include the loss of its fundamental, biblically driven warrior-king motif.

It seems to me that the very sort of theological framework that is required to explain the shift from the popular conception of Messiah toward the conceptual trajectory exhibited within the post-Easter community is to be found in the uniquely conceived "already—not yet" eschatological schema that Dunn himself convincingly shows to be characteristic of Jesus' conception of the kingdom of God.[80] Two of the chief impressions left on the tradition vis-à-vis Jesus' distinctive eschatological kingdom teaching are especially relevant here. First, there is the memory of Jesus' nonviolent, agape-oriented stance toward *all human beings*—including (most decisively for our purposes) his human "enemies" (Matt 5:43–47).[81]

Second, there is the memory of Jesus' identification of the spiritual antagonist—Satan, along with his demonic hordes—as the *true enemies of God's people*. Wright has properly grasped the import of this shift initiated by Jesus during his ministry:

> One of the key elements in Jesus' perception of his task was therefore his *redefinition* of who the real enemy was. . . . The pagan hordes surrounding Israel [including Rome] were not the actual foe of the people of YHWH. Standing behind the whole problem of Israel's

---

buck this tendency. I submit that he would do well to challenge it once again when it comes to the question of the genesis of the "Jesus as Messiah" motif.

[80] Dunn, *Jesus Remembered*, 467. For Dunn's lengthy argument toward this end, see pp. 406–67.

[81] In a phrase ripe for unpacking, Marcus Bockmuehl anticipates, I believe, my own conclusion here: "The themes of non-violent resistance and messianic redemption are for the ministry of Jesus two sides of the same coin." M. Bockmuehl, "Resistance and Redemption in the Jesus Tradition," in *Redemption and Resistance: The Messianic Hopes of Jews and Christians in Antiquity* (ed. M. Bockmuehl and J. C. Paget; New York: T & T Clark, 2007), 73.

exile was the dark power known in some Old Testament traditions as the satan, the accuser. The struggle that was coming to a head was therefore cosmic.[82]

Dunn himself has emphasized the connection made by Jesus between the arrival of the kingdom in his exorcisms and the defeat of Satan.[83] It is certainly no unwarranted leap from this recognition to the more comprehensive observation that before Jesus ever redefined and embraced the title and role of Messiah, he first fundamentally *redefined Israel's enemy* against which Messiah was anointed to do battle. For Jesus, no longer is Rome (or any other pagan or Gentile collective) the primary enemy of Israel. Rather, it is the nefarious cosmic entity known as Satan, along with the demonic hosts over which he rules, that constitutes Israel's real foe—and thus it is Satan and his demonic powers that serve as the rightful target of Messiah's warrior calling. In this light, it is quite plausible to imagine that, at one level, Jesus—the binder of the satanic strongman—would have continued to understand himself in terms of the messianic warrior-king. But with the true enemy of Israel now redefined and relocated to the cosmic heavenly realms, the notion of Israel's Messiah would also have to undergo an equally appropriate conceptual transformation if he was to be a messianic warrior-king appropriate to the cosmic task at hand.[84] I would suggest that this sort of transformative eschatological

[82] Wright, *Jesus and the Victory of God*, 450–51; emphasis in original. Although I believe Wright is absolutely correct on this point, I have argued elsewhere that this conviction raises questions as to whether his view of the nature of Second Temple Jewish apocalyptic eschatology offers a sufficiently robust *solution* to this admittedly cosmic *problem*. See Eddy, "(W)Right Jesus," 47–48.

[83] Dunn, *Jesus Remembered*, 457–61.

[84] This, of course, raises the question of how the (redefined) Messiah will wage warfare and gain victory over the (redefined) enemy, one who is located in the spirit-realm and thus against whom the common physical weaponry of human warfare will be of no avail. The answer seems ready at hand in the tradition. Dunn, *Jesus Remembered*, 817–18, himself concludes that Jesus anticipated his own death and gave theological meaning to it, and rightly so. More to the point, Jesus is remembered in the tradition as holding to the conviction that, paradoxically enough, it would be through his own death that he would obtain victory over Israel's cosmic enemy. As it turns out, Jesus may not have been the only Jew who imagined that it would be through the suffering of an eschatological figure that deliverance for others would come—as texts such as 4QTLevi (a.k.a. 4QAhA) and the LXX of Isaiah 53 may

thought fits well with what we know of Jesus' own unique perspective on the kingdom of God and that it is thus most historically plausible to trace the origin of the early Christian consensus on the identity of the (redefined) Messiah back to the very self-understanding of Jesus.[85]

suggest. See G. J. Brooke, "4QTestament of Levi[d](?) and the Messianic Servant High Priest," in *From Jesus to John: Essays on Jesus and New Testament Christology in Honour of Marinus de Jonge* (ed. M. C. de Boer; JSNTSup 84; Sheffield: Sheffield Academic Press, 1993), 83–100; M. Hengel, with D. P. Bailey, "The Effective History of Isaiah 53 in the Pre-Christian Period," in *The Suffering Servant: Isaiah 53 in Jewish and Christian Sources* (ed. B. Janowski and P. Stuhl-macher; trans. D. P. Bailey; Grand Rapids: Eerdmans, 2004), 75–146.

[85] Chester appears to be pushing in a similar direction; see "Nature and Scope of Messianism," 322–23.

12

JAMES D. G. DUNN ON THE RESURRECTION OF JESUS

STEPHEN T. DAVIS

Introduction

First let me express my deep appreciation for James D. G. Dunn's work, *Jesus Remembered*.[1] The book is amazingly comprehensive, stunningly well-informed, and it advances an interesting and provocative thesis. Moreover, for the most part, the book is sensibly argued. Having agreed to write this review chapter, I must say that I was somewhat discouraged when the book arrived and I saw that it contained 1,019 pages and, as I count, 3,896 footnotes. But when I worked up the courage to start the book, I actually found it a pleasure to read and not at all arduous.

Let me say at the outset that I am not a New Testament (NT) scholar but rather a philosopher of religion. I have written about the resurrection of Jesus, however, and I do try to keep up with major trends in NT studies. That perhaps qualifies me, although admittedly just barely, to write without embarrassment about Dunn's book in an

---

[1] J. D. G. Dunn, *Jesus Remembered* (vol. 1 of *Christianity in the Making*; Grand Rapids: Eerdmans, 2003).

academic setting. But I am aware that it is an honor for me to have been asked to contribute to this book on an important work of one of the foremost NT scholars in the world.

The "Official Doctrine" of *Jesus Remembered*

I have been asked to write about Dunn's take on the resurrection of Jesus, and I intend to say something about that. But first I have a question about what looks to be one of the book's central theses.

Dunn is convinced that we do not have access to Jesus; he stresses what he calls "the impossibility of getting back to Jesus himself."[2] All that the evidence gives us, he insists, is the way Jesus is remembered.[3] The Jesus tradition, he says, is simply the deposit of how Jesus was heard by those who responded positively to his message; that is, it is Jesus seen through the eyes of those who followed him.[4] So the best we can do is arrive at the earliest impact that Jesus made on people. There are no "objective facts" about Jesus; all we have are interpreted data; we cannot clear away all the tradition and call what remains "the historical Jesus."[5]

So let us call this the "official doctrine" of the book: *we do not have access to Jesus himself but only to the earliest memories of Jesus.*

Now in one sense the official doctrine is relatively innocuous. In that sense, what Dunn says about Jesus is true of all historical figures who did not write anything that has survived or leave any other artifacts. In such cases, all that we have access to is what other people remembered and wrote about them. Fair enough. But let us think for a moment about human memory. We all have memories, and we are aware that memory is fallible. We easily forget things (can you remember what you had for lunch three days ago?), and we misremember things (occasionally we are obliged to learn that our memory of a certain event is faulty). So it seems that some human memories are accurate and others are inaccurate, or at least partially inaccurate.

---

[2] Ibid., 490.
[3] "All we have," Dunn says, "are the impressions which Jesus made, the remembered Jesus." Ibid., 329.
[4] Ibid., 131, 340, 616, 827.
[5] Ibid., 672.

Now suppose we can successfully get back to the ways in which Jesus was remembered by his earliest followers, as Dunn admits that we can. But that fact would immediately raise the question whether those memories are accurate. And if we are able to judge that some of them *are* accurate, have we not succeeded in getting back to Jesus and not just to the remembered Jesus?

I recognize that many NT scholars would consider naïve any claim to the effect that historical scholarship can arrive at Jesus himself. This perhaps is one of the points where Bultmann's legacy continues. But let us consider an example. Suppose we are able to judge that in all probability the evangelist Mark was correct in remembering that Jesus died on a cross. Does that not mean that we now know something about Jesus and not just the remembered Jesus, namely, that he died on a cross?

Doubtless, Dunn can clear up the muddle we appear to be in. But if the piece of reasoning we have just gone through is convincing, it looks as if the official doctrine—that we do not have access to Jesus himself but only to the earliest memories of Jesus—is false. If some of the memories about Jesus that are recorded in the NT are, so far as we can judge, accurate, then it seems that we *do* have access to Jesus himself.

And the odd fact is that Dunn himself seems to recognize this point. When he gets past methodological and background issues early in the book and starts talking about Jesus, we find him, again and again, quite apparently reaching conclusions about Jesus and not just the remembered Jesus:

- The evidence indicates, Dunn says, that Jesus saw no deficiency in the status of women or in their innate capacity for service and ministry.[6]
- Much of Jesus' teaching and conduct, Dunn says, was controversial and even outrageous.[7]
- The case for accepting the NT claim that Jesus threatened the Temple, Dunn says, is "surprisingly strong."[8]

---

[6] Ibid., 537.
[7] Ibid., 615.
[8] Ibid., 631.

- The probability is beyond plausible rebuttal, Dunn says, that the issue of Jesus' alleged messiahship was raised at the hearing before Caiaphas.[9]
- There is a wide consensus among scholars, Dunn says, that "Jesus did indeed engage in a symbolic act in the Temple."[10]
- It cannot be seriously doubted, Dunn says, that Jesus' use of "Amen" in the Gospels "began with Jesus and was a distinctive feature of his own teaching style."[11]
- Jesus spoke of himself, Dunn insists, as the "the Son of Man."[12]
- The NT claim that Jesus was crucified on the direct authority of Pilate himself, Dunn says, "need not be doubted for a minute."[13]
- There can be little doubt, Dunn says, that Jesus anticipated that his message would be rejected in Jerusalem, that he would suffer, and that he would share the fate of the prophets.[14]

So the point where I am puzzled is that what I am calling the official doctrine seems both false and, in practice, frequently abandoned by Dunn himself.

Now I think I know, and certainly have sympathy for, the overall position that Dunn is trying to take here. I think he sees himself as marking out a middle position between two extremes. He wants to reject the views of uncritical conservatives who say that the Gospels give us, without varnish or interpretation, the real historical Jesus. But he also rejects the views of critical skeptics who hold that the Gospels give us not Jesus but late first-century Christian faith about Jesus. Again, I am sympathetic to this overall purpose. But the problem I am worried about still remains. If we can arrive at "Jesus remembered," then do not any accurate memories that may be there tell us about Jesus? And if the best we can ever do is arrive at "Jesus remembered," then why is Dunn apparently so confident at so many points that he knows what Jesus said and did?

Late in the book, Dunn reaffirms his methodological principle that "our only viable subject matter for historical investigation is the

---

[9] Ibid., 633–34.
[10] Ibid., 36–37.
[11] Ibid., 700.
[12] Ibid., 39, cf. 759.
[13] Ibid., 775.
[14] Ibid., 805.

impact made by Jesus as it has impressed itself into the tradition." But then, almost by way of an afterthought, he goes on to say, "I hope in what I have already written I have not been misunderstood to mean that nothing can be said about what (the one who) made the impact."[15] But I cannot avoid thinking that this point is at least prima facie inconsistent with Dunn's stated views earlier in the book—that is, with the official doctrine.

It seems to be that there are several responses that Dunn might make to the criticism that I am raising. Let me mention three.

First, Dunn might reply that our only available methods for deciding which memories about Jesus are accurate and which are inaccurate would themselves depend on "the remembered Jesus." That would be true enough, but of course an analogous claim would be true of any historical investigation of any figure from the past who did not leave writings, for example, Socrates, Alexander the Great, or Joan of Arc. Despite controversies and difficulties surrounding all three of these figures, historians seem happy to accept that we know things about them.

Second, Dunn might, so to speak, place figurative brackets around everything that he apparently says about Jesus in his book and then say of the bracketed material, "Here I am only speaking about Jesus as remembered." Indeed, perhaps something like that is what Dunn actually intends. But then we would still face the problem noted earlier, namely, that any items in the tradition of the remembered Jesus that seem to us to be accurate apparently tell us something about Jesus himself.

Third, perhaps Dunn's deepest point is about probabilities. Perhaps he would agree that *if* we could be sure that, say, Mark correctly remembered something Jesus once said or did, we would then know something about Jesus and not just the remembered Jesus. But perhaps Dunn will deny that we can ever be sure that Mark was correct; the probabilities that we will be able to generate by our evidence will always fall below certainty.[16] So we can never be certain that we have

---

[15] Ibid., 876. I entirely agree with Dunn against Marxsen in the main point that he is making here, namely, that the resurrection was something that happened to Jesus rather than to the disciples.

[16] "Any judgment [made by a historian] will have to be provisional." Ibid., 103.

reached back to Jesus himself. Moreover—so Dunn might argue—even if there are some points where we can find accurate memories of Jesus, we have not reached back to Jesus because those memories will be selective and interpreted.

In some cases, that seems to me a fair response. Did Jesus meet and talk with the centurion whose slave was ill (as in Matt 8:5–13) or did the two never in fact meet (as in Luke 7:1–10)? Did Jesus tell the disciples to take a staff on their journey (as in Mark 6:8) or to take no staff (as in Matt 10:9–10 and Luke 9:3)? Although there are undoubtedly such debatable points about Jesus, there are also others where, so far as I can tell, we can be about as sure as we ever are of anything in history, for example, that Jesus died on a cross. Moreover, I have no desire to deny that what we find in the Gospels are selected and interpreted memories of Jesus. That seems quite obviously true. But, again, as a purely logical point, it seems that if they (or some of them) are accurate memories, then we have arrived not just at the remembered Jesus but at Jesus.

So I will conclude this first point by asking Dunn whether he thinks our belief that Jesus died on a cross tells us something about Jesus himself. If the answer is yes, then what I am calling Dunn's official doctrine is apparently false.

Dunn's View on the Resurrection of Jesus

Let me now turned to my assigned task, namely, to comment on Dunn on the resurrection of Jesus. And here I am happy to report that, despite a few differences, I am largely in sympathy with Dunn's approach. I appreciate his clear affirmation of the resurrection, his conviction that physical views of the resurrection of Jesus were early, his cogent responses to arguments of Marxsen and Lüdemann, his refutation of the idea that there once existed a version of Christianity that did not affirm the resurrection, and his conviction that the earliest believers encountered the risen Jesus.

I will mention only two points of disagreement. The first has to do with the vexed question of whether the resurrection of Jesus is "historical." It is almost a commonplace of biblical scholars of the past 100 years that it is *not* historical, and one can appreciate the reticence of scholars on this point. There is no denying that if "God raised Jesus from the dead," that event was not an ordinary historical event, like the outcome of a battle or the motivation of a certain leader. It is not the kind of event that can be explained in ordinary naturalistic terms. It occurred only as a result of God breaking into history and bringing about an event that would not otherwise have occurred. That makes the resurrection of Jesus in important ways disanalogous to all ordinary historical events. It cannot be fully explained or understood purely in terms of natural causes.

Dunn's discussion of this point is brief. He views the resurrection as "not so much a historical fact as a foundational fact or a meta-fact."[17] It is a fact that determines how one evaluates the significance of Jesus and his life and death. I agree with him at this point. He further holds that the empty tomb and the appearances are interpretations of data (where "data" are historical sources like records, texts, memories, and artifacts). He calls these interpretations "historical facts" in the sense that they, like all historical facts, are interpretations of available data.[18] The resurrection, then, is a kind of second-order fact—an interpretation (made by contemporary historians) of an interpretation (that was originally made by the people from whom we derive our data).[19]

I am not sure to what extent I will be disagreeing with Dunn here, but let me suggest a different approach. The crucial question—as Dunn recognizes—is how to define the term "history." Perhaps history is just *whatever happened in the past*. If Caesar did indeed cross the Rubicon, then that event is part of history. If Jesus was indeed raised by God from the dead, then that event too is part of history. Here history is, so to speak, already there; it is not invented by historians. Or perhaps history is *whatever historians discover about what happened in the past*. On this view, the aim of historians is to find out and explain what actually occurred in the past; the past in itself is inaccessible to us, but history is attainable just in the sense that it is sometimes possible for historians to succeed. What we call

---

[17] Ibid., 878.
[18] Ibid., 102.
[19] Ibid., 877.

"history," then, is created by human beings. It is not events in the past but the attempts of historians to discover and recreate what happened in the past. Or perhaps history is *whatever historians can discover about the past that can be explained by natural causes* or even *whatever might be accepted as having occurred in the past by historians who do not believe in God.* Here, of course, the resurrection of Jesus is not an event in history.[20]

It is impossible for me to say everything that I would want to say about the resurrection of Jesus no matter which of the three definitions of "history" is preferred. On the third definition, I would have to say that the resurrection was not an event in history but still occurred. But precisely because that construction seems paradoxical, I would prefer to proceed on the basic of the first definition,[21] always keeping in mind the point that the resurrection of Jesus was not an *ordinary* event in history.

I prefer the first definition because it seems axiomatic that if the resurrection of Jesus occurred, then it is a fact about the past that occurred. And if the word "history" is understood as *whatever happened in the past*, then the resurrection of Jesus is an event in history. Certainly the statement "God raised Jesus from the dead" would never appear in a history written by someone who did not believe in divine intervention. Nevertheless, if the event actually occurred, then it *should* appear in all relevant historical writings. Why should believers in the resurrection accept the idea that the only items that count as history are those that secular historians will allow? It is true that such an event cannot be explained naturalistically, as most events can. Still, if an event occurs that looks to be naturalistically inexplicable and fits well in a given religious context (i.e., the sort of thing that God—understood in that context—might be expected to do), then it can be sensible for people who belong in that religious context to take it as an act of God.

---

[20] One suspects that many of those scholars who deny that the resurrection is an event in history are working with some such definition of "history" as this.

[21] "History is what occurs, and which forms the content of the writings about it." T. Rockmore, "Subjectivity and Objectivity in the Ontology of History," *The Monist* 74 (April 1991): 190. See also the other essays in this issue of *The Monist*, devoted to "The Ontology of History."

Did Paul's View of Resurrection Differ Significantly from That of Matthew, Luke, and John?

The second point where I disagree with Dunn on the resurrection has to do with his claim that Paul's view of resurrection differs from that of Matthew, Luke, and John in not being physical or bodily.[22] Dunn's hypothesis is that since Paul was operating in a much more characteristically Hellenistic milieu than the evangelists, which "took for granted a greater discontinuity between flesh and spirit than the Jewish conception of the body,"[23] Paul moderated the heavy physicality of the resurrection appearance stories in the Gospels.

But I do not think this thesis is quite correct. What is certainly true is that (a) Paul crucially uses the term "spiritual body" (*pneumatikon sōma*) and (b) nowhere tells resurrection appearance stories. But I think it is overstepping the evidence to say that Paul has "a different conception of the resurrection body" from the evangelists. Dunn asks, "Where is the evidence that a *Pauline* church believed in a *physical* resurrection?"[24] Dunn insists that Paul holds that the resurrection body will be "a different body from that put into the ground at death."[25]

There are three issues here to be sorted out. First, *Did Paul have in mind a physical theory of resurrection?* It seems to me that the answer is clearly "yes." He used the term "resurrection (*anastasis*)," which carries with it heavy connotations of bodiliness. And he used the term "body" (*sōma*), which also entails physicality. So, to answer Dunn's pointed question, the evidence that Pauline churches believed in *bodily* resurrection is right there in 1 Corinthians 15. Moreover, I think the concept of "spiritual resurrection," popular among some interpreters of the resurrection in the past century, is of doubtful coherence (nobody to my knowledge has ever made clear what it means) and, to the extent that it differs from immortality of the soul, is largely a twentieth-century invention. Paul did insist that "flesh and blood cannot inherit

---

[22] Dunn, *Jesus Remembered*, cf. 839–40, 870–72.

[23] Ibid., 840.

[24] Ibid., 840n62. I agree, however, with the point that Dunn is making here against Michael Goulder.

[25] Ibid., 839.

the kingdom of God" (1 Cor 15:50), but that clearly means that the old body cannot inherit the kingdom of God—not that no bodily or physical thing can do so.

Second, *Did Paul deny that the resurrection body is the same body as the pre-mortem body?* The answer depends on what is meant by "the same." Let us say that two things, X and Y, are *qualitatively* identical if they share all their properties. Notice that in this sense my present body is not qualitatively identical with my body of five years ago. My present body has more wrinkles and gray hairs than the previous one, for example. And let us say that two things, X and Y, are *numerically* identical if the terms "X" and "Y" are two ways of referring to one and the same thing. I certainly hold that my present body, despite the changes, is the same thing as (is numerically identical to) my body of five years ago.

We can now answer Dunn's question: Paul definitely held that the resurrection body is not qualitatively identical to the old body; obviously, as Paul makes clear (see 1 Cor 15:35–49), there will be too many dramatic changes for that. But it certainly seems that Paul would hold that the two bodies are numerically identical. They are two stages in the life of one and the same person. Moreover, the second or "spiritual" body comes into existence not by an act of creation ex nihilo but via changes made in the old body. Thus Paul can make repeated statements like, "It is sewn in dishonor, it is raised in glory." The English pronoun "it," which is correctly used here in translating the Greek, refers to the one numerically identical thing that undergoes the changes.

Third, *Does Paul's view of resurrection differ from that found in Matthew, Luke, and John?* There is indeed a difference in emphasis, but I would argue that that is all the difference amounts to. I do not accuse Dunn of going this far, but it is frequently argued that Paul's early "spiritual" theory of the resurrection is inconsistent with the crudely physical and apologetically motivated theories found especially in Luke and John. But I am not convinced that there is a big discrepancy at this point.[26]

---

[26] I do not deny that there are discrepancies between the various resurrection appearance accounts in the NT that are extremely difficult if not impossible sensibly to harmonize.

Let us call the "physical accounts" those that entail the empty tomb or have the risen Jesus walking, eating, retaining the premortem wounds or being touched. And let us call "spiritual accounts" those that imply that Jesus' body had strange new properties that natural human bodies do not have. Then we notice immediately that "physical" and "spiritual" motifs are combined in the same narratives. In the Emmaus story (Luke 24:13–35), the risen Jesus walks, talks, and breaks bread (physical) but then strangely vanishes from their sight (spiritual). In the two appearances to the disciples in the Fourth Gospel (20:19–25,26–29), Jesus appears in the room, despite "the doors being shut" (spiritual), but then shows them his hands and sides and encourages Thomas to feel his wounds (physical). This fact at least suggests that there is no inconsistency here. Authors do not often offer as true explicitly inconsistent accounts of events.

So rather than identifying Paul with some sort of "spiritual" or at least only weakly bodily view, as Dunn does, I would prefer to follow another path. I think it is possible to understand the puzzling Gospel resurrection stories in terms of 1 Corinthians 15, which, despite being earlier, does more explicit theologizing about the resurrection than the evangelists do. Paul's theory amounts to an intermediate position between two extremes—bodily resuscitation (the kind of "resurrection" that Lazarus underwent and that occurs occasionally in modern hospitals) and dualistic spiritualism (which is more like the Platonic theory of the immortality of the soul than bodily resurrection).

The resuscitation theory—which holds that resurrected persons are restored to their old manner of life—was certainly present in contemporary Jewish thinking (see 2 Baruch 50:2). Spiritualistic theories were also in the air in Paul's day—Platonic and proto-Gnostic body/ soul dualisms that held that the soul is imprisoned in the body and at death escapes to live on eternally. In opposition to both extremes, Paul seems to me to argue for resurrection as a kind of bodily transformation, whereby the old natural body is changed into a new "spiritual body" (i.e., a body that is fit for the kingdom of God) in such a way that material continuity and personality are preserved. So Paul's term "spiritual body" does not mean a body that is made up of spirit (whatever that might mean) but rather a body that has been glorified or transformed by God and is now fully dominated by the power of the Holy Spirit (see 1 Cor 2:15; 14:37; Gal 6:1).

In the end, I do not agree with Dunn that Paul's concept of resurrection differs significantly from that of the evangelists. Despite different audiences and theological purposes, I think Paul, Matthew, Luke, and John agree to an amazing degree in rejecting resuscitation and immortality in favor of bodily resurrection.

Conclusion

I am sure than Dunn can respond coherently to my three points of disagreement. And in the end I want again to thank him for *Jesus Remembered*. The guild of NT scholars, as well the Christian community, owes him a debt of gratitude. We look forward to the volumes that will follow.

13

REMEMBERING JESUS' RESURRECTION

RESPONDING TO JAMES D. G. DUNN

GARY R. HABERMAS

James D. G. Dunn is a first-rate researcher whose initial installment of his multivolume set *Christianity in the Making* has continued to make an immediate impact on the field of "Jesus studies." He and I met first in Dallas, Texas, in 1986, where we were invited to participate in a series of extended dialogues. Then, as now, I greatly appreciated his depth of scholarship and commend his willingness to grapple with issues regarding the data and their best interpretation; these issues sometimes get (frankly) ignored by certain other scholars.

After some very brief comments regarding Dunn's overall methodology, I will begin my assessment by summarizing a number of what I think are the more important points of agreement between our positions on the subject of Jesus' resurrection. Then I will pursue in further detail just three important areas where we differ.

Dunn's Historical Methodology

I begin as Dunn does by treating three key terms (events, data, and facts) that he defines differently than certain other scholars. Acknowledging the weight of critical scholars such as Gotthold Lessing and Ernst Troeltsch, Dunn regards all past *events*—the actual occurrences in space and time—as "irretrievable." To be sure, we do have *data* regarding many of these events, and these are the evidential materials with which the historian works, such as memories, eyewitness reports, archaeological artifacts, and circumstantial information. Events and the data concerning them lead to the emergence of *facts*. These are always and necessarily the data as interpreted by others.

The data and the facts will bear "some degree of approximation to the event." As such, they will yield "carefully graded judgments" from "almost certain" to just "possible." In our context "of historical scholarship, the judgment 'probable' is a very positive verdict." Accordingly, historical judgments are couched in terms of various levels of probability and are always provisional.[1] This is true for all of past historical events and their explication.

Dunn waits until after this brief discussion to address his own philosophical perspective: critical realism. Following Ben Meyer and agreeing generally with the emphases of certain other scholars such as N. T. Wright, Dunn proposes an alternative that falls between the two antitheses of naïve realism, with its positivistic overemphasis on the objective element of history, and idealism, which exaggerates the subjective component. Rather, Dunn offers a path that acknowledges the existence of real events of the past but that can only be accessed through dialogue between the historian and the history that is reported (110–11).

The bridge between these historiographical considerations and Dunn's reflection on the historical Jesus is the chief idea that forms the central thesis of this volume. The Synoptic Gospels supply evidence not precisely for what Jesus actually said or really did "but for what Jesus was *remembered* as doing or saying by his first disciples" (130). In other words, the "earliest retellings" of what became the synoptic tradition "are the memories of the first disciples—not Jesus himself." Thus, the Jesus we know is "the remembered Jesus" (130–31).

---

[1] J. D. G. Dunn, *Jesus Remembered* (vol. 1 of *Christianity in the Making*; Grand Rapids: Eerdmans, 2003), 102–3. Further page references to this volume will be listed in the previous text.

When we plug into Dunn's version of critical realism, we can never arrive at some "objective historical reality" that is somehow distinct from the memories of his disciples. We simply do not have the ability to get back to a Jesus that is any earlier than the remembrances of those who knew him best. But on the other side of the critical realistic equation, neither is this such a negative historical conclusion. We still have the potential for discovering eyewitness reminiscences as seen and heard by Jesus' first disciples (131).

So Dunn begins with the remembrances of Jesus' followers, as these were impressed into the early Christian tradition that they handed down. This tradition was transmitted orally and later committed to writing. But was the material passed on faithfully?

Here Dunn subjects select passages from the Synoptics and Acts to a painstaking though somewhat brief analysis in terms of both its oral narrative tradition as well as its oral teaching tradition (210–38). Dunn concludes that variations in different versions of the same stories "do not indicate a cavalier attitude to or lack of historical interest in the events narrated." The result "is clearly *the same story*." Further, where differences were introduced, the changes were not radical, concerning either the substance or the character of the story (223–34). Most significantly, the bottom line on the whole is that *"developments in the Jesus tradition were consistent with the earliest traditions of the remembered Jesus"* (224; Dunn's emphasis).

After his analysis of the oral teaching tradition, Dunn concludes similarly, that Jesus' teachings "remained constant in the process or rehearsing and passing on that teaching in disciple gatherings and churches" (237). The variations chiefly concerned how the material was arranged and adapted or the additional lessons that were garnered, all consistent with the tradition of Jesus' own initial impact (238).

In sum, Dunn concludes that the importance of remembering Jesus and his teachings "is attested as early as we can reach back into earliest Christianity, in Jewish as well as Gentile churches" (253). Thus, this "oral traditioning process was probably established more or less from the beginning." Far from having only a late layer from which to draw our conclusions, we have "the living tradition of Christian celebration which takes us with surprising immediacy to the heart of the first memories of Jesus" (254).

How does Dunn's method impact his approach to the resurrection of Jesus? He asserts that the resurrection is not to be listed among the data[2] that have come down to us, neither is the empty tomb nor appearances themselves. Rather, we must offer the qualification that "the data are *reports* of empty tomb and of seeings/visions of Jesus." From these data, the facts[3] "are at best the fact of the empty tomb, and the fact that disciples saw Jesus." Then to say that Jesus was raised from the dead is "a second order 'fact' . . . an interpretation of an interpretation" (876–77).

If this delineation of Dunn's argument is correct, what we have, then, are the data, consisting of the early reports of the empty tomb and visions of Jesus, followed by a fact—the interpretation of that same report on the part of the early believers. This is followed by a secondary interpretation that Jesus had been raised from the dead. His conclusion, then, is anchored in the reported data of the early Christian tradition, with additional interpretations being derived from this report with each being removed one step from the data.

Perhaps this is a clue to what Dunn means when he states, "My own focus remains, as throughout, on the impact on the disciples and eschews any attempt to get behind that belief to some objectively conceived event" (875). It is difficult to know *exactly* what he means here, since, in the same chapter (esp. 841–66), he *does* attempt to unpack some of these layers and address the issue of what may have occurred, as we will see.

Particularly in light of his initial discussion of historiography, Dunn could be reflecting here on several things by this last statement. Perhaps his chief point is that *no* historical event can itself ever be known objectively (101–9). Or, following from the theme of the entire volume, he does not intend to take the discussion beyond what history is capable of producing—either to the "real" Jesus behind the remembrance of his earliest disciples (130–31, 827) or to discuss the theological likelihood that *God was the One who raised Jesus* (cf. 877–79).

---

[2] Recall that by Dunn's definition, the data are the materials with which the historian works: testimony, artifacts, and so on.

[3] For Dunn, recall that the facts are interpretations of the known data.

Shared Emphases

The majority of the time, as I read Dunn's treatment of Jesus' resurrection, I found myself nodding in agreement, often enthusiastically. In most of these areas, even where we do not share entirely the same philosophical perspectives or the same reasons for holding them, there is a crucial core on which we agree. I will list briefly some of the more important items that we share, at least in many of the essentials.

First, I agree with Dunn that the specifics of historiography ought to be addressed carefully before one launches into a discourse on one's personal views. It is also especially helpful to delineate the particular approach that one takes, as he does (chaps. 3–6). I also prefer critical realism as a methodology. In such matters, Dunn follows a trail taken by a few recent historical Jesus scholars such as Ben Meyer[4] and N. T. Wright.[5] The application of his historical methodology led Dunn to mine a number of gems, though I will disagree with some of his conclusions, as is inevitable.

Unfortunately, too few contemporary historical Jesus scholars have laid similar foundations, and therefore some of their contributions appear to drift without a theoretical anchor. Moreover, speaking more formally, we need to step back even before our historiographical underpinnings in order to construct a prior philosophy of history, but that is a matter for another time.

At any rate, although I differ with Dunn on some of his key definitions and their application (see further discussion), I agree with him that there are no such things as "hard historical facts" that exist apart from researchers with their particular perspectives, angles, and prejudices. Thus the resulting historical conclusions must necessarily be couched in probabilistic terms that are corrigible. If we are going to align ourselves with the historical method, that is the best we can accomplish. But as he notes throughout, this need not keep us from arriving at carefully constructed cases that favor the historical data.

---

[4] B. F. Meyer, *The Aims of Jesus* (London: SCM, 1979), chaps. 4–5; idem, *Critical Realism and the New Testament* (Princeton Theological Monographs; Allison Park: Pickwick, 1989).

[5] N. T. Wright, *The New Testament and the People of God* (vol. 1 of *Christian Origins and the Question of God*; Minneapolis: Fortress, 1992), part 2, chaps. 2–5.

Second, the application of Dunn's methodology to the Synoptic Gospels, particularly his conclusions regarding the underlying oral traditions in the narratives and teaching texts, provides crucial parallels to other recent work that has placed special emphasis on the consistent transmission of the original data.[6] These conclusions provide a solid factual foundation on which to answer questions such as identifying as best we can what occurred in the last days of Jesus' life.

Third, moving more specifically to questions pertaining to the resurrection accounts, Dunn agrees with virtually all-recent commentators that these discussions must acknowledge the crucial importance of the postdeath experiences of Jesus' followers, who thought that they had witnessed the risen Jesus. Critical scholars almost always acknowledge that this is the key to this discussion.[7] These experiences were reported by both the disciples (841–57) and especially in Paul's eyewitness testimony to this own experience (856, 864). After an overview, Dunn emphasizes especially the strong considerations that favor the postdeath experiences of the women (843), of Peter (843–44), of the 11 disciples (849–51), of the other experiences reported in the pre-Pauline creed in 1 Cor 15:3–7 (854–55), and of Paul himself (856, cf. 210–12).

Fourth, more particularly, Dunn emphasizes the *sort* of occurrences experienced by Jesus' followers. Unquestionably, the central belief that the disciples, James the brother of Jesus, and Paul had experienced was that each one thought that he had *seen* Jesus after his death. This may perhaps be the single most important, "core" aspect of the discussion (858–66, 872–77). Dunn affirms confidently that "no one who has studied the data can doubt that the Christian witness on this theme began from a number of experiences understood as seeings of Jesus alive after he had been dead." Then Dunn continues, "The stories were remembered as visual or visionary experiences, because that is how they were experienced; that was the impact crystallized in the core tradition. They not only *believed* they had seen the Lord, they had *experienced* a seeing of the Lord alive from the dead" (861). I agree

---

[6] Most notably, see R. Bauckham, *Jesus and the Eyewitnesses: The Gospels as Eyewitness Testimony* (Grand Rapids: Eerdmans, 2006).

[7] See G. R. Habermas, "Experiences of the Risen Jesus: The Foundational Historical Issue in the Early Proclamation of the Resurrection," *Dialog* 45 (2006): 288–97.

wholeheartedly and have said often that the disciples' "seeings" are crucially important for any discussion of the resurrection traditions.[8]

Fifth, again agreeing with virtually all recent critical scholars, Dunn also shares the conclusion that the resurrection appearance tradition reported in the pre-Pauline creed in 1 Cor 15:3–7 dates from immediately after these events (142–43, 826, 836, 864). In fact, Dunn declares rather forcefully that "we can be entirely confident" that this exceptionally early confession dates from *"within months of Jesus' death"* (855; Dunn's emphasis). As with some of Dunn's other research, this proclamation has been affirmed recently by other influential critical scholars as well.[9] The value of having such crucial testimony from the very beginning of Christianity, particularly when it concerns the vital message of the Gospel proclamation, cannot be overestimated.

Sixth, moreover, the resurrection message was the central proclamation for all forms of early Christianity. There was no group (including the Q community) for which the resurrection was not celebrated. Put briefly, "as a historical statement we can say quite firmly: no Christianity without the resurrection of Jesus" (826; cf. 836).

Seventh, Dunn's emphasis on other early creedal statements in Paul (855–57, 864, 869), Acts (826), and elsewhere in the New Testament (826, 843–44) is also in line with that of the majority of recent scholars. This broadens the very early testimonial basis on which resurrection faith can be built. But some of Dunn's groundbreaking work on the value of the traditions included in the Synoptic Gospels adds even more to expand this foundation (192–254), especially when several of the particular Gospel passages deal specifically with various aspects of the resurrection testimony. Dunn's work can also help to affirm the reliability of these latter remembrances (841–54, 857–66).

Eighth, Dunn's evaluation of the empty tomb accounts in the Gospels once again aligns him with most contemporary scholars. But

---

[8] G. R. Habermas, "Resurrection Research from 1975 to the Present: What Are Critical Scholars Saying?" *JSHJ* 3 (2005): esp. 149–52.

[9] For similar affirmations, see L. W. Hurtado, *How on Earth Did Jesus Become a God?* (Grand Rapids: Eerdmans, 2005), esp. 4–5, 25–30; idem, *Lord Jesus Christ: Devotion to Jesus in Earliest Christianity* (Grand Rapids: Eerdmans, 2003), 71–72, 168–76; Bauckham, *Jesus and the Eyewitnesses*, especially chap. 11. Though older, see also the helpful distinctions in G. O'Collins, *Interpreting Jesus* (London: Geoffrey Chapman, 1983), chap. 4.

he presents more details here than the majority of his peers, beginning his discussion by identifying the characteristics of the core tradition of the empty tomb (829–31). Dunn concludes that these features are explained best as dating to the earliest Christian beginnings and resulting from the "oral traditioning process." The most likely source for the empty tomb accounts is those individuals who had been present themselves (831–32), as the tradition appears to be anchored in eyewitness testimony (840–41). Dunn adds that the story of the empty tomb "was probably being told in Jerusalem shortly after the event" (836). Dunn thinks that these conclusions are warranted by the facts that he presents, such as the centrality of female testimony, the nature of Jewish burial practices, the absence of any reports of Jesus' tomb being undisturbed, the lack of any tomb veneration, and Paul's probable knowledge of the empty tomb, all attesting to the veracity of his conclusion (832–41).

Ninth, although he only entertains a few alternative options, Dunn rejects several attempts to explain the empty tomb and resurrection appearances in natural terms (831–32, 838, 873–79). Elsewhere, he is much more direct, stating conclusively that "alternative interpretations of the data fail to provide a more satisfactory explanation."[10]

Tenth, an intriguing turn regarding the nature of Jesus' resurrection appearances is that Dunn rejects what is perhaps the most popular critical view, which holds that, over the years, the Gospel teachings gradually developed from a less to a more material view. It is usually said that early Christians desired to counteract critical questions regarding the reality of the appearances, so the latter grew increasingly more palpable.[11]

Dunn finds that this common position fails to account adequately for several traits of the early tradition, including the empty tomb, the early appearance reports, as well as the predominant Jewish view of resurrection (870).[12] To the contrary, Dunn begins his discussion of Jesus' resurrection body with the assertion that "the initial conceptualization of 'resurrection' was most likely in quite physical terms . . . to

---

[10] J. D. G. Dunn, *The Evidence for Jesus* (Philadelphia: Westminster, 1985), 76; cf. 71–72.

[11] For example, P. Perkins, *Resurrection: New Testament Witness and Contemporary Reflection* (Garden City, N.Y.: Doubleday, 1984), 94–95.

[12] Cf. also J. D. G. Dunn, *Jesus and the Spirit: A Study of the Religious and Charismatic Experience of Jesus and the First Christians as Reflected in the New Testament* (London: SCM, 1975), 116–22.

a life just like the present (that is, physical) life but now beyond the reach of death" (870). I have argued elsewhere that this is a growing recognition among contemporary critical scholars.[13]

As mentioned earlier, I agree with a great many of the positions that Dunn holds regarding the resurrection of Jesus, found at many of the crucial junctions. Still, I also think that a few aspects of his discussion need further clarification. It is to a few of these issues that I turn now.

Some Areas of Concern

Historiography

When defining the key terms that occupy much discussion in the study of historiography, Dunn employs an irregular and somewhat even peculiar usage. In the end, it even seems to exert some influence on his conclusions. To review briefly, "event" indicates occurrences in the irretrievable past for which we only have historical evidence, or "data." A study of the past can yield "facts," but unlike their usual meaning, these are neither the events nor the data but "are always an *interpretation* of the data" (102).

Dunn's second- and third-level distinctions here between the "data" (the historian's evidence) and the "facts" (their interpretations) are puzzling, if not confusing. It needlessly adds an extra step into the process, thereby shoving the unrecoverable event itself even further into the background. After all, why differentiate between the evidence and the interpretation, when arguably, as most recent researchers have noted, the historian cannot and should not meaningfully consider one without the other. Actually, separating them is more problematic. Generally, except in a pristine sense, knowing the evidence is very difficult, if not actually impossible, to separate from one's angle in viewing that data, at least in matters that are crucially important to us.[14]

---

[13] G. R. Habermas, "Mapping the Recent Trend toward the Bodily Resurrection Appearances of Jesus in Light of Other Prominent Critical Positions," in *The Resurrection of Jesus: John Dominic Crossan and N. T. Wright in Dialogue* (ed. R. B. Stewart; Minneapolis: Fortress, 2006), 78–92.

[14] M. White, *Foundations of Historical Knowledge* (New York: Harper & Row, 1965), chap. 1.

Against this backdrop, Dunn mentions the conclusions of Paula Fredriksen. But I think she is much closer to the normal usage when she refers to "facts" as the events as they are interpreted. Just as Dunn notes, in common parlance at least, facts *are* taken as the historical event plus its interpretation (102–3n5), though he actually avoids that delineation by separating these aspects.

Dunn's historiography is a study in contrasts. On the one hand, his critical realist methodology correctly postulates that complete objectivity is an illusion and that there are no such things as brute historical facts (107–9). But still, in spite of our own biases, our historical data are capable of rendering "very probable" and even "almost certain" verdicts on what actually occurred (102–3).

Therefore, when this method is applied to studies of Jesus' words and actions, it is unrealistic to think that we can arrive at some completely objective verdict, for we must keep in mind that the Gospels do not so much record what Jesus actually did or said but what he was *remembered* as doing or saying. Nonetheless, many of these reminiscences about Jesus come from the eyewitnesses (130–31) and they potentially present "us with surprising immediacy to the heart of the first memories of Jesus" (254).

Yet, Dunn appears to overemphasize the subjective direction by extending unnecessarily the secondary nature of the resurrection. Near the close of the volume, he inquires regarding the sense in which the resurrection might be considered as a historical event. He concludes that neither the resurrection itself, nor the appearances of Jesus, nor the empty tomb may be considered as historical data (i.e., as the historian's evidence). But strictly, neither is the statement that "Jesus has been raised from the dead" a "fact" (i.e., an interpretation of the data). Rather, the resurrection of Jesus is a second-order fact, one that is at best considered as an interpretation of an interpretation (876–77).

It is not immediately clear, however, whether Dunn thinks that this evaluation would also be the case with Paul's testimony regarding his own appearance. Is Paul's report any closer to the event itself? Dunn is clear "that with the appearance to Paul we have the closest thing to a firsthand personal testimony to a resurrection appearance" (856). Then is Paul's actual experience the irretrievable "event" and his later conclusions concerning it the "data"? It is difficult to know Dunn's precise position on this.

These distinctions are important for more than one reason. More is at stake here than simply defining and discussing the definitions of key terms in the study of historiography. We must emphasize that the better the quality of the evidence and the closer it is to the event(s) in question, the more probable it is that we may arrive at a solid conclusion regarding what really happened to Jesus. Although we are dealing with the canons of probability, we must not lose sight of the goal that the closer we can get to the convergence of eyewitness with early testimony, the more solid our historical conclusion becomes. Without this ability, most of our historical research would be in vain. Though corrigible and therefore open to future research, this does not negate the need to arrive presently at the most likely verdict that we can.

Dunn has said more than once that he does think that we can know things about the historical Jesus, his ministry, teachings, and actions (876, 882). Presumably, this results from the proper application of the data and facts. But he ought not to shrink back when we arrive at a carefully constructed case.

The Nature of the Resurrection Appearance to Paul

After concluding that "the core belief of the first Christians was of Jesus' bodily resurrection" (872), Dunn perhaps surprisingly adds that Paul's conception of the resurrection body (*pneumatikon sōma*), however, was more spiritual in nature. The "spiritual" portion of Paul's emphasis is due to his giving a bit of ground to his "Hellenized interlocutors," whereas the apostle's insistence on a real "body" was due to "his Jewish heritage" (871). If Paul witnessed the resurrected body of Jesus, then "what he saw was more like a 'light body'" (871, cf. 873), or as Dunn refers to it elsewhere, this was Paul's "great light experience on the Damascus road" (857). Thus, when Paul makes reference to the light of the Gospel or the glory of Christ, he "probably alludes" to Jesus' glorious appearance to him (857).

After Dunn's previous reasoning regarding the initial reports of the physical nature of Jesus' resurrection body, this conclusion was somewhat disappointing, and for more than one reason. Initially, a number of scholarly studies,[15] even by some of those who reject the historicity of Jesus' resurrection,[16] have recently concluded that the New Testament position is that of bodily resurrection. And each of these skeptical scholars is careful to point out that this includes Paul. This may even be the predominant scholarly position at present.[17]

Why especially would scholars like Lüdemann and Crossan reject the historicity of the resurrection but still hold that Paul at least thought that he saw bodily appearances of Jesus? Reasons such as those that Dunn himself allows for the other appearances carry much weight, even for Paul: the predominant Jewish view of resurrection, the nature of the appearance traditions, and the empty tomb reports.[18]

Other reasons could also be adduced for the conclusion that Paul held the same bodily view as did the other early believers. By far, the primary meaning and usage of *anastasis* in ancient accounts prior to AD 200, including pagan, Jewish, and Christian writings, is that of *bodily* resurrection. That even ancient opponents of resurrection would still use the term to refer to the raising of the body is significant. This is indeed a weighty argument.[19]

Further, Paul had identified himself with the Pharisaic tradition (Phil 3:4–6). A typical way to understand Josephus's emphasis (*Wars*

---

[15] For examples, see the sources listed here by L. W. Hurtado, N. T. Wright, and R. Gundry, as well as S. T. Davis's chapter in this volume. D. Allison, *Resurrecting Jesus: The Earliest Christian Tradition and Its Interpreters* (New York: T & T Clark, 2005), 226–27, 265–66, 317, 324–25. I cite many more scholars in "Mapping the Recent Trend toward the Bodily Resurrection Appearances," 88–90, especially nn48–59.

[16] Examples include J. D. Crossan and J. L. Reed, *In Search of Paul: How Jesus' Apostle Opposed Rome's Empire with God's Kingdom* (San Francisco: Harper, 2004), 6–10; G. Lüdemann, with O. Ozen, *What Really Happened to Jesus: A Historical Approach to the Resurrection* (trans. J. Bowden; Louisville: Westminster John Knox, 1995), 103.

[17] Habermas, "Mapping the Recent Trend toward the Bodily Resurrection Appearances," 90–92.

[18] While Paul does not mention the empty tomb directly, recall Dunn's reasoning that the apostle probably knew about it (839).

[19] N. T. Wright, *The Resurrection of the Son of God* (vol. 3 of *Christian Origins and the Question of God*; Minneapolis: Fortress, 2003), especially parts 1–3. In recent agreement with Wright's conclusions on the nature of *anastasis* as bodily resurrection, even for Paul, Crossan affirms that "I was already thinking along these same lines" ("Mode and Meaning in Bodily Resurrection Faith," in Stewart, ed., *The Resurrection of Jesus: John Dominic Crossan and N. T. Wright in Dialogue*, endnote 3).

of the Jews 2:8.14; *Antiquities of the Jews* 18:1.3)[20] is that the Pharisees held firmly to bodily resurrection. Also, if we accept the Acts interpretation that Paul also agreed with the Pharisees specifically on the notion of bodily resurrection (Acts 23:6–8), this would seem to form a crucial strand of argument. Although there is much discussion at this last point, this may possibly explain the Greek protest of Paul's resurrection message (Acts 17:31–32), due to the Hellenistic view that only the soul was immortal.

Further, Paul's anthropology provides additional details regarding his view of bodily resurrection. The apostle hoped that he would experience an "out-resurrection from among the dead ones" (*tēn exanastasin tēn ek nekron*; Phil 3:11), possessing a resurrection body like Jesus' glorified *body* (Phil 3:20–21). Paul also asserted similarly in 1 Cor 15:12, a text that Ben Witherington thinks indicates by itself that Paul held to bodily resurrection.[21] Robert Gundry has argued that many other passages in the authentic Pauline corpus clearly indicate that the apostle's anthropology calls for a bodily notion for the term *sōma*.[22]

Moreover, Paul's sociology favors bodily resurrection. He always speaks of the resurrection of the dead in the plural—all believers will be raised corporately. And the resurrected saints will inherit a renewed earth (Rom 8:18–23), which also seems to favor a bodily experience.

A last matter should also be mentioned. A majority of contemporary critical scholars, including Dunn, affirm the historicity of the empty tomb. Almost two dozen reasons have been identified that indicate this conclusion.[23] For those who hold that Paul implied that the tomb was empty (as Dunn seems to think; 833, 839), this is yet another

---

[20] In spite of the seeming contrast in Josephus, even the *Antiquities* passage (18:1:3) points out that the righteous are rewarded and the wicked are imprisoned, favoring the view of resurrection bodies.

[21] B. Witherington III, *The Paul Quest: The Renewed Search for the Jew of Tarsus* (Downers Grove: InterVarsity, 1998); for these and similar thoughts, cf. 18, 51, 138, 147–51, 210–13.

[22] R. H. Gundry, *Soma in Biblical Theology, with Emphasis on Pauline Anthropology* (Cambridge: Cambridge University Press, 1976; repr. Grand Rapids: Zondervan, 1987); see especially "The *soma* in Death and Resurrection," in ibid., 159–83.

[23] See G. R. Habermas, "The Empty Tomb of Jesus: Recent Critical Arguments," forthcoming article.

indication favoring the notion that Jesus' *body* was raised. What went into the tomb is what came out again (1 Cor 15:3–5).

But did Paul teach that his resurrection appearance was an experience of light, a less than bodily manifestation, as Dunn holds? This contention seems to be tenuous. At no point does Paul explicitly describe any resurrection appearance in terms of light. (For that matter, perhaps surprisingly, neither do the Gospel accounts.[24]) So to emphasize light appears to force the issue a bit.

More crucially, for those who emphasize the Acts accounts of Paul's conversion on the road to Damascus (Acts 9, 22, 26), even light appearances would not prove that Paul's appearance was less than bodily. Paul's personal statements that he saw Jesus (1 Cor 9:1; 15:8) are firsthand accounts that provide the key insights to his appearance. The Pauline data take precedence.[25] Then, if Paul supports bodily appearances in other ways, some of which we just mentioned, this further clarifies the situation. To favor the Acts implications over Paul's testimony, or to use them as the paradigm for interpreting Paul, seems strange.

For such reasons, I would argue that Dunn's own contentions as to why the early non-Pauline believers taught the bodily nature of the resurrection appearances should be extended to Paul's own view, as well. Paul's connection with the Pharisees, along with his anthropology, sociology, and implied empty tomb, argues in this direction as well. Especially in light of the absence of clearly contrary data, I conclude that Paul's position was most likely that of the Pharisees and virtually all others in the ancient world—that the term *anastasis* indicates bodily appearances.

The Probable Resurrection Appearance Scenario

In the first response, I dealt chiefly with Dunn's notions of historiography, his definitions of key terms, and the subject of his critical realist

---

[24] This is a reference to Jesus' appearances, not to the shining garments of the angels at the tomb, as mentioned in Matt 28:3 and Luke 24:4.

[25] Because they take Paul's own statements to exert priority over the accounts in Acts, Crossan and Reed "bracket that blinded-by-light sequence and imagine instead a vision in which Paul both *sees* and hears Jesus as the resurrected Christ, the risen Lord." Crossan and Reed, *In Search of Paul*, 8.

methodology. In the second rejoinder, I commented on his notion of the form taken by Jesus in Paul's resurrection appearance.

In this last response, I would like to pursue the more historical upshot of how these two previous conclusions actually affect Dunn's research on the subjects of the empty tomb and postresurrection appearances of Jesus. I might just add that the issue here appears to be more than just a clarification of meanings; the tension appears deeper than that. This seems all the more clear when we recall that the notion of historical research does not determine which philosophy of history suffices to better explain the data.

One concern is Dunn's conceptualization of the product of historical investigation in relation to Jesus.[26] We have said that his theme from the outset is to study the remembrances of Jesus by his followers, as they were impressed into the early Christian tradition. But certain more stunning statements are dispersed throughout the volume. For example, "I do not envisage 'getting back to Jesus' himself" (329). Or, the remembered Jesus "is as close as we will ever be able to reach back to him" (335). Finally, "our approach throughout has stressed the impossibility of our getting back to being Jesus himself" (490).

Yet, provocatively, Dunn also cautions his readers that this "impossibility" should not be misunderstood as Dunn saying that "nothing" can be said about Jesus (876). Perhaps this is because "we can certainly hope to look behind that impact to *the one who made that impact*" (882; Dunn's emphasis). It seems that even some of us who are sensitive to his work and actually think that he has made some very positive strides in historical Jesus research will still be confused by this seeming dialectic.

It appears to me that there is a reasonable amount of tension here: if we are not careful, we will constantly walk the tightrope between what the early disciples remembered of Jesus and what we can (or cannot) say about the accuracy of their comments. This tension carries over to our subject of the resurrection of Jesus. We have seen that Dunn clarifies that his focus is on the disciples' remembrance and "eschews

---

[26] Several more theoretical discussions lurk in the background. A crucial issue is provided here by recent discussions in philosophy of history and its outworking into the practices of historiography.

any attempt to get behind that belief to some objectively conceived event" (875). It is unclear whether he is simply questioning the discovery of "objective" conclusions, which are not the domain of historical inquiry (as per 102–5), or if it is getting behind the remembrances in any form that concerns him, or both. But we want to guard carefully against philosophical presuppositions determining in advance what history can and cannot conclude.

Then, just a page later, he sums up this immediate discussion. The early tradition "pushes us to the conclusion" that the perceptions such as the empty tomb and appearances actually pertained to *Jesus* and were "not just something which happened to the *disciples*." This leads Dunn to the "more plausible explanation for the origin and core content of the tradition itself" and consists of "something" that actually happened to Jesus on the original Easter Sunday (876).

It seems that his conclusion, then, is that we are justified in holding at the very least that "something" happened to Jesus. The original, outward remembrances of this "something" were the empty tomb and appearances. But even as I attempt to state carefully this interpretation, I am unsure if I am properly nuancing the dialectic that appears to be present throughout Dunn's work. I do not wish to force Dunn's thesis into a different shape.

I will leave aside for the moment the proper relation between the disciples' remembrances and any possible characteristics of Jesus. Instead, I will briefly draw on a thesis that I have proposed in many publications on this topic. I will suggest that we might establish a minimalistic approach to "peek" behind the New Testament accounts. I will begin with the virtually unanimous critical agreement that the relevant sources sufficiently establish that Jesus died by crucifixion.[27]

---

[27] Crossan states, "I take it absolutely for granted that Jesus was crucified under Pontius Pilate." J. D. Crossan, *The Historical Jesus* (San Francisco: HarperCollins, 1991), 372. Crossan further asserts, "That he was crucified is as sure any anything historical can ever be." Idem, *Jesus* (San Francisco: HarperCollins, 1994), 145. Marcus Borg comments that "the most certain fact about the historical Jesus is his execution as a political rebel." M. Borg, *Jesus, A New Vision* (San Francisco: HarperCollins, 1987), 179. Compare the similar comment by Dunn: "That Jesus was crucified on the direct authority of Pilate himself need not be doubted for a minute" (775). These three scholars do not hesitate to provide details regarding some of the facts that may be known about crucifixion (Crossan, *The Historical Jesus*, 372–76; Borg, 178–84; Dunn, *Jesus Remembered*, 774–81).

Further, hardly any critical scholars will deny that Jesus' followers had experiences (singly and in groups) that they thought were appearances of the risen Jesus.[28] If with Dunn and the majority of recent scholars we also allow the tradition of the empty tomb, what we get is the following scenario, based on the earliest remembrances of the witnesses: Jesus died by crucifixion. Afterward, his followers believed that they saw him alive. His burial tomb seemed to be empty, as well.

Following Dunn again we can arrive at a similar minimal but powerful conclusion: "No one who has studied the data can doubt that the Christian witness on this theme began from a number of experiences understood as seeings of Jesus alive after he had been dead" (861). We need *not* introduce here what Dunn terms the secondary miraculous interpretation that God raised Jesus from the dead (877), concentrating simply on the best space-time cause of these experiences, whatever they were. Still, we are left with the fairly straightforward conclusion that, on several occasions, the best data indicate the belief that a dead man was witnessed or seen as being alive again. When we add the less probable but still likely empty tomb, the thesis expands further.

It seems that few should object here, since these data are exceptionally well established and are allowed as historical even by skeptical scholars. As Bart Ehrman states, "Historians, of course, have no difficulty whatsoever speaking about the belief in Jesus' resurrection, since this is a matter of public record. For it is a historical fact that some of Jesus' followers came to believe that he had been raised from the dead soon after his execution."[29] One could always, if desired, espouse naturalistic alternatives to account for these reports.[30]

Although quite minimal, does this give us the best glimpse (or even the most educated guess) of what may lie behind the New Testament

---

[28] For a list of 60 critical scholars who acknowledge this, see G. Habermas, *The Risen Jesus and Future Hope* (Lanham, Md.: Rowman & Littlefield, 2003), chap. 1, esp. 46–48n148. For an additional, very recent acknowledgment here, see B. D. Ehrman, *Jesus, Interrupted: Revealing the Hidden Contradictions in the Bible (And Why We Didn't Know about Them)* (San Francisco: HarperCollins, 2009), 177–78.

[29] B. D. Ehrman, *Jesus: Apocalyptic Prophet of the New Millennium* (Oxford: Oxford University Press, 1999), 231; see also 230.

[30] For those few scholars who would dispute Jesus' death or the later experiences by Jesus' followers, the data for each, as well as additional reports, should of course be discussed freely.

accounts of *why* Jesus was remembered this way? Is this the closest we can come?[31]

But this may be the clinching point, especially for those like Dunn[32] (as well as the majority of other scholars[33]) who reject naturalistic accounts of the resurrection appearances. May we at least conclude in these cases only that it is a warranted stance that Jesus was dead and was probably (in some sense) seen alive later, without reference to the cause or purpose of this event? After all, we have multiple early reminiscences of the *seeings* of Jesus (854–62), formulated as tradition within just months of the crucifixion (855). Crucially, "the more plausible explanation for the origin and core content of the tradition itself" is that whatever occurred was thought to have happened to Jesus himself and not merely to his disciples (876). If so, then something *must* lie behind these experiences as their foundation and cause. For the many for whom natural alternatives cannot account viably for the data, we have a further hint. Significantly, to say as we have that whatever the "something" was most plausibly happened to Jesus himself is *already* to take a huge step in this direction.

Reminiscences do not merely hang in space, of course. I am not asking here about the *interpretations* that we give these occurrences but only about the accuracy of the core, remembered accounts. May we affirm with E. P. Sanders that Jesus appearing to his followers after his death is one of the "secure facts," even though one may add that exactly what form the appearances took is difficult to say?[34]

---

[31] Dunn's position in *The Evidence for Jesus* is similar in many respects to that in *Jesus Remembered*. In the former, he seems to come closer to an affirmation like mine at the close of this chapter (73–75). But as I said earlier, statements in *Jesus Remembered* such as the conclusion on p. 876, referred to earlier, certainly could be either this or, in a more subjective sense, of not being able to draw any further conclusions.

[32] Both in *Jesus Remembered* (838, 873–79), as well as elsewhere (*The Evidence for Jesus*, 68, 71–72, 76).

[33] For an extensive description and overview of the naturalistic positions held by some recent scholars, see G. R. Habermas, "The Late Twentieth-Century Resurgence of Naturalistic Responses to Jesus' Resurrection," *TJ*, NS 22 (2001): 179–96. For a survey of how these thinkers compare to the much larger number of scholars who reject naturalistic hypotheses, see Habermas, "Mapping the Recent Trend toward the Bodily Resurrection Appearances," esp. 91–92.

[34] E. P. Sanders, *The Human Figure of Jesus* (London: Penguin, 1993), 11; cf. similarly, 13, 278, 280.

Even more succinctly, we have many very early remembrances of the initial disciples actually seeing Jesus again, almost immediately after his death. Particularly for those like Dunn who hold that natural alternative hypotheses are not feasible, the most likely explanation is that Jesus did indeed appear to them. So I ask Dunn, especially since he holds that behind the remembrances of Jesus' disciples most plausibly lie actual events that involved Jesus himself and not just his followers alone, at least for those who eschew natural alternatives, are these not most likely the postdeath appearances of Jesus? If this is not so, how else may we learn about the Jesus behind the remembrances, as Dunn maintains is possible?

14

IN GRATEFUL DIALOGUE

A RESPONSE TO MY INTERLOCUTORS

JAMES D. G. DUNN

How do I adequately thank colleagues and friends who do me the great honor of contributing to a volume devoted to the discussion of my attempt to join the debate about what and how much can be said today regarding the beginnings of the history of Jesus of Nazareth? I can at least say, "Thank you," and I do so with a glad and grateful heart. Thanks also to Bob Stewart for suggesting the enterprise and for gathering such a great band of contributors. More than that, however, I can contribute to the dialogue of which these contributions are such a welcome part. I cannot think of a more fitting response.

Many years ago, I entertained briefly the foolishly audacious thought that one day I might write such a masterfully polished piece that it would be counted as definitional ("the last word") for a generation. But the thought did not last long, for it was already more than obvious to me that by myself I could never attain such a comprehensive and well-informed view of a subject as might merit such esteem. There is a corporate dimension to knowledge that means that any individual sees only partially and can present only a limited or restricted perspective. Knowledge, and growth in knowledge, in other words, is unavoidably dialogical—complementary, interacting, and reacting. Knowledge

includes the humility of acknowledging how little one knows. We
need to dialogue, to hear what others have to say, to let their contributions improve, correct and reshape what others recognize as truth
telling, and to trash whatever has gone badly wrong.

So I have always hoped that what I write will be helpful to more
than the other 40 scholars in the world who share my particular interests. I have hoped that others will feel it sufficiently worth their time
to raise questions, to ask for clarifications, to draw attention to the
many inadequacies, to suggest better ways to make valid points, and
so on. In lectures, I regularly seek to be more provocative than I need
(or want) to be, in the hope that the questions or discussion following the lecture will give me the opportunity to make a more rounded
presentation, drawing attention to issues I passed by or treated too
briefly, allowing me to rephrase what has come across differently from
what I had intended, and so on. My hope is always that any dialogue
that a lecture or a book provokes will give me a better insight into the
subject, will suggest improvements on the way I can present it, and
will, of course, be of benefit or value to the others who take part in the
dialogue. This is very much how I have approached the challenge of
responding to the chapters of this book.

Since I regard this as a conversation in seminar style, I will refer
to my conversation partners by their first names and hope I am not
being too presumptuous.

1. **Bob Stewart** does a fine job of "situating" my *Jesus Remembered*
in the history of Jesus research. I agree with him that I am probably
closest to my Durham colleague Tom Wright (bishop of Durham), as
shown by our shared "critical realism" methodological approach to the
subject and with his evaluation of my differences with Tom. I accept
his semirebuke that I could have made more use of speech-act theory,
though I confess that I have never really been "turned on" by it. I am not
sure how "the role that worldviews play in communication and interpretation" would or should have affected my methodological section and
subsequent findings. I would certainly be interested in fuller dialogue
with specialists in philosophical hermeneutics on my use of Gadamer.

I think I would like to have seen more attention given to what
are, for me, key features of *Jesus Remembered* and what are probably the
book's most distinctive features. One is what I take to be an a priori

probability: that Jesus was a figure whose mission, in its character and its teaching, made a considerable *impact* on his immediate followers. It is this fact that I am confident can be taken as given, which allows me to speak of *faith* as already a factor before Easter. It is this fact that enables me to argue that high esteem for Jesus (faith) should not be set aside or stripped away from the data as post-Easter and "nonhistorical."

The second is that the synoptic tradition of Jesus' mission provides a remarkably consistent and coherent portrayal of Jesus. Even allowing for all the diversity of the individual compilations and emphases, as of course we must do, the Jesus portrayed is recognizably the same. That doyen of British New Testament (NT) scholars, C. H. Dodd, expressed it well: "The first three gospels offer a body of sayings on the whole so consistent, so coherent, and withal so distinctive in manner, style and content, that no reasonable critic should doubt, whatever reservations he may have about individual sayings, that we find here reflected the thought of a single, unique teacher."[1]

The distinctiveness of my approach is to bring these two features together, both the a priori given and the evident character of the synoptic tradition. My argument, in brief, is that the second is the outworking of the first. More fully, my argument is that the impact made by Jesus was first expressed more or less by his disciples in sharing stories about Jesus and in reflecting on forms of his teaching that were integral to the disciples' own preaching and teaching, both before Jesus' death and after his resurrection.

It is in filling out this link that the terms "memory" and "oral tradition" come into play. My argument is that the synoptic tradition still provides clear indication of how Jesus was remembered and that the undoubted period of oral tradition explains how both the unity and variety of the synoptic tradition came about—that is, how the synoptic tradition gained the character that it still has.

2. The chapter by **Markus Bockmuehl** is everything that one could hope for in the dialogue on the questions and issues raised by *Jesus Remembered*, and I am grateful for his generous remarks. He justifiably notes the lacunae and blind spots in the early chapters, probably inevitable in an all too brief attempt to outline what seem to

---

[1] C. H. Dodd, *The Founder of Christianity* (London: Collins, 1971), 21–22.

me to be the characteristic emphases, key issues brought to light and deficiencies of the earlier life of Jesus research. But naturally I focus on the five issues he raises.

In response to the first question, I acknowledge at once that I did not do justice to Birger Gerhardsson, a failure that I have tried to compensate for in subsequent lectures and in correspondence with Birger. The reasons were several. (a) The anecdotal accounts of Kenneth Bailey of how foundational and other tradition worked orally within Middle East congregations in the twentieth century explained, as nothing I had previously encountered, the character of the synoptic tradition. Years of leading seminars on the Huck *Synopsis* of the Gospels had started from and inevitably returned to the same feature: that the Synoptic Gospels told the same stories, repeated the same teaching, but *differently*. Why this basic feature— the *same* yet *different*? The traditional literary analyses in terms of written sources copied and redacted only went so far. They explained where the differences were small or where the reasons for redaction were obvious. But they did not explain why in half of the synoptic parallel material, the differences were great and inconsequential. Performance variation, typical in celebration and transmission of oral tradition, seemed to shed light on this and, an added bonus, also gave insight into the way the Jesus tradition had evolved and been used in what more or less everyone accepts was a 20- to 40-year period of oral transmission.

(b) In seeking to mark out my approach as distinctive, I overplayed the difference between Bailey's local congregation model and Birger's rabbinic school model. That was not fair, since Birger, particularly in the sequels to his great *Memory and Manuscript*, had also emphasized that his model recognized and accounted also for the variation in the synoptic tradition. The value for me of the Bailey model, however, was that it extended beyond the teaching context (equivalent to a rabbinic school) to embrace the local congregation being fed by and relishing the Jesus tradition in informal as well as formal gatherings. I will come back to this in my third point.

In response to the second question, yes, I did not provide a theory of memory, and that left me very vulnerable to the criticism of a volume titled *Jesus Remembered*. As Markus notes, I have tried to make some amends for this weakness in subsequent writing.[2] But I should perhaps explain that my primary object was to reach a better understanding of the character of the synoptic tradition—the same yet different. As I have already indicated in response to Bob Stewart, memory for me is what provided the explanatory link between the impact made by Jesus and the Jesus tradition in its same yet different character. That, for me, was self-evidently how the memories of the first disciples had worked. I did not see a need to provide a theoretical model of how memory works, no more than did Birger in his *Memory and Manuscript*. The synoptic tradition was for me (as I assume also for Birger) the evidence and proof of how the first disciples' memories had worked.

Regarding the third question, Markus justifiably echoes the criticisms of Samuel Byrskog and Richard Bauckham that I have not given enough attention and emphasis to the eyewitness testimony and authority attributed to the apostolic witnesses. I probably deserve the rebuke, though I always did emphasize the role of Jesus' own first disciples in forming and shaping the Jesus tradition. How could I fail to do so, since my whole thesis depends on recognizing the impact that Jesus made on these disciples? And its basic thrust is precisely that these disciples (eye- and ear-witnesses) were the responsible agents in formulating and beginning the process of spreading the Jesus tradition. Of course, I recognize the vital role of the first disciples in the whole process! What I did not want to do was to make the authority and value of the Jesus tradition dependent on being able to trace it back to specific eyewitnesses. Richard tries to do so, but the difficulty of tracing Q tradition back to named sources is fairly obvious, as is the difficulty of finding any indication that the importance of that tradition was thought to depend on the tradents being able to cite apostolic authority for the tradition (an interesting parallel to the neglect of Paul and James to cite Jesus as the authority for their references and allusions to his teaching). Without questioning for one minute the vital role of the first disciples (a larger group than the apostles) in

---

[2] Particularly J. D. G. Dunn, "Social Memory and the Oral Jesus Tradition," in *Memory in the Bible and Antiquity* (WUNT 212; ed. L. T. Stuckenbruck et al.; Tübingen: Mohr Siebeck, 2007), 179–94.

beginning the process of formulating and passing on the Jesus tradition, my concern was rather to account for the congregations where apostles as such were at best occasional visitors, and founding figures, like Epaphras in Colossae and the other churches of the Lycus valley, were at one or several removes from the first apostles.

Similarly, I do not emphasize sufficiently that much of the shape of the Jesus tradition was given by Jesus' own teaching style. I suppose I took it for granted that it would be more appreciated, than has proved to be the case, that the impact made by Jesus was made in large part by his teaching, both content and style. And the importance of the role of teachers in the early Christian communities, again a larger and more local group than named apostles, I regarded as equally obvious.

It is, of course, true that I pay little attention to John's Gospel. That was simply because to do John sufficient justice would have required a full discussion of its date and character. That will be one of the principal tasks of volume 3 of *Christianity in the Making*, and I hope that in that volume I can provide an adequate account both of the relationship of John's testimony to that of the Synoptics and of its own distinctive merits.

In response to the fourth question, I am slightly surprised by Markus's fourth point. As he noted, I have affirmed both Markan priority and a second written source of Matthew and Luke (Q), though I think that much of the "Q" material is better understood as oral and not yet written tradition. So I have no problem with recognizing source and redaction when the data calls for that as the best explanation. My criticism has been that the literary explanation of the Synoptics has been assumed when it does not provide any obvious explanation for many or most of the *divergences* between Synoptic Gospels. In contrast, it makes historical sense to me that Jesus tradition was much more widely known in oral form even after written material and Gospels began also to be circulated. That, for example, Matthew knew different versions of stories and teaching in Mark, and that in a good number of cases preferred the familiar oral version to Mark's, seems to me the most obvious explanation on several differences between Mark and Matthew.

I am also slightly puzzled over why Markus does not see the obvious linkage between the "impact" made by Jesus and the Jesus who made that impact. I work with the obvious image of the stamp: the pattern of the stamp leaves its image by the impact it makes on the wax stamped; from the impact, we can readily discern the character of the one who made the impact. I could quote C. H. Dodd (n1) again. So it poses no problem to me to affirm both that we can get back only to the remembered Jesus, to the impact made by Jesus, still evident in the content and character of the Jesus tradition, and that we can speak with some confidence about the one who made that impact and reflect realistically about his aims and even his self-understanding.

In response to the fifth question, I resonate with much of what Markus says here, as I do with much of what Bob Morgan says in the similar dialogue we have had over *Jesus Remembered*.[3] My concern in *Jesus Remembered* was simply to attain a realistic historical appreciation of the impact Jesus made on his first disciples. That for me is what the Quest is all about. On the assumption that Jesus is historically significant, in the first place, because he made a powerful impact on his first disciples, the endeavor is to grasp as far as possible the character and force of that impact (perhaps even, in a real sense, to experience something of that impact as the Jesus tradition is read and reflected on today). Of course, the Christology that emerged (and emerged quickly) from the "Jesus event" found it necessary to speak of Jesus in terms of divinity. And that will become clear as *Christianity in the Making* proceeds. What I want to avoid is any suggestion that the impact made by Jesus during his mission in Galilee and Judea cannot be appreciated without a prior assumption that the Christology of the next four centuries is true, any assumption that the Jesus tradition can be rightly read only through the lenses that subsequent Christology provides. The subsequent Christology was certainly the outcome of the impact made by Jesus, but it is the initial impact itself that I set out to discern and describe, though always with the thought (and hope) in mind that someone who recognizes (and experiences) that impact from encountering the Jesus tradition today will be encouraged to follow out the further trail of that impact.

---

[3] R. Morgan, "James Dunn's *Jesus Remembered*," *ExpT* 116 (2004): 1–6; J. D. G. Dunn, "On Faith and History, and Living Tradition," *ExpT* 116 (2004): 13–19; R. Morgan, "Christian Faith and Historical Jesus Research: A Reply to James Dunn," *ExpT* 116 (2005): 217–23; J. D. G. Dunn, "A Letter to Robert Morgan," *ExpT* 116 (2005): 286–87.

3. I found **Scot McKnight's** chapter both perceptive and helpfully informative, particularly in his latter discussion of contemporary historiography. Taking Flannery O'Connor as the starting (and concluding) point is a great tweak to what can easily become a rather dull literary debate. Nevertheless, I was slightly confused by his talk of "(data that are embedded in) facts,"[4] since it still seems important to me to distinguish "data" from "facts," in that "(historical) facts" are more accurately described as "interpreted data."[5] But the main points for discussion are the six that Scot lists early in his chapter.

We should start by clarifying the question of what we mean by the "historical Jesus." When they have asked that question, the leading Questers have usually been clear that they mean the figure of Jesus as reconstructed by historical method. Nevertheless, in more common speech, the phrase "the historical Jesus" is used to refer to the Jesus of Nazareth who walked, lived, and taught in Galilee (probably) in the late AD 20s. This is where the distinction between data and facts comes in: "the historical Jesus," properly speaking, is a figure composed of the facts deduced from the evidence available—that is, of the "interpreted data."

My protest at this point is against the working assumption that the interpretations of previous generations of Questers, stretching back indeed to the earliest interpretations of the first Christians, have to be and can be stripped away, like the strata of an archaeological tell, to reveal an uninterpreted artifact ("the historical Jesus" = Jesus as he actually was) beneath all the strata. I try to reverse the process, abandoning the assumption that "interpretation" (faith) is always something that needs to be stripped away if the "brute facts" are to be recovered in their pristine originality. I argue that the impact made by Jesus actually forms the first layer of interpretation—already a diverse layer, since various individuals are involved. Or, rather than use the too static image of "layers," my argument is that the beginning of the process of ongoing interpretation is precisely the impact made by Jesus and that the synoptic form of the Jesus tradition provides clear evidence of how that process proceeded during the first generation of Christianity.

---

[4] McKnight, chapter 3, p. 56.
[5] J. D. G. Dunn, *Jesus Remembered* (vol. 1 of *Christianity in the Making*; Grand Rapids: Eerdmans, 2003), 102–4. Jens Schröter takes up this point helpfully in his chapter.

My point, which Scot fully takes, is that we do not have a sufficiently diverse range of data (the views of Jesus and reactions to Jesus of other of Jesus' contemporaries in their own terms) to enable us by triangulation to plot the location and position of Jesus—which would give the modernist historian the opportunity to make "objective" interpretation of the data and judgment about Jesus. All we effectively have is the Jesus of the Gospels—the Jesus who made the impact that the Gospels express and embody. But that is the Jesus, the Jesus who made that impact, who the historian inquiring into the beginnings of Christianity surely wants to "find."

In his first question, Scot seems to me in danger of falling into this old trap—of suggesting that one can speak informedly and meaningfully about a "historical Jesus" who is distinct from "the remembered Jesus." There are cases where we can speak of a historical figure other than in terms of the way he was remembered—when we have speeches and writings that the figure made and have survived. But with others, as with Jesus, it is true that all we have is the remembered figure—the impact he made, the influence he exercised. My point, already made in an earlier response, is that by recognizing this fact in the case of Jesus, that all we have is the impact he made, we can actually discern the character of the person who made that impact and the character of his mission. So it is possible to distinguish the impact from the one who made the impact but only through and by means of the impact as evidenced in the Jesus tradition.

Scot speaks of a threefold distinction—between a "historical Jesus," a "remembered Jesus," and the evangelists' (or Church's) Jesus. If we once again avoid the confusion of what is meant by the "historical Jesus," my point can be put thus: whereas earlier Questers worked with a clear and often sharp distinction between the "historical Jesus" and the evangelists' (or Church's) Jesus, I want to insist that "the remembered Jesus" actually forms the link and bridge between the other two. "What good is the remembered Jesus?" asks Scot. I reply, precisely in that he bridges the gap between Jesus' otherwise virtually unattested mission in the late 20s and the narrative Jesus of the 70s and 80s, precisely because the remembered Jesus shows us the impact and influence of Jesus through that half century, how his mission was remembered, and its significance assessed and spoken about.

Of course, we can distinguish the remembered Jesus from the evangelists' Jesus but not in the sense that they are clearly distinct and mutually exclusive. On the contrary, the synoptic evangelists show how the shared Jesus tradition could be slanted and further interpreted. But the shared commonality (I refer once again to Dodd), the remembered Jesus, remained a stable element in the interpreted tradition. And I try to avoid the term "authentic," because, as Scot recognizes, the evangelists' Jesus indicates and expresses the continued outworking of the original impact, the impact in its varied expressions in varied situations. I do not regard it as appropriate, for example, to label Mark 7 as "authentic" and Matthew 15 as "inauthentic"; both indicate the diverse impact made by Jesus' teaching on purity. But I do recognize that it is the overall narrative form that brings out the significance of Jesus' mission and the coherence of its different elements. What I would resist is the suggestion that the narrative structure was imposed on the Jesus tradition only by the evangelists, and what I would like to discuss further is the extent to which the narrative structure of Jesus' mission was given by the mission itself and was already in the earliest preaching of the gospel (as in Acts 10:34–43).

Scot's fourth question seems to miss the point. It is true that "the faith-impact on the nature of the Gospel traditions" has been a factor in the Quest. But surely in the sense that it is that post-Easter faith that Questers sought to strip away in order to pursue a historical Jesus in more "objective" terms, untrammeled by the blinkers of a faith perspective. My point is that faith came in at the first level—the faith-creating impact made by Jesus—so that it cannot be stripped away to leave an unfaith core (the onion has no core, contains no kernel). Of course, you could say there is some unfaith data (that Jesus came from Galilee, that he was crucified in Jerusalem, etc.), but such data do not begin to give an account of or to explain the significance of Jesus, "the historic Jesus."

Scot's fifth question still stumbles on the confused use of the term "historical." The bare datum (that Jesus was crucified in Jerusalem in AD 30) is just that—a bare datum. The "redemptive" character of the event (its *geschichtliche* character) is the impact that it made on the disciples and the significance they recognized in it and in the resurrection of Jesus that they saw to be its sequel. I will have to return to this subject in a later discussion (#12).

And the final issue raised by Scot seems to express a hankering after the old days when the synoptic tradition could and should be analyzed exclusively in literary terms, of copying and redacting written sources—a skill in which I remember Scot excelled. But I am fascinated by the fact that Matthew and Luke do not always copy Mark; they sometimes prefer a different version of the story. And they know other material (for a start, "Q"), some of which overlaps with Markan tradition. So I am by no means driven to conclude that Mark (i.e., an already written Mark) is the core or sole form of the Jesus tradition on which Matthew and Luke could draw. For myself, the thought that Matthew and Luke, until they received their copies of Mark, were wholly ignorant of the Jesus tradition that Mark contains is historically incredible if not ludicrous. My response in an earlier conversation, which Scot quotes (n14), "Of course, we can't know if it is oral," is simply an acknowledgment that all the Jesus tradition has come down to us (inevitably) in written form. But that is hardly to affirm that the Jesus tradition was always and only circulated in written form. And if we cannot say anything about the Jesus tradition in its oral form, we have to accept that we cannot say much, if anything, about the first 30 or so years of the Jesus tradition—not a conclusion I want to be left with.

4. **Samuel Byrskog** poses another great set of issues that really require an extended conversation to begin to do them justice. This in fact is the second round in our conversation on the subject of oral tradition and oral history,[6] but the mutual clarification of what our agreements and disagreements amount to would take several more rounds. So let me simply try to clear away some of the confusions I have caused so that the conversation can focus on the issues on which positive progress may be made.

Samuel begins by justifiably asking me what is "new" about what I went on to characterize as "a new perspective on Jesus." A Swede has justification for asking this question, a justification that few if any others have, for focus on "oral tradition" has been a major contribution

---

[6] S. Byrskog, "A New Perspective on the Jesus Tradition: Reflections on James D. G. Dunn's Jesus Remembered," *JSNT* 26 (2004): 459–71; J. D. G. Dunn, "On History, Memory and Eyewitnesses: In Response to Bengt Holmberg and Samuel Byrskog," *JSNT* 26 (2004): 473–87.

of Swedish biblical scholarship, as Samuel points out. So I should not overemphasize that claim (a "new perspective") too much. It should be remembered, though, that it was not a term of which I made anything in *Jesus Remembered*. The "new perspective" characterization came in only with my briefer *A New Perspective on Jesus*,[7] in which I attempted to clarify in a more focused way both my protests at dominant features of the earlier Quests and my own alternatives. Without over-emphasizing the "newness" of my approach, I still find it necessary to protest both against the predominantly negative view of "faith" in the traditional quest for the "historical Jesus" and against the almost exclusive analysis of the history of the Jesus tradition in literary terms. My emphasis on the impact made by Jesus as the starting point for a historical appreciation of the Jesus tradition, on oral tradition as the way that impact continued to have an effect in the earliest Christian communities, and on the Synoptic tradition as embodying and expressing that impact is, if not entirely "new," then arguably "new" enough to merit some of the attention that this volume gives it.

In all the issues that Samuel goes on to raise, it is important for me to say again that the moving force in my thesis is not a theory of memory, of oral history, or even Kenneth Bailey's model of informal controlled tradition. My motivation is the synoptic tradition itself—finding the most satisfactory explanation of its "same yet different" character. So I have no doubt whatsoever that Jesus was an effective teacher and that the impact still visible in the Jesus tradition well expresses his intention as a teacher.

Nor do I have any problem whatsoever with a theory of oral history, when its primary focus is on individuals telling their own stories, giving their own accounts of the impact Jesus had made on them. Indeed, I find such a theory entirely complementary to my historical imagining of the first disciples telling their stories and passing on the teaching that they learned from Jesus. I find oral history less attractive as an explanatory model when its illustrations are of late twentieth-century historians seeking out World War II or London blitz veterans, who had previously tried to forget the horrors of the

[7] J. D. G. Dunn, *A New Perspective on Jesus: What the Quest for the Historical Jesus Missed* (Grand Rapids: Baker Academic, 2005).

early 1940s, and encouraging them to remember and tell the stories they had tried to exclude from their memories. That depiction of oral history is too much like the parody of the evangelists trying to compose their Gospels by dredging up forgotten memories of Jesus. I do not for a moment think that is what Samuel has in mind, which is why I do not regard his probing here as undermining my thesis in any substantive way.

Similarly, I have no problem with a process of "traditioning" that is both a remembering and an interpreting. Here again it seems to me that the synoptic tradition shows precisely how that worked out in the early years of Christianity—both a substantive and coherent impression made by Jesus (remembered), and an ordering, grouping, and interpreting of that tradition typical, I assume, of the ways in which the Jesus tradition was used, taught, and transmitted across the diverse range of early churches. And that would include the early gatherings in house and apartment churches in the Mediterranean cities as Christianity expanded. I would find it hard, for example, to understand how Paul could assume such knowledge of Jesus' character and teaching as he does, unless the Jesus tradition was part of the regular communal gatherings of these churches.

Nor do I have any problem with asserting both the role of key individuals, local teachers, and the community as a whole. Of course, we should not "dismiss Papias and Irenaeus as unreliable."[8] The idea is more than mildly ridiculous. I thought I had emphasized the crucial role of the first disciples in first formulating and spreading the Jesus tradition. And there need not be any doubt that when one of these first disciples (apostles) visited a church, say in Macedonia or Asia, the local Christians would have been as anxious to hear from them firsthand, not necessarily only to learn something about Jesus they did not already know, but also to have confirmed "from the horse's mouth" what they were already familiar with, or even stories that had personally involved the visitor. My appeal to the model suggested by Bailey's *haflat samar* was never intended as an alternative that excluded the continuing role of first disciples and apostles. It was intended rather to show how the Jesus tradition would probably have functioned when

[8] Byrskog, chapter 4, p. 70.

no such visitors were present, as would probably be the case most of the time.[9]

Samuel at times skirts the danger of taking one of my affirmations as excluding other alternatives. I do not think I said that early church teachers "simply reinforced their church's corporate memory." That they did reinforce that corporate memory I do affirm. But that corporate memory was formed not least *by* the teaching—that is, the teaching of the Jesus tradition, which the founding apostles and teachers had already given them. And I note that Samuel goes on to speak of "joint acts of co-remembering,"[10] which moves back to what I had in mind in talk of communal remembering.

What is needed in all this, it seems to me, is a much more flexible depiction of the whole process from Jesus to the Gospels: a process begun by first disciples and apostles, a process for which they ultimately took responsibility, a process involving explicit catechesis and teaching, visiting apostles, and teachers interpreting the tradition for which they took local responsibility. A process in which congregations were involved as teaching on one subject set echoes of other teaching resonating through their minds and where bolder spirits did not hesitate to question when interpretation moved too far from what they were familiar with. This process allows room for and takes account of different kinds of orality, to be sure, and of the rhetorical character of the traditioning process, no doubt. It is a process where evangelists can be envisaged as writing down their church's Jesus tradition (expressive of their community's collective memory), as well as seeking out eyewitnesses and earwitnesses of Jesus' own mission (and how different would the result be?) as well as giving their own "spin" to the tradition they record.

Samuel seems to want a conceptual model that would embrace and explain all these flexibilities and more. I am not so enamored of sociological models and prefer to look for an explanation that is sufficient and makes best sense of the character of the Jesus tradition in

---

[9] Here I may refer to my interaction with Richard Bauckham in "Eyewitnesses and the Oral Jesus Tradition," *JSHJ* 6 (2008): 85–105, and say how much I look forward to Samuel's interaction with Richard also (Byrskog, chapter 4, 71n40).

[10] Byrskog, chapter 4, p. 72.

its function as the key link between Jesus and the Gospels. I still think I have found that explanation. And I am not so very far from Samuel, even if he wants to press me for more refinement.

5. I am grateful to **Craig Blomberg** for his focus on the parable tradition within the synoptic tradition. In writing *Jesus Remembered*, I was aware of the desirability to do more work on the parables, for the reasons Craig states,[11] but I was also conscious that my manuscript was becoming overlong. I wish I had known his *WTJ* article at that time[12] but appreciate that he has here contributed such a detailed study on the subject and not limited himself to critiquing *Jesus Remembered*. Since his article is overall very supportive of the main thrust of my oral tradition thesis, I need do little more than dot a few i's and cross a few t's.

Early on, Craig refers to the critique of Kenneth Bailey's theses made by Ted Weeden. I should perhaps note that Ted's critique and my response to Ted—a critique and response that was the fruit of many years of discussion—are now published.[13] And I naturally resonate with Craig's positive evaluation of my challenge to the still prevailing literary default setting and to the monograph of Terence Mournet. I have never denied that it is in principle possible to explain all synoptic variation on the presupposition of one evangelist drawing on and redacting another. What I object to is the argument that if such an explanation can be offered (however implausible in at least some instances), then no other explanation need be looked for. The corollary that we cannot say anything about the Jesus tradition during the presumably 30 or so years before the Jesus tradition was written down extensively is not acceptable, nor is the alternative of having to argue that the Jesus tradition was extensively committed to writing at a much earlier stage on the presupposition that it would otherwise have to be regarded as unreliable.

Craig's estimate of statistics that may be regarded as indicative of oral tradition may be rather generous but are certainly a welcome

---

[11] Blomberg, chapter 5, p. 99.

[12] Ibid., 91n38.

[13] I refer to my "Kenneth Bailey's Theory of Oral Tradition: Critiquing Theodore Weeden's Critique," *JSHJ* 7 (2009): 44–62, in response to T. J. Weeden, "Kenneth Bailey's Theory of Oral Tradition: A Theory Contested by its Evidence," *JSHJ* 7 (2009): 3–43.

departure from the assumption that if a variation can be interpreted as redaction of a written source then it should be. I welcome his examination of the passages I cite. My point about the Last Supper traditions is that the variations between the Matthew and Mark version and the Luke and Paul version are best explained by liturgical tradition developing slightly differently in different centers. The significance for me is that these variations demonstrate that even what we may well describe as already "sacred tradition" was remembered and celebrated slightly differently—a foreshadowing of the similar variations in different liturgical celebrations of the eucharist today. I see the same in the Lord's Prayer, even when the differences are not very great.

I agree not least with Craig's protest against the assumption that Jesus never gave particular teachings more than once or never told differing parables with the same message. But of course! What teacher past or present ever taught the chief points of his message only once? Craig also rightly highlights one of the chief insights to emerge from an oral tradition perspective on the Jesus tradition, namely, that the concept of "originality" has to be rethought. For if Jesus taught the same thing in different forms, then which form is "original"? If the remembered Jesus was the Jesus who impacted different eye- and ear-witnesses differently, which of the varied testimonies is "original"? If a characteristic feature of oral tradition is the varied forms of its retelling and celebration, then variation is of the essence of the tradition—the same, yet different. The significance of this point has still to be fully grasped: that differences between the Synoptic Gospels are not inherently a problem, are not to be designated as "contradictions"; they are simply testimonies to the way that the oral Jesus tradition functioned. And that points to the further corollary regarding the "authenticity" of the Jesus tradition. "Original" usually goes hand in hand with "authentic"—"original" and therefore "authentic." But if "original" is no longer an appropriate term to use, then it is not appropriate to conclude that variation from the "original" is "inauthentic." There are lots of consequences that follow from that insight.

Craig's discussion of the *Gospel of Thomas* tradition is very interesting and one to which I will have to return when I examine the ways in which the Jesus tradition developed into the second century. Suffice it to say that now I am less confident than Craig that Thomas presupposes knowledge of and is derived from the written canonical Gospels. I suspect that more allowance has to be made for Thomas as evidence of presynoptic oral tradition that developed independently of the synoptic tradition. But I will be returning to the question in *Christianity in the Making*, volume 3, and its intriguing corollary: if the Synoptic (and Johannine) variations of the oral Jesus tradition can properly be describes as "authentic," why should the same judgment be withheld from Thomas? And if not, why not? Whether groups "remembering Jesus" in ways diverse from what became mainstream Christianity should also be designated as "Christian" remains an issue.

6. One of the delights for me of the last decade or so has been getting to know and dialoguing with **Jens Schröter** (we first met at the Society for New Testament Studies meeting in Durham in 2002). His *Habilitationsschrift* was one of the things that encouraged me to press forward with my principal thesis in *Jesus Remembered*,[14] and this exchange is a second round—in large measure, a rerun—of our earlier dialogue in *Zeitschrift für Neues Testament*.[15] Here space prevents me from elaborating the points that I need to make in response to Jens's chapter.

I appreciate Jens's emphasis on history as a hermeneutical enterprise. This insight remains fundamental for all historical Jesus research. I wonder, however, whether he fully appreciates the link I see between "the remembered Jesus" and the impact made by Jesus. Central to my thesis is the claim that "the remembered Jesus" of the Jesus tradition is the primary and still visible expression of that impact. So I would not accept Jens's reformulation of my thesis as "that *the remembered Jesus*, not the 'earthly Jesus' . . . belongs to the formative components of Christianity."[16] To be sure, we can get back only to the remembered Jesus. But in doing so, we can be confident that "the remembered Jesus" is the effect of the impact made by the "earthly Jesus."

Jens questions this in that he believes the Jesus tradition to be composed of a mix of material. He maintains that "the impulses of the earthly Jesus . . . were probably enriched very early with motifs from

---

[14] J. Schröter, *Erinnerung an Jesu Worte: Studien zur Rezeption der Logienüberlieferung in Markus, Q und Thomas* (WMANT 76; Neukirchen-Vluyn: Neukirchener, 1997).

[15] J. Schröter vs. James D. G. Dunn, "Der erinnerte Jesus als Begründer des Christentums," *ZNT* 20 (2007): 46–59.

[16] Schröter, chapter 6, p. 133.

the Hellenistic Jewish tradition and transmitted as paraenesis and catechesis of the early communities,"[17] and it is this mixed tradition that
is taken into the Synoptic Gospels. Here Jens remains faithful to one
of the principal claims of the earliest form critics. In principle, I do
not dispute that the synoptic tradition includes elaborated and interpreted Jesus tradition. But Jens's basic supporting argument is seriously flawed.

He bases it on the fact that Paul, 1 Peter, James, and Didache show
no interest in remembering Jesus' teaching. I dispute that. They show
little or no interest in *attributing* teaching *explicitly* to Jesus. But the
echoes and allusions to Jesus tradition are sufficiently clear as to provide
a good case for these writers, and the communities for which they wrote,
to have been well enough aware that some of the teaching and metaphors of the early church paraenesis were the heritage of Jesus. When,
for example, there was no precedent in Second Temple Judaism for
abstracting Lev 19:18 from its context and giving it such high prominence as we find in Mark 12:31 pars., it was hardly necessary to trumpet
attribution to Jesus in the similar references to Lev 19:18 in Paul and
James. And was it really necessary for Jas 5:12 to attribute its teaching
explicitly to Matt 5:37 for the point to be recognized? No more did
James have to cite chapter and verse in his echoes of Proverbs and ben
Sira for his audiences to recognize what he was doing. I have already
suggested elsewhere that such references and allusions are examples
of "in-group" language, where explicit attribution is unnecessary and
indeed would break the bond formed by the in-group language.[18]

Where I find Jens's argument most surprising and, indeed, rather
forced is his unwillingness to recognize that in 1 Cor 7:10; 9:14; and
even 11:23–25, Paul was not making explicit reference to teaching that
Jesus was remembered as giving during his mission. That Paul uses the
formal language for passing on tradition hardly constitutes a denial
that the tradition began with Jesus himself. And that Paul elaborates
the tradition (1 Cor 7:10–13) or dispenses with it (1 Cor 9:14–18)

---

[17] Ibid., 136.

[18] J. D. G. Dunn, "Jesus Tradition in Paul," in *Studying the Historical Jesus: Evaluation
of the State of Current Research* (vol. 19 of *New Testament Tools and Studied*; ed. B. Chilton and
C. A. Evans; Leiden: Brill, 1994), 155–78; also idem, *The Theology of Paul the Apostle* (Grand
Rapids: Eerdmans, 1998), 189–95.

does not mean that its origin as Jesus' teaching was unimportant for Paul. It tells us rather how Jesus' teaching was recalled and used—charismatically interpreted, we might say, in the light of circumstances different from those envisaged by Jesus. That Paul attributed these commands to the Lord certainly implies that Paul regarded them as still conveying the mind of the exalted Christ, but it hardly implies that Paul either did not know that the teaching came from Jesus during his mission or disowned it as such (along the lines of the old misinterpretation of 2 Cor 5:16).

In response to my emphasis on the impact of Jesus' mission as faith forming, Jens asks, "Is there not a difference between pre-Easter reactions and post-Easter faith—although there might be continuity? Is there only one kind of 'faith' or should we not think of a multitude of confessions, better described as different kinds of faith for which Jesus is of different importance?"[19] I am surprised by the first question, since I have never affirmed that pre-Easter faith was the same as post-Easter faith. Of course, the further impact of crucifixion and resurrection resulted in a significantly different and developed faith. And of course, there were different reactions to Jesus. My point in affirming that the only Jesus we have is the Jesus we reach through the picture of him in the Gospels was not to deny that there were other reactions to Jesus but to remind people like Jens that the reactions he cites come to us through the witness of the Jesus tradition of the disciples—that is, through the testimony of faith—hardly an independent source.

As indicated in my response to Craig Blomberg, I think it is more than likely that the *Gospel of Thomas* is evidence of Jesus' impact having different and divergent effects on others. The question for me is whether that was the immediate impact of Jesus himself or of the early (Q-type) Jesus tradition. Put another way, should the non-Q-like tradition in Thomas be dated as early as the Q-like tradition, or seen as itself the result of further reflection on the Q-like tradition? I need to do more work on this before reaching a clear decision. What I do quarrel with is Jens's too easy attribution of my confidence in the Jesus tradition to an uncritical reading of Acts. He misses or ignores the point that I have already made more than once in this response: the

---

[19] Schröter, chapter 6, p. 137.

primary consideration for me is that the synoptic tradition gives such a coherent and consistent impression of the one who made the impact that the Jesus tradition embodies, that we can have high confidence in the reliability of its testimony; from the coherence and consistency (not uniformity) of the impact made, we gain a clear enough picture of the one who made that impact.

A final note: I am delighted to see someone taking up my suggested distinction of Q and q; I am intrigued that Jens wants to strengthen my "overall perspective of continuity between Jesus' activity and the origins of early Christology,"[20] but I am puzzled by his unwillingness to recognize an allusion to Isa 53:5 in a passage like Rom 4:25. Even Morna Hooker recanted at that point![21]

7. The chapter by **Craig Evans** is a welcome corrective to the sometimes too strong reaction against the use of the criteria of dissimilarity in assessing what in the synoptic tradition can be traced back to Jesus with confidence. The criteria have been unfairly treated. Failure to meet the criteria did not in itself constitute proof that the tradition had originated independently of Jesus—although sometimes used in that way. It simply meant, for those ready to accept that the early churches supplemented Jesus tradition with Jewish and Hellenistic wisdom, that a tradition with Jewish or early Christian features could not be traced back to Jesus with any confidence; only the dissimilar material could be attributed to Jesus with confidence. The real problem was that such material was too easily treated as characterizing Jesus' teaching and as providing the norm for authenticity. Worse still, it fed the unsavory presupposition of so much historical Jesus research, that what was of lasting value in the Jesus tradition (in Jesus' mission) was his distinctiveness and distance from both his native Judaism and early Christian evaluation of Jesus. The dissimilar Jesus could neither have been influenced by Second Temple Judaism nor have influenced those who followed him as his disciples. It was the self-evident unrealism of that presupposition that has caused the reaction of the Third Quest, in its search for the Jewish Jesus.

---

[20] Ibid., 142.

[21] Dunn, *Jesus Remembered*, 811n222; idem, *Beginning from Jerusalem* (vol. 2 of *Christianity in the Making*; Grand Rapids: Eerdmans, 2009), 230n300.

The reaction, however, can easily go too far the other way. The gap between the mission of Jesus and the gospel as proclaimed by Paul remains a problem for students of Christianity's beginnings. But its challenge cannot be met simply by closing the gap between Jesus and his fellow Jews, for that may only open once again the gap more widely between the Jesus of Galilee and the Christ proclaimed by the early Church. The response of Craig has to be the right way forward—that is, by looking for features in the Jesus tradition that *both* demonstrate their rootedness in Jewish tradition *and* help explain how Jesus stood out within his context to the extent that he did. The response to abuse of the criterion of dissimilarity with Judaism is not to abandon the criterion altogether but to use it more astutely and with fuller information.

The examples that Craig chooses to illustrate both Jesus' similarity with Judaism and dissimilarity are highly effective. He makes a strong case in regard to Mark 12:1–12, though I continue to wonder whether the sequel to the parable (Mark 12:10–12) was an early elaboration of the Jesus tradition. And I am very dubious about his assertion of "a post-Easter understanding of the Christian community as an entity distinct from Israel."[22] The argument that Jesus was influenced by Hos 6:2 is intriguing, though I continue to be puzzled as to why the passage featured so little in the NT, despite the earliest Christians' extensive use of scripture to make sense of what had happened to Jesus.

Like Craig, I was impressed by Peter Stuhlmacher's argument that the best explanation for Mark 10:45 is Jesus himself contrasting his conception of his own role as *bar 'enasa* with that of the one like a Son of Man in Dan 7:14—as one who came not to be served but to serve. And I like the case he makes for seeing Matt 11:25–26 as a neat play on Dan 2:20–23. But I would like to have seen Craig's response to my suggestion that Mark 12:35–37a is best seen as an example of Jesus posing a riddle[23] rather than necessarily making a Christological claim. And I remain unsure whether Ps 110:1 was part of the original exchange with the High Priest in Mark 14:62.[24] On the other hand, the saying about the unknown exorcist (Mark 9:38–40) has always impressed me as

---

[22] Evans, chapter 7, p. 150.
[23] Dunn, *Jesus Remembered*, 634–35.
[24] Ibid., 749–51.

demonstrating the openness of Jesus, though I found Craig rather too generous in his estimate of the claims made by the seven sons of Sceva!

Craig has made a considerable specialism of (to use shorthand) the NT's use of the OT, a specialism from which we have all benefited. His chapter in this volume is an excellent example of the value of this approach and clearly demonstrates its indispensability if Jesus (and the first Christians) is to be properly located within their context.

8. **Bill Warren's** contribution is very welcome for its reminder that textual criticism should not be ignored in attempts to illuminate the character and content of the Jesus tradition. The work of David Parker and others parallels and complements my own approach to the Jesus tradition. My attempt to penetrate behind the synoptic tradition calls for a conscious alteration of the default setting of the literary mind-set—differences between the Synoptic Gospels should not be analyzed exclusively in terms of copying and redacting written sources. But textual critics had already been making an equivalent protest against a too exclusively literary explanation for textual variations—differences were not exclusively the result of scribal error or inattention. In each case, there is a rejection of the idea (or ideal) of an "original" version that had been departed from in the course of transmission and that could, in principle, be recovered by sophisticated form-critical or text-critical tools. In each case, there is a questioning of the assumption of an original fixity, with any variation from that fixity being regarded as a defective form of the tradition. I welcome this newer conception of text criticism, not least because it reinforces our appreciation of the degree of fluidity in the Jesus tradition, not just during the oral phase, but still, in lesser degree perhaps, in the literary phase. To appreciate that variant texts should not be regarded as inferior texts but as the authoritative texts for different churches is an important step forward in our attempts to gain as clear as possible a picture of early Christian diversity.

I accept Bill's gentle rebuke that in *Jesus Remembered* I did not pay more heed to textual variants of the Gospel tradition. And his suggested "guiding principles for identifying the variant readings most likely to interface with Dunn's emphasis on oral tradition"[25] are well chosen and potentially valuable. I am just a little dubious as to how

---

[25] Warren, chapter 8, p. 164.

valuable they might be for historical Jesus research. His opening example (Mark 1:1) is hardly a case of early Jesus tradition; it is obviously part of Mark's written introduction to his Gospel. Bill's sequence of examples of "additional" material can certainly be attributed to performance variations and elaborations of oral tradition, though we should also remember that initial writing down was probably in closer continuity with oral tradition, as being itself a form of performance of the Jesus tradition, with similar variations and elaborations. The difficulty of "getting back" to the oral phase of the Jesus tradition, when all that we have comes to us as written, remains. So recognition of the similarity of and continuity between oral and written is important.

In fact, Bill seems content to point to the likelihood that some of the textual variant material provides evidence of oral tradition in the post-70s or early second-century period. This is not so very relevant to historical Jesus research as such, though, of course it may tell us more about how the Jesus tradition was still being handled orally into the second century. I was a little surprised, however, that he did not take up my suggestion regarding Luke 23:34—that the echo in Acts 7:60 may suggest that Luke was familiar with the Luke 23:34 tradition,[26] a rather earlier attestation than that of Irenaeus! Otherwise, I remain unclear how a fuller reference to textual variants than I gave would have made any even modestly significant alteration to my substantive depiction of the remembered Jesus.

9. **Charles Quarles** focuses entirely on the birth narratives and raises a number of important issues, which I can deal with only briefly here.

One is the strong appeal made by Samuel Byrskog and Richard Bauckham to eyewitness testimony as strengthening the case for the historicity of the birth narratives—Mary, Jesus' mother, being the obvious (and only real?) candidate for that role here (Luke 2:19,51). I certainly agree that Luke was very likely to have used one or more visits to Jerusalem (Acts 21:17–18) to search out the eyewitness testimony to which he refers in Luke 1:2–3[27]—though it would appear

---

[26] Dunn, *Jesus Remembered*, 780n86.
[27] I may refer to my *Beginning from Jerusalem* (§§ 21.2–3) on the historical value of Acts.

from Acts 1:21–22 that the eyewitness testimony he probably had in mind began from Jesus' baptism by John. I am less confident than Charles that we can assume that Luke followed the same working principle for Luke 1–2. For example, Charles does not say anything about the canticles that are such a major feature of Luke 1–2 and that are so distinctive within Luke–Acts as a whole. He also avoids the problem of the Quirinius census, not to be resolved by merely hypothesizing an earlier Quirinius or an otherwise unknown universal census throughout the Roman empire, but if not, what then? And on the wider appeal to eyewitnesses, I have to say that talk of Luke 4:38 and 24:34 as forming "a literary *inclusio*"[28] is at best a very strained use of such a literary feature.

On Charles's objection to my use of "midrash," I have to admit that I am at some disadvantage since I am unfamiliar with and have been unable to access his *Midrash Criticism*. It will have to suffice for me to say that I use "midrash" loosely to describe everything from a straight exposition of an OT passage to elaborations of the OT text, such as we find in *Jubilees*.[29] Also, in trying to be sensitive to allusions to and use made of OT material, we must avoid looking too woodenly for literary dependence. I suggest that a detail like Matthew's moving star indicates a readiness to tell the story in terms of vivid symbolism that modern historiography would regard as inappropriate. Ulrich Luz has highlighted Matthew's readiness to tell his story using what he calls "fictionality," as well as by demonstrating loyalty to tradition.[30] We may well regard such features of ancient historiography as unacceptable for us today, but we should not conclude that they were unacceptable for the ancients. What we must not do is judge them by our own standards and demand that their writing conform to these standards.

I find Charles's argument regarding Mark 12:35–37 and Matt 22:42 also rather forced, as implying (far less "mentioning") both Jesus' Davidic sonship and divine sonship. The context is clear: "Whose son is he?" invites the answer, "The son of David." Charles plausibly draws

---

[28] Quarles, chapter 9, p. 175.
[29] What Jim Charlesworth refers to as "expansions of the Old Testament." J. H. Charlesworth, *The Old Testament Pseudepigrapha* (vol. 2; London: DLT, 1985).
[30] U. Luz, *Studies in Matthew* (Grand Rapids: Eerdmans, 2005), chap. 4.

in Mark 14:60–61 to strengthen the case of a "Son of God" reading of Mark 12:35–37. And I agree that Jesus probably did think of God as his Father in very intimate terms. But much the stronger case for the basic assertion is given by the Gospels' account of Jesus' anointing with the Spirit at Jordan (the heavenly voice). It hardly seems necessary to press for it to have derived from Mary's telling Jesus about the circumstances of his birth, when there is no supporting evidence.

Charles keeps referring to my "rejection" of the historical value of the birth narratives. I do not think I ever use that word ("reject"), and to express his reaction to #11.1 in *Jesus Remembered* in these terms really misses the point. My concern was to build as substantive a case as possible for the historical value of the Jesus tradition. When my method seems to give such strong results regarding Jesus' mission itself, it seemed neither wise nor necessary to build more on the birth narratives, which provide too thin results to bear much historical weight. I do not reject the birth narratives but remain largely agnostic on most of their factual details. The difficulty, for example, of demonstrating Jesus' birth in Bethlehem makes it doubtful whether too much should be made to depend on it in historical terms. And I question whether we can say with confidence that "multiple sources attested to the virginal conception of Jesus well before the composition of Matthew and Luke";[31] at best it is wise to admit that such a statement depends on a good deal of speculation. And it remains an interesting question, whether belief in Jesus' virginal conception was a source of early high Christology or a corollary to it, but to pursue that issue further would take us too far from the main subject.

Nevertheless, the main question that Charles's chapter puts before me is whether we should value the birth narratives only or primarily for their historical worth. To do so, I suspect, is to be less respectful to Matthew and Luke than we usually think. In fact, I am in broad agreement with Ray Brown in large part because he had given such a definitive treatment of these narratives that I did not feel bad about passing over them so cursorily. I still find it making more sense of the content and spirit of the birth narratives to interpret them primarily as evidence of how Jesus was celebrated early on in Palestinian Christian circles.

---

[31] Quarles, chapter 9, p. 189.

10. **Ben Witherington III** begins with some very kind comments on *Jesus Remembered* and expresses well-informed appreciation both of my protests against features and assumptions of the earlier Quests and of what I offer as an alternative model or, perhaps more accurately, as a complementary alternative, since, as Ben also notes, I still believe in the priority of Mark and in some form of the Q hypothesis, and I also have no doubt that a good many of the differences between the Gospels are best explained as Matthew's and Luke's redactions of Mark.

It is slightly amusing, not to say ironic, that Ben's memory of my lecture to the Lightfoot Society in Durham in the late 1970s is rather different from mine. He recalls it as a lecture on "glossolalia." In fact (I think I can fairly put it this way), it was a lecture on the charismatic dimension of Christianity, past and present—the spin-off of my early work on *Baptism in the Holy Spirit* and *Jesus and the Spirit*. What I infer was "extraordinary" for my venerable Durham predecessors was my suggestion that the "charismatic renewal" then growing and developing was a modern expression of the third strand of (Western) Christianity, which has often disappeared below the surface but has bubbled up afresh every so often and which might provide hope for renewal of the whole church today. So Ben's recollection is, for me, not such a good example of what I envisage in my talk of "remembering Jesus," since glossolalia was only one element within a much broader talk and not the most important aspect of it. Rather, as so often in this larger subject, any mention of glossolalia is so fascinating and off-putting that it eclipses other and more important themes in an audience's response.

Ben's main criticism takes us back to the earlier discussion with Markus and Samuel: he thinks that I do not give enough emphasis to the role of eyewitnesses in the traditioning process that climaxed in the Gospels or to Samuel's emphasis on oral history. I have already responded to Samuel on this point, and may refer to #4, where I note that if "oral history" is another name for eyewitness testimony, then I have no problem with it. Where the misunderstanding begins to emerge, as in Richard Bauckham's similar critique of *Jesus Remembered*, is in the suggestion that I was putting forward merely a variation of the form-critical assumption of traditions passed through anonymous communities, a variation that in effect dispensed entirely with eyewitnesses. If this is the criticism, then I say again, it seems to miss the point. It is central to my thesis that the process by which the Jesus tradition has come down to us began with the first disciples (eyewitnesses); obviously I could have emphasized the point more fully! My thesis is designed to meet and include the situations where the tradition was being passed on and elaborated in congregations where no eyewitness was present. My concern has been to argue that even in such circumstances the tradition remained substantially stable, as illustrated by the synoptic tradition, or by the overlap between Mark and Q.[32]

The point evidently requires some elaboration. My argument is that Richard and Ben are in effect dependent on being able to make a direct connection between eyewitnesses (themselves) and the synoptic tradition as we now have it. I assume that in at least much of the tradition (the Q material being the obvious example) such a *direct* or immediate connection cannot be assumed. My argument is that it is not actually necessary to make or assume such a direct connection—a connection, yes, since eyewitnesses were at the start of the whole process and contributed to that process to a significant extent but were not personally responsible for the whole process in all the scattered and burgeoning churches or able to exert the personal control that Richard seems to want to argue for. My argument is that even without such direct supervision of the traditioning process, the character of that process, as evidenced by the synoptic tradition, ensured the coherence and consistency of the tradition.[33]

If the issue focuses on the actual evangelists themselves, then I doubt whether Q supports the view that the Gospel writers wrote down only what they learned directly from the mouths of eyewitnesses. And in any case, my thesis in *Jesus Remembered* focuses on the period before the Jesus tradition was written down. Nevertheless, I should perhaps make it clear that I do not think the Gospels are the "product of community tradition" and never say or imply that the communities

---

[32] See again n9.

[33] I have no idea why Ben refers to what I have in mind as the traditioning process of "Palestinian nomads" (chapter 10, p. 207) and his criticism of Bailey, that he "simply thinks that orality works the same way regardless of what sort of stories and sayings one is relaying and retelling to others" (chapter 10, pp. 207–8), is entirely unfounded and unfair.

created the tradition;[34] but *Jesus Remembered* stops well short of the transition from oral to written tradition, though I have no doubt that Luke did as he said he had (Luke 1:1–4). What I do say is that the synoptic tradition *reflects* the content and character of the varied communities' Jesus tradition, of the Jesus tradition as rehearsed, celebrated, drawn on for instruction, and transmitted, in congregations where no eyewitnesses were present. So, *pace* Ben, I do not have to rebut Richard or Samuel to defend my thesis. What I have in mind is complementary to their thesis, as providing a theory for the periods and churches that their emphasis on eyewitnesses does not cover.

With regard to the Papias testimony on which Richard and Ben build so much, I read it slightly differently. As I have already said, I take Papias to be talking about eyewitnesses confirming what he already knew from the Jesus tradition in his own church. He was not implying that all he heard from Aristion and John he was hearing for the first time. Rather, I infer, he wanted what he was already familiar with *confirmed* by an eyewitness—as almost anyone would who had heard a good story or teaching but never from someone who was an eye- or ear-witness. But how did he know that tradition? The implication presumably is that the tradition he already knew had *not* been told him by one of the first disciples.

Ben is also overconfident, in my view, that the great bulk of the differences between the Synoptic Gospels can be explained by Matthew's and Mark's redactions of their literary source (Mark). To repeat, I do not dispute a considerable degree of such redaction, but Ben ignores other cases where it makes better sense if Matthew knew a different version of the story or teaching and preferred to use it rather than Mark's version. And he rather misses the point about the three Acts accounts of Paul's conversion. My point is that the three accounts exemplify precisely how the same story could be told differently—an example of multiple storytelling by the *same* author, which I infer was typical of how such stories could be told variously—as in the synoptic tradition. As for the rebuke that I paid too little attention to rhetoric (mea culpa), perhaps all I need to say here is that rhetoric is another way of saying that oral delivery was shaped by the intentions

---

[34] Witherington, chapter 10, pp. 221, 226.

of the speaker and the circumstances addressed. If the rules of rhetoric explain how the tradents worked, that is very helpful. My primary concern, however, was to take more seriously the fact of inconsequential variations in the synoptic tradition. My argument is that stories about Jesus and the teaching of Jesus circulated in varied forms from the beginning, without denying that some differences are best explained by evangelists' editing—though I also want to say that such editing may be another way of saying "performance variation." What I was objecting to was the working assumption that all such editing was the editing of a written source or of a fixed "original" version.

11. I wondered whether any of the contributors to this volume would take up the tension between my double assertion that we have access only to the remembered Jesus and that we can nevertheless speak with historical integrity of Jesus' self-consciousness. I am grateful to **Paul Eddy** for doing so and for his further bibliographical references, some of which I missed.

Despite the various positive things Paul says about *Jesus Remembered*, he reads chapter 15 of that book as concluding that Jesus rejected the title Messiah. In contrast, Paul wants to argue strongly for the view that Jesus had a strong and full "messianic self-consciousness" or, more briefly, that Jesus saw himself as the Messiah.

What I find unhelpful here, and rather missing the point I was trying (unsuccessfully!) to make, is the assumption that there is a concept of "Messiah" that can be abstracted from the actual expectations regarding Israel's Messiah. My claim is that by "Messiah," Jesus' contemporaries would mean (in the words of Loren Stuckenbruck, whom Paul quotes) "an eschatological ruler, chosen by God to act decisively against the wicked on behalf of the righteous of God's people Israel."[35] That I agree was the predominant concept of "Messiah"; the only other "Messiah" that we hear of in the expectation of the period was the priestly Messiah, but that never seems to have been a factor in Jesus' mission or in early Christology. My point in *Jesus Remembered* is that if this was the only real content of "Messiah" at the time of Jesus, a royal, military figure who would deliver his nation from its oppressors, then this is what "Messiah" meant to most people. It was probably this role

---

[35] Eddy, chapter 11, p. 250.

that lies behind, for example, Peter's confession and Jesus' execution. This presumably gives the reason for Jesus' hesitation over accepting the title and its concomitant role.[36]

Paul recognizes my argument here—that Jesus rejected the role of Messiah that others tried to push him toward or fit him into. But he wants to distinguish a concept of Messiah from what would appear to have been the only popular conception of Messiah available. He believes that Jesus thought of himself as a different kind of Messiah, but as Messiah nonetheless, and criticizes me for claiming that Jesus rejected the title altogether.[37] Now there may not be much between us, actually, and it may be a matter of words, but it may also be important, since Paul may be lapsing back into the idea of a Platonic ideal concept of Messiah that underlies all the early Jewish hope and expectation—what he calls "the title per se."[38] But we know that early Jewish expectation and hope took different forms. My question is whether it should all be described as "messianic." Some early Jewish expectation did not feature an intermediary figure; God would intervene directly. Some had in view a prophetic figure. To be sure, if he was to be anointed (Isa 61:1), then in that sense he was "messianic." But was that figure regarded as a "Messiah"? So my first question is whether it is justified and wise to use the term "messianic" too undiscriminatingly. Does it add anything to the facts we can deduce if we can speak of a "messianic" teacher, a "messianic prophet," a "messianic exorcist"?

Here I remain not persuaded that at the time of Jesus there was a Son of Man messianology current so that in his use of the *bar 'enasa* phrase, even when alluding to the "one like a Son of Man" in Dan 7:13 (RSV), it can be inferred that Jesus saw himself as the Son of Man or Messiah. I have given my reasons sufficiently in *Jesus Remembered*,[39]

---

[36] On the issue of how Jesus replied to the high priest (Mark 14:62), I still find it less likely that Matthew and Luke changed Mark's confident or confessional "I am" affirmation than that the present Markan text makes explicit what came across as hesitating or ambivalent.

[37] In fact, I think it is only once that I use the word "reject" in this context, in the conclusion to chapter 16 of *Jesus Remembered*: "We have to conclude as likely that Jesus made no attempt to lay claim to any title as such; also that he rejected at least one which others tried to fit him to." Dunn, *Jesus Remembered*, 761.

[38] Eddy, chapter 11, p. 244.

[39] Dunn, *Jesus Remembered*, 730–33.

though obviously, once again, I have not succeeded in convincing everyone! Here I need simply repeat that for me the decisive consideration is that the question, "Is Jesus the Son of Man?" is never raised in the Gospel tradition, nor the confession ever voiced, "You are/he is the Son of Man." I find that hard to understand if there had already been a substantive Son of Man messianology in Israel at the time of Jesus.

My key question to Paul is whether it is actually necessary (as well as justified) to argue that Jesus believed himself to be the Messiah, to speak of a "*messianic* consciousness." Is it not sufficient to conclude that Jesus had a clear sense of his own mission and of its outcome (suffering, death, and vindication), which was definitive for the first Christians and became the definitive factor in redefining the concept of Messiah? I do not dispute (quite the contrary) that the redefined role of the Messiah originated with Jesus' own self-understanding and its outcome in his death and resurrection. It is just a question whether we can historically and fairly describe it as a "messianic" self-understanding. And here I find it significant that we have no record of Jesus redefining his role in messianic terms—that is, as a correction giving the true sense of "Messiah,"—"the title per se." What we do have is the first Christians going out of their way to explain and define Messiah, that—surprise, surprise—the Messiah must suffer (Luke 24:26–27,46; Acts 3:18; 17:3). Does it actually matter whether we can describe Jesus' self-awareness as expectation of suffering, death, and vindication without using the term "messianic"?

Paul does not hesitate to refer to "Dunn's complete elimination from the self-consciousness of Jesus any sense of a more personal identification with Yahweh."[40] So perhaps I should just add the note that Richard Bauckham and Larry Hurtado focus their discussions on post-Easter worship of Jesus, even when noting that, for example, the worship referred to by Matthew in his retelling the story of Jesus walking on the water (Matt 14:33) reflects early Christian worship. But such a discussion would have to define "identification" and include reference also, for example, to Luke's emphasis on Jesus' practice of prayer and to Jesus' response in the temptations narrative,

---

[40] Eddy, chapter 11, 237n41.

"Worship the Lord your God and him only shall you serve" (Matt 4:10 RSV; Luke 4:8 RSV).[41]

12. I am delighted that **Stephen Davis** was able to take part in this exercise and particularly on the question of Jesus' resurrection, since I know him basically through our mutual friend, Gerry O'Collins, who has probably written more books on that subject than most people read in a lifetime.

Stephen first of all raises, once again, the issue of history and memory. He begins by generalizing, rather too glibly in my view, from contemporary experience of memory in our modern highly literate societies, whereas it should be obvious, almost a priori, that memory in a predominantly oral society would function differently. His main point, however, is his assertion that we can speak in meaningful historical terms of "accurate" memory. I find that unhelpful for three reasons.

First, Stephen acknowledges that the historian can deal only in probabilities—in my terms, that historical "facts" are interpretations of such data as are available to the historian. Is it helpful or wise to use the term "accurate" to describe a probability, even a very strong probability? In this "language game," the term "accurate" goes with the term "certain." But probability is not certainty—nor can probable findings helpfully be described as "accurate."

Second, what is an "accurate" memory? That X was impacted in a particular way by someone else or by some event? But that can hardly be "accurate" in the sense that anyone in X's position would have been impacted in the same way. So "accurate" is a term that is appropriate only on an objectivist or historicist view of history—that there are concrete things (events) that lie at the bottom of the archaeological tell of history that can be uncovered, touched, felt, and experienced just as X did. I hope I had sufficiently dealt with this issue in #6.3 of *Jesus Remembered*.

Third, of course we can easily access basic data regarding Jesus—that he was from and lived out his mission principally in Galilee, that he was crucified by the Romans, and so on. But how does the fact that Jesus died give us access to Jesus himself? Is Stephen not falling back on to the wrong side of Martin Kähler's famous antithesis—opting for the *historische Jesus* rather than the *geschichtliche Christus*? That is, he would be content, it would appear, to "know things about" Jesus,[42] even if only to the extent that Jesus exercised missions in Galilee and was executed on a cross! But surely historians, Christian or otherwise, want to know not just the bare data about the man Jesus (*Historie*); they want to know about the historic Jesus (*Geschichte*), the significant Jesus, the Jesus who made the impact that he did. And here we go beyond the reach of some objective idea of "accuracy." We ask not only what he did but also what it signified. We ask not only what he said but also what he meant—not forgetting that at best we have his teaching already translated into Greek. And the traditions of both his doings and his sayings attest clearly enough the impact Jesus made, but the variations in these (Greek) traditions prevent us again and again achieving the "accuracy" that Stephen aspires to.

So, do I contradict myself in saying that we can speak with confidence of many of the things Jesus did and said? I do not think so. I still think it fair to say that we can recognize the character of the one who made the impact that he did from the impression left by that impact. I know we only have a one-sided remembering—from those positively impacted by Jesus; so no real triangulation is possible. And I do not for a moment resile from my observation that the varied memories prevent us from any "certainty" as to the "accuracy" of particular details in the Jesus tradition. But I do remain confident that the record of the actual impact made by Jesus enables us to get as clear a picture of the one who made that impact as is both possible and necessary.

On Stephen's third section, with its distinction between three different senses of "history," I suppose, if I had to choose between the three in reference to the resurrection of Jesus,[43] I would have to go with the second (*whatever historians discover about what happened in the past*). I think the first (*whatever happened in the past*) less appropriate for discussion of the resurrection as a "historical event." My problem is that "history" on any definition is a function of time. And I do not think the timelessness of eternity (or of heaven) can meaningfully

---

[42] I echo Stephen's phrase on Davis, chapter 12, p. 259.

[43] Davis, chapter 12, p. 261.

be described as "historical." "History" comes into play in human, time-bound observation (vision) of or reflection regarding heaven. Alternatively, it is the interaction of heaven with the time and space continuum that constitutes "history." In that context, "resurrection" almost by definition is an exit from history and so not properly speaking "historical." We can speak of the historical data of accounts of the empty tomb and "resurrection appearances" and of the interpretation given to what they experienced by the first disciples. But since they did not experience or witness the resurrection (Jesus being raised), the talk of "resurrection" takes us only to their interpretation of what they did experience. It is more confusing than helpful to describe an event that in principle is not subject to historical examination as "historical."

In his final section, Stephen insists that Paul understood the resurrection as physical: "body . . . entails physicality."[44] I am afraid I simply have to disagree. In my view, "body" for Paul denoted the embodiment that makes relationship and communication possible—in a physical context, of course, a physical body—but in a different context?[45] And of course Paul believed in a *bodily* resurrection (1 Corinthians 15), but it does not follow that he believed the resurrection body to be "physical." It is true that we cannot say what Paul means by a "spiritual" body—except what he says it is not! In the list of antitheses Paul draws up to distinguish the resurrection body from the body of this life, "flesh and blood" (15:50 RSV) belong on the "this body" side of the antitheses—along with "corruption," "dishonor," "weakness," "natural body," "earthly," "corruptible," and "mortal" (15:42–54).[46] For Paul, "flesh and blood" = physical = what decays and corrupts—what the "spiritual body" is not and does not!

13. It is a pleasure also to reengage with **Gary Habermas** principally on the same subject that has engaged so much of his attention over the past years. I naturally welcome his sense of positive resonance with what I say regarding historical method and on the points where we stand shoulder to shoulder on the subject of Jesus' resurrection.

---

[44] Davis, chapter 12, p. 263.

[45] I dealt with this at some length in my *Theology of Paul*, §3.2.

[46] See further my "How are the Dead Raised? With What Body do They Come? Reflections on 1 Corinthians 15," *SwJT* 45 (2002–2003): 4–18.

I could quibble with his formulations at one or two points, but that would not forward the discussion. More important probably is that my pleasure is tinged with a certain degree of frustration at what seems to me an element of misunderstanding or confusion in the points on which Gary expresses his several concerns.

The first is, once again, my distinction between event, data, and fact, and my unwillingness to replace "data" with "historical facts." As Gary notes more than once, I think it important to recognize that "facts" are interpretations of the data. Gary, however, thinks that Paula Fredriksen "is much closer to the normal usage when she refers to 'facts' as the events as they are interpreted."[47] If I take his point, Gary seems to me to be confusing the issue. For one thing, unlike the "event," the "data" are present to the historian in the here and now—records, reports, and so on from the past, yes, but available to the historian for firsthand encounter and evaluation. When I speak of "interpretation," I am referring to *historians'* interpretations of the data available to them. In some contrast, Gary seems to be thinking of the interpretation given by the first believers in Jesus' resurrection—"facts . . . as the historical event plus its interpretation."[48] But the interpretation given to what they experienced by the first believers is not the *historian's* interpretation; it is not "interpretation" in the way I use it in elaborating the distinction between event, data, and fact. The interpretation of the first disciples (what Gary seems to be referring to) is *part of the data*, which the historian has to evaluate. And of course we have to take account of that data—that is, of the interpretation given to their experiences by the first disciples—but let us not confuse the interpretation given by the first disciples (part of the available data) with the interpretation that historians give and that may enable them to speak confidently of certain historical "facts."

I should perhaps draw attention here to the importance I give to the first disciples' interpretation of their experience. For them to have understood that they were seeing the crucified Jesus as *risen from the dead* rather than as (simply!) translated or glorified was quite extraordinary. That it led them to the conclusion that God had raised

---

[47] Habermas, chapter 13, p. 276.
[48] Ibid.

Jesus from the dead, that Jesus had been raised as the beginning of the end-time general resurrection of the dead, was exceptional and unprecedented. That is why I am more confident than a dispassionate reviewer of the data might think proper, that this first Christian interpretation deserves a very high respect, and that Christians, on its basis, need have no qualms about affirming their faith in Jesus as risen. But it still remains the case that any historian's conclusion, that Jesus was raised from the dead, is a second order fact, "an interpretation of an interpretation."[49]

The other misunderstanding takes us back to the discussion with Stephen Davis, and on the same point that by "body" Gary understands *physical* body. I can scarcely take it in when Gary seems to doubt my acceptance that Paul believed in a *bodily* resurrection.[50] Of course he did; how could it ever be in dispute after passages like 1 Cor 15:42–49 and Phil 3:21? Gary is concerned that I give too much weight to the emphasis on light in the Acts accounts of Paul's conversion, ignoring not only the likelihood that in writing 2 Cor 4:4–6 Paul had his own conversion very much in mind—not to mention Dan 12:3! But the crucial point, as with Stephen, is that Gary seems simply to presuppose that "body" means "physical" body. I have already dealt with this assumption, what seems to me a misinterpretation of Paul's understanding of the resurrection body as *spiritual* body. But here I may simply add one of my disquiets over Tom Wright's otherwise magnificent *The Resurrection of the Son of God*, that it does not do enough justice to the variegated ways in which Christian hope was expressed, including Mark 12:25 and Phil 1:21–23. It is, of course, always attractive to reach a single elegant solution to the complexities of the data, to draw a single grand narrative out of the diversity of facts and fragments of different stories, but does it do justice to all the data, all the stories, including the variety of images and conceptualizations used by the first Christians?

---

[49] Dunn, *Jesus Remembered*, 877; also quoted by Habermas, chapter 13, p. 276.

[50] Gary thinks he is describing my view in the clause, "Paul's appearance was less than bodily" (Habermas, chapter 13, 280).

What a stimulating time I have had reading through all these reactions to my *Jesus Remembered*. I can only repeat my heartfelt thanks to them all for the positive ways they responded and for the time they have given to reading such a massive volume (but an excellent doorstop). I am even more grateful for the questions and probings that have forced me to rethink and restate my theses at various points. And I can only hope that my own response has clarified at least some points of obscurity, answered legitimate criticisms with some effect, and helped move the dialogue on all the issues positively and fruitfully.

Name Index

SUBJECT INDEX

SCRIPTURE INDEX